The Aztecs

New Perspectives

ABC-CLIO's
Understanding Ancient Civilizations

The
AZTECS

New Perspectives

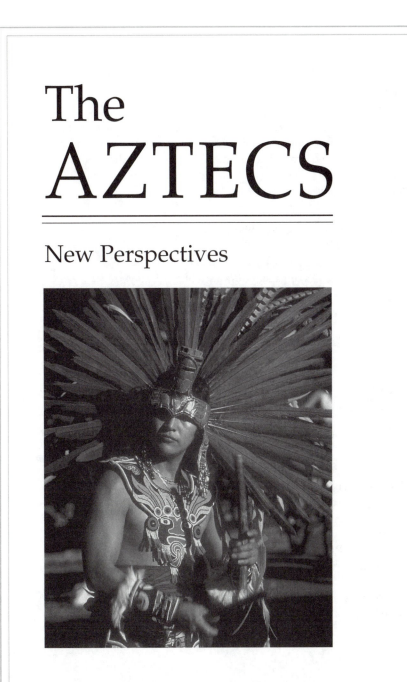

DIRK R. VAN TUERENHOUT

A B C · C L I O

Santa Barbara, California • Denver, Colorado • Oxford, England

Library of Congress Cataloging-in-Publication Data
Van Tuerenhout, Dirk R.
    The Aztecs : new perspectives / Dirk R. Van Tuerenhout.
       p. cm. — (ABC-CLIO's understanding ancient civilizations)
    Includes bibliographical references and index.
    ISBN 1-57607-921-X (hardback : alk. paper) — ISBN 1-57607-924-4 (ebook)
1. Aztecs—History.   2. Aztecs—Kings and rulers.   3. Aztecs—Social life and customs. 4. Mexico—Antiquties.   I. Title.   II. Series: Understanding ancient civilizations.

F1219.73.V35 2005
972.018—dc22

2005003598

08   07   06   05   /   10   9   8   7   6   5   4   3   2   1

This book is also available on the World Wide Web as an e-book.
Visit abc-clio.com for details.

ABC-CLIO, Inc.
130 Cremona Drive, P.O. Box 1911
Santa Barbara, California 93116-1911

This book is printed on acid-free paper.
Manufactured in the United States of America.

To Rosalinda and Sara

Contents

List of Maps

Series Editor's Preface

In recent years there has been a significant and steady increase of academic and popular interest in the study of past civilizations. This is due in part to the dramatic coverage, real or imagined, of the archaeological profession in popular film and television, and to extensive journalistic reporting of spectacular new finds from all parts of the world. Because archaeologists and other scholars, however, have tended to approach their study of ancient peoples and civilizations exclusively from their own disciplinary perspectives and for their professional colleagues, there has long been a lack of general factual and other research resources available for the nonspecialist. The *Understanding Ancient Civilizations* series is intended to fill that need.

Volumes in the series are principally designed to introduce the general reader, student, and nonspecialist to the study of specific ancient civilizations. Each volume is devoted to a particular archaeological culture (e.g., the ancient Maya of southern Mexico and adjacent Guatemala) or cultural region (e.g., Israel and Canaan) and seeks to achieve, with careful selectivity and astute critical assessment of the literature, an expression of a particular civilization and an appreciation of its achievements.

The keynote of the *Understanding Ancient Civilizations* series is to provide, in a uniform format, an interpretation of each civilization that will express its culture and place in the world, as well as qualities and background, that make it unique.

Series titles include volumes on the archaeology and prehistory of the ancient civilizations of Egypt, Greece, Rome, and Mesopotamia, as well as the achievements of the Celts, Aztecs, and Inca, among others. Still others are in the planning stage.

I was particularly fortunate in having Kevin Downing from ABC-CLIO contact me in search of an editor for a series about archaeology. It is a simple statement of truth that there would be no series without him. I was also lucky to have Simon Mason, Kevin's successor from ABC-CLIO, continuing to push the production of the series. Given the scale of the project and the schedule for production, he deserves more than a sincere thank you.

JOHN WEEKS

MAP 1. General Location of the Aztec Realm vs. that of the Maya and Inca

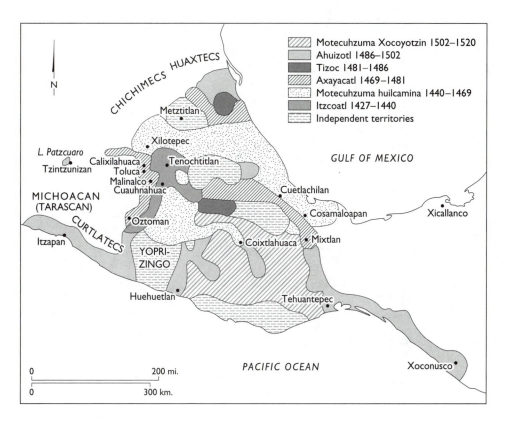

MAP 2. Aztec Conquests

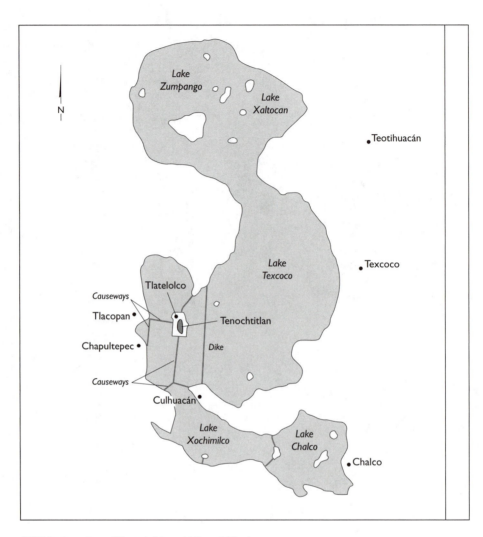

MAP 3. Location of Tenochtitlan – Valley of Mexico

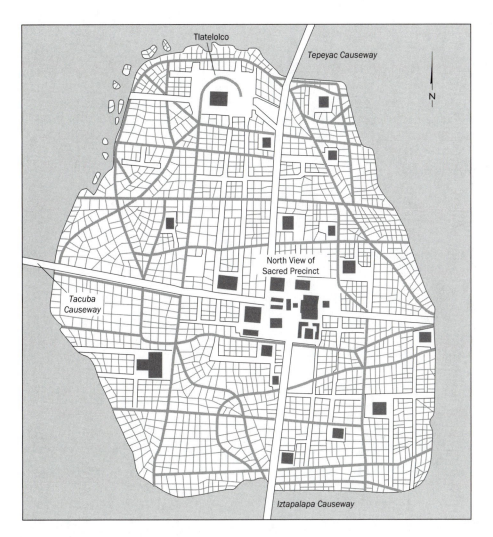

MAP 4. Tenochtitlan Layout

PART I

Introduction

Introduction

OVERVIEW

This book is about the Aztec culture. Our knowledge of Aztec culture is based on the contributions made by many specialists. The list starts with anthropologists and historians, and continues with animal and plant specialists, geneticists, astronomers, and even astronauts. As our means to extract information from the past expand, so will the number of different fields of study that can help us better understand a culture like that of the Aztecs. Because I am an anthropologist, I will begin with a discussion of anthropology and its contributions to our knowledge of Aztec culture.

THE ISSUE OF JARGON TERMINOLOGY VERSUS "PLAIN ENGLISH"

We will begin with a disclaimer: as with any field of study, anthropology is "guilty" of employing all kinds of technical jargon, usually words derived from Latin and Greek words. The reader will find these terms interspersed throughout the chapters that follow; however, whenever they appear, I have inserted the "plain English" versions as well. Why not therefore go with just the plain English versions? I made the assumption that anyone interested in learning more about this subject of the Aztecs would be going through a great number of books and articles. In that case, one should be familiar with the terminology. One could see the following pages as a general introduction where the reader can get acquainted with some of the language employed by specialists in the cultures of the region. Aside from Greek and Latin words, the following text also includes a lot of words in Nahuatl, the language spoken by the Aztec before the arrival of the Spanish. There is a glossary in the back to get the definitions and explanations of these terms.

This use of multisyllabic words (in itself a good example of jargon) is not limited to anthropologists. There are many disciplines that are "guilty" of this policy of obfuscation. The continued use of words with Latin and Greek roots can be considered an echo of a distant past in which the language of science was Latin, not English (and before that ancient Greek).

ANTHROPOLOGY: WITH WHAT KIND OF ANIMAL ARE WE DEALING?

The word *anthropology* in itself is also a good example of the use of complex terminology. What is meant by this? When one goes back to the roots of the

An anthropology researcher examines the remains of an Aztec-period skull unearthed at the Templo Mayor archaeological site in downtown Mexico City. The site was the ceremonial center of the Aztec city of Tenochtitlan. (Keith Dannemiller/Corbis)

word, *anthropos* and *logos,* then we have the study of human beings, with *anthropos* referring to humans and *logos* meaning "study of." Anthropology as a field of study in the United States has traditionally encompassed four different, yet complementary, fields of study: physical (or biological) anthropology, archaeology, linguistics, and cultural anthropology.

Among the general public, the subfield of **archaeology** is the best known of the four fields just mentioned. An archaeologist is someone who studies (the "logos" component shows up here as well) things that are "old." In more specific terms, an archaeologist is someone who is interested in reconstructing what people did at one point in time in one particular place or area. Most important, an archaeologist will base his or her reconstruction of this past behavior on the material remains of that behavior. In plain English, this could translate to the following: when we get up in the morning, we prepare breakfast, and then go off to work or school. What are some of the material indicators left behind at our homes that signal that we had breakfast? The coffee pot might still have coffee in it. We may have left dishes in the sink. There may be dishes left on the table with food on them. Archaeologists are people who look for these kinds of clues when excavating the homes of people who lived in the past. It is sometimes said that archaeologists are people who dig up other people's garbage, and there is some truth to that.

Physical (or biological) anthropology deals with human bones. One could be digging up a nineteenth-century site in upstate New York or an early farming community in Europe and come across human remains. What does one do then? This is typically where physical anthropologists step in and carefully excavate the human remains and then study them. You may have heard the expression, "you are what you eat," and this certainly applies to the results of the work of physical anthropologists. These anthropologists, who study the physical remains of past people, can extract a lot of information about the lives of these individuals. Even as a complete amateur, one can make the distinction between an adult and a child found in a grave; however, could you tell how old that child or adult might have been? Could you tell us if an individual had suffered from malnutrition at one point in his or her life? What about evidence of sickness, or violence? For what clues would you be looking? Physical anthropologists have most of the answers. Among physical anthropologists, there are people who specialize in the study of ancient mummies and others who study the remains of our earliest ancestors. The latter group is sometimes referred to as *paleoanthropologists,* or people who study ancient humans (where the term *paleo* means "ancient" or "old").

One important aspect has to be mentioned with regard to the field of physical anthropology. The handling of human remains is an issue that often elicits strong reactions. Among several ethnic groups, including some of the American Indian tribes, there is strong resistance to any handling of human remains. Those who object to the study of human remains will tell you it reflects a lack of respect toward the deceased, which they cannot accept.

Cultural anthropologists are people who study the human behavior of contemporary people. Because of one important fact—the subjects of their study are still around—anthropologists have the luxury of asking these people why they are engaged in certain practices or what the meaning and importance is of certain design elements in their pottery or textiles. This is undoubtedly a great advantage that cultural anthropologists hold over archaeologists, especially those studying cultures long gone; however, let us not forget that we are dealing with people. One is reminded of a famous (at least within anthropologist's circles) cartoon by Larson. It shows a scene inside a hut somewhere in a forest. The "primitive natives" are depicted frantically running around with a TV and VCR under their arms. Through a window in the background one can see a canoe with pit helmet–wearing anthropologists disembarking and getting ready to trek into the village. The caption reads: "Anthropologists! Anthropologist! Hide the stuff!" People will sometimes deliberately deceive anthropologists, whether because they think it is fun or because they want to please and will therefore provide an answer that they think the other side wants to hear.

Anthropology quite often involves communicating with others in a foreign language. **Linguistic anthropologists** are people who will study the language of their subjects, providing a better insight into the grammar and vocabulary of one of the roughly 6,000 languages that are currently around. A subspecialty, historical linguistics, involves greater time depth than just the contemporary world. This approach allows us to reconstruct the family tree of existing languages. This involves drawing up relationships between languages by comparing their vocabularies and ascertaining how many basic words have changed. The resulting count provides an approximation of how much time has past since two languages evolved out of a common language.

The study of the Aztecs relies on the insights of all four of these fields within anthropology. The Aztec past is the domain of archaeologists, physical anthropologists, and even historical linguists. The descendants of the ancient Aztecs can be studied today by cultural anthropologists and linguists alike. In the following pages, you will be introduced to the world of the Aztec; we will be guided by the results of the investigations conducted by all the different kinds of anthropologists just mentioned.

CONTRIBUTIONS MADE BY OTHER FIELDS OF STUDY

Aside from archaeologists researching the Aztec past, historians also make major contributions to this topic. Both approaches complement each other. Imagine being an archaeologist studying our own society. When we are tasked to reconstruct what people in the twenty-first century were up to, using only the material record, we would be tempted to insert what we know ourselves to connect the dots and fill in the blanks. That is what the study of historic (or written) documents does. That is the importance of what historians can contribute: more raw information (a.k.a. more "dots"), but most importantly, the context that links all these dots.

The reader will be provided with a brief overview of some of these written documents and the authors that produced them in Chapter 3. Lest we become overconfident that we can bring the Aztecs back to life with this magic mix of archaeology and history, we need to remind ourselves that the archaeological record is spotty and that authors did not always write down the truth. In other words, when we read the early colonial chroniclers, we need to remember that they were writing for a reason, and that reason was not necessarily to give us future readers an impartial report of what happened. Instead, these early chroniclers wrote to promote themselves or even defend themselves against allegations of concentrating too much power. For example, they were prone to exaggerate the number of enemy forces that were vanquished, or to depict in overly sensationalist terminology some of the ceremonies that they observed (the latter approach should ring familiar to anyone who has scanned the tabloid headlines in our supermarket checkout lanes).

Animal and plant specialists are quickly becoming major players as well. In the earliest excavation reports, the discussion of animal and plant remains was often relegated to the last sections of the publication. This is no longer true. We now have the technology to capture tiny plant fragments or animal remains, all of which can help us reconstruct the environment in which the Aztecs lived as well as what was on their menu. Aside from the technology making this possible, there is also a shift in impetus: researchers now intentionally set out to answer these types of questions. Gone are the days sometimes described by a French expression as "histoire bataille," or history focusing on major battles and rulers. We are no longer just interested in who ruled the kingdom, we also want to know who the remaining 99.9 percent of the people were that built the temples and pyramids, tilled the fields, and kept the upper crust fed and protected. That is why plant and animal specialists have become part of archaeological projects.

In some cases, and the Aztecs were no exception, a culture engaged in advanced stargazing. The Aztec were accomplished in this endeavor and ordered their lives around celestial events that they were able to observe. Modern astronomers and historians have been working on documents pertaining to Aztec knowledge of the sky.

The segue from astronomy to astronaut comes naturally: astronauts have occasionally been enlisted to train their cameras (using infrared and visible light) on our planet. Because of their efforts, we have truly had the opportunity to see the "big picture"; in fact, it does not get any bigger. Various road networks have been identified after analysis of some of these photographs taken aboard the space shuttle. That in turn has allowed us to reconstruct connections between communities, and even find unknown sites located at the intersections of these roads.

As our knowledge of genetics progresses with leaps and bounds, more of this kind of data will amplify our understanding of the past. The skeletal remains of Aztec-period people are recent enough to allow us—given the right conditions of preservation—to extract DNA. Once a sufficiently large database has been compiled, it should become possible to establish relationships between population groups to a degree that our present-day sources of information do not allow us to do.

With all these approaches in mind, and mindful of the various cautionary remarks just made, let us proceed with this next set of questions.

WHO WERE THE AZTECS?

Before we get started, there are a few questions that we need to answer. One refers to who the Aztecs were, and a subsequent question deals with the reasons why one could be, or even should be, interested in learning more about them. These questions are addressed next. This chapter ends with an overview of the other chapters that follow; however, we will start with the two questions just posed.

Even though the Aztecs were among the shortest-lived Precolumbian cultures, they are probably one of the best known. In addition, their short-lived history, at least as far as their Precolumbian history is concerned, left quite a legacy, including a widely spoken language that evolved from Nahuatl, the ancient Aztec language, and continued religious practices.

The term *Aztec* refers to Nahuatl-speaking people who settled in the Basin of Mexico during the thirteenth century AD. They managed to extend their territorial control over much of Northern Mesoamerica over the two centuries that preceded the arrival of the Spanish in the region.

Gilberto Losada teaches a Nahua-language class in Milpa Alta, a Nahua neighborhood on the outskirts of Mexico City. Nahua is spoken by the descendants of the Aztecs. Photo taken ca. 2003. (Robert van der Hilst/Corbis)

WHY IS IT IMPORTANT TO STUDY THEM?

When you mention the term *Aztec*, the image that is usually conjured up among the general public is one of a culture that is extremely violent and militaristic. References to human sacrifice and, occasionally, cannibalism are never far behind. When it comes to placing when and where the Aztec existed, there tends to be less agreement. Some people might locate them in South America, whereas others place them much earlier in time. For these reasons, the general public might be interested in going through these pages to find out more about a culture that carries their interest. An additional reason to focus on the Aztec is to appreciate some of their achievements. For example, how could the Aztec sustain a city the size of Tenochtitlan using Stone Age technology and still be successful? We might still be able to learn a few things from these earlier people and put them to good use in our world. There is, of course, also an intrinsic reason: the Aztec are interesting because of who they were. It is both fun and thought provoking to learn how civi-

Drummer in red and blue feather headdress at Aztec traditional dance performance. (Wolfgang Kaehler/Corbis)

lizations arose and then disappeared. People are interested in reading about achievements of past cultures and how they stack up against other cultures. In that regard, Precolumbian people are often compared with European civilizations, and the comparison of the Aztec with the Romans is one that is often made.

A ceramic mask from Teotihuacan. It has a "butterfly" nosepiece and disc earflares. (National Museum of Anthropology, Mexico, D.F.) (Charles & Josette Lenars/Corbis)

Contemporary people living in Mexico have their own reasons to be interested in the Aztecs. For one, a lot of people in that country, especially those living in the Basin of Mexico, consider themselves descendants of this high civilization. Most of these people are probably correct in making this assumption, and they are justified in the pride they show in their heritage. This brings up one final point: the Aztec culture is not totally gone. There are still aspects of it today, especially in the realms of religion and language. For that reason alone, if we are to understand large portions of Mexican society, indeed Hispanic communities in the United States as well, we need to know more about the roots and the origins of some of the beliefs and behaviors we might observe around us. We need to know who the Aztec were before we can understand who their descendants are.

OVERVIEW BY CHAPTER

In order for us to better understand the proper geographic and ecological context in which the Aztec civilization evolved, we start with this information in Chapter 2. The Aztecs found themselves wandering into an area that was both rich in resources and filled with other competing cultures. Their success in achieving dominance throughout large portions of what is now Central Mexico and areas to the south of it is a testimony to their tenacity and adaptability.

The rise of the Aztecs from a wandering tribe to the last indigenous empire in North America is detailed in Chapter 3. The reader will follow the Aztecs on their migration from a mythical place called "Aztlan." After all their peregrinations and repeated run-ins with various powerful political entities already established in the Valley of Mexico, we will witness the founding of the city of Tenochtitlan. This marks the beginning of a meteoric rise to Aztec hegemony, first on a regional basis and eventually throughout most of Northern Mesoamerica. Chapter 3 will introduce the reader to all of the known Aztec rulers. The astounding detailed information that is available to us is a testimony to the rich source material, retrieved from both written sources and the archaeological record. This chapter also identifies the various categories of written sources we have, with a special emphasis on those early documents written as eyewitness accounts by the Conquistadors as well as those written by the former Aztec elite as they were assimilated into a new culture.

The origins, growth, and decline of the Aztec civilization are discussed in Chapter 4. The archaeological antecedents of the Aztecs in Central Mexico are highlighted. Of great importance in this regard is the ancient metropolis of Teotihuacan, located to the northeast of the Aztec capital. As the reader will see, this city figured prominently in the history and the ceremonies of the Aztec elite. Once the Aztecs had achieved military and political supremacy in the Valley of Mexico, the question arises: Can we refer to an Aztec empire or not? Chapter 4 reviews how various specialists have defined this concept and then applies this notion to the Aztecs. The latter portion of this chapter is devoted to the rapid defeat of the Aztecs by the Spanish.

Although the Aztecs may be best known in popular culture for their violent and bloodthirsty image, they were accomplished traders. Chapter 5 deals with Aztec economics with a series of questions. These include such queries as, "What was the role of the markets in the realm," "What was traded," "When did markets take place," "How did the Aztec determine the value of the items being exchanged," and "How did goods get to the market?" Part of the Aztec economic system included a complex system of levying taxes, which will be discussed in this chapter. Chapter 5 also addresses one of the more notorious aspects of Aztec long-distance trade: the role of the pochteca. Finally, we will discuss the Aztec subsistence methods, or how the Aztec managed to feed themselves. The reader will learn about various agricultural production methods, as well as about the Aztec diet. The discussion of the latter should bring home the important contributions on the part of various indigenous American civilizations. Without them, our cuisine would be lacking a wide array of essential ingredients, which are outlined toward the end of Chapter 5. To offset the general perception of the Aztecs as brawny rather than otherwise sophisticated, there is a review of Aztec food etiquette at the end of the chapter.

One of the best-known aspects of Aztec civilization is the well-defined social organization, especially its social stratification. Our sources abound with references to many social classes. These details, as well as the extent to which Aztec citizens were able to move up the ladder, are discussed in Chapter 6. Most of this chapter addresses a "what if" situation. The reader is invited to imagine being an Aztec. What would your life have been like? Where would you have lived and how? This chapter ends with an attempt to figure out how many Aztecs there may have been in Precolumbian days. The reader is given an introduction to the way archaeologists try to tackle this issue.

We delve into Aztec politics in Chapter 7. The chapter focuses on the supreme Aztec political figure; that of the emperor. His position was never an easy one, as we will see. One of the constantly recurring aspects of Aztec political life was the heavy emphasis on the military. The Aztec rulers were almost always challenged when they ascended to the throne. This aspect, combined with powerful neighbors who successfully resisted Aztec attempts to incorporate them into their empire, led to a very sophisticated form of waging war on the part of the Aztecs. What this entailed is reviewed in the latter part of this chapter.

The Aztec shared an intricate belief system with other Mesoamerican civilizations. Chapter 8 consists of two main parts: one deals with the Aztec belief system, and the other highlights the close connection between politics and religion. It will become clear to the reader that the Aztec did not believe in separation between church and state.

We will assess one of the main reasons we know so much about Aztec culture in Chapter 9. Whereas the most important source of information is still the written record, the contributions of archaeologists are rapidly adding important chunks of information. Because of the nature of their work, what the archaeologists most often deal with is referred to as "material culture," terms that refer to the tangible, material remains of various aspects of Aztec life. The material culture reviewed here includes architecture, ceramics, stone tools, mural paintings, stone sculpture, and metallurgy.

As mentioned earlier, violence and warfare played an important role in Aztec politics. As a result of an extensive body of work on this aspect of Aztec society, the modern public perception of the culture tends to overemphasize it and neglect other aspects and achievements. Chapter 10 elaborates on such Aztec intellectual achievements as mathematics, the calendar, astronomy, writing, and their educational system. The final chapter deals with some controversies surrounding the Aztecs, including the issue of Aztec cannibalism. The chapter ends with a review of new trends in Aztec archaeology, especially how rural Aztec sites are being investigated in greater numbers, adding much-needed information to a database that still heavily favors the capital.

SOURCES OF INFORMATION ON THE AZTECS

As outlined, the reader will have an opportunity to get better acquainted with the breadth of indigenous and colonial-period sources in the chapters of this book. In addition to these important sources, there is a multitude of archaeological reports out there. The reader will be referred to such contributions, which continue to be published, throughout this book. Publishing these days is a term that encompasses both the printed word as well as the web.

Websites Related to Aztec Culture

A word of caution before we get started with these websites: as anyone familiar with the Internet knows, links can become outdated. The references that are listed were valid at the time of writing. In most cases, these are links to solid resources, such as universities, museums, and academic publishers. The reader is advised to look for additional material using the web's many good search engines.

General Information

http://www.Mesoweb.com This site is devoted to Mesoamerica, and the many cultures that were once part of it, including the Aztec culture. It provides links to other websites and to online articles on a wide variety of topics.

http://www.ancientmexico.com/ This website, created and designed by Patrick Olivares, provides a wealth of information on ancient Mexico. General categories of information include: maps, gods, conquest, time lines, documents, and history.

Aztec/Nahua Culture

http://www.ipfw.edu/soca/Nahua.htm This is the online version of *The Nahua Newsletter* published by the Center for Latin American and Caribbean Studies at Indiana University. This publication (both paper and electronic versions) provides articles, and book reviews on ancient Aztec and modern Nahua culture.

Bibliographies

Anyone interested in compiling bibliographic references on Aztec culture should go to the following sites:

http://www.famsi.org/research/bibliography.htm This site belongs to FAMSI, the Florida-based Foundation for the Advancement of Mesoamerican Studies, Inc. Follow the link to the *Bibliografia Mesoamericana* and type "Aztec" into the search engine and watch how thousands of references are generated.

http://www.doaks.org/Pre-Columbian.html This address will take you to Dumbarton Oaks, a Washington, D.C.–based research center specializing, among other things, in Precolumbian cultures, including the Aztec. You can access their excellent research library by starting on this site and then following links to ACORN, the online catalogue of the library. A search engine allows one to look for exact words or by category.

http://www.lib.utexas.edu/benson/ The Benson Library at the University of Texas, Austin, contains a wealth of publications and manuscripts referring to the Precolumbian world, especially Mesoamerica.

http://lal.tulane.edu/ The Latin American Library at Tulane University in New Orleans also has an incredible range of publications on Mesoamerica.

These resources can be accessed online by following the link given earlier. The collection incorporates the resources of Tulane's Middle American Research Institute.

http://lal.tulane.edu/latamcolls.html A useful link found at the website of Tulane's Latin American Library (see earlier entry) is a page that lists Latin American and Caribbean Archives and Libraries outside the United States.

Calendar

http://www.azteccalendar.com/ If you want to know what today's date looks like in the Aztec calendar, then this is the place to go.

Law

http://www.law.utexas.edu/rare/aztec/Home.htm If you are interested in learning more about Aztec law before conquest, then visit the website of the Law School at the University of Texas, Austin. The university's Tarlton Law Library put together a series of topics that can be perused, including Aztec courts, attorneys and judges, property law, and family.

Museum Collections

http://www.mna.inah.gob.mx/ The premier Aztec collection in the world can be found at the Museo Nacional de Antropología in Mexico City. Enter the site and select the option "salas," and then open the section dedicated to the "Mexica."

http://www.conaculta.gob.mx/templomayor/ This website presents information about one of the best-known Aztec structures, the Main Temple, or Templo Mayor, in the Aztec capital. Very rich in visuals, this site presents, among other topics, a time line of the construction and ultimate destruction of the temple.

Nahuatl Language

http://www.public.iastate.edu/~rjsalvad/scmfaq/nahuatl.html This website will put you on the right track if you are interested in learning more about Nahuatl, the ancient Aztec language.

Journals

A number of journals are dedicated to the archaeology of Mesoamerica. More information, and occasionally even articles, can be accessed online at the following websites:

http://www.cambridge.org/ Type in "Ancient Mesoamerica" and this link will take you to the pages of the semi-annual publication dedicated to the archaeology of Mesoamerica. A free sample issue of this publication is available online. Articles cover both Northern and Southern Mesoamerica.

http://www.arqueomex.com/ This address will take you to the pages of the magazine *Arqueologia Mexicana.* Some articles are available online. These are mostly Spanish-language contributions, although contributions are occasionally made in English

http://www.mexicon.de/index.html If you are interested in frequent and speedy updates on what is going on in the field of Mesoamerican archaeology, then Mexicon is the source to tap into. Its companion website allows for a search by key words, so tracking down articles on the Aztecs is easy.

http://www.saa.org/Publications/LatAmAnt/latamant.html Published by the Society for American Archaeology, this journal, called *Latin American Antiquity*, occasionally features articles on Aztec civilization. The website allows for a search by volume and provides a synopsis of the articles.

Rural Aztec Sites

http://www.albany.edu/~mesmith/rural.html This website highlights the research undertaken by Dr. Michael Smith, a leading Aztec specialist at the State University of New York at Albany. Here you will find additional links to his work, including excavations at rural Aztec sites.

Tenochtitlan—Virtual Reality

http://www.berg.heim.at/kaprun/430112/tenochtitlan/Vr_main.htm While this is a German-language website, the virtual reality reconstructions speak for themselves, with wonderful renderings of what the city might have looked like. These reconstructions are based on archaeological data and descriptions left by the Spanish.

Conquest

http://www.pbs.org/conquistadors/ PBS website. Click on "Cortés" to access the story of the Spanish conquest of the Aztec empire.

PART 2

Aztec Civilization

CHAPTER 2

Location of the Aztec Civilization and Environmental Setting

LOCATION

An Archaeologist's Concept: Mesoamerica

Open any book on the Aztec or Maya and chances are that the word *Mesoamerica* is mentioned on the first page. Paul Kirchhoff coined this term in 1943 (Kirchhoff 1943). Mesoamerica refers to a specific geographic area, covering parts of Mexico, as well as the entire territory of Guatemala and Belize and parts of Honduras and El Salvador. Kirchhoff intended to define a culture area that was distinct from those adjacent to it. To the north of Mesoamerica anthropologists recognize a culture area encompassing the present–day Southwestern United States and Northern Mexico; to the south of Mesoamerica there is the Chibcha culture area (named after a language family in Central America and Colombia).

Kirchhoff identified this geographic region as one in which cultures shared similar traits. He distilled these traits from early colonial descriptions of Precolumbian cultures. In other words, the term *Mesoamerica* reflects shared traits as they existed at the time of contact. This has implications with regard to the borderline between Mesoamerica and its neighboring culture areas. It is very likely that as we go back in time, shared traits were not always shared throughout the same region, and that as a result the borderline must have undulated back and forth as cultures acquired or shed traits.

Among others, the traits as identified by Kirchhoff encompass subsistence, agriculture, religion, dress, technology, and trade.

Although the term *Mesoamerica* refers to traits shared within a certain geographic area, we should not confuse it with well-defined geographic regions, such as North or Central America. We should not use Central America and Mesoamerica as interchangeable terms, if for no other reason than Mexico, portions of which are part of Mesoamerica, is part of North America.

The Valley of Mexico: The Heart of Aztec Civilization

The area in which the Aztec built their capital is traditionally referred to as the Valley of Mexico. This is where the capital of modern Mexico is located as well, on top of the ruins of the ancient Aztec capital and the subsequent colonial-period city. Two phenomena have conspired to produce these impressive population densities throughout this region: mountain ranges that acted as barri-

Subsistence:
Maize: corn softened with ash
  • large cooking plates (comales)
  • three-stone hearths
Beans
Squash
Cacao (chocolate)—also used as
  money
Tobacco (for smoking and healing)
Barkless dogs ("Mexican hairless")
Agriculture
Intensive agriculture
  • terracing of slopes
  • chinampas ("floating gardens")
Architecture
Stepped pyramids
Arrangement of buildings around
  a plaza
Construction with stone, mortar,
  and plaster
  • stucco floors
  • dedicatory caches in pits
    or cists
Roads paved with stone
Stone and clay construction
Hanging bridges
Religion
I-shaped ball courts
Ball game: game played with latex
  (rubber) balls
Bar-and-dot numerals

Complex pantheon of gods
260- and 365-day calendars
Barkcloth and deerskin books
  (codices), folded accordion
  style
Self-sacrifice (bloodletting):
  drawing blood from ears,
  tongue, or penis.
Live heart removal
Ritual cannibalism
Dress
Earspools
Lip plugs
Turbans
Sandals
Cotton armor
Technology
Pyrite or magnetite mirrors
Copper working
Obsidian
Ceramics
Clubs with embedded stone
  chips
Spinning and weaving
  • cotton cloth
  • rabbit-hair textiles
Trade
Exchanges of valuables among
  elites to establish political ties
Specialized markets
"Ports of trade"

Traits Shared By Mesoamerican Cultures

ers to human movement across the landscape and a series of interconnected lakes that enticed people to stay close to the shores.

The Valley of Mexico is an extended elevated basin surrounded by high mountain chains on three sides: the Sierra Nevada to the east, the Sierra Las Cruces to the west, and the Sierra Ajusco to the south. A series of low and discontinuous hills marks the northern edge of the Valley (Sanders 1971: 4). The Valley covers close to 8,000 sq. km (or slightly more than 3,000 sq. miles). Several majestic snowcapped mountains ring the Valley on its southern edge. One of these mountains is Mexico's highest: Pico de Orizaba (also known by its Aztec name, Citlaltépetl), rising 5,700 m above sea level. Other famous snowcapped mountains include Popocatepetl volcano (5,450 m) and

Men work in the shadow of the Popacatepetl volcano. (Charles & Josette Lenars/Corbis)

Ixtacihuatl (5,290 m) (Smith 1997: 11). They are affectionately known as "Popo" and "Ixta" today. Human presence above the tree line (4,000 m) during Precolumbian times was limited to the exploitation of the forest resources and pilgrimage to a few mountaintop shrines (Smith 1997: 11).

Although one will frequently find the term *Valley* in the literature when referring to this region, we should remind ourselves that during Precolumbian times, the "Valley" constituted a closed hydrographic unit. Because of this lack of a natural outlet, it would be more appropriate to use the term *basin* rather than *valley* (Gibson 1964: 1).

The higher elevations of the mountains surrounding the lakes supported a heavy forest cover during Precolumbian times. These higher areas yielded much-needed raw material for lumber, firewood, and charcoal (Smith 1997: 11). As a result of soil erosion in the higher elevations, the lower regions of the slopes as well as the basin floor had a very thick soil cover. Given the volcanic nature of the mountains, these soils were able to support a very productive agricultural system (Gibson 1964: 1).

As mentioned earlier, the presence of these high mountains conspired to keep much of the population concentrated on the basin floor. Today, these mountains are also the cause of a perennial problem in the Mexican capital:

smog. The pollution created by car exhausts and factory chimneys is kept in this huge natural bowl that is the Basin of Mexico. Because of this, today it is often difficult to see these majestic mountains surrounding the city.

Waters coming from the snowfields up in the mountains, the local springs, and the seasonal streams all collected into a series of lakes. Three interconnected lakes went along a north–south axis: Lake Xaltocan-Zumpango in the north, Lake Texcoco in the middle, and Lake Chalco-Xochimilco in the south. This lake system covered 1,000 sq. km, or about one-eighth of the total area of the Valley of Mexico. Lakes Texcoco and Xaltocan were salty; Lake Chalco-Xochimilco was a freshwater lake (Sanders 1971: 4).

Although these lakes were interconnected, they were not all located at the same elevation. This affected the salinity levels throughout the lake system. Lakes Chalco and Xochimilco were more elevated than the adjacent Lake Texcoco. As a result Lakes Chalco and Xochimilco were less saline than was Lake Texcoco. The Aztecs took advantage of this difference in salinity, and constructed their famous floating gardens, or *chinampas,* in the freshwater areas of the lake system. The lakes also served as efficient highways: goods and people moved across the lakes in hundreds, perhaps even thousands, of canoes. We know that agricultural produce was brought to the main market of the Aztec empire by means of canoes crossing the lakes.

Aside from opportunities, the lakes also presented problems to those living on their shores. Because of recurring flood problems, both the Aztecs and later the Spanish inhabitants tried to contain the floodwaters. During Aztec times, a dike system was built. Later, in colonial times, the Spanish dealt resolutely with the problem of flooding by draining most of the lakes. (See Chapter 9 for a discussion of a dike system built during the Aztec era.)

Surrounding the Valley of Mexico are several other valleys and plains. To the west of the Valley of Mexico is the Toluca Valley; to the east is the Puebla Valley. Both have environments very similar to the Valley of Mexico (Smith 1997: 11).

There were no mountains to close off the Basin of Mexico to the north. As one goes north, the climate becomes increasingly drier. This northern area of the Basin is ultimately what constitutes the northern border of the culture area known as Mesoamerica. During Precolumbian times, the agricultural potential of this northern region was poor. It still is today (Smith 1997: 11). One of the most important crops cultivated was the maguey plant. Another resource, of great importance during Aztec times, was obsidian, or volcanic glass.

The region becomes considerably lower to the south of the Basin of Mexico, with portions of the modern Mexican states of Morelos and Puebla about 1,000 m lower than the Valley of Mexico itself. Because of the lower elevation, temperatures are higher, which in turn permits the cultivation of such tropical crops as cotton and fruits (Smith 1997: 12).

Aztec Conquest: The Extent of Aztec Territorial Control

After the Aztecs settled in the Valley of Mexico, it took them very little time to establish control, first over the heartland, and later of a large number of territo-

Illustration of Aztecs building a chinampa. (Charles & Josette Lenars/Corbis)

ries. The Aztec possessions encompassed both the Valley of Mexico as well as the neighboring Toluca Valley. The Aztec also exerted control over the modern Mexican state of Morelos, the Gulf Coast area of Mexico, and parts of the modern state of Oaxaca. We find them as well in what is called Soconusco, an area in southern Mexico along the Pacific Ocean. Because of the pleasantness of the climate in what is now Morelos, and the great fertility of the soil, it was an area in which a great number of Aztec eventually settled. Archaeologists have found that Aztec-period sites are abundant and very well preserved (Smith 1997: 13).

At this stage I will refrain from using the expression, "Aztec empire." In Chapter 4, we will review whether or not we can use this terminology when discussing the extent of Aztec control over their possessions outside the Valley of Mexico.

ENVIRONMENTAL SETTING

Climate

The Valley of Mexico is part of what is called the *tierra fría* area, an area with fairly low mean-annual temperatures (Mexico City today records an average of 14.7∞C) (Sanders 1971: 3). Rainfall data collected in the Basin of Mexico since the end of the nineteenth century show a gradient within the region: in the northern and central plains of the Basin, the rainfall amounts range from 450 to 650 mm; this amount increases by about 20 to 50 percent in the piedmont areas bordering these plains. This seems like it would favor agriculture in these piedmont areas, but unfortunately the thinner soils and more rapid runoff in the same locations effectively nullify the advantage of increased rainfall (Sanders et al. 1979: 222). Annual rainfall amounts increase considerably in the southern portion of the Basin, where about 1,000 mm of rain will fall (Sanders 1971: 4).

One of the dangers inherent in making general statements such as these is that they reflect modern conditions. It is believed that these numbers have a considerable time depth to them; in other words, people assume that the same figures apply to Aztec times. The reader should also know that these modern rainfall figures are averages. We know that in modern times the rainy season has never completely failed, although in some cases there were severe droughts (Sanders et al. 1979: 225). Again, we are to assume that similar episodes of diminished rainfall must have occurred in Prehispanic times.

Soils

The soils in the Basin of Mexico come in a variety of types and thickness. Some are more suited than others to sustain agriculture. This variation is due to several factors, including altitude and slope. It should come as no surprise that almost half of the agricultural land (45 percent to be exact) in the Basin of Mexico is subject to erosion (Sanders et al. 1979: 225; Smith 1997: 10). Because erosion is an ongoing process, and one which is very difficult to reverse, we may surmise that Aztec farmers in Prehispanic days had access to slightly thicker soil cover than do their modern counterparts. The Aztec employed an intricate system of field walls to retain soils and prevent them from completely washing down slope.

The soils on the slopes of the foothills leading up to the mountain ranges are very rich and easy to work using simple technology, like the hand tools used by the Aztec. Still, because of the variation in soil depth throughout the Basin, plant cultivation was considerably harder in the northern portions of the Valley. This was primarily due to reduced rainfall, more hilly terrain, and limited soil cover encountered in that region. Conditions were much more favorable in the southern portion of the Valley, with a more humid climate, fewer hills, and thicker soil cover (Sanders 1971: 5).

Flora

We all owe a debt of gratitude to Prehispanic farmers, who domesticated a number of plants that have made it into our world, and more specifically, onto

Aztecs cultivating crops using a coa, or digging stick. (Bettmann/Corbis)

our plates. Perhaps the best known of these domesticates, as these plants are called, is maize or corn.

The earliest known evidence of domesticated maize comes from the Highlands of Mexico, either the Tehuacan Valley or the Basin of Mexico (Feddick 2001: 10). These earliest known corn cobs were puny, looking very similar to the so-called baby corn that we can find in our specialty food stores today. They date back to about 5000 BC, or roughly 7,000 years ago. Ancient farmers in Mexico were among the first in the Americas to domesticate squashes and pumpkins. Among other regions, it appears that central Mexico may have been one of the centers of domestication (Feddick 2001: 10).

Maguey, or agave, plants grow in a field west of Oaxaca. Once the sap-filled hearts are cut from these plants, they are collected, roasted in outdoor ovens, then crushed to extract the juice for distillation into mescal and other spirits. (Danny Lehman/Corbis)

For those among us who like spicy food, the chile peppers we know today may have been derived from wild chiles collected in Central Mexico by 5,000 BC. These peppers became domesticated and were then cultivated by farmers around 3,500 BC (Feddick 2001: 10).

One of the more typical plants from modern Mexico is the agave or maguey, no doubt because of its role in the production of such alcoholic beverages as tequila and mescal. The Aztec never indulged in the production of said beverages, so we should turn our attention instead to the Precolumbian uses of this plant.

The term *agave* refers to more than 100 species that grow throughout the Americas. In Central Mexico, the *agave* will grow at high altitudes, higher than 1,800 m above sea level (or more than 5,900 ft). In Prehispanic context the agave plant was used in a great variety of applications. Its sap was used to produce nonalcoholic beverages; its fiber, known as *ixtle,* was the basis for spinning and weaving textiles. The flesh of the plant's leaves, which can weigh up to 8 kg (or more than 20 lbs), was cooked and eaten. In some parts of Mesoamerica, the leaves were also used as roofing materials, whereas the stalk of the plant (*quiote*) served as construction material. In some cases these stalks were even turned into beehives (Parsons 2001: 5).

Agave is attractive to farmers because it grows all year long and will thrive at great altitudes in poor soils. With proper care, therefore, a farmer can extend the area in which to grow food, such as the *agave*. With their extensive root system, these sturdy plants also provide protection against soil erosion (Parsons 2001: 5). Moreover, in those areas that were either treeless or had been deforested, the *agave* also served as fuel.

Fauna

The Basin of Mexico is part of one of the richest biotic zones in the world. This means that the region extending from the northern Mexican border to the Isthmus of Panama has an incredible diversity of animal species (Emery 2001: 255). Although we should be aware that this statement is based on observations of animal life that can be observed today, we can extend this observation into the past based on finds of animal remains in archaeological contexts.

Of the mammals present in the Basin in Mexico, there are several species of opossum. Today they are hunted and eaten. The Aztecs may have eaten opossum as well, but they certainly used it in concoctions administered to women giving birth. Nine bat species have been reported for the larger area just mentioned. Free-tailed bats are the most common in the Basin (Emery 2001: 256).

The Aztec were familiar with carnivores, primarily cats, although a few members of the family of canids, or dogs, also occurred. Red fox, coyote, and wolf extend their range into northern Mexico. Dogs as we know them today did not occur in their contemporary variety in Aztec times. In general, Precolumbian peoples tended to have small domesticated dogs. These were both pets and served as a source of food. Bears today are restricted to the Highlands of Mexico. It is very likely that this observation also applied to Precolumbian times. Although these bears are almost extinct today, they may have formed the basis of a legendary monster known by its Nahuatl name as *cuetlachtli* (Emery 2001: 256). Among the big cats that live through Middle America, only the mountain lion would have lived in the Aztec heartland (Emery 2001: 256).

The lake environment that made up large portions of the Basin of Mexico undoubtedly contained its fair share of badgers, skunks, and river otters. One of the Aztec rulers was named after the river otter *Ahuizotl*. It is said that this creature operated at the command of the rain god Tlaloc, drowning greedy fishers and innocent victims (Emery 2001: 256).

White-tailed deer are very common throughout the region. They were hunted and eaten during Aztec times as they are today. The Aztec, as well as other Precolumbian people, considered the deer a primary fertility symbol. It was most often associated with the sky and the sun (Emery 2001: 257). Aside from venison, rabbit and hares were often featured for dinner among Mesoamerican peoples.

The bird population in Mexico and Central America, both permanent and overwintering, represents more than 100 families, comprised of more than

2,000 species. Of greatest importance to people are the so-called galliformes, a scientific term referring to such birds as the currassows, chachalacas, guans, pheasants, grouse, quails, and turkeys. Most of these animals were featured on the menu at one point or another. These birds were not very adapted to domestication, although there are indications that they were quite frequently captured and then kept alive in holding pens. Waterfowl, including ducks, herons, cranes, and rails, were also hunted (Emery 2001: 258). Egrets were also used as a source of feathers. These birds, together with such others as the quetzals living in the highland areas of Guatemala, as well as the hummingbirds found throughout large portions of Mesoamerica, all contributed to the manufacturing of dazzling feather-decorated objects (Emery 2001: 258).

Amphibians and reptilians were abundant in the region. Most of the amphibians encountered today can be classified into ten frog and toad families. Based on what we know of the Aztec diet, and the animals that were part of it, it is tempting to say that the Aztec would have felt at home in French restaurants. Aztecs consumed frogs in huge quantities; they were included in stews and tamales. Tadpoles were considered a delicacy. Another amphibian considered a delicacy was the mole salamander found in the Highlands of Mexico. The Spanish apparently also liked it, and the animal almost became extinct by the eighteenth century as a result (Emery 2001: 258). Of great interest to people today is a salamander, known by its Aztec name, the *axolotl*, which remains in its larval stage throughout its entire life. The Aztec did take advantage of the animal resources available in the Central Mexican lakes. These salty lakes provided the Aztecs with a wide range of food resources, including fish, turtles, insect larvae, blue-green algae, and salt (Smith 1997: 9).

Middle America has a great variety of snakes, with almost 500 species making up eight families. Among these 500 species, there are about seventy-five considered dangerous to humans, including a group of snakes called the pitvipers. The latter include moccasin vipers, copperhead vipers, lanceheads, bushmasters, and rattlesnakes (Emery 2001: 259). Some of these also occurred in the Mexican Highlands.

Faunal Exploitation in Prehispanic Times

Compared with their predecessors, modern archaeologists have become better at retrieving animal remains from their excavations. Even so, it is difficult to reconstruct in detail what the ancient Aztecs had on their menu. The available data only allow us to paint a picture in very broad strokes. It appears that the Aztecs focused on the exploitation of a few key animal species: white-tailed deer, cottontail rabbit, domestic dog, domestic turkey, and several varieties of migratory waterfowl, especially duck (Sanders et al. 1979: 282). The latter should not surprise us, given that the Basin of Mexico is located on a very busy migration route for birds.

White-tailed deer can be found throughout Mesoamerica. Their optimal foraging areas are the pine-oak woodlands that can be found in the Basin of Mexico, as well as Puebla, Toluca, Oaxaca, and Guerrero. Studies conducted in the 1950s have revealed a high density of thirteen to fifteen deer per square

An axolotl is a salamander species that retains its larval external gills as an adult. (Devin Schafer/Corbis)

kilometer (Sanders et al. 1979: 282). These deer tend to have relatively small home ranges, frequently traveling the same trails. This makes them very good targets for predators, human and animal. Because of the white-tailed deer's great breeding success, these animals can withstand an annual culling rate of 20–40 percent today (Sanders et al. 1979: 282). A factor that might have kept the deer in close contact with their human predators, despite all the culling going on, might have been that the animals were attracted to secondary grasses and weeds. Human agricultural practices, especially fallow agriculture, in which fields were allowed to "rest" after a few years of use, would have ensured that the deer stayed close to humans because they wanted to exploit these grass resources (Sanders et al. 1979: 282).

Precolumbian hunters used traps and snares to catch rabbits. Cottontails are very successful breeders and must have been extremely numerous throughout the Basin of Mexico. Archaeologists have found the bones of these animals well represented in the faunal remains at archaeological sites; however, given the small size of the animals, one had to wonder what the importance of the food value by weight would have been. Some have suggested that it was extremely low (Sanders et al. 1979: 284).

As mentioned earlier, the Basin of Mexico and its rich lake environment is one of the end points on migration routes for waterfowl. This migration route, today referred to as the Central Flyway, is used by ducks flying down from western Canada during the fall. A duck census conducted in 1952 indicated that more than 33,000 migratory ducks were present in Lake Texcoco. Given that the lakes in the Basin are but a shadow of their Prehispanic self, the number of waterfowl that might have traveled south during Aztec times may have numbered in the millions. It seems that nets as well as bows and arrows were used to bag some of these birds. Although large numbers of these birds may have been consumed, their overall dietary contribution was low—a situation similar to that of the cottontails (Sanders et al. 1979: 284–285).

Of passing interest is the apparent absence of fish remains from the material record. This is probably due to a lack of fish consumption among the Aztec, or, as is more likely, the perishable nature of fish bones, making it highly unlikely we will encounter a representative sample at a site (Sanders et al. 1979: 285).

REFERENCES

Emery, Kitty. 2001. Fauna. In *Archaeology of Ancient Mexico and Central America. An Encyclopedia*. Edited by Susan Toby Evans and David L. Webster, pp. 255–265. New York: Garland Publishing.

Feddick, Scott. 2001. Agriculture and domestication. In *Archaeology of Ancient Mexico and Central America. An Encyclopedia*. Edited by Susan Toby Evans and David L. Webster, pp. 7–15. New York: Garland Publishing.

Gibson, Charles. 1964. *The Aztecs under Spanish Rule. A History of the Indians of the Valley of Mexico 1519–1810*. Stanford: Stanford University Press.

Kirchhoff, Paul. 1943. Mesoamerica; sus límites geográficos, composición étnica y carácteres culturales. *Acta Americana 1: 92–107*. Washington, D.C.

Parsons, Jeffrey R. 2001. Agave. In *Archaeology of Ancient Mexico and Central America. An Encyclopedia*. Edited by Susan Toby Evans and David L. Webster, pp. 4–7. New York: Garland Publishing.

Sanders, William T. 1971. Settlement Patterns in Central Mexico. In *Handbook of Middle American Indians*. Vol. 10, part 1. Archaeology of Northern Mesoamerica. Edited by Gordon Ekholm and Ignacio Bernal, pp. 3–44. Austin: University of Texas Press.

Sanders,William T., Jeffrey R. Parsons, and Robert S. Santley. 1979. *The Basin of Mexico. Ecological Processes in the Evolution of a Civilization*. New York: Academic Press.

Smith, Michael E. 1997. *The Aztecs*, 2nd ed. Blackwell Publishers: Oxford.

CHAPTER 3

Historical and Chronological Setting

AN OVERVIEW OF AZTEC STUDIES

Colonial Period Interests into Aztec Culture

There was initially very little interest on the part of the Spanish conquerors to preserve any of the Aztec structures in the capital or anywhere else. We know instead that Cortés decided to use the rubble of the demolished temples and palaces as building materials for the first European-style houses in the colonial capital of Mexico City (López Luján 1999). Cortés himself had a palace built on the ruins of Motecuhzuma II's palace (Evans 1999, 2001).

Cortés paradoxically did generate widespread interest in European capitals in things from the New World. In an attempt to curry more favor with Emperor Charles V, Cortés sent shiploads of objects, animals, and even people from the new dominions to the Old World. We know from written sources that these shipments made a great impression on anyone who saw them. These eyewitness accounts included the well-known artist Albrecht Dürer (Rupprich 1956, I: 155; Parker 1999: 135). Most of the objects that were sent over eventually disappeared (Saville 1920: 58–100). The few pieces that did survive are now among the most prized possessions of museum collections (Anders 1978; Nowotny 1960; Pasztory 1998: 279–280).

This pattern of disregard of a rich Precolumbian past continued for more than 250 years after the conquest. It was not until the end of the eighteenth century that incidental discoveries of archaeological materials were preserved rather than destroyed or discarded.

On August 13, 1790, a monumental sculpture was found in the main plaza of Mexico City. This sculpture is known today to represent the goddess Coatlicue, and is currently in the National Museum of Anthropology in Mexico City. Not long after this discovery followed that of the famous Calendar Stone. Both sculptures were the subject of a publication by Don Antonio de León y Gama in 1792. The Calendar Stone was left in front of the Cathedral in Mexico City for more than 2 years. It was eventually buried by friars who must have felt uneasy at the thought of relics from a pagan past being uncovered and displayed. In 1803, Baron Alexander von Humboldt had the Calendar Stone disinterred so that he could study it (Matos Moctezuma 2003: 92–95).

Calendar Stone. (Philadelphia Museum of Art/Corbis)

Aztec Studies After Mexican Independence: Nineteenth and Early Twentieth Century

The French incursion into Mexican affairs included an effort to study the indigenous culture. Some of the Mexican documents held at French repositories today were obtained during this period.

W. H. Prescott's work on the conquest was one of the first written in English (Prescott 1843). Prescott, together with Alexander von Humboldt (1810), introduced the term *Aztec* to the public. This term has stuck with us since (see later).

At the beginning of the twentieth century, Batres undertook excavations in the center of Mexico City. At the end of the nineteenth century and the beginning of the twentieth century, work on the construction of a drainage canal in the area where the Templo Mayor once had stood had destroyed all evidence found. Batres undertook emergency excavations and was able to collect information on a portion of the Templo Mayor (Batres 1902).

About a decade later, from 1913 to 1914, Gamio excavated in the temple precinct as well, and uncovered one of the corners of the Templo Mayor. He also found a carved stone sculpture of a serpent's head at the bottom of one of the stairs going up the temple. Gamio did realize that he had found remains of the Templo Mayor (Gamio 1917, 1921).

Aztec Studies since 1940

Even though archaeological research ground to a halt in Europe in the 1940s, it was still possible to pursue scholarly interests in Mexico. In particular, scholars continued focusing on Central Mexico, heartland of the Teotihuacan and Aztec cultures. George Vaillant published his *Aztecs of Mexico* in 1941. In this book, he addressed the issue that had vexed archaeologists for a long time: the chronicles referred to Tollan, a site long considered to have been mythical. Vaillant argued that it might have been the megalopolis of Teotihuacan that was meant by that term (Vaillant 1941). Arguments quickly ensued, with others putting forward another archaeological site, Tula, as the candidate for the mythical Tollan.

In 1942, the archaeologist Pedro Armillas started work at Teotihuacan. He also began studying the phenomenon of the *chinampas,* or so-called floating gardens. He saw in this very productive agricultural system the explanation for the incredible growth of urban centers in the southern portion of the Valley of Mexico (Armillas 1950, 1971). Toward the end of the decade, excavations at the Templo Mayor continued. In 1948 Moedano and Estrada Balmori dug at the site, expanding the area around the temple's corner already exposed by Gamio. An important study was published in the same year by Cook and Simpson, who in a meticulous way tried to reconstruct the population numbers during the early colonial period. To do so, they accessed tax records, as well as military and clerical documents (Cook and Simpson 1948).

During the 1950s, researchers followed the suggestion made by Armillas earlier: to make good use of the written record to reconstruct Late Postclassic society in Central Mexico—in other words, the Aztecs. One of the topics that scholars addressed this way was that of land tenure: Who owned the land? Kirchhoff (1954) and Caso (1959) both published on that subject.

A work of epic proportions appeared in 1964, when Gibson published his work on the Aztec during the colonial period (Gibson 1964). In the late 1960s Vega Sosa coordinated research in the Sacred Precinct of Tenochtitlan (Vega Sosa 1979). Matos Moctezuma uncovered an altar in 1964. It appeared that it had once been used inside the Great Precinct (Matos Moctezuma 1992: 23; Matos Moctezuma 1964).

During the 1970s, Aztec culture became a topic of theoretical concern when studies on state formation proliferated. *The Handbook of Middle American Indians,* a major undertaking emanating from Tulane University, was the platform on which some of these studies appeared (Carrasco 1971; Gibson 1971).

Up until the late 1970s, a lot of scholarly contributions had concentrated on the Aztec capital. A new emphasis was added in 1979, when the first systematic study of Aztec settlement patterns, as the distribution of sites across the landscape is called, was published (Sanders et al. 1979).

The Coyolxauhqui, a large stone statue, was found during excavations in the Templo Mayor area of Tenochtitlan/Mexico City. (Philippe Desmazes/AFP/Getty Images)

A year earlier, in February 1978, workers for the Mexican electrical company discovered a monumental sculpture, now known as the Coyolxauhqui. This discovery eventually led to 4 years of very intense excavations. The Templo Mayor project lasted from 1978 to 1982, and greatly increased our knowledge of the temple structure (Boone 1987; Matos Moctezuma 1988). The Templo Mayor project continued during the 1990s (López Luján 2001: 714).

Investigations in the Ceremonial Precinct have brought to light evidence that the Aztecs themselves were interested in the past of the region. Archaeologists found figurines and masks from Teotihuacan and even an Olmec mask while uncovering offerings inside the Templo Mayor (López Luján 1989; Matos Moctezuma 1979; Olmo Frese 1999: 41). The so-called House of the Eagles, encountered at Tenochtitlan, is now considered to be a revival of the Palacio Quemado in Tula. It appears that the Aztec also excavated in the ruins of the ancient Toltec capital of Tula (López Luján 2001: 715; in press).

Tremendous progress has been made since the late 1970s in our understanding of how Aztec society was organized outside the Basin of Mexico, as well as how Aztec society operated internally. Insights into the latter have been helped by the wealth of information produced by the Templo Mayor project. Work at sites outside the Valley of Mexico also took off during this period, especially in ancient Aztec rural communities (Brumfiel 1980; Smith 1992, 1993). A good example of this type of research is the work undertaken at the Aztec town of Yautepec in Morelos, Mexico (Hare and Smith 1996; Smith 1996, passim; 1997; Smith et al. 1994; Smith 2003b). As a result of this work outside Tenochtitlan, we now know that there was a great diversity in economic activity throughout the empire. For example, the inhabitants of Otumba seem to have been accomplished craftsmen (Smith 2003a: 4). Our knowledge of Aztec farming techniques has also benefited greatly by the excavations outside the Valley of Mexico. Aztec farmers were capable of adjusting their ways of tilling the soil to suit the local conditions (Hodge 1998).

Even though great progress has been made, Aztec scholarship continues to face problems and shortcomings. Some might be overcome by an improved means of communication among North American and European scholars; others only after barriers of provincialism have been breached. Smith (2003a) outlines the following problems that still affect Aztec scholarship:

1. *A lack of systematic catalogs of Aztec material culture.* Although compendia of Aztec written documents are generally available, similar published source materials dealing with Aztec material culture are still nonexistent.
2. *Lack of communication between scholars from different, but overlapping, fields.* Archaeologists, art historians, and historians commonly see each other with suspicion and are only vaguely aware of the significant contributions that their fields can make to the greater good: a better understanding of Aztec culture. Related to this is the lack of communication among scholars because of a language barrier. Researchers in Mexico, North America, and Europe do not always know of each other's work, quite often because it has been published in a language that the other side cannot read. (I would add that in addition to a lack of linguistic prowess on the part of some researchers, progress is further hampered by a lack of available journals and books on the subject in the geographic areas just mentioned. Perhaps the Internet can provide a partial solution here by making these publications available in an electronic format.)

CHRONOLOGICAL FRAMEWORK

Origins: Aztlan (pre-AD 1100)

The Aztec relate to us that they came from a place called Aztlan. This term, which forms the basis of the word *Aztec,* can be translated as "Place of the Herons" (Smith 2003c: 35), or "place of the storks," or "of whiteness" (Matos Moctezuma 2003: 3). We should note, however, that those people we refer to today as Aztecs did not use that term for themselves at the time of contact. In codices, such as the Telleriano-Remensis, annotators use the term *Mexica* instead (Quiñones Keber 1995: 107). Another term that applies is *Tenochca*, meaning "inhabitants of Tenochtitlan" (Quiñones Keber 1995: 107).

Scholars today cannot agree whether Aztlan refers to an actual place or to a mythical homeland of the Aztec. Among those who argue in favor of Aztlan being a real place, there is still no agreement about its location on the map. Some have argued in favor of a location in the Southwestern United States (Vollemaere 1992), whereas others have suggested the Valley of Mexico itself (Matos Moctezuma 2003: 3). Several Mexico scholars do not believe in the historicity of the Aztlan site (Acosta Saignes 1946; Jiménez Moreno 1974; Kirchhoff 1958; López-Austin 1973: 80–85; Townsend 2000: 58). Smith (1984) tries to find the middle of the road. He argues that the origin stories often belong in the realm of myth, but that there is also a high degree of historical validity in these stories. Smith derives this validity from the insertion of origin stories in the historical sections of Precolumbian or colonial manuscripts rather than in the ritual or mythological sections (see also Quiñones Keber 1995: 193).

Days of Wandering (AD 1100–1250)

Colonial documents such as the Tira de la Peregrinación relate how the Aztec migrated into Central Mexico. They seem to have moved from north to south, an idea supported by historical studies into the origins of the Nahuatl language (Kaufman 1976). Some accounts refer to seven tribes who at one point of their migration visit Chicomostoc, the "Place of the Seven Caves" (Smith 1996: 39). The migration from Aztlan to what would become Tenochtitlan took several generations to complete. As they wandered around, in search of a place to settle permanently, the Aztec occasionally stopped to build houses and temples. They carried out rituals, and we are led to believe that they also cultivated food (Smith 1996: 39; Townsend 2000: 59). The migrants were led by priests who carried effigies of Huitzilopochtli, their patron god (Smith 1996: 40; Townsend 2000: 59).

Matos Moctezuma suggests that Huitzilopochtli may have been a historical figure, who, upon his death, became a god. According to a sixteenth-century chronicler, Cristóbal del Castillo, there was at one point a priest called Huitzil. He served the god Tetzauhteotl. In a story that reminds one of that of Moses and the exodus from Egypt, Cristóbal del Castillo relates how Huitzil led the Mexica out of Aztlan. At one point, as he was near death, he addressed the Mexica, saying that he was about to die, that the gods were going to transform him, and that they would give his remains to the god Tetzauhteotl. At that point he becomes Huitzilopochtli Tetzauhteotl, a god in his own right (Matos Moctezuma 2003: 6).

The wandering Mexica are subject to dissention, and as a result, three groups are referred to in the written record. The largest group was led by Huitzil or Huitzilopochtli. A second group, sometimes referred to as a clan (Matos Moctezuma 2003: 6), was led by Malinalxochitl, the sister of Huitzilopochtli. A third group of wanderers was headed by another female figure, Coyolxauhqui. The latter figure was also related to Huitzilopochtli. She took charge of the clan of the Huitznahua (Matos Moctezuma 2003: 6–7).

An important episode in the wandering days of the Aztec arrives when they decide to settle in the area around Coatepec Hill (Hill of the Serpent), close to Tula, the capital of the Toltec civilization. According to tradition, the Mexica apply the knowledge of water management, and build a dam. They then proceed to produce shrimp, fish, aquatic plants, and birds. It appears that this episode of settlement at Coatepec led to internal friction. Those who represented the clan of the Huitznahua wanted to stay at Coatepec and settle for good, a decision that Huitzilopochtli opposed. The story of the Aztec exodus relates how this conflict was "diffused." At midnight the Mexica heard a great noise, and the next day the leaders of the clan of the Huitznahua, including Coyolxuahqui, were found dead. All had their chests opened and their hearts removed (Matos Moctezuma 2003: 7).

This battle among mortals may have been so important in Aztec history that it took on its own life, whereby the human protagonists in the fight are transformed into gods (Matos Moctezuma 2003: 9).

Arrival in the Valley of Mexico and Founding of Tenochtitlan (AD 1250–1324)

After the events around Coatepec, the Aztec continued their march southward. According to tradition, later recorded by the chroniclers, they passed through Atitalaquia, Atotonilco, and then reached the shores of Lake Texcoco, where they went by Tzompanco, Ecatepec, and Pantitlan (Matos Moctezuma 2003: 16). They eventually settled in the area of Chapultepec, or "Grasshopper Hill," a desolate and rather undesirable spot (Smith 1996: 40). They did not stay there forever, as they were attacked by established settlers and forced to flee (Townsend 2000: 63). The survivors reached the town of Culhuacan and begged for protection. They were given land to settle on near a place called Tizaapan, another rather inhospitable location (Townsend 2000: 63).

This, however, was not to be the end of their wanderings. The Aztecs managed to invoke the wrath of their hosts by sacrificing one of the daughters of the Culhuacan ruler to the god Huitzilopochtli. In the ensuing fight, the Aztecs were driven out and were forced to flee to one of the uninhabited islands in Lake Texcoco. The Aztecs were by no means an independent political force once the city had been founded. After they had escaped the wrath of the Culhuacan ruler, they placed themselves under the protection of the ruler Azcapotzalco, home of the Tepaneca people. This protection came at a price: the Aztec became his vassals and were required to send tribute and to participate in military campaigns undertaken by Azcapotzalco (Matos Moctezuma 2003: 16). This was a very convenient arrangement for the ruler Azcapotzalco. He assigned the Aztecs an area in which they could settle; an island in the lake, located on the border between his domain and that of Culhuacan. This provided Azcapotzalco with a buffer against any aggression from Culhuacan, while at the same time also ensured a steady flow of lake products sent to the city as part of the tribute requirement (Matos Moctezuma 2003: 17).

Aztec tradition glosses over these events and instead suggests that the reason why they settled on the island was because they had seen an eagle perched on a nopal cactus. They interpreted this as a sign from Huitzilopochtli to settle. All sources do agree that Tenochtitlan was founded in the year 2 House, AD 1325 (Heyden 1989; Smith 1996: 44–45; Townsend 2000: 64–65).

The name *Tenochtitlan* means "Among the Stone-Cactus Fruit." This is mirrored in the glyph representing the city's name: it depicts a fruited nopal cactus growing out of a stone (Smith 2003c: 43; Townsend 2000: 65). It reflects the foundation story of the city just mentioned. A sister community of Tlatelolco was established on the northern side of the island where Tenochtitlan was founded (Townsend 2000: 65). One of the first structures to go up was a shrine to Huitzilopochtli. This location would eventually grow into the Sacred Precinct, considered by the Aztec to be the center of the universe.

The early inhabitants of Tenochtitlan faced daunting prospects. Living on an island, they were surrounded by hostile neighbors, they lacked adequate building materials, and had to cope with limited agricultural opportunities.

Still, Tenochtitlan slowly grew, primarily because of economics. The inhabitants took advantage of the abundance of resources available: migratory birds and aquatic animals were hunted and collected. These resources, as well as green algae, were taken to the markets of larger communities along the edges of Lake Texcoco and sold there. Markets were eventually established inside Tenochtitlan and Texcoco as well (Townsend 2000: 65–66).

As commercial ties with neighboring communities grew, the Aztec also established family ties with their commercial partners by intermarrying with them. Early on, the Aztec also started efforts to improve the agricultural potential of their island home by constructing "floating gardens," the famous *chinampas* (Townsend 2000: 67).

A Century of Imperial Rule (AD 1325–1428)

A problem involved with *chinampa* agriculture was to separate the salty waters of Lake Texcoco from the fresh waters of Lakes Chalco and Xochimilco. The early Aztecs achieved this by constructing a dike and canal system (Smith 1996: 46).

Through trade, successful intermarriage, and alliance building, Tenochtitlan grew. During this first century of Tenochtitlan's history, the Aztec had to contend with the presence of much more powerful entities along the lakeshores. Two cities in particular had begun their rise to power: Azcapotzalco, capital of the Tepanecs, and Texcoco, capital of the Acolhua (Smith 1996; 46). As we have seen, the Aztec had allied themselves with the Tepanecs, and part of their tribute requirement included military service.

About 50 years after the founding of Tenochtitlan, in 1372, the Aztec sought to have their own king, or *tlatoani*. To achieve this, they looked for help from the king of Culhuacan, a city that had granted them protection more than a century earlier. As a result of this diplomatic endeavor, a high-ranking Aztec

Page from the Codex Mendoza referring to the founding of Tenochtitlan. The center of this image is repeated in Mexico's flag. (Gianni Dagli Orti/Corbis)

individual married the daughter of the Culhuacan king. Their son, Acamapitchli, was to become the first Aztec *tlatoani* (Smith 1996: 46).

The Triple Alliance (AD 1428–1519)

The term *Triple Alliance* refers to a close bond that was established by emperor Itzcoatl between the cities of Tenochtitlan, Texcoco, and Tlacopan. The Alliance came into being in 1428, in the wake of the Tepanec civil war. As will be outlined in Chapter 4, this alliance had both military aspects and very specific economic ones, especially pertaining to the distribution of tribute among the members of the alliance. This alliance lasted for 91 years. The Spanish conquest ended it.

Spanish Conquest (AD 1519–1521)

When the Spanish landed in what is now the state of Veracruz, they were drawn further inland by stories of a great empire in the interior. The fact that the Aztec envoys sent by emperor Moctecuhzuma Xocoyotzin tried to entice the Spanish to return home by providing them with gifts of gold was completely counterproductive to the Aztec's aspirations and served only to encourage further Spanish exploration.

As will be elaborated upon in Chapter 4, several factors contributed to the downfall of the Aztecs. The fragile nature of this system, built on the extraction of tribute rather than absolute territorial control, provided the Spanish with the allies they needed. Superior armor and tactics, as well as a silent ally in the form of diseases, all contributed to the dissolution of the Aztec realm. Given the centralized nature of the political system in the Aztec world, the conquest of this entity took much less time than did the conquest of other Mesoamerican cultures (i.e., the Maya).

THE AZTEC IMPERIAL LINEAGE

Acamapichtli (1372–1391)

Acamapichtli was the son of a high-ranking Aztec individual and a Culhuacan princess. He became the first Aztec king, or *tlatoani*. His rule lasted for 19 years, from 1372 to 1391. Acamapichtli also married a noblewoman from Culhuacan. Their son, Huitzilihuitl, became the second Aztec king (Smith 1996: 47).

Huitzilihuitl (1391–1415)

Huitzilihuitl was the second Aztec *tlatoani*. He ruled for 24 years, from 1391 to 1415. Under his rule, Tenochtitlan grew considerably. Huitzilihuitl continued the practice of cementing Tenochtitlan's position in the Valley of Mexico by arranging successful marriage alliances between his noblemen and aristocratic women from neighboring cities. Because Aztec nobles practiced polygamy, this network grew very quickly over a short period of time (Smith 1996: 47).

Huitzilihuitl married the daughter of Tezozomoc, the Tepanec ruler. Their son, Chimalpopoca, became the third Aztec *tlatoani*. Upon the death of Tezozomoc's daughter at a young age, Huitzilihuitl married the daughter of a powerful ruler of the Cuauhnahuac dynasty in what is now the state of Morelos. The ruler apparently initially rebuffed Huitzilihuitl's advances. In an endearing story that has survived until today, we learn how the Aztec king was able to woo his future bride and convince his future father-in-law by shooting a hollow arrow shaft filled with jewels into the princess' room. They were soon married (Alvarado Tezozomoc 1975: 94–95; Smith 1996: 48). The son of this union, Motecuhzuma Ilhuicamina, was to become one of the great Aztec leaders.

Chimalpopoca (1415–1426)

When his father died in 1415, Chimalpopoca took over as third Aztec king. Under his rule, Tenochtitlan-Tlatelolco continued to grow. The cities attracted newcomers and proved to be a growing economic power. The market at Tlatelolco, which was to become one of the most important in the Aztec world, began to offer luxury goods under his rule. Such items as parrot feathers and jewelry offered for sale imply that there was enough of an emerging Aztec elite who wanted them and could afford to purchase them (Smith 1996: 48).

The political clout of Tenochtitlan also grew during this period. A war broke out between the Tepanecs, with whom the Aztec were allied, and the Acolhua of Texcoco. With Aztec help, the Tepanecs defeated Texcoco. As a reward for their assistance, the Aztec received Texcoco as a tribute-paying community (Smith 1996: 48–49).

The year 1426 proved to be eventful for both the Tepanecs and the Aztecs. In that year, Tezozomoc, the Tepanec king, died and a civil war broke out. Two factions vied for power, with the Aztecs backing the heir apparent. They seem to have bet on the wrong horse, as the other faction, heavily anti-Aztec, took control. Not too long thereafter, Chimalpopoca was killed under suspicious circumstances. The Aztecs chose the brother of Huitzilihuitl, Itzcoatl, as their new leader.

Itzcoatl (1426–1440)

Itzcoatl proved to be the right man at the right time for the Aztecs. He was not about to give in to the Tepanecs under their new ruler, who was hostile to the Aztecs. Itzcoatl was assisted by two able ministers, Motecuhzuma Ilhuicamina, his nephew, and Tlacael. The latter was a half-brother of Motecuhzuma (Smith 1996: 49).

Hostilities with the Tepanecs lasted for 2 years, 1426–1428. Itzcoatl combined forces with other cities; Texcoco, Tlacopan, and Huexotzinca. In 1428 these new allies defeated the Tepanec king. Tenochtitlan, Texcoco, and Tlacopan formed a more formal alliance, which we know as the Triple Alliance. Huexotzinca did not participate and withdrew back to its own domain in the Tlaxcalla-Puebla area, south of the Valley of Mexico (Smith 1996: 49–50).

Itzcoatl proved to be an astute politician as much as an able commander on the battlefield. He realized the power of the written word and made an attempt to rewrite history by ordering the destruction of Aztec history manuscripts (Boone 2000a: 20–21). We can only assume that these older documents, dealing with the history of the Aztec, provided information that was considered offensive to or that did not conform to the preconceived notions of the then ruler, Itzcoatl (Thomas 1995: 23).

Itzcoatl initiated an expansion of Aztec-controlled territory, first by conquering southern portions of the Valley of Mexico. One of the most important conquests in this part of the Basin of Mexico was that of Xochimilco. This was an important food-production center along the lake, with its inhabitants specializing in floating garden, or *chinampa*, agriculture (Matos Moctezuma 2003: 22).

He expanded his realm outside the Valley as well by attacking towns like Cuauhnahuac and Huaxtepec in what is now Morelos. Itzcoatl also looked after the needs of the capital. Access to drinking water was of great importance to the citizens of Tenochtitlan. The water in the surrounding lake was not suitable to be drunk, so an aqueduct was constructed during Itzcoatl's reign, bringing water from the springs of Chapultepec across the lake (Matos Moctezuma 2003: 74).

In 1440, shortly after the conclusion of the Morelos campaign, Itzcoatl died. Motecuhzuma Ilhuicamina succeeded him (Smith 1996: 50–51).

Motecuhzuma Ilhuicamina I (1440–1468)

Scholars refer to this ruler as Motecuhzuma I to distinguish him from his great-grandson, Motecuhzuma Xocoyotzin. Motecuhzuma Ilhuicamina completed the conquest of the Valley of Mexico by defeating Chalco, a holdout in the southern part of the Valley. This campaign was followed by a systematic effort to consolidate Aztec power within the conquered areas. This effort took about 10 years (Smith 1996: 51).

From 1450 to 1458, the emperor turned to internal affairs. The construction of the Templo Mayor was initiated during this part of his reign. A legal code was drafted that resulted in a widening gap between the aristocracy and the commoners; however, he also made provisions for social mobility, by creating a new title, *quauhpilli* or eagle lord (Smith 1996: 52).

During this emperor's reign, the Aztecs faced natural disaster in the form of a long-lasting drought. From 1450 to 1454, a severe drought hit the Valley. Crops were failing and people were starving. At the end of the 4 years, the empire was in complete chaos, with people roaming the countryside looking for food. The rains returned in 1455, and the people started on the long road to recovery (Smith 1996: 53; Thomas 1995: 30).

In 1458, Aztec forces from Tenochtitlan and Texcoco embarked on a campaign that would expand the boundaries of the Aztec territory dramatically. The city of Cuauhnahuac, which had been under Aztec control once before, had to be reconquered. The Aztec armies then established control over the remaining parts of Morelos, the Gulf Coast, and portions of what is now Oaxaca (Smith 1996: 53). Ten years after initiating this massive campaign, the emperor died.

According to some reports it is possible that this emperor was succeeded by his daughter Atotoztli (Carrasco 1984: 44; Chimalpahin 1965: 64). She may have served as a *tlatoani* for a period of 6 years that is alleged to have existed between the reigns of Motecuhzuma Ilhuicamina and Axayacatl (Marcus 2001: 333). Van Zantwijk (1985: 188, 191) argues that we know very little of Atototztli's reign because the official Aztec scribes, exhibiting a male bias, were prone not to mention female rulers. Instead of mentioning her, Van Zantwijk argues, the scribes may have preferred to fill this 6-year gap between male kings either by extending the reign of Motecuhzuma well past his death, or by starting the reign of Axayacatl much earlier than his actual accession date.

Axayacatl (1468–1481)

This emperor spent most of his reign consolidating the conquests his grandfather had made. Just like his predecessors, Axayacatl had to reconquer some cities that had thrown off the yoke of the Aztec empire and its demands for tribute.

The twin-city arrangement between Tenochtitlan and Tlatelolco came to an end during his reign. Up until now, Tlatelolco had been ruled by an independent *tlatoani*. It seems that the king of Tlatelolco had his mind set on complete independence from Tenochtitlan. He rejected his wife, the sister of the Aztec emperor, as part of severing his ties with Tenochtitlan (Thomas 1995: 36). Axayacatl was left no choice but to intervene. The Tlatelolco *tlatoani* committed suicide and was replaced with a military governor. This created ill-will among the inhabitants of Tlatelolco, and they eagerly looked forward to the day that they could repay the emperor. As we know, that day eventually did come.

The only expansion of the empire during his reign took place in the Toluca Valley, located to the immediate west of the Valley of Mexico. This conquest proved to be of great strategic importance. The Toluca Valley became a buffer zone between the Aztec heartland and the Tarascan empire. Around 1478 or 1479, the Aztec armies were soundly defeated by the Tarascans in a head-on battle in the Toluca Valley. The emperor himself was severely wounded (Hassig 1988: 186–187; Smith 1996: 55; Thomas 1995: 36). He did not survive very long. Axayacatl died in 1481 and was succeeded by his brother, Tizoc.

Tizoc (1481–1486)

Tizoc seems to have been keen on self-aggrandizement and nothing else. He did not engage in major campaigns and as a result added little to Aztec territory. He did start a war immediately upon ascending to the throne. His opponent, the independent kingdom of Metztitlan, met and beat the Aztec army. This did not stop Tizoc from having himself depicted on a carved stone monument, known as Tizoc's stone, as a ruler victorious in many battles. Moreover, during this period, the title of the emperor changed from simply "tlatoani," or "speaker/king" to "huehuetlatoani," or "old/supreme king" (Smith 1996: 55). The king "was helped to die" 5 years after becoming ruler, probably because of his ineptitude and perceived loss of prestige (Isaac 1983: 125). Tizoc was succeeded by Ahuizotl, his brother.

Ahuizotl (1486–1502)

Ahuizotl had to reconquer parts of the empire. This included putting down a rebellion by the Huaxtec along the Gulf Coast (Smith 1996: 55). Ahuizotl also pursued a policy of containment of the Tarascan threat. Having learned a lesson from their defeat in 1478 or 1479, the Aztecs refrained from attacking the Tarascans, and started establishing client states along the Tarascan border instead. A system of fortifications was set up and colonists from the Valley of

Mexico were brought in to settle the border area (Smith 1996: 56). The Aztec, too, were familiar with the policy of containment.

The Aztec realm grew considerably during this emperor's reign. He established control over the Valley of Mexico and Soconusco, a region along the Pacific coast of Mexico. These were among the most remote territories under Aztec control. They contained within them important trade routes, funneling exotic (for the Aztec, at least) lowland products, such as cacao and quetzal feathers to the capital (Smith 1996: 56).

Ahuizotl gradually assumed the primacy among the rulers of the Triple Alliance. It was abundantly clear which one of the alliance members was in control by the end of his reign (Smith 1996: 56–57).

Moctecuhzuma Xocoyotzin (1502–1520)

Moctecuhzuma Xocoyotzin was the son of Axayacatl and great-grandson of Moctecuhzuma Ilhuicamina I. He is also referred to as Mochtecuhzuma II. During his reign, the character of the monarchy changed considerably.

Moctecuhzuma II abolished the rank of *quauhpilli,* or eagle lord. This effectively took away any opportunity for upward social mobility that commoners might have had. Instead, important military and government positions were given to members of the hereditary aristocracy (Smith 1996: 57).

Instead of relying on a system of co-opting capable officials and rulers in subjugated territories, this emperor decided to rule through sheer terror (Thomas 1995: 45). Wars and terrible omens characterized Moctecuhzuma II's reign. The long-standing conflict with the Tarascans continued, as did the battle against Tlaxcalla. The Aztec would never manage to subdue either region (Smith 1996: 57).

In 1519, the Spanish arrived on the scene. On November 8, 1519, the Spanish entered Tenochtitlan. The emperor died in 1520, a captive of the Spanish. The exact circumstances of his death are not known. Some sources claim that he was killed by a stone thrown by one of his own subjects (Townsend 2000: 37), whereas other sources state that the Spanish executed him (Smith 1996: 280).

While the Spanish were present, they observed how every day 600 high-ranking men would visit the imperial palace, accompanied by their attendants. Cortés noted that all were fed by the emperor (Bayard Morris 1991: 96).

Cuitlahuac (1520)

Even before Moctecuhzuma's death in 1520, the ruling council in Tenochtitlan had decided to depose him and have him replaced by his brother, Cuitlahuac (Townsend 2000: 36–37). He did not rule for very long, even though his reign was very eventful. In June 1520 the Spanish were expelled in what has become referred to (by the Spanish chroniclers) as "la noche triste," or "the sad night" (Townsend 2000: 37–39). It delayed the inevitable downfall by about another year. Cuitlahuac did not witness this ultimate cataclysm. He died of smallpox during the final siege by the Spanish and their native allies (Smith 1996: 280–281).

Moctecuhzuma II (1466-1520) was the emperor of the Aztecs from 1502 until his death. When the Spanish invasion came, Moctecuhzuma offered Hernan Cortés treasure and money to try to keep him out of the capital, Tenochtitlan, but was taken hostage by Cortés instead. When trying to address his people, who were disappointed by his seemingly easy submission, Moctecuhzuma was stoned and shot at. He died of his injuries. (Corbis)

Cuauhtemoc brought captive before Cortés. (Bettmann/Corbis)

Cuauhtemoc (1520–1525)

Cuauhtemoc was a nephew of Moctecuhzuma II. He succeeded Cuitlahuac in 1520. The siege of Tenochtitlan ended in 1521. On August 13, 1521, the emperor was captured by the Spanish (Smith 1996: 281–282; Townsend 2000: 41–42). The emperor remained in Spanish captivity for years. On October 12, 1524, Cortés left Tenochtitlan for what is now Honduras to put down a mutiny. Cortés took with him Cuauhtemoc, as well as other deposed leaders, fearing that they might start a rebellion if left behind in the former Aztec capital. These fears may have been well founded. Documents retrieved from the Archives of the Indies in Seville, Spain, refer to an attempt by Cuauhtemoc to entice a Maya ruler to join in a conspiracy against the Spanish. Unfortunately for Cuauhtemoc, he was betrayed and Cortés ordered the execution of the last Aztec ruler. With the death of Cuauhtemoc in late February 1525, the chapter of Aztec independence came to an end (Sharer 1994: 735-736).

WHERE DO WE GET THE DATES FOR AZTEC CHRONOLOGY?

One of the interesting aspects of Aztec history is that we have very secure dates for the reigns of the rulers. The chronological framework for the preceding periods, dealing with the exodus from Aztlan and the subsequent odyssey, is fuzzier but still remains fairly well accepted.

We should be aware, however, that these remarks, especially the strong chronological framework for the emperors' reigns, apply mainly to Aztec settlement in the Valley of Mexico. Archaeologists dealing with material remains in the countryside, and in cities far away from the heartland, have to rely on other methods to date their discoveries.

In archaeology, there are two approaches used to date objects. One such approach encompasses techniques that will provide an absolute date. This term, *absolute date,* refers to our ability to date an object with regard to a fixed point in time. We can provide an absolute date for the arrival of the Spanish on the shores of Veracruz: AD 1519. That date refers to the number of years that have expired since a particular fixed event in time, in this case the birth of Christ. Not every culture uses this particular fixed point in time, and, as a result, even in today's world archaeologists might use different absolute dates depending on their own cultural background and the fixed point in time that is considered important in that culture.

It is sometimes impossible to provide an absolute date, and archaeologists resort to statements such as "object X or event X is older than object Y or event Y." Although we do not have any idea exactly how old these objects or events are, we at least know which ones are older with regard to each other (not with regard to a fixed point in time).

We all prefer being able to refer to absolute dates. In the absence of inscriptions or texts mentioning specific dates, we seek recourse in a number of scientific dating methods that can provide us with an approximation of an absolute date. In the following pages, we will look at two absolute dating methods and explain how they work. We will then compare those two approaches with two relative dating methods.

Absolute Dating Methods

Radiocarbon Dating

Radiocarbon dating came into being in the years following World War II. In our atmosphere, we can encounter three isotopes of carbon: C12, C13 (both stable), and C14 (unstable or radioactive). Out of these three isotopes, C12 and C13 make up the overwhelming majority of carbon in the atmosphere. Carbon 14 represents only 0.00000000010 percent of the total amount of carbon found in the atmosphere.

C14 is created in the upper atmosphere through the effect of cosmic rays on nitrogen 14. This carbon 14 becomes part of the food chain. It is ingested or absorbed by all living organisms, plant and animal alike. For as long as an organism is alive, the ratio in which carbon 14 is present in the organism will remain similar to the ratio outside this organism, in the atmosphere. Things change when the organism dies. Absorption of any carbon, or any other material for that matter, ceases completely. The importance here is that the radioactive carbon will start to decay. This will eventually result in the complete disappearance of C14 from the organism.

The decay of radiocarbon happens at a constant rate. If we wait long enough, the amount of C14 will have been reduced to half of its original amount. We would have to be extremely patient though to witness such reduction: scientists have figured out that it takes 5,568 years (plus or minus 30 years) for half of the C14 in the original sample to have decayed. This period of 5,568 years is known as the half life. If we wait another 5,568 years, the amount of radiocarbon present in the sample will have been reduced by half again. There is a technical limit to our ability to apply this technique to date samples from the past. After about ten half lives, or about 50,000 to 60,000 years, we can no longer detect the traces of the remaining C14. Our current machines are simply not sophisticated enough to pick up on these traces, which at this age have now become incredibly infinitesimal.

Because the Aztecs were around much more recently than 50,000 years ago, we do not have to worry about this lower limit inherent in this dating technique. As a consequence, C14 dating can be applied to Aztec archaeological remains. A quick glance through site reports on Aztec site excavations reveals that radiocarbon dating is carried out with great effectiveness.

Thermoluminescence

The term *thermoluminescence dating* refers to a dating technique that measures the amount of light that is released when rocks, minerals, and pottery are heated up. In other words, there is light (luminescence) that is generated when heat (the "thermo" part of the term) is applied. This technique has a range of 300 to 10,000 years, effectively making this a candidate to date Aztec objects.

Minerals, pottery, and rocks are exposed to radiation. This exposure results in trapping electrons within the matrix of these materials. When clay is heated during the manufacturing process, it will release all these trapped electrons and do so in the form of a brief flash of light. This flash is minute and cannot be detected by the naked eye. Once a pot is cooled off, it will once again start absorbing radiation, which will in turn once more cause electrons to be trapped in imperfections within the clay. When we heat the pot up in laboratory conditions to a temperature that resembles that of the kiln, the accumulated electrons will be released once again. Modern tools at our disposal allow us to measure the intensity of the light that is released in this process. It is the measurement of this light release that gives us a pointer as to the amount of time that has passed since a pot was last at that temperature. It is important to catch that last nuance: presumably the last time that a pot was heated to that temperature was when it was fired in a kiln. If we accept this thinking, then the measurement will tell us when the pot was manufactured. This approach is open to pitfalls. It is always possible that a potsherd gets exposed to kilnlike temperatures. This will reset its thermolumi-nescence values and ultimately produce an incorrect date. Still, with all its imperfections, this dating approach has also been applied to Aztec archaeo-logical sites.

Relative Dating Methods

Stratigraphy

The term *stratigraphy* is derived from a Latin term *stratum,* meaning layer. When archaeologists excavate, they tend to follow either easily definable lay-ers or artificial layers in increments of a few centimeters. The general rule is that the deeper one digs, the further back in time one goes. This is based on the assumption that layers are added on top of each other. The oldest would there-fore be encountered at the bottom of the sequence, the more recent ones closer to the top of the excavation.

This does not always apply. Archaeologists sometimes encounter what is called "reverse stratigraphy." Imagine large-scale earth-moving equipment digging up a large section of a given area. As the earth-moving process starts, soil will be moved out of context and piled somewhere else. As the digging proceeds, the excavated layers will continue to be deposited somewhere else, but what we have now is a case of reverse stratigraphy. The most recent layers will be at the bottom of the new pile, while older layers will be closer to the top. This reflects the sequence in which each of these layers is removed and re-deposited. Archaeologists need to be aware of the possibility of reverse stratig-raphy; if not, they could make very embarrassing mistakes.

WRITTEN SOURCES: PRECOLUMBIAN AND COLONIAL DOCUMENTS

Written documents are an important source of information. Anthropologists and historians always establish first what exists in terms of indigenous written sources. The information provided by these materials, combined with that from contact-period eyewitnesses, gives us a wider context than archaeology can by itself.

Only fifteen preconquest manuscripts from various cultures have survived. Four Maya manuscripts survived, as did five documents from the Mixteca and six Borgia group manuscripts. (For a discussion on the origin of the Borgia group, see Nicholson 1966 and Sisson 1983. For a general overview of these documents, see Boone 1992 and Alcina Franch 1992.)

We can add to those about 500 early colonial manuscripts. These documents, often written on behest of the new administration, were compiled by indige-nous writers. Their writing reflects the native tradition in which many of the authors had been steeped. An extensive scholarly literature exists on these early colonial writings. Some scholars have devoted their entire careers to these types of documents (Robertson 1959 and Glass 1975).

The Aztecs used pictographs as a form of writing. The Spanish-language notes seen on this page were added in colonial times. (Hulton/Getty Archives)

Precolumbian Documents

Aztec Writing System

The Aztec were one of five known Mesoamerican cultures that used writing. The others were the Maya, the Zapotec, the Mixtec, and the successors to the Olmec. The Aztec writing system was much more limited than was that of the Maya (Nicholson 1973b). The Aztecs apparently used their system as a mnemonic device—to remind them of the story to be told—rather than as a system that could record a spoken language, like the Maya (Smith 2003c: 13, 243).

Aztec Bookmaking

Aztec manuscripts were painted on deerskin, cloth, or on *amate*, a substrate made out of the inner bark of a wild fig tree. (For information on Aztec codices and "paper," see von Hagen 1944; Sandstrom and Sandstrom 1986; and Wyllie 1994.)

Aztec papermakers would use the bark of various types of fig trees (see Standley 1944 for more details). These types of fig trees are very abundant in the present-day state of Morelos. Many Aztec-period towns in Morelos were specialized in papermaking (Smith 2003c: 239–240).

The Aztec used paper to produce documents, such as trial records, maps, and genealogies. They also incorporated paper into their religious ceremonies: paper was sometimes burned as a form of sacrifice (von Hagen 1944: 78–88). Father Bernardino de Sahagún, a Franciscan monk and one of the first people to write extensive books on the Aztec (see later), outlined some of the ceremonial uses to which paper was put. A merchant guild would cover the statue of the patron god of merchants with paper (von Hagen 1944: 80). People who had been sacrificed were sometimes dressed in paper, covered with rubber (von Hagen 1944: 81).

Types of Precolumbian Documents

Aztec writing has survived in a small number of manuscripts as well as on stone, wood, and ceramic objects. We traditionally refer to the pictorial manuscripts as "codices" (singular: codex) rather than as books. We can assume that the Aztecs left most of their written information on the surface of their codices rather than on wood and stone; however, as we have seen, most of these books have been lost.

These codices served various purposes. Religious books were one such category, and one example of this was the *Codex Borgia* (1976). The *Borgia* contained information on the 260-day calendar and depictions of gods and rituals (Smith 1997: 247), and was used by priests to divine the future and to regulate rituals. Historical books present a year-by-year overview of events in the history of a dynasty. Examples of such documents were a section of the *Codex Mendoza* and the *Codex Boturini* (*Tira de la Peregrinación*). Administrative books include tribute lists, land records, and maps of city–state territories (Smith 1997: 247). Examples of such records can be found in the *Codex Mendoza* (1992). Among the codices dealing with Aztec migration are the following examples: *Azcatitlan, Boturini, Aubin, Mexicanus, Mendoza, Telleriano-Remensis,* and *Vaticanus A/Ríos.* This group of documents should also include the *Mapa Sigüenza* and the *Tira de Tepechpan* (Boone 2000: 213). The so-called *Historia de los Mexicanos por Sus Pinturas,* although a prose contribution, should also be included in this same category of primary-source documents (Boone 2000a: 8; Radin 1920: 4).

Hundreds of manuscripts existed at the time of the Aztecs. All but eleven disappeared with the arrival of the Europeans. The majority were destroyed in a bonfire ordered by Juan de Zumárraga in 1535. According to tradition, beautifully painted historic, ritual, and genealogic documents were gathered in the marketplace at Texcoco and burned (Carrasco 2003: 133).

Specific Precolumbian Documents Pertaining to Aztec History

Codex Mendoza

In the early days of Spanish presence in what is now Mexico, the viceroy of Mexico, Don Antonio de Mendoza, received orders from Spain to collect information on the political organization and tribute system of the Aztecs. Mendoza invited artists and scribes, who were being trained at the Franciscan college in Tlatelolco, to convene in a workshop where they were to create the document requested by the Spanish Crown. This document is known as the Codex Mendoza.

The physical aspect of the codex includes seventy-one folios on Spanish paper, painted in the native style but bound at the spine in the manner of European books (Carrasco 1999: 19). The codex consists of three sections, with the first two apparently drawing inspiration from now lost Precolumbian documents. Part one narrates and illustrates the Precolumbian history of the capital Tenochtitlan. The story starts with the founding of the city and ends in the year AD 1523. A second portion elaborates on the vast amounts of tribute that was sent to the capital. The third and final section provides a wealth of information regarding daily life, education, warfare, priestly training, crime and punishment, and social stratification in Prehispanic days (Carrasco 1999: 20).

Modern researchers believe that they can discern the input of known individuals in the compilation of the Codex Mendoza. Among these possible contributors we find the name of a student of Sahagún, J. Martin Jacobita, who had attended the Colegio de Santa Cruz in Tlatelolco. Martin Jacobita's contribution may have been the insertion of Spanish annotations into the document. The pictorial part was the responsibility of Francisco Gualpuyogualcal, known as a "maestro de Pinturas" (Carrasco 1999: 20).

Although the Spanish Crown had requested the manuscript to be put together, it never took possession of it. Shortly after the codex had been sent on a Spanish ship bound for Spain, it was taken by French sailors who had attacked the ship. Thus, we instead find the Codex Mendoza ending up at the French Court, in the hands of the royal cosmographer, André Thevet. This was not to be the final resting place for this document, however. After 1587 Thevet sold it to an Englishman, the famous navigator Richard Hakluyt. This transferred the codex to British soil, where it can still be found today at the Bodleian Library at Oxford (Carrasco 1999: 21).

Colonial Documents

There is an immense collection of colonial documents pertaining to the New World in general, and to the Aztec in particular. There are the reports sent home by the conquerors, the books written by compilers, and the documents generated by the colonial administration. Descendants of the Aztecs also left us with documents, including pictorial manuscripts and prose contributions. With regard to the pictorial documents, we should note that it was people of indigenous descent trained in the European ways who produced most of these documents. Their efforts represent the last gasp of a long, and now largely destroyed, preconquest tradition of pictorial manuscripts (Boone 2000a: 245). For a good overview of historical documents of Central Mexico, consult Nicholson (1971) and the three-volume part of the Handbook of Middle American Indians, entitled *Guide to Ethnohistorical Sources* (vols. 13–15).

Most of the colonial documents have traditionally been classified as secondary sources because they often relied on older pictorial documents or on other written documents (Boone 2000a: 8; Radin 1920: 4). These original sources are in turn known as primary sources. Although the classification of our sources into primary and secondary categories implies a ranking among them, we should note that both are equally important in preserving history. This observation holds true today as much as it did in the early colonial days (Boone 2000a: 20).

Colonial-period documents range from genealogies and histories of towns to documents to support a family's claims to property in the courts. In the following paragraphs I will introduce these sources and then outline their contributions and their drawbacks.

Eyewitness Accounts Written by the Conquerors

As soon as the dust settled those conquerors who could, ensured the preservation of their legacy by committing their memoirs to paper (Fuentes 1963). Cortés (1962) wrote a series of letters to Emperor Charles V. One of his companions, Bernal Díaz del Castillo (1963), left us with a vivid description of what the Spanish soldiers experienced in their conquest.

Despite their importance as eyewitness accounts, these documents are biased. Enemy numbers were exaggerated, as was the alleged pervasive cruelty of the native peoples. All of this served to make the Spanish source look good back home. Modern historians are aware of these biases, and can extract valuable information on Aztec society because of this awareness.

The Works of European Chroniclers

Aside from the soldiers who were directly involved in the submission of the Aztec, others followed in their wake and left their impressions behind. Some of these authors were members of the many religious orders who set out to convert the native population.

Bernardino de Sahagún. Bernardino de Sahagún was born around 1499. His family may have been of Portuguese origin, as his family name was Ribeira (Bandelier 1932: 3). He studied at the University of Salamanca, but he did not finish; instead, he became a Franciscan monk. Upon joining the order, he was given a new name, Sahagún, reflecting a town in the Spanish province of Leon in which he grew up (Bandelier 1932: 3).

He arrived in New Spain in 1529. He spent the first few years of his stay (1530–1533) in the convent of Tlamanalco, at the foot of the Iztacihuatl and Popocatepetl volcanoes (Bandelier 1932: 4). In 1536 he became a Latin teacher at the college of Santa Cruz.

While he was teaching Latin, as well as Spanish, to the native population, he learned Nahuatl from them. In 1545 he appeared in Tlatelolco, and very likely became Superior of the convent in that location (Bandelier 1932: 5). The following year, in 1546, Sahagún nearly died after contracting the plague. The

Franciscan Order sent him to Michoacan around or just before 1558 to act as an inspector of the Franciscan convents (Bandelier 1932: 6–7).

His fluency in the native language facilitated his research into Aztec history, making him one of the most prolific early chroniclers (D'Olwer and Cline 1973). He wrote a treatise in Nahuatl on the Aztec, entitled *Tratado de la retórica y filosofía moral y teología de la gente mexicana*. He is best remembered for his *Historia de las cosas de la Nueva España* (Sahagún 1950–1982). This work was written in Nahuatl as well. He worked on this from 1558 to 1566. He finished it around 1569 (Bandelier 1932: 7). By 1578, the manuscript had been copied eight times, the last one being a version in both Spanish and Nahuatl (Bandelier 1932: 11). Ten different copies were ultimately made (Bandelier 1932: 12). Sahagún passed away in 1590, as a result of a cold (Bandelier 1932: 16).

Sahagún's work on the conquest was refreshingly different in various ways: instead of presenting the events as seen from the victors' perspective, he related these occurrences from the native point of view. In his own words, this is how Sahagún refers to writing the chapters on the conquest of Tenochtitlan: "Those who helped me with this description were old chiefs, well-versed in all things, idolatrous practices as well as their government and its offices and who were also present in the war when this city [i.e., Tenochtitlan/Mexico City] was conquered" (Bandelier 1932: 11).

Another reason why Sahagún's work is so important pertains to its geographic coverage. Most of our sixteenth-century sources center on Tenochtitlan, with informants hailing from this city or else providing information about that city. The countryside and the lesser communities within the Aztec realm are less well represented. Because Sahagún relied on informants from such smaller communities as Tepepolco, we are presented with a view of late prehispanic culture through the eyes of a subordinate community. In this aspect Sahagún is paralleled only by the *Relaciones geográficas*, a source to be discussed later (Nicholson 1973a: 208).

Diego Durán. Another European chronicler was Diego Durán, a Dominican priest who wrote a history of the Aztec (Durán 1967). He arrived in New Spain around 1545. He was ordained a priest and spent most of his life traveling around Mexico. His work was divided into three parts. The first part dealt with the political and social history of the Aztecs, the second part describes their religious customs, and the third presents an analysis of the Aztec calendar (Warren 1973: 79–80; Smith 2003c: 16).

Native Colonial-Period Documents

Descendants of native Mexican elites left us written documents, either histories or papers used in litigation over land (Nicholson 1971). One of the native authors was Alva Ixtlilxochitl. He came from the royal family of Texcoco and took his name from one of his ancestors, Ixtlilxochitl, who ruled from 1409 to 1418. He wrote a work in Nahuatl on the expansion of the Aztec empire as seen from the perspective of the members of the Triple Alliance (Alva Ixtlilxochitl 1975–1977).

Another native source was Domingo Francisco de San Antón Muñón Chimalpahin Quauhtlehuanitzin. As a distant relative of the ruling elite of Amecameca, a city subject to Chalco, he authored a book on the history of that part of the Valley of Mexico. He started with the Toltecs and ended his story in 1612 (Chimalpahin 1965). He, too, wrote in Nahuatl.

Although these indigenous authors are invaluable, ethnohistorians have increasingly become aware that they also come with two serious drawbacks. They did not spend a lot of ink on the commoners, and instead focus on their own aristocracy. Their narratives also lack detail in the description of the Aztec realm. Our archaeological data and colonial-period administrative documents present a more varied picture, reflecting the variation that truly existed (Smith 1997: 21–22). We turn next to this fourth category of documents.

Colonial-Period Administrative Documents

A counterbalance to the often much-generalized view of Aztec society provided by the chroniclers comes from the great variety of colonial-period administrative documents. As soon as the conquest was concluded, the Spanish bureaucracy started its prolific output of paperwork. Native peoples trained in the European traditions of writing were engaged in drawing up wills, deeds, and baptismal and death records. The so-called *Relaciones Geográficas* were of particular importance (Acuña 1984–1987; Cline 1972). The Crown prepared a questionnaire in 1577. This list of fifty questions covered local customs, population demographics, political jurisdictions, language(s) spoken, physical terrain, native vegetation, and resources available. Of all the communities contacted, 191 sent in replies. Out of these we know where 167 are located today. In addition to written answers to the questions posed by the Spanish administration, the respondents often also included maps of their communities. Extensive information on these documents can be found in the *Handbook of Middle American Indians,* in an article authored by Howard Cline (Cline 1972) and in a study by Barbara Mundy (Mundy 1996).

REFERENCES

Acosta Saignes, Miguel. 1946. Migraciones de los Mexica. *Memorias de la Academia Mexicana de la Historia* 5 (2): 177–187.

Acuña, René, ed. 1984–1987. *Relaciones Geográficas del Siglo XVI.* 9 vols. Mexico City: Universidad Nacional Autónoma de México. (Originally written 1578–1582)

Alcina Franch, José. 1992. *Códices Mexicanos.* Madrid: Fundación Mapfre.

Alva Ixtlilxochitl, Fernando de. 1975–1977. *Obras históricas.* 2 vols. Translated by Edmundo O'Gorman. Mexico City: Universidad Nacional Autónoma de México. (Originally written 1600–1640)

Alvarado Tezozomoc, Fernando, 1975. *Crónica Mexicáyotl.* Translated by Adrián León. Mexico City: Universidad Autónoma de México. (Originally written in 1609)

Anders, Ferdinand. 1978. Der altamerikanische Federmosaikschild in Wien. *Archiv für Völkerkunde,* XXXII, pp. 67–88. Vienna.

Armillas, Pedro. 1950. Teotihuacan, Tula y los Toltecas. *Runa* (3): 37–70. (Argues in favor of identifying Teotihuacan as the site referred to as Tollan in Mesoamerican myth)

———. 1971. Gardens on Swamps. *Science* 174: 653–661. (Discussed the role played by the *chinampas* in supporting complex and extensive urban centers in the southern portion of the Basin of Mexico)

Bandelier, Fanny R. 1932. *A History of Ancient Mexico by Fray Bernardino de Sahagún.* Translated by Fanny R. Bandelier from the Spanish version of Carlos Maria de Bustamante. Nashville: Fisk University Press.

Batres, Leopoldo. 1902. *Exploraciones Arqueológicas en la Calle de Escalerillas, Mexico City.* Inspección y Conservación de Monumentos Arqueológicos de la República Mexicana.

Bayard Morris, J. 1991. *Five Letters of Cortés to the Emperor.* (Reissue of 1969 edition) New York: W. W. Norton and Company.

Boone, Elizabeth Hill, ed. 1987. *The Aztec Templo Mayor.* Washington, D.C.: Dumbarton Oaks.

Boone, Elizabeth Hill. 1992. Pictorial Codices of Ancient Mexico. In *The Ancient Americas. Art from Sacred Landscapes.* Edited by Richard F. Townsend, pp. 197–210. Chicago: The Art Institute of Chicago.

———. 2000. *Stories in Red and Black. Pictorial Histories of the Aztecs and the Mixtecs.* Austin: University of Texas Press.

Brumfiel, Elizabeth M. 1980. Specialization, Market Exchange, and the Aztec State: A View from Huexotla. *Current Anthropology* 21: 459–478.

Carrasco, Davíd. 1999. *City of Sacrifice. The Aztec Empire and the Role of Violence in Civilization.* Boston: Beacon Press.

Carrasco, Pedro. 1971. Social Organization of Ancient Mexico. In *Handbook of Middle American Indians.* Edited by Robert Wauchope. Vol. 10. Austin: University of Texas Press.

———. 1984. Royal Marriages in Ancient Mexico. In *Explorations in Ethnohistory: Indians of Central Mexico in the Sixteenth Century.* Edited by Herbert R. Harvey and Hanns J. Prem, pp. 41-81. Albuquerque: University of New Mexico Press.

Caso, Alfonso. 1959. La tenencia de la tierra entre los antiguos Mexicanos. *Memorias del Colegio Nacional* 4: 29–54. Mexico.

Chimalpahin, Domingo Francisco de San Antón Muñón. 1965. *Relaciones Originales de Chalco Amequemecan.* Translated by Sylvia Rendón. Mexico City: Fondo de Cultura Económica. (Originally written 1606–1631)

Cline, Howard F. 1972. The Relaciones Geográficas of the Spanish Indies, 1577–1648. In *Handbook of Middle American Indians.* Edited by Robert Wauchope. Vol. 12, part one. *Guide to Ethnohistorical Sources,* pp. 183–247. Austin: University of Texas Press.

Codex Borgia. 1976. *Codex Borgia.* Edited by Karl NowotnyAkademische Druck-u. Graz: Verlagsanstalt.

Codex Mendoza. 1992. *Codex Mendoza.* Edited by Frances F. Berdan and Patricia R. Anawalt. Berkeley: University of California Press.

Cook, Sherburne, and L. B. Simpson. 1948. *The Population of Central Mexico in the Sixteenth Century.* Ibero-Americana, no. 13. Berkeley and Los Angeles: University of California Press. (The authors provide a census of the population in Central Mexico in the years following the Spanish conquest. They used written documents to compute the numbers.)

Cortés, Hernando. 1962. *Five Letters of Cortés to the Emperor.* Edited and translated by J. Bayard Morros. New York: W. W. Norton and Company. (Originally written 1519–1526)

D'Olwer, Luis Nicolau, and Howard F. Cline. 1973. Bernadino de Sahagún, 1499–1590. A. Sahagún and His Works. In *Handbook of Middle American Indians.* Edited by Robert Wauchope. Vol. 13, part two. *Guide to Ethnohistorical Sources,* pp. 186–207. Austin: University of Texas Press.

Díaz del Castillo, Bernal. 1963. *The Conquest of New Spain.* Translated by J. M. Cohen. New York: Penguin. (Originally written 1560s)

Durán, Diego. 1967. *Historia de Las Indias de Nueva España.* 2 vols. Edited by Angel M. Garibay K. Mexico City: Porrúa. (Originally written between 1570 and 1581)

Evans, Susan Toby, 1999. Aztec Palaces. In *Palaces of the Ancient New World.* Edited by Susan Toby Evans and Joanna Pillsbury. Washington, D.C.: Dumbarton Oaks.

———. 2001. Tenochtitlán: Palaces. In *Archaeology of Ancient Mexico and Central America. An Encyclopedia.* Edited by Susan Toby Evans and David L. Webster, pp. 718–719. New York and London: Garland Publishing, Inc.

Fuentes, Patricia de, 1963. *The Conquistadores: First-Person Accounts of the Conquest of Mexico.* London: Cassell.

Gamio, Manuel. 1917. Investigaciones Arqueológicas en Mexico, 1914–1915. Annals of the XIX International Congress of Americanists. Washington, D.C., pp. 125–133.

———. 1921. Vestigios del Templo Mayor de Tenochtitlan descubiertos recientemente. *Ethnos* I (8–12), November 1920–March 1921: 205–207.

Gibson, Charles. 1964. *The Aztecs under Spanish Rule: A History of the Indians of the Valley of Mexico (1519–1810).* Stanford: Stanford University Press. (Monumental and detailed study of such topics as religion, encomienda and corregimiento, tribute, labor, production and exchange during the colonial period. Meticulous endnotes.)

———. 1971. Structure of the Aztec Empire. In *Handbook of Middle American Indians.* Edited by Robert Wauchope. Vol. 10. Austin: University of Texas Press.

Glass, John B. 1975. "A Survey of Native Middle American Pictorial Manuscripts," and "A Census of Native Middle American Pictorial Manuscripts." In *Handbook of Middle American Indians,* 14. Edited by Robert Wauchope and Howard F. Cline, pp. 3–80, 81–225. Austin: University of Texas Press.

Hare, Timothy S., and Michael E. Smith. 1996. A New Postclassic Chronology for Yautepec, Morelos, Mexico. *Ancient Mesoamerica* 7: 281–297.

Hassig, Ross. 1988. *Aztec Warfare. Imperial Expansion and Political Control.* Norman: University of Oklahoma Press.

Heyden, Doris. 1989. *The Eagle, the Cactus, The Rock: The Roots of Mexico-Tenochtitlan's Foundation Myth and Symbol.* BAR International Series 484. Oxford: BAR.

Hodge, Mary G. 1998. Archaeological Views of Aztec Culture. *Journal of Archaeological Research* 6:197–238.

Humboldt, Alexander von. 1810. *Vues des Cordillères et Monuments des Peuples de l'Amériques.* Paris: F. Schoell.

Isaac, Barry. 1983. Aztec Warfare: Goals and Battlefield Comportment. *Ethnology* XXII, 2: 121–131.

Jiménez Moreno, Wigberto. 1974. La Migracíon Mexica. In *Atti del XL Congresso Internazionale degli Americanisti, Roma and Genova,* 1972. Vol. I, pp. 167–172.

Kaufman, Terrence. 1976. Mesoamerican Indian Languages. In *Encyclopedia Britannica, Macropedia*, vol. 11, pp. 956–963. New York: Encyclopedia Britannica.

Kirchhoff, Paul. 1954. Land Tenure in Ancient Mexico, a Preliminary Sketch. *Revista Mexicana de Estudios Antropológicos* 14: 351–361.

———. 1958. "La ruta de los tolteca-chichimeca entre Tula y Cholula. In *Miscellanea Paul Rivet: Octogenaria Dictata*. I: 485–494. Mexico City: UNAM.

López-Austin, A. 1973. *Hombre-Dios: Religíon y Política en el Mundo Nahuatl*. Mexico City: UNAM.

López Luján, Leonardo. 1989. *La Recuperación Mexica del Pasado Teotihucano*. Mexico: INAH/GV editores/Asociación de Amigos del Templo Mayor (Colección Divulgación).

———. 1999. Water and Fire: Archaeology in the Capital of the Mexica Empire. In *The Archaeology of Mesoamerica. Mexican and European Perspectives*. Edited by Warwick Bray and Linda Manzanilla, pp. 32–49. London: British Museum Press.

———. 2001. Tenochtitlán: Ceremonial Center. In *Archaeology of Ancient Mexico and Central America. An Encyclopedia*. Edited by Susan Toby Evans and David L. Webster, pp. 712–717. New York and London: Garland Publishing, Inc.

———. (in press). *La Casa de las Aguilas: Un Ejemplo de Arquitectura Sacra Mexica*. Instituto Nacional de Antropología e Historia/Princeton University/Mexican Fine Arts Museum Center, Mexico City.

Marcus, Joyce, 2001. Breaking the Glass Ceiling: The Strategies of Royal Women in Ancient States. In *Gender in Pre-Hispanic America*. Edited by Cecilia F. Klein, pp. 305 - 340. Washington, D.C.: Dumbarton Oaks Research Library and Collection.

Matos Moctezuma, Eduardo. 1979. Una máscara olmeca en el Templo Mayor de Tenochtitlan. *Anales de Antropología* XVI: 11–19.

———. 1988. *The Great Temple of the Aztecs: Treasures of Tenochtitlan*. New York: Thames and Hudson.

———. 1992. Templo Mayor. Guide Officiel. Mexico City: INAH-SALVAT.

———. 1999. *Excavaciones en la Catedral y el Sagrario metropolitanos. Programma de Arqueología Urbana*. Mexico City: Instituto Nacional de Arqueología e Historia.

———. Eduardo, 2003. Aztec History and Cosmovision. In *Moctezuma's Mexico. Visions of the Aztec World*. Revised Edition. Edited by Davíd Carrasco and Eduardo Matos Moctezuma, pp. 3–97. Boulder: University Press of Colorado.

Mundy, Barbara E. 1996. *Mapping of New Spain: Indigenous Cartography and the Maps of the Relaciones Geográficas*. Chicago: University of Chicago Press.

Nicholson, Henry B. 1966. "The Problem of the Provenience of the Members of the 'Codex Borgia Group': A Summary." In *Suma Antropológica en Homenaje a Roberto J. Weitlaner*, pp. 145–158, Mexico City.

———. 1973a. Bernadino de Sahagún, 1499–1590. B. Sahagún's Primeros Memoriales, Tepepolco, 1559–1561. In *Handbook of Middle American Indians*. Edited by Robert Wauchope. Vol. 13, part two. *Guide to Ethnohistorical Sources*, pp. 207–218. Austin: University of Texas Press.

———. 1973b. Phoneticism in the Late Pre-Hispanic Central Mexican Writing System. In *Mesoamerican Writing Systems*. Edited by Elizabeth P. Benson, pp. 1–46. Washington, D.C.: Dumbarton Oaks Research Library and Collections.

Nowotny, Karl Anton. 1960. *Mexicanische Kostarbeiten aus Kunstkammern der Renaissance im Museum für Völkerkunde Wien und in der Nationalbibliothek Wien.* Vienna: Museum für Völkerkunde.

Olmo Frese. Laura del. 1999. *Análisis de la ofrenda 98 del Templo Mayor de Tenochtitlan.* Mexico City: INAH. (Colección Científica)

Parker, Geoffrey. 1999. The Political World of Charles V. In *Charles V and His Time. 1500–1558.* Edited by Hugo Solis, pp. 113–225. Antwerp: Mercatorfonds.

Pasztory, Esther. 1998. *Aztec Art.* Norman: University of Oklahoma Press.

Prescott, W. H. 1843. *History of the Conquest of Mexico.* New York: Random House.

Quiñones Keber, Eloise. 1995. *Codex Telleriano—Remensis. Ritual, Divination, and History in a Pictorial Manuscript Aztec Manuscript.* Austin: University of Texas Press.

Robertson, Donald. 1959. *Mexican Manuscript Painting of the Early Colonial Period: The Metropolitan Schools.* New Haven: Yale University Press.

Rupprich, H. 1956. I *Dürer: Schriftlicher Nachlass.* Berlin: Deutscher Verein für Kunstwissenschaft.

Sahagún, Bernadino de. 1950–1982. *The Florentine Codex: General History of the Things of New Spain.* Translated by Arthur J. O. Anderson and Charles Dibble. Santa Fe: School of American Research and the University of Utah Press.

Sanders, William T., Jeffrey R. Parsons, and Robert S. Santley. 1979. *The Basin of Mexico: Ecological Processes in the Evolution of a Civilization.* New York: Academic Press.

Sandstrom, Alan R., and Paula E. Sandstrom. 1986. *Traditional Papermaking and Paper Cult Figures of Mexico.* Norman: University of Oklahoma Press.

Saville, Marshall H. 1920. The Goldsmith's Art in Ancient Mexico. Museum of the American Indian, Heye Foundation, *Indian Notes and Monographs,* No. 7. New York.

Sisson, Edward. 1983. Recent Work on the Codex Borgia Group. *Current Anthropology* 24: 653–656.

Smith, Michael E. 1984. The Aztlan Migrations of the Nahuatl Chronicles: Myth or History? *Ethnohistory* 31(3): 153–186.

———. 1992. *Archaeological Research of Aztec-Period Rural Sites in Morelos, Mexico.* Vol. 1: *Excavations and Architecture.* Memoirs in Latin American Archaeology, No. 4. Department of Anthropology, University of Pittsburgh, Pittsburgh.

———. 1993. Houses and the Settlement Hierarchy in Late Postclassic Morelos: A Comparison of Archaeology and Ehnohistory. In *Prehispanic Domestic Units in Western Mesoamerica: Studies of the House, Compound and Residence.* Edited by Robert S. Santley and Kenneth G. Hirth, pp. 191–206. Boca Raton: CRC Press.

———. 1997. Life in the Provinces of the Aztec Empire. *Scientific American,* September, 76–83.

———. 2003a. A Quarter-Century of Aztec Studies. *Mexicon XXV,* 1 (February 2003): 4–10.

———. 2003b. *Tlahuica Ceramics: The Aztec-Period Ceramics of Morelos, Mexico.* Institute of Mesoamerican Studies Monographs, vol. 13, Albany.

———. 2003c. *The Aztecs,* 2nd Ed. Malden: Blackwell Publishing.

Smith, Michael E., Cynthia Heath-Smith, Ronald Kohler, Joan Odess, Sharon Spanogle, and Timothy Sullivan. 1994. The Size of the Aztec City of Yautepec: Urban Survey in Central Mexico. *Ancient Mesoamerica* 5: 1–11.

Standley, Paul C. 1944. The American Fig Tree. In *The Aztec and Maya Papermakers.* Edited by von Hagen, pp. 94–101. (1999 Reprint) Mineola, NY: Dover Publications.

Thomas, Hugh. 1995. *Conquest. Montezuma, Cortés, and the Fall of Old Mexico.* New York: Simon and Schuster.

Townsend, Richard F. 2000. *The Aztecs.* (Revised edition). London: Thames and Hudson.

Vaillant, George. 1941. Aztecs of Mexico. New York: Doubleday. (The author outlines his theory that the mythical site of Tollan should be identified as the site of Teotihuacan.)

Van Zantwijk, R. 1985. *The Aztec Arrangement: The Social History of Pre-Spanish Mexico.* Norman: University of Oklahoma Press.

Vega Sosa, Constanza. 1979. *El Recinto Sagrado de Mexico-Tenochtitlan. Excavaciones 1968–69 y 1975–76.* Mexico City: Instituto de Antropología e Historia.

Vollemaere, Antoon. 1992. *De Mythe van Aztlan.* Mechelen: Quetzal Press.

von Hagen, Victor W. 1944. *The Aztec and Maya Papermakers.* New York: J. J. Augustin. (Dover Reprint, 1999).

Warren, J. Benedict. 1973. An Introductory Survey of Secular Writings in the European Tradition on Colonial Middle America, 1503–1818. In *Handbook of Middle American Indians.* Edited by Robert Wauchope. Vol. 13, part two. *Guide to Ethnohistorical Sources,* pp. 42–137. Austin: University of Texas Press.

Wyllie, Cherra. 1994. *How to Make an Aztec Book: An Investigation Into the Manufacture of Central Mexican Codices.* Unpublished MA thesis, Department of Anthropology, Yale University, New Haven.

IV CHAPTER 4

Origins, Growth, and Decline of the Aztec Civilization

The Aztecs present us with many unique features. Their history is one that is relatively well known. Their origins remain murky, despite accounts from Aztec sources and ongoing archaeological investigations to identify the location of Aztlan, the alleged Aztec homeland. The growth of Aztec society is something we know much more about. Their meteoric rise to prominence, first throughout most of the Basin of Mexico and later throughout huge portions of northern Mesoamerica, has generated scores of publications. The decline of Aztec society does not fit the predictable rise and fall of complex societies, where the downward trajectory is usually one that takes several centuries to complete. In the case of the Aztecs it was all over in the span of about 2 years, a mere blink of the eye in human history.

AZTLAN: PLACE OF ORIGIN

Through Aztec Eyes: The Origin Story

The story of the Aztecs wandering from their homeland mysteriously known as Aztlan was outlined in Chapter 3. It is wrought with references to supernatural realm and locations that people are still trying to identify on a map. Although some of these may never be found, or indeed may have never existed, the story is theirs, representing how the ancient Aztecs perceived their origins.

Through Our Own Eyes: The Origin Story as Told by Archaeology

The Basin of Mexico stands out in the history of complex societies. Over a timespan of more than a millennium, this relatively small region gave rise at least twice to large metropolitan communities: the earliest one was known as Teotihuacan, the other one was the Aztec capital, Tenochtitlan.

Teotihuacan

The Aztecs were fully aware of the existence of Teotihuacan, a huge city that once dominated the Valley of Mexico and influenced large portions of Mesoamerica. About 1,000 years before the Aztecs, the Teotihuacanos, as the inhabitants of this city are known, were busy constructing their own sprawling metropolis.

Although the city was long abandoned in Aztec times, and the population in the region was reduced to small farming hamlets (Evans 1985; Gibson 1964: 90, 96), we know that the Aztec reverently referred to the greatness that once was "there in Teotihuacan" (Thomas 1995: 29). To the Aztecs, Teotihuacan was the place where the present creation, known as the Fifth Sun, got its start (Boone 2000b: 372; Codex Chimalpopoca 1975: 121; Sahagún 1959–1975, book 3: 1, book 7: 4–8 and 7: 42–58). We do not know what the original inhabitants called their city, as the current name of the city, Teotihuacan, came to us from the Aztecs. In Aztec lore, Teotihuacan was the "City of the Gods" (Boone 2000b: 371).

Aside from naming the city, the Aztecs also created names for important landmarks in this ancient city. Some of these Aztec toponyms, or place names, have survived into the colonial period and ultimately into our times. A good example of this is a reference to the "tower or hill of the moon," a structure we call the Pyramid of the Moon today (Boone 2000b: 373).

Our sources also indicate that the Aztecs were trying to make sense out of this massive site, and tried to explain how it had gotten there. For example, the Aztecs were convinced that some of the larger structures at Teotihuacan must have been built by a race of giants (Boone 2000b: 375). The Aztec also considered Teotihuacan to be the place where their own system of government and legal system first saw the light of day (Boone 2000b: 375–376).

We know that the Aztec emperors made regular pilgrimages to the ruins. The organization of Teotihuacan into quadrants, the presence of main arteries laid out in the form of a cross, and the existence of apartment complexes as the dominant domestic unit all find parallels in much later Tenochtitlan. Even though we should not argue that the Aztecs sought their inspiration among the ruins of this illustrious predecessor, they certainly followed a path that closely mirrored that of Teotihuacan.

Modern archaeologists have been busy excavating this massive city to unravel its history. Based on their findings, we know that the history of human presence at Teotihuacan goes back to the middle Preclassic period, as early as 800 BC (Millon 1981: 207). The city reached its zenith in the fifth to seventh centuries AD (Millon 1981: 203). By the tenth century AD, the city had collapsed.

When we look at the archaeological map of the city, one aspect that strikes us immediately is the precision with which the streets were laid out. At Teotihuacan the street pattern was organized along a prominent north–south axis, intersecting with a less dominant east–west axis. These streets effectively divided the city into quadrants. The north–south axis is known by its Aztec appellation, the Street of the Dead. It was flanked by some very impressive ceremonial architecture, including two of Mesoamerica's best-known pyramids, the Pyramid of the Sun and the Pyramid of the Moon. The northern end of this Street of the Dead was also the location of palatial elite residences. Among the best known of these is the Palace of the Quetzalpapalotl, referring to the Quetzal butterfly motive that was used to decorate the building's walls.

These elite residences were complemented by a great number of residential compounds inhabited by lower-ranking citizens. More than 2,000 residential

Tourists explore the Street of the Dead at Teotihuacan, Mexico. Teotihuacan is laid out on a grid with the Street bisecting the city. It is among the earliest examples of urban planning in Mexico. (Corel Corp.)

compounds have been identified and mapped throughout the entire city. This number continues to grow as ongoing mapping efforts continue to add to this tally. These residential compounds encompassed domestic areas—places where entire families lived—in conditions that can best be described as an apartment complex (Millon 1981: 203). The compounds varied in size and complexity, yet they seem to have been organized around a religious focus, such as a small temple building and an interior courtyard. The compounds were typically one-story buildings, and in that they differ from the image that is conjured up in our mind when we hear the word *apartment*.

Each of these compounds included several semi-private apartments. The compounds themselves were separated from other compounds by high walls and narrow alleys. There is strong evidence that these apartments were occupied for centuries and that they underwent several rebuilding phases (Millon 1981: 203). Construction was sturdy, with interior walls often being made of stone and covered with plaster. The floor surfaces were frequently covered with plaster as well. Careful preconstruction planning is evident in the presence of elaborate networks of drainage channels laid out underneath these dwellings. These channels would drain excess rainwater away from the central

Pyramid/Temple of the Sun and the ruins of the ancient Mexican city of Teotihuacan. (Corel Corp.)

courtyards, delivering it either to drains outside the compound or to underground storage reservoirs within the compounds (Millon 1981: 203).

Investigations of these compounds started in 1961 (Séjourné 1966) and have continued ever since. It has become clear that these compounds were all different from each other. In other words, there does not seem to have been a limited number of master plans from which prospective homeowners could choose. Moreover, their specific layouts were preserved for centuries, long after the original inhabitants had disappeared from the scene. A compound measuring about 60 ◊ 60 m may have had anywhere from 60 to 100 people living in it (Millon 1981: 206).

Because of such estimates and because a rough number of residential compounds is known, archaeologists could not resist the temptation to produce a figure representing the total number of inhabitants. Millon (1981: 208), for example, has put forward a probable population of 125,000 people, with a maximum number of 200,000 people at the height of the city's history.

Excavations in the compounds have brought to light a sizeable population of skeletal material. Analysis of the DNA coming from male human remains shows how similar, and therefore probably related, these men were to each other. On the other hand, the remains of women found in the compounds have been described as "genetically more diverse" (Millon 1981: 208). In practical terms this may indicate that men remained in the compound where they were born, and their spouses came from other residential units, outside the compound.

Archaeologists have noted that the timing of the construction of the apartment compounds coincided with two major events: the development of craft production throughout the city and the expansion of the city's influence beyond the Valley of Mexico. This imposition of a lifestyle (the compound), as well as the yielding of power well beyond the traditional homeland, are signs of a strong central authority.

The size of the city and its public architecture, such as the preponderance of the apartment compound as the standard residential unit, all point to a highly stratified society. The elite must have had enough authority or prestige to press the overwhelming majority of the population into carrying out its wishes or master plan with regard to the city's governance (Millon 1981: 212).

Modern archaeological research in the Aztec capital has also revealed the importance of Teotihuacan to the Aztecs. Teotihuacan-specific architectural features, such as the talud-tablero masonry arrangements, also show up in the Aztec capital. They built at least four Teotihuacan-style temples inside the sacred precinct in Tenochtitlan (Boone 1985: 179; 1987: 52–53, 56; 2000b: 388; Gussinyer 1970, 1972; Heyden 1987: 125; Matos Moctezuma and López Luján 1993: 159–161; Umberger 1987: 86–88). We also know that the Aztec unearthed carved masks, stone figurines, and ceramics at Teotihuacan and placed these antiques inside the Templo Mayor as part of an offering (Batres 1902: 17, 19, 24; Boone 2000b: 388; Umberger 1987: 67). A Teotihuacan Thin Orange vessel was found inside the ruins of the House of the Eagles, an important Aztec structure adjacent to the Templo Major. It appears in this case that the Aztec obtained this vessel from Teotihuacan and then, almost 1,000 years after it was made, reused it as an urn for the ashes of an important Aztec individual (López Luján, Neff, and Sugiyama 2000: 220). A discovery in December 2003 identified a Teotihuacan presence in the southern portion of the Valley of Mexico. Archaeologists working in the area of Chapultepec castle unearthed Teotihuacan pottery and remnants of a structure (Camila Castellanos, The Associated Press, Jan. 29, 2004).

During its heyday, Teotihuacan was a powerhouse in Mesoamerica. We find extensive evidence of Teotihuacan-style objects and architecture throughout this culture area (Hirth and Angulo 1981). As the Teotihuacan state reached out across wide swaths of Mesoamerica, there was reciprocity. We find, throughout the city, very strong evidence of the presence of non-Teotihuacano people. People who originated in what is now Oaxaca inhabited a specific neighborhood, or barrio, in the city (Millon 1981: 210). These neighborhoods were organized by ethnicity, and we also have evidence of economic activity organized by barrio. Some of these neighborhoods specialized in pottery making, others in stone tool making (Millon 1981: 223–225).

It remains a mystery what brought this giant metropolis down. It appears that the city was the victim of internal strife rather than the target of an invading force. Although the latter explanation is always a popular one, the material evidence does not support it. Even though the city does not seem to have had European-style fortifications in the forms of walls, bastions, and moats, it nonetheless must have been a tough nut to crack for an invading force. Imagine the incredible losses a population determined to resist could have inflicted on an enemy force as they tried to fight their way through the maze of narrow alleys that separated the residential compounds. This is exactly what we know happened at the end of Tenochtitlan's history, when the Aztec fought courageously for their survival, and in the process lost their city. Teotihuacan shows signs of destruction, but it is not widespread destruction. The damage seems to have been carefully inflicted in well-defined areas of the city, most conspicuously sparing residential zones, and targeting public areas and buildings. This has led archaeologists to suggest that the city succumbed to an internal revolt, perhaps the result of pent-up frustrations. An angry mob of citizens rather than an invading force may have heralded the end of Teotihuacan (Millon 1981: 235–238). The torch then passed to another city in the Basin of Mexico: Tula.

Tula

Another city that featured in the mind of the Aztec was the city of Tula, located in the northern portion of the Basin of Mexico. Its history extends back to about AD 700. Human presence continued well into early colonial times (Diehl 1981: 280, Table 9-1). Settlement surveys, aimed at delineating the size of the community, have been conducted in the 1970s. Based on the data collected through this mapping effort, archaeologists have suggested that Tula may have had a population of 32,000 to 37,000 inhabitants (Diehl 1981: 284).

Tula's economy depended predominantly on agriculture. Its farmers grew maize, nopal cacti, persimmons, and very likely beans. There is good evidence that they constructed agricultural terraces; the evidence for irrigation is less solid (Diehl 1981: 287).

Aside from agriculture, the inhabitants of Tula were engaged in craft production. Our main source of information here is Sahagún, who lists lapidaries, stonecutters, metalworkers, woodcarvers, feather workers, scribes, potters, spinners, and weavers (Diehl 1981: 287). As far as the production of these elite goods is concerned, the production of travertine vessels is the only nonagricultural economic activity for which we have archaeological evidence (Diehl 1981: 288).

Nonelite goods were also produced, and in larger numbers, with obsidian tool manufacturing being the most important of these activities. It appears that obsidian tool production took place in a residential context instead of in a specialized workshop environment (Diehl 1981: 288). A specialty seems to have been the production of polyhedral cores; large preprepared chunks of obsidian, from which rectangular-shaped slivers of obsidian (known as blades) would be struck (Healan et al. 1983). The very large number of such cores recovered in excavations has led archaeologists to suggest that they produced these forms for export as well as for their needs (Diehl 1981: 288).

Ceramics, both pottery and figurines, were also produced on a large scale.

Warrior Columns at the site of Tula. These 15-foot-tall basalt columns may have supported the roof of a building. Tula predates the Aztec culture. (Corel Corp.)

The Founding of Tenochtitlan

As we have seen elsewhere, the Aztec started out as a wandering band of nomads. Their own migration stories refer to a homeland called Aztlan, land of the Heron. Opinions vary as to whether Aztlan was ever a real location. There are many scholars, however, who argue that it was, and suggest several possibilities. These range from areas just north of the Valley of Mexico to the Southwestern United States (Smith 1996: 38).

Our sources identify up to eight tribes that left Aztlan. They include the Matlatzinca, the Tepaneca, the Tlahuica, the Malinalca, the Alcolhua, the Xochimilca, the Chalca, and the Huexotzinca (Smith 1996: 39, Fig. 2.4). At one point, these migrants reached Chicomostoc, the "place of seven caves." Although our sources cannot agree on the number of participating tribes, there seems to be agreement on the overall timing of three contingents of migrants (Smith 1996: 40). The first arrivals settled in the Valley of Mexico, but the second settled in the surrounding areas because they found the Valley itself already occupied by the first wave. The Mexica were the last group to arrive in Central Mexico, around AD 1250. Because all choice real estate had already been snapped up by the other two waves of immigrants, the Aztecs were forced to settle in Chapultepec, or "Grasshopper Hill." Chapultepec today contains museums, parks, and choice restaurants, but there was none of that when the Aztecs arrived. It was the least desirable of all locations, which explains why none of the earlier immigrants had bothered settling there.

The early Aztec's neighbors were weary, however, and conflict eventually broke out. The Aztecs were forced to leave Chapultepec and ask the ruler of Culhuacan for asylum, which he gave them. They settled in a snake-infested place called Tizaapan. The Culhua ruler is alleged to have noted, "Perhaps they will die there, eaten by the serpents, since many dwell in that place" (Smith 1996: 44). The Aztecs, however, managed to survive. They started trading in the Culhuacan market and offered the Culhua king their services as warriors. Because of a timely intervention of Aztec warriors in a battle that the Culhua were about to lose, attitudes toward these Johnnies-come-lately started to change. This was not to last, however, as we have learned from semimythical accounts that the Aztecs sacrificed the daughter of the local ruler who had come to the settlement to be worshipped as a goddess. Once again the Aztecs were forced to flee. They wandered through the swamps around the lakes of the Valley of Mexico. The Aztec god, Huitzilopochtli, conveyed to his followers that they should settle on the spot where they would observe an eagle perched on top of a cactus devouring a snake. In the year 2 House, AD 1325, the Aztec did encounter this scene and founded what eventually became known as Tenochtitlan, the Aztec capital. The etymology, or meaning, of the city's name refers to this episode: Tenochtitlan meant "Place of the cactus fruit" (Smith 1996: 45). The image of the snake on top of the cactus eating a snake has survived until today in the flag of modern Mexico.

The first century of Aztec history is marked by a rapid population explosion. New Aztec settlements were founded, and the landscape was modified to accommodate intensive agricultural techniques required to feed a growing population. The Aztecs turned the perceived disadvantages of their island city to their advantage. The area abounded with wild plants and animals, especially waterfowl. These resources, combined with the abundant harvests from their raised fields that ringed their city, allowed the Aztecs to sustain a rapid population growth. Large-scale engineering works in the lake separated the salty waters of Lake Texcoco from the freshwater in Lakes Chalco and Xochimilco. The presence of the lakes also greatly facilitated water-borne trade with other lakeside communities. The Aztecs were soon looked upon as equals by other communities in the Valley. The Aztecs allied themselves with two cities, Azcapotzalco on the western shores of Lake Texcoco, and Texcoco on the eastern shore (Smith 1996: 45–46). The Triple Alliance was born.

THE HEYDAY OF THE AZTEC

The Triple Alliance

As outlined in Chapter 3, the Triple Alliance came into being as a result of the war between Tenochtitlan and its allies, Texcoco, Tlacopan, and Huexotzinca. When Tenochtitlan backed one of the factions in the Tepanec kingdom fighting to succeed Tezozomoc in 1426, they found themselves backing the losing party.

An eagle perched on a cactus, as seen in this Mexican flag, repeats an image seen in the Codex Medoza. (Hans Georg Roth/Corbis)

With the subsequent murder of the then-Aztec ruler, Chimalpopoca, and his succession by Itzcoatl, the stage was set for a struggle that was to last 2 years. Even though the fortunes of war favored both sides over those 2 years, the Aztecs ultimately emerged victorious. They did not prove to be magnanimous in their victory; instead, they pursued the vanquished Tepanec foes into the hills, until the last one of them had laid down his arms. The defeated Tepanec then promised the Aztecs land to build on and houses built for the Aztecs, as well as work in the fields for them. They engaged in sending tribute in perpetuity, including stone, lime, and wood, as well as large quantities of corn, beans, sage, chile, and all the vegetables that they would eat (Matos Moctezuma 2003: 21–22).

With the defeat of the Tepanecs in 1428, the Aztecs formed a new alliance with Texcoco and Tlacopan. This new alliance is known to us as the Triple Alliance. The parties in this confederation agreed to abstain from military action against each other, and to cooperate in wars of aggression against other communities. They also resolved to divide any future tribute along the following lines: two-fifths were to go to Tenochtitlan, two-fifths to Texcoco, and one-fifth to Tlacopan (Smith 1996: 50). This alliance lasted 91 years and ended when the Aztec civilzation came to an end. The tribute-sharing arrangement was honored until the end (Smith 1996: 51).

One of the first areas the Triple Alliance turned its attention to was the southern portion of the Valley of Mexico. Towns like Coyoacan, Xochimilco, and Cuitlahuac were conquered. This gave Tenochtitlan access to the *chinampas*, or floating gardens, around Lake Chalco and Lake Xochimilco (Smith 1996: 50).

The Triple Alliance then expanded its influence over territories outside the boundaries of the Valley of Mexico. Emperor Itzcoatl took charge of conquering portions of what is now the state of Morelos, south of the Valley of Mexico.

Empire or Not?

A traditional definition of an *empire,* as defined by Karl von Clausewitz, involves concerns with territorial expansion, internal control of conquered areas, and the maintenance of secure borders. This requires a standing army, and fortifications to defend one's territory (Finer 1975: 85–86; Hassig 1988: 11; Tilly 1975: 73). If one were to use this definition, then the lack of a standing Aztec army and the absence of widespread garrisoning of troops in conquered territories would argue against the existence of an Aztec "empire" (Hassig 1988: 11–12).

After defeating an enemy, the Aztecs faced two options. They could incorporate the territory into their domain and replace the existing leadership with Aztec governors. On the other hand, they could also leave the previous leadership in place and extract a pledge of allegiance from them (Hassig 1988: 17). The Aztecs usually chose the second of these options (Hassig 1988: 17–18).

Hassig argues in favor of defining the Aztec system as an "empire":

The salient features of the Aztec empire were (1) achieving political expansion without direct territorial control, (2) maintaining internal security by exercising influence over a limited range of the subordinate states' activities (usually political and economic matters), and (3) achieving the latter by generally retaining rather than replac-

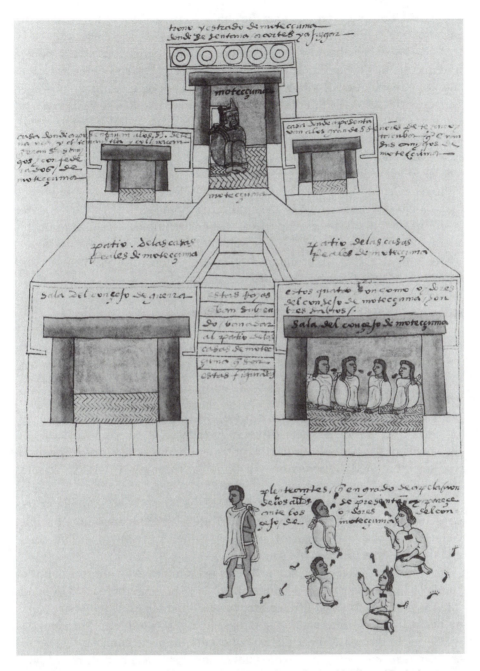

Nobility shown in the palace of Moctecuhzuma. Image from: Codex Mendoza. (Corbis)

ing local officials" (Hassig 1988: 19). In the remaining pages of this book, we will follow Hassig's lead and employ the term "empire."

The incorporation into the Aztec empire brought with it a range of new obligations, such as paying tribute, providing logistical support for the Aztec army, and even having local contingents join the Aztec army. There was a major benefit, however, and that was the ability to participate in the Aztec long-distance trade network (see Chapter 5).

As we have seen, the Aztecs preferred leaving the indigenous elite in power, and making them responsible for the maintenance of law and order, as well as requiring that they send tribute to the capital of their new overlords; however, the Aztecs occasionally felt the need to establish garrisons. The written record has left us with the names of at least eight identifiable locations (Carrasco 1991: 106–108). Spanish colonial documents, especially the ones known as the *Relaciones Geográficas*, mention many more. These are quite frequently much harder to identify (Carrasco 1991: 108). Most of the known military garrisons were established in tributary provinces of the Aztec empire.

It should be pointed out that the application of the term *empire* to the Aztec realm has not met universal approval. Other terminology has been put forward, including "hegemony," "macrostate," "loosely knit empire," "confederation," and "mercantile economy backed by military force" (Conrad and Demarest 1984: 5; Thomas 1995: 28).

THE CONQUEST

Contact

The Aztecs heard about the presence of the Spanish years before the Europeans had set foot on the mainland. Aztec merchants working in the Maya area relayed rumors of what they had heard. At one point they even sent a manuscript depicting the Spanish sailing ships that they had observed (Thomas 1995: 40). In the years leading up to contact, a trunk was collected on the shores of the Gulf of Mexico. It contained the possessions of a Spaniard. The emperor gifted the contents to the kings of Tacuba and Texcoco (Thomas 1995: 40).

Around the same time that word reached the Aztecs about a foreign presence in the Caribbean, several omens were observed presaging trouble. Comets were observed repeatedly, mysterious fires broke out in various cities, and the lakes rose and flooded some houses.

Finally, in 1518, Moctecuhzuma II received another eyewitness account of "big hills floating in the sea" (Thomas 1995: 48). The emperor reacted by sending trusted aides to the Gulf Coast to look for themselves. Upon their return, he heard that the rumors and eyewitness accounts were true. More envoys were sent to the coast, this time carrying gifts from the emperor. The Aztec emissaries made contact and were allowed on board one of the Spanish vessels. Gifts were exchanged. In that fateful year of 1518, the Aztecs and the Spanish had finally come eye to eye (Thomas 1995: 49–51).

Conflict and Conquest

In February 1519 Cortés left Cuba with a force of 500 men transported in eleven ships. This departure took place against the backdrop of political intrigue on the highest level. The governor of Cuba, and highest-ranking representative of the Spanish Crown in the Americas, was Diego de Velásquez. The

Hernando Cortés. (Library of Congress)

governor and Cortés were both very ambitious men and were extremely wary of each other's intentions.

When Cortés started making preparations for the expedition to the mainland, funding ended up being split between the Spanish Crown and Cortés himself. As the ships set sail, Governor Velásquez had second thoughts about the wisdom of letting Cortés depart, so he tried to recall the fleet and intended to imprison its leader. He was not successful.

The Spanish set sail in a direction already familiar to them: toward the Caribbean coast of the Yucatan Peninsula. There, on the island of Cozumel, the Spanish encountered a Spanish sailor, by the name of Gerónimo de Aguilar, who had been shipwrecked in the area years earlier. Although his survival in this region was remarkable, he also brought with him a basic knowledge of the

Yucatec Maya language. From Cozumel the Spanish followed the coastline west, rounding the peninsula, and proceeding south–southwest. They stopped at Potonchan on the Gulf Coast. After a brief battle with local forces, the Spanish met with the local chiefs, who ended up offering the Spanish gifts. Among these "gifts" was a young woman, named Malintzin, who spoke both Nahuatl and Maya. She was originally from a Nahuatl-speaking part of Mexico and had apparently been sold into slavery into the Maya area.

Malintzin, or, as she was also known, La Malinche, formed the last link in an arduous chain of translations that were to take place between the Spanish and the Aztecs. The other initial link was Gerónimo de Aguilar. Conversations between the Spanish and the Aztec would have to go through Gerónimo and then Malintzin and back. Although this was not exactly the most efficient way to communicate, it was extraordinary that Malintzin of all people joined the expedition at this early stage.

When the Spanish landed in what is now the state of Veracruz, close to what is now the city of Veracruz, they were awaited by emissaries from the emperor. There were no immediate hostilities, as both sides were trying to ascertain the scope of the other's forces, and even, as far as the Aztec were concerned, the very nature of the new visitors. Were these strange people humans or were they gods? To obtain an answer to this question, the Aztecs ended up subjecting the unwary Spanish to various tests, and all of them involved food. As soon as the Spanish had met with envoys of the Aztec emperor, they were offered food. As it turned out, the Aztecs sent different kinds of food, some intended for humans, and other "items," such as slaves, just in case the Spanish were gods. As Sahagún (1950–1982: 12, 21–22; Coe 1994: 71) relates:

> And he sent the commanders, the strong ones, the braves, to purvey all that was needed for food, among them turkeys, turkey eggs, white tortillas; and that which they might demand, as well as whatsoever might satisfy their hearts. They would watch them well. He sent captives so that they might be prepared if perchance they would drink their blood. And thus the messengers did it.

The Spanish failed the test. They acted as mere mortals would, not as the gods that the Aztecs thought they were. So we read (Sahagún 1950–1982, 12: 21–22; Coe 1994: 71):

> And when they [the Spanish] saw this, they were nauseated, they spat, they blinked, they shut their eyes, they shook their heads. For the food, which they had sprinkled and splattered with blood, greatly revolted them, for it strongly reeked of blood.

Later, as they approached the Aztec heartlands, the Spanish were tested one more time, again with food. Again, they reacted as mortals would. In this case:

> They sent Cortés five slaves, incense, domestic fowl, cakes, so that if he was, as they had heard, a fearsome god, he could feed on the slaves, if a benevolent one he would be content

with the incense, and if he was human and mortal he would use the fowl, fruit, and cakes that had been prepared for him. (Coe 1994: 74–75; Hernández 1945: 207)

Aside from sending food and slaves, the emperor also engaged in gift exchange with the new arrivals. Within the context of Aztec society, these imperial gifts represented dominance: these were tokens of imperial power and munificence that could not be matched; however, the tradition that such gifts should be made with extreme humility was also part of Aztec society. In other words, traditional Precolumbian recipients of such gifts would recognize the value of these gifts, even though the act of giving would have been accompanied with required statements of belittling their importance. The Spanish were not traditional Prehispanic recipients of such gifts. Cortés took their ritual denigration of the gifts and the gift giving at face value and interpreted them as signs of submission, or even clumsy attempts at bribing the Spanish. As the Spanish went further inland and drew closer to the Aztec capital, the variety and opulence of the Aztec gifts grew. Because of their great interest in gold, and because they were unfamiliar with the Precolumbian context of imperial gift giving (hardly a surprising aspect), the Spanish missed the point the Aztec were making: we are powerful, we are incredibly rich, and we expect you to submit or even leave the realm (Clendinnen 2000: 269).

The Spanish forces did not march inland immediately. Instead, Cortés set up camp in the part of what is now modern Veracruz state that used to be Totonac territory. The Totonacs were part of the Aztec empire. Their initial encounters with the Spanish apparently entailed some skirmishes as well as more peaceful contacts. Cortés took advantage of the resentment among Totonacs vis-á-vis the Aztec and their tribute requirements. In a clear show of his power, Cortés ordered some Aztec tribute collectors captured, a move that surprised the Aztecs and impressed the Totonacs. When Cortés suggested to Totonac nobility that he would free them from Aztec domination, they accepted, and he had made his first allies (Smith 1996: 277–278).

In the months following their arrival on the mainland, the Spanish had also learned about territories further inland. They had been apprised of the existence of Tenochtitlan, about the wealth and power of the Aztec empire in general, and how some kingdoms had been successful in resisting the Aztecs. One of these kingdoms was that of the Tlaxcalans.

When Cortés finally decides to march inland, his aim was to make contact with these Tlaxcalans. The Spanish undoubtedly wanted to make more allies because they had heard that the Aztecs could field armies with thousands of soldiers. At this stage of the tense interaction between the two worlds, the Spanish were still at a considerable numerical disadvantage, even though they had just made their first alliance with local people.

The encounter with the Tlaxcalans did not start off under the best of conditions for the Spanish because they were challenged by the Tlaxcalans. Cortés eventually skillfully negotiated what he had hoped to achieve, and the Tlaxcalans agreed to join the Spanish in their march on the Aztec capital. The

In 1530, Nuño de Guzman and his Tlaxcalan allies are victorious in the Battle of Michoacan. The Spanish were aided by indigenous troops in their fight against the Aztecs. (Hulton Archive/Getty Images)

Spanish had begun to seriously address the issue of their numerical inferiority (Smith 1996: 278).

The next stop on the road to Tenochtitlan was the city of Cholula. Although the Spanish were well received, they feared an ambush and ended up killing thousands of unsuspecting and unarmed Cholula warriors. The Spanish then forced the people of Cholula to declare their loyalty to Spain (Smith 1996: 278). The Spanish, it had become clear to the indigenous population, were no different than the Aztec when it came to imposing their dominance.

Despite additional gifts from the emperor and messages to entreat Cortés to return to Spain, the Conquistadors continued their march inland. They eventually reached the Valley of Mexico and for the first time laid eyes on the island city of Tenochtitlan. The Spanish approached the city by entering one of the causeways that linked it to the mainland. This causeway was the place where the Aztec emperor, Moctecuhzuma II, and Cortés met for the first time. Upon learning that the Spanish had reached the capital, the emperor went to meet them. He was carried in a litter and was accompanied by a large retinue of noblemen. Once the two sides met, the emperor descended from his litter. Cortés

Hernando Cortés and Aztec ruler Moctecuhzuma meet in November 1519 on his expedition to conquer Mexico. (Library of Congress)

dismounted from his horse and embraced the emperor. Both protagonists appear to have treated each other with the utmost respect and dignity. Moctecuhzuma II gave Cortés a gold necklace. The entire scene was witnessed by great crowds who had gathered on the rooftops of the nearby city, and from canoes in the lake (Smith 1996: 278–279).

On November 8, 1519, the Spanish entered Tenochtitlan. Moctecuhzuma made available the palace of his father, Axayacatl, for the Spanish to stay. Things became tense very fast. Using the pretext that Spanish soldiers had been attacked by Aztec warriors, Cortés took the emperor hostage in his own capital. Over the next few months, Cortés ruled the city by using the emperor as his spokesperson. Even with the Aztec emperor hostage, the Aztec ceremonial calendar continued to be observed, and that meant that human sacrifice continued to be performed. The Spanish tried to stop this practice, but were only partially successful (Smith 1996: 280).

In April 1520, Cortés learned that a second Spanish force had landed in Veracruz. The governor of Cuba had sent these men to arrest Cortés and return him to the island. This lead Cortés to divide his forces and he set off to face this threat himself. The soldiers remaining in Tenochtitlan were placed under the orders of Pedro de Alvarado (Smith 1996: 280).

Cortés convinced the newly arrived troops to join his side. Once more, Cortés emerged from a potentially career-ending situation much strengthened, whereas his opponent, in this case the Governor of Cuba, was weakened by the outcome. Cortés returned with these new troops to the capital, where Pedro de Alvarado and his troops were locked in battle with Aztec forces. The hostilities had ensued after Alvarado had tried to stop preparations for human sacrifice. In order to achieve the goal of stopping human bloodshed, he had ironically ordered thousands of unsuspecting participants in the ceremony to be slaughtered. The Aztecs then attacked and tried to take Axayacatl's palace. Cortés returned to the city at this time, and managed to fight his way into the city to reinforce the Spaniards in the palace.

The ruling council deposed Moctecuhzuma at that time, and elected a successor, his brother Cuitlahuac. The fighting continued, and Moctecuhzuma died shortly thereafter. Some sources claim that he was killed by the Spanish. The Spanish later indicated that it was the Aztecs themselves who killed their emperor with a stone (Smith 1996: 280). Either way, the former emperor had ceased to be relevant to the Spanish and the Aztecs, and he paid with his life.

As the siege of the palace continued, the Spanish realized that they were doomed unless they were able to escape the city; therefore, they planned a bold exit on the night of June 30, 1520. In what was to become known to the Spanish as "la noche triste," or "sad night," greed proved to be the undoing of many a Spaniard as he tried to flee to the mainland. Instead of just trying to save their lives, many of the Conquistadors also tried to take as much treasure with them as possible. They did initially slip out of the city unnoticed, but then were seen and pursued. One Aztec strategy involved removing the wooden bridge segments that had been built into the causeways. The fleeing Spaniards were now forced to jump or swim across these gaps. Because they were so heavily laden, many did not make it. Those that did escape joined Cortés on his flight back to the coast.

The Aztecs did not pursue the Spanish, and thereby allowed Cortés ample time to reorganize in Veracruz. There he received reinforcements both in the form of additional Spanish troops as well as more indigenous allies. Several months after "la noche triste" Cortés set off for the capital once more. He brought with him seven hundred Spanish troops and 70,000 native troops (Smith 1996: 280–281). This time his intentions were clear to the Aztecs.

The new Aztec emperor sent troops to cities on the route of the Spanish to block their advance. Possibly to confound this strategy, Cortés divided his approaching force into two parts, and each approached the capital from a different direction. As cities were defeated, native rulers throughout the empire started switching alliances. At this stage the Spanish no longer had to contend with the issue of numerical inferiority. The Aztecs started suffering horrible losses of population at this time because of their exposure to European diseases. One of these diseases claimed the life of the Aztec emperor.

Still, the capital did not fall immediately. The Aztecs did not give up without a fight. The conflict between these two worlds was brutal. Neither side gave quarter. Bernal Díaz del Castillo left us with this impression of the conflict (Carrasco 1999: 50–51):

When we retreated near to our quarters and had already crossed a great opening where there was much water, the arrows, javelins, and stones could no longer reach us. Sandoval, Francisco de Lugo, and Andrés de Tapia were standing with Pedro de Alvarado each one relating what had happened to him and what Cortés had ordered, when again there was sounded the dismal drum of Huichilobos and many other shells and horns and things like trumpets and the sound of them all was terrifying, and we all looked towards the lofty Pyramid where they were being sounded, and saw our comrades whom they had captured when they defeated Cortés were being carried by force up the steps, and they were taking them to be sacrificed. When they got them up to a small square in front of the oratory, where their accursed idols are kept, we saw them place plumes on the heads of many of them and with things like fans in their hands they forced them to dance before Huichilobos and after they had danced they immediately placed them on their backs on some rather narrow stones which had been prepared as places for sacrifice, and with some knives they sawed open their chests and drew out their palpitating hearts and offered them to the idols that were there, and they kicked the bodies down the steps, and the Indian butchers who were waiting below cut off the arms and feet and flayed the skin off the faces, and prepared it afterwards like glove leather with the beards on, and kept those for the festivals when they celebrated drunken orgies and the flesh they ate in chilmole.

The struggle went on for months. Sometime during these months of siege, Cuitlahuac died of smallpox and the last Aztec emperor, Cuauhtemoc, took over. The final act of Aztec resistance followed the crowning of Cuauhtemoc. The Aztecs decided to dress the bravest warrior they had in the most potent battle array they had, the "Quetzal-Owl" uniform. Cuauhtemoc allegedly addressed the remaining warriors thus: "these regalia belonged to my father, the great warrior Ahuitzotl. Terrify our enemies with it. Annihilate our enemies with it. Let them behold it and tremble" (León-Portilla 1990: 112). The emperor then placed the Serpent of fire in the hands of the warrior. This was considered the most powerful Aztec weapon. Its power was derived from Aztec mythology, referring to the weapon used by Huitzilopochtli to sever Coyolxauhqui's head and body (Carrasco 1999: 213). The warrior, looking impressive in his quetzal feather costume, then marched toward the Spanish and their allies. He was accompanied by four Aztec captains. They apparently managed to impress and awe the enemy line briefly because Aztec sources relate how the enemy "quaked with dread, as if they thought a mountain were about to fall on them." These brave Aztec warriors eventually disappeared from view. The battle stopped—silence reigned—and nothing more happened as night fell (Carrasco 1999: 213).

The end came when the last emperor was captured on August 13, 1521. In the ensuing days, the Tlaxcalan allies went on a rampage through the remnants of the city, massacring the survivors (Smith 1996: 282). The last emperor's words upon his capture by the Spanish are preserved: "Lord, Malinche, I have done what I am obliged to do in the defense of my city and can do no more. Since I am forced to come as prisoner before your person and power, take that dagger on your waist and kill me with it now" (Matos Moctezuma 2003: 86). By making this request, the emperor, personifying the ultimate warrior, is following the tradition by which a captive warrior is sacrificed and thus freed to follow the sun on its daily trek through the sky. The Spanish, unfamiliar with this custom, granted him a pardon (Matos Moctezuma 2003: 86).

Cuauhtemoc did accompany Cortés and his army on a march to Honduras to suppress a rebellion among Spanish soldiers. As we have seen in a previous chapter, he never made it because he was executed on Cortés' orders during the march. Thus, the imperial lineage of the Aztecs had come to an end.

Epilogue

Through eyewitness accounts and artistic renderings, as well as because of objects and people that were sent over to Europe, we have a fairly good understanding of the chronology of the fall of the Aztecs and the incredible complex nature of their civilization. We know, for example, that Cortés had sent gifts to the court of Emperor Charles V in Brussels. We have a description of some of these items, as described by the famous German artist, Albrecht Dührer (Wood 2000: 15–16):

> I saw the things that had been brought to the King from the new land of gold, a sun all of gold a whole fathom broad, and a moon all of silver of the same size, also two rooms of the armor of the people there, with all the manner of wondrous weapons, harness, spears, wonderful shields, extraordinary clothing, beds and all manner of wonderful objects of human use, much better worth seeing than prodigies. These things are all so precious they are valued at 100,000 florins. All the days of my life I have seen nothing that touches my heart so much as these things, for I saw amongst them wonderful works of art, and I marveled at the subtle ingenia of men in foreign lands. Indeed I cannot express my feelings above what I saw there . . .

Today, a visitor to Mexico City can go to Tlatelolco and look for a marble tablet at the site. It reads "Tlatelolco fell to the power of Hernan Cortés. This was neither a triumph nor a defeat, but the painful birth of a mixed race that is the Mexico of today."

REFERENCES

Batres, Leopoldo. 1902. *Archaeological Explorations in Escalerillas Street, City of Mexico, by Leopoldo Batres, General Inspector of Archaeological Monuments, Year 1900.* Mexico City: J. Aguilar Vera and Co.

Boone, Elizabeth Hill. 1985. The Color of Mesoamerican Architecture and Sculpture. In *Painted Architecture and Polychrome Monumental Sculpture in Mesoamerica.* Edited by Elizabeth H. Boone, pp. 173–186. Washington, D.C.: Dumbarton Oaks.

————. 1987. Templo Mayor Research. In *The Aztec Templo Mayor*. Edited by Elizabeth H. Boone, pp. 5–69. Washington, D.C.: Dumbarton Oaks.

————. 2000a. *Stories in Red and Black. Pictorial Histories of the Aztecs and the Mixtecs*. Austin: University of Texas Press.

————. 2000b. Venerable Place of Beginning. The Aztec Understanding of Teotihuacan. In *Mesoamerica's Classic Heritage. From Teotihuacan to the Aztecs*. Edited by Davíd Carrasco, Lindsay Jones, and Scott Sessions, pp. 371–395. Boulder: University of Colorado Press.

Carrasco, Davíd. 2003. Toward the Splendid City: Knowing the Worlds of Moctezuma. In *Moctezuma's World. Visions of the Aztec World*. Revised Edition. Edited by Davíd Carrasco and Eduardo Matos Moctezuma, pp. 99–148. Boulder: University Press of Colorado.

Carrasco, Pedro. 1991. The Territorial Structure of the Aztec Empire. In *Land and Politics in the Valley of Mexico. A Two Thousand Year Perspective*. Edited by H. R. Harvey, pp. 93–112. Albuquerque: University of New Mexico Press. (Reviews and discusses the categories of territory within the empire and the types of tributary obligations and land tenure that prevailed.)

Clendinnen, Inga, 2000. *Aztecs. An Interpretation*. Cambridge: Cambridge University Press.

Codex Chimalpopoca. 1975. *Códice Chimalpopoca: Anales de Cuauhtitlán Y Leyenda de los soles*. Translated and edited by P. F. Velázquez. Mexico City: UNAM-IIH.

Conrad, Geoffrey W., and Arthur Demarest. 1984. *Religion and Empire. The Dynamics of Aztec and Inca Expansion*. Cambridge: Cambridge University Press.

Diehl, Richard, 1981. Tula. In *Archaeology*. Edited by Jeremy A. Sabloff, pp. 277-295. Handbook of Middle American Indians, Supplement, 1. Austin: University of Texas Press.

Evans, Susan T. 1985. Cerro-Gordo Site; a Rural Settlement of the Aztec Period in the Basin of Mexico. *Journal of Field Archaeology* 12(1): 1–18.

Finer, Samuel E. 1975. State- and Nation-Building in Europe: The Role of the Military. In *The Formation of National States in Western Europe*. Edited by Charles Tilly. Princeton: Princeton University Press.

Gussinyer, Jordi. 1970. Un adoratorio azteca decorado con pinturas. *Boletin del INAH* 40: 30–35.

————. 1972. Rescate de un adoratorio azteca en México, D.F. *Boletin del INAH*, segunda época 2: 21–30.

Healan, Dan M., Janet M. Kerley, and George J. Bey III. 1983. Excavation and preliminary analysis of an obsidian workshop in Tula, Hidalgo, Mexico. *Journal of Field Archaeology* 10(2):127-145.

Hernández, Francisco. 1945. *Antiguedades de la Nueva España*. Mexico City: Pedro Robredo.

Heyden, Doris. 1987. Symbolism of Ceramics from the Templo Mayor. In *Aztec Templo Mayor*. Edited by Elizabeth H. Boone, pp. 109-130. Washington, DC.: Dumbarton Oaks.

Hirth, Kenneth G. and Angulo, Jorge. 1981. Early State Expansion in Central Mexico; Teotihuacán in Morelos. *Journal of Field Archaeology* 8(2): 135-150.

León-Portilla, Miguel. 1990. *The Broken Spears: The Aztec Account of the Conquest of Mexico.* Boston: Beacon Press.

López Luján, Leonardo, Hector Neff, and Saburo Sugiyama. 2000. The 9-Xi Vase. A Classic Thin Orange Vessel Found at Tenochtitlan. In *Mesoamerica's Classic Heritage. From Teotihuacan to the Aztecs.* Edited by Davíd Carrasco, Lindsay Jones, and Scott Sessions, pp. 219–249. Boulder: University of Colorado Press.

Matos Moctezuma, Eduardo. 1964. El adoratorio decorado de las Calles de Argentina. *Anales del INAH* 17: 127–138.

Matos Moctezuma, Eduardo, and Leonardo López Luján. 1993. Teotihuacan and its Mexica Legacy. In *Teotihuacan: Art from the City of the Gods.* Edited by K. Berrin and E. Pasztory, pp. 156–165. New York: Thames and Hudson/The Fine Arts Museum of San Francisco.

Millón, René. 1981. Teotihuacan: City, State, and Civilization. In *Archaeology.* Edited by Jeremy A. Sabloff, pp. 198-243. Handbook of Middle American Indians, Supplement, 1. Austin: University of Texas Press.

Nicholson, H. B. 1971. Pre-Hispanic Central Mexican Historiography. In *Investigaciones contemporáneas sobre historia de México: Memorias de la Tercera Reunión de historiadores mexicanos y norteamericanos, Oaxtepec, Morelos, 4–7 de noviembre de 1969*, pp. 38–81. Mexico City: Universidad Nacional Autónoma de México, El Colegio de México and Austin: University of Texas Press.

Radin, Paul. 1920. The Sources and Authenticity of the History of the Ancient Mexicans. *University of California Publications in American Archaeology and Ethnology* 17(1): 1–150.

Sahagún, Fray Bernadino de. 1950–1982. *Florentine Codex: General History of the Things of New Spain.* Translated and edited by C. E. Dibble and A.J.O. Anderson. Santa Fe: The School of American Research/University of Utah.

Séjourné, Laurette, 1966. Arquitectura y pintura en Teotihuacan. Siglo XXI Mexico.

Thomas, Hugh 1995. *Conquest: Montezuma, Cortés, and the Fall of Old Mexico.* New York: Touchstone.

Tilly, Charles, 1975. Reflections on the History of European State-Making. In *The Formation of National States in Western Europe.* Edited by Charles Tilly. Princeton: Princeton University Press.

Umberger, Emil. 1987. Antiques, Revivals, and References to the Past in Aztec Art. *Res: Anthropology and Aesthetics* 13: 62–105.

White, Christine D., Michael W. Spence, Fred J. Longstaffe, Hilary Stuart-Williams, and Kimberley R. Law. 2002. Geographic Identities of the Sacrificial Victims from the Feathered Serpent Pyramid, Teotihuacan: Implications for the Nature of State Power. *Latin American Antiquity* 13 (2) 217–236.

Wood, Michael. 2000. *Conquistadors.* Berkeley: University of California Press.

CHAPTER 5

V

CHAPTER 5

Economics

THE INTERNAL ECONOMIC SYSTEM

"Local Trade versus Long-Distance Trade" a False Dichotomy?

Several questions arise when we consider the economics of the Aztecs. What was the role of the markets within the realm? What were some of the items being exchanged? When did the markets take place? How important were the shipments of food to the capital? Did the Aztecs have anything that approximated our concept of money? How were prices set? How did goods get to the market? Before we discuss these topics, we should address the dichotomy presented in this chapter between local trade and long-distance trade.

Presenting local and long-distance trade as opposite concepts in the realm of economics has been labeled a false dichotomy (Hassig 1993: 24–28). Hassig specifies his position by referring to people's perception of long-distance trade as being "elite" trade more so than local trade. The notion of long-distance trade most often connotes elite goods being moved around; however, goods intended for general, rather than elite, consumption are sometimes transported over great distances. In such cases (among others, the transport of salt in the Precolumbian world) we cannot argue that the dichotomy between local trade and long-distance trade is a false one.

Hassig points out that some goods, such as corn, are very bulky and would tend to be transported only over short distances. If transported over long distances, there would come a point where the carrier of corn would have consumed the equivalent of the load carried. In this instance it would not make sense to attempt to transport food over greater distances (Hassig 1993: 27). On the other hand, gold, a very rare and precious commodity, can be transported over great distances without transportation costs amounting to any sizeable amount of the final cost of the gold (Hassig 1993: 25).

In the pages that follow, we will look at the Aztec economic system and identify both a local and a long-distance component. We will keep in mind that some goods intended for general consumption may be transported over long distances.

Markets

What Was the Role of the Markets in the Realm?

Throughout the Aztec realm, a great variety and well-developed hierarchy of market systems existed. After a region had become incorporated into the Aztec system, they would typically make changes on the level of regional markets, while leaving the lower-level market arrangements mostly untouched.

They did change the regional commerce system by rearranging the dates that these regional markets would be held, and they introduced the pochteca as the designated engines of that trade (Hassig 1993: 110).

As a result of such intervention, a well-developed and fairly well-balanced economic exchange system existed throughout the Aztec realm. Markets were operating in all sizeable communities. We know that these markets were held on a regular basis (Hassig 1982) and that sometimes, especially in large population centers, markets specialized in certain products, as we will see later (Smith and Hodge 1994: 12). Hicks (1987) argued that the Aztec economy was verging on being a "market-integrated" one. He outlined four requirements to achieve such an economy:

1. the presence of full-time specialists, who do not produce their own food
2. the presence of people who produce these necessities (including food)
3. a market economy to bring the previously mentioned two layers together
4. the presence of a state to maintain order, and to provide mechanisms for dispute resolution

What Was Traded?

The local markets played an important role in the lives of Precolumbian peoples. This is where they could obtain the necessities of life, which they were not producing themselves. It is estimated that a household produced enough surplus to be able to meet its own needs as well as to fulfill tribute obligations (Hicks 1994: 100).

The *Tianquiztli,* or great market, was one of the main commercial centers in the Aztec capital. One could see and buy anything that was available in the empire and beyond: gold and silver objects, cotton textiles, feather work, cacao, ropes, sweet-root, stone, stamps used in decorating pots and weavings, beans and maize, skins of otters, jaguars, and much more (von Hagen 1944: 79).

These constitute the raw materials and essential foodstuffs needed in the capital. In return, the craftsmen residing in the capital produced secondary goods that were exported to other parts of the empire (Blanton 1996: 48; Parsons 1980; Sanders, Parsons, and Santley 1979: 180). A sample of goods that reached the markets in the capital included such bulk materials as stones, sand, wood, maize, grain, salt, meat, fish, fruits, flowers, and vegetables. When perishable goods were transported, the preferred time to ship them was at night to ensure their freshness by the time they reached their destination (Hassig 1993: 64).

Smaller, regional markets tended to provide items that were of local origin. Note that our information in this regard is often derived from early colonial data collected by the Spanish. The assumption is made that these early colonial markets reflected situations going back to Prehispanic days. Such early colonial documents refer to a market at Coyacan specializing in wood and wood products (Blanton 1996: 75). In general terms, however, we can say that local markets would provide access to ordinary goods for use in daily life, whereas the regional markets provided both access to such mundane wares as well as exotic goods much sought after by the elite (Hassig 1993: 111).

The availability of natural resources dictated to a great extent the range of raw materials being offered. For example, Otompan (or Otumba), located in the Valley of Teotihuacan, was a major source area for and a major market in obsidian (Blanton and Hodge 1996: 244–245). The market at Coyoacan was well known for its wood products, derived from nearby forests. The market in Cholula was the place to get chiles and maguey honey (Berdan 2002: 42–43). Some markets specialized in goods that one could not readily describe as raw materials. The Acolman market excelled in selling dogs, Texcoco was famous for its ceramics, and Azcapotzalco and Itzocan were the premier slave markets (Berdan 2002: 43).

Cloth, especially decorated cloth garments, was the favorite exchange medium. It was much in demand, it was readily accepted, easy to carry, and did not spoil easily (Hicks 1994: 100). Aside from cloth, cacao beans also were an important exchange medium (Hicks 1994: 101). The advantage of cacao beans was that they could be used to buy cheap commodities, and that they also could be used to make up the difference in value between two barter items (Hicks 1994: 101; Las Casas 1958: 236).

When Did Markets Take Place?

Within the Aztec realm, sources refer to two daily markets: Tlatelolco and Texcoco (Blanton 1996: 68). The market would start in the morning and end in the evening. Just like Wall Street today starts the proceedings with a bell being rung, the Aztec would start their trade at the sound of a drum. The drum would also announce the end of the market day (Hassig 1993: 67).

Aside from the major daily market events in the capital and other major Aztec cities, the Aztec realm has market events occurring every 5, 8, 9, 13, and 20 days. It has been suggested that there was a direct correlation between the size of a community and the frequency with which markets were being held there. In other words, the larger the city the greater the frequency with which markets were held (Hassig 1993: 75, 81–82). The decision to organize markets at the intervals just listed relied, in part, on the Aztec calendar system, except for the 8-day market cycle. It appears that this 8-day market cycle is a colonial-period phenomenon that is not related to any indigenous Prehispanic calendar (Hassig 1993: 79).

Regardless of when markets would be organized, they were the only sanctioned location for trade to occur. The Aztecs had regulations that markets be held and attended on a regular basis. They also prohibited exchanges from taking place outside the markets (Hassig 1993: 69).

The question remains to what extent the Aztecs relied on a system of regional markets to move goods throughout the empire. That topic will be elaborated upon later under the header of long-distance trade.

The Tlatelolco Market in the Capital

Located on the same island as the capital, Tenochtitlan, the Tlatelolco market was one of the largest in the Aztec realm. It was held in a space especially built for it. It was located close to the residences of the rulers. As is still the case in many open-air markets in large Latin American cities, the commodities were sold in separate sections (Hassig 1993: 67).

The Tlatelolco market was a daily market. According to colonial descriptions, it was big enough to accommodate 60,000 people coming and going every day (Soustelle 1961: 25). As this was the main market in the capital, everything was available: food items as well as precious materials were brought in from all over the realm. One aspect that struck the Spanish observers of this market was the orderliness. Despite the enormous size of this location, each kind of merchandise was allocated its own customary space. This aided in maintaining order, and also made it easier for customers to know where to go. Another feature that struck the Spanish was the behavior of the Aztec crowd. Even though there were thousands of people milling about, they were not very noisy; instead, they hummed and murmured (Soustelle 1961: 27).

Although the market had economic exchange as its primary function, it served another important function as well: it was a place where people would congregate to socialize. Anyone who has visited open-air markets in other countries will be able to relate to the impression that such markets make upon one's senses. First is the incredible array of colors displayed in the goods that are offered for sale. Then there are the smells, some delectable, some odiferous, wafting through the air. The sounds of people interacting—some talking, some laughing, others crying—are all very different from what is a sanitized and socially circumscribed experience in Western supermarkets. Finally, imagine being there at the time of the Aztecs. There would have been people from all over the empire trying to sell their wares. Imagine seeing a famous long-distance *pochteca* trader. What stories they may have to tell, and what incredibly rich goods they may have been offering at the time you walked by.

Even though the Spanish remarked how well organized and relatively quiet this market was, there was a need to maintain order. There were the *tianquizpan tlayacaque,* overseers who patrolled the vast square. Any disputes regarding theft or cheating led to the parties concerned being walked off the market to see a court that was in permanent session. Three judges took turns presiding over this court to settle these disputes.

Provincial Markets

The Tlatelolco market did not operate in a void. It may have been the largest market within the Aztec empire, but it was not the only one. Almost every Aztec city and town had a *tianquiz,* as markets were called. Early Spanish chroniclers remark that there were such regional markets, but did not leave us many descriptions. We may assume that these markets were smaller and held less frequently than the market in the Aztec capital (Smith 1996: 117).

Some of the provincial markets specialized in particular products. Anyone interested in purchasing a dog, for example, went to the market at Acolman. A chronicler describes what he saw when he visited Acolman around 1577. There were more than 400 dogs tied up in crates. Some of them were for sale, and others had already been sold. As can be expected in a situation like this, the writer complained that he was overwhelmed by the stench created by the piles of ordure (Smith 1996: 119). Other markets excelled in other goods. For example, slaves were traded in the markets of Azcapotzalco and Itzocan (Smith 1996: 119).

The Tlatelolco market and those in Itzocan and Azcapotzalco all fell within a well-established hierarchical framework of markets. Within the Valley of Mexico, a four-tiered system of markets operated. The top of the hierarchy was occupied by Tlatelolco. No market even came close. The second tier was taken by markets in such cities as Texcoco and Xochimilco. These markets owed their high rank to the size of the community they served. Markets at Acolman, Otumba, and Coyoacan made up the third level in this hierarchy, whereas the markets at the smaller towns and villages throughout the Valley took up the bottom wrung of the ladder. These markets stood apart from each other in terms of the number of people who bought and sold goods there, the quantity and variety of goods and services that were offered, and the frequency with which they were held (Smith 1996: 119). With regard to frequency we know that the highest-level markets met daily, the city–state markets were held once every 5 days and, finally, the smallest markets met less frequently (Smith 1996: 1996).

The periodic nature of most markets served a purpose. Most people did not need to go to the market on a daily basis. Moreover, a staggered market schedule allowed traders to travel from one market to another throughout the region. This way they could serve a much larger customer base without being excluded from most of the markets because of a calendar conflict (Smith 1996: 120).

The social function remarked upon for the Tlatelolco market applied to other markets as well. People undoubtedly took advantage of market days to see friends, learn the latest news, and even to meet potential spouses, while at the same time taking care of the purchases for the family. We also know that most of the markets had a shrine dedicated to a god who supervised the proceedings. Market days had several important functions then, covering the economic, social, and religious needs of a community (Smith 1996: 120).

How Did the Aztec Determine the Value of the Items Being Exchanged?

The administration set the prices only on rare occasions, as, for example, at the market in Tlatelolco (Berdan 1975: 263; Blanton 1996: 48). Aside from this one example, it seems that people had a general idea of the value of the items that were being bartered, and that the exchange that took place was determined by supply and demand.

A special and very poorly understood case is the role that land or real estate may have played in transactions. Was it ever sold? Was it ever used in a barter context? We know that the emperor often resorted to paying his officials by assigning them plots of land. This is a workable system, until the land runs out (Thomas 1995: 31). Those studying the Prehispanic Aztec economy do not know of any examples of land being part of a barter economy; that is, a situation where land would have been part of an exchange of goods (Hicks 1994: 101).

How Did Goods Get to the Market?

Goods made it to market either by road or by boat. As was true for other Mesoamerican peoples, the Aztecs never used wheeled transportation, even though they were familiar with the concept of the wheel. Wheeled toys have been found (Ekholm 1946; Thomas 1995: 31). A traditional explanation for the absence of wheeled transportation refers to the lack of draft animals. Any burdens, therefore, were carried on the back of *tlamemes,* professional carriers. One cannot wonder and make the following observations: given that preconquest people were familiar with the wheel, and that they were willing to engage large numbers of people carrying burdens across the landscape, why then did they never employ people to pull carts? It has been done in other cultures, and it was done in the Americas very shortly after the arrival of the Spanish. When Cortés prepared for his conquest of Tenochtitlan, he had carts built to transport his artillery. These carts were pulled by Totonacs from the Gulf Coasts, not by horses (Thomas 1995: 227). Moreover, once the conquest was complete and the construction of the colonial capital was started, the surviving Aztecs readily used carts and wheelbarrows (Thomas 1995: 563).

Canoe transport would bring in bulk goods and food items from all over the Basin of Mexico. The southern lakes in the Valley of Mexico produced great amounts of food because the *chinampa* system was greatly developed in that area. That food was sent to the capital in great quantities and in the most efficient way: across the lakes by canoes. Canoes would tend to return from Tenochtitlan with finished goods. The natural configuration of the lakes, with the peripheral lakes being of higher elevation than the central area around the capital, also facilitated this type of transportation. As canoes made their way to Tenochtitlan laden with goods, the current would assist their voyage. The return trip would take place against the current because the return, if there was any, would involve finished products of smaller bulk and lower weight (Hassig 1993: 61). Going against the current was less of a problem with a lighter load.

We have early colonial documents that refer to the extent of the canoe trade in the Valley of Mexico. We can only guess that during Precolumbian times the number of canoes plying the waters of the lakes in Central Mexico may have been about the same. Early colonial sources estimate that there were anywhere from 50,000 to 200,000 canoes of various sizes afloat on the lakes around Tenochtitlan (Hassig 1993: 62). We should also note that the size of the canoes ranged from 15 to 50 feet. In some of these canoes, a single man was said to be able to transport 1 ton of corn (Hassig 1993: 62). Aztec canoes were simple craft, made from a single tree. People would use oars or poles to propel themselves in their canoes. Sails were apparently not used in the Valley of Mexico (Hassig 1993: 56–57).

Full-Time Versus Part-Time Craft Specialization

Full-Time Production

Feather working was a full-time craft specialization. In the Valley of Mexico, Tlatelolco, Texcoco, and Huaxtepec were important centers of feather working.

Feather workers were also present at the capital. Several guilds of *amanteca,* or feather workers, worked at the palace. Some made feather objects for the emperor for his personal use or to be used as gifts; other specialists made the emperor's ceremonial costumes (Pasztory 1998: 278).

Aside from feather working, the manufacture of obsidian blades may also have been a full-time craft specialization. This is suggested by ethnographic accounts and experimental data (Nichols 1994: 185; Sanders and Santley 1983; Sanders and Webster 1988: 542–543).

Part-Time Production

Most of the people engaged in production of goods worked part time. Moreover, they tended to be male, who also tilled the land to help support themselves and their family (Hicks 1994: 95).

Textile production was such a part-time endeavor, albeit one in which both men and women participated. Women were traditionally the cloth makers; the men took it upon themselves to prepare the maguey fibers for spinning (Hicks 1994: 104, n. 1; Medina and Quezada 1975: 82). Thanks to detailed descriptions left to us by several colonial-period authors (Sahagún 1950–1982: bk. 8, 47; Suaarez de Peralta 1878; Torquemada 1975: v. 2, 488), we know that the techniques used to make textile have largely survived. We can still observe people weaving in the same way as their Precolumbian ancestors.

Cloth was made out of either cotton or agave fiber. Both raw materials had to be prepared before spinning. Again, a division of labor among men and women applied: men would prepare the agave fibers, whereas the women would work on the cotton fibers. Preparing the agave fibers was a laborious task. They would be roasted, then fermented, beaten, scraped, washed, and treated with maize water (Hicks 1994: 90). These fibers could be spun and woven only after this process (Anawalt 1981: 12; Bernard and Salinas 1989: 322–330; Medina and Quezada 1975: 79–86; Nolasco 1963: 170–172; Parsons and Parsons 1990: 145 ff.).

Tribute

During the Triple Alliance days, tribute was levied in an organized fashion, and with regional variations that illustrate a deep understanding on the part of the Aztecs of the varied nature of the people they ruled.

One of our most important sources on the Aztec tribute system is the Matrícula de Tributos; another is the second part of the Codex Mendoza. Both documents provide a detailed list of what was sent by the cities and towns throughout the empire. Some things stand out. For example, the Aztecs were very keen to obtain feathers from the people that they had conquered. The Matrícula document indicates that out of the more than thirty provinces in the Aztec empire, at least twenty-two were asked to send feathers as part of their tribute payments (Broda 1978: 129; Pasztory 1998: 278). Over time, the nobility and the emperor came to rely upon tropical fruits and cacao. Aristocrats apparently received an annual supply of more than 200,000 cotton cloaks of different sizes. They also had a sweet tooth: Tenochtitlan took delivery of 15,000

A page from an Aztec tribute roll, known as the "Codex Mendoza." This page shows that seven subjugated towns annually paid 2,800 mantles and tunics, one live eagle, and two war costumes and shields to their Aztec overlords. (Bill White/Instructional Resources Corp.)

jars of honey on an annual basis (Molíns Fábregas, 1952–1953: 315; Thomas 1995: 31).

Payment schedules of tribute varied from four times, to twice, or to once a year. These differences in schedule depended upon the nature of the tribute.

For example, warriors' outfits and staple foodstuffs were sent in once a year. Clothing items were due either twice or four times a year. In practice, provinces paid various kinds of tribute items, which meant that they were subject to all the payment schedules just mentioned (Berdan 1994: 308, n. 7).

As mentioned in previous chapters, upon conquering an area, the Aztecs usually left the local dynasties in place as long as they swore allegiance to the emperor. The Aztecs occasionally did leave garrisons behind in border provinces. Their role was primarily to ensure border security; however, their presence undoubtedly also "encouraged" compliance with tax levies (Berdan 1994: 303). Absorption into the Aztec political and economic system was further promoted by marriage alliances, gift exchanges, and participation in religious ceremonies and political events (Berdan 1994: 299; Berdan 1996: 122).

Even though they left the traditional political and economic structure in place, the Aztecs quite often also imposed their own tribute collection structure. This was a hierarchical arrangement, with *calpixque*, or tax collectors, stationed in various cities (Berdan 1982: 38; Smith 1994: 315). In turn, they reported to a governor: a head tax collector who oversaw the collection of taxes in a region. It is very likely that the local system of collecting taxes and the network of tax collectors imposed by Tenochtitlan operated in parallel. We assume that the tribute collected by the *calpixque* went to the emperor, whereas the local tax-collecting infrastructure brought in the tribute intended for the local ruler (Berdan 1994: 299). In some case studies, such as that of the state of Morelos (Smith 1994: 333–338), four levels of tribute requirements have been identified. These involved tribute paid to the Triple Alliance, payments made by dependent city–states to the capitals of the conquest states, support sent by the local noblemen to the local rulers, and tribute to sustain the local nobility.

Tribute requirements differed from one province to the next. At this point we need to distinguish between those provinces that were located at the edge of the empire and those that were not. It appears that the strategically important border provinces met their requirements by providing services, while only occasionally sending tribute (Berdan 1994: 300–305). For example, the city of Tetela sent battlefield captives to Tenochtitlan. This was their "tribute." In return, they received arms (Berdan 1994: 307). This differential treatment of provinces based on their location within the empire allowed the Aztecs to maintain their borders at minimal cost to themselves (Berdan 1994: 307).

As mentioned earlier when discussing transportation modes to get goods to the markets, the Aztecs used humans as carriers. The same applied to taxes moving from the provinces: huge columns of these men would bring tribute to the capital, crossing rivers and mountains to get there.

Within the empire a great number of people were exempt from paying tribute. They included the nobility, priests, children, minor or local administrators, leaders of the *calpultin*, merchants, and teachers (Thomas 1995: 34). The tax base encompassed laborers or *macehuales* who worked the land, and the serfs or *mayeques* who worked on other people's land, especially that of the aristocracy (Thomas 1995: 34–35).

A Special Case of Tribute Requirement: Rotational Labor

Early colonial documents refer to a system of tribute requirement in which people were asked to donate their time and labor. In the case of Texcoco, we know that groups of people living in small communities surrounding the city were subject to labor service in Texcoco. It seems that these requirements pertained to an entire community. It would have included people of almost all ages, and of both sexes. Youths and the elderly were exempt. Men and women were asked to perform different tasks (Hicks 1984: 161). It is likely that labor squads from nearby places went home every night. Those from more distant places must have been given quarters in Texcoco (Hicks 1984: 162).

The requirement to provide labor was not made because there were not enough laborers available in Texcoco; we know there were. It should have been possible for the outlying communities to send in food and raw materials to be used by a full-labor force indigenous to Texcoco, and yet that did not happen. Hicks (1984: 165–166) suggests that other, political reasons may have been at play here:

- By requiring people from outlying areas to come in to the city, the kings may have promoted the unity of their territory
- The system had built-in flexibility: by relying on a workforce that is brought in when necessary, one could also send them back home when the job was done. This cuts down on unemployed masses of people in the city.

As a result of this arrangement, Texcoco did not grow into a tight urban agglomeration, as was the case with Tenochtitlan.

Currency

The Aztecs bartered. They exchanged one item for another because they lacked what we would call coins. As mentioned earlier, cloth was the most commonly used item in an exchange. Economists have referred to cloth as "commodity money" (Dalton 1971). It could be used in an exchange to "buy" something else, yet it also had uses other than being money (i.e., being a commodity) (Hicks 1994: 101). There was little demand by the Aztec for something whose only use was that of money (Hicks 1994: 101).

The closest the Aztecs came to the concept of money would be cacao beans and cotton cloaks. Cacao beans were most often used to make small purchases, whereas cotton cloaks represented a higher value (Berdan 2002: 43). Cacao beans were sometimes used to pay tribute as well (Hicks 1978: 135). Cacao would be carried to the Basin of Mexico on the backs of professional carriers, the *tlamemes*. A normal load apparently consisted of 24,000 beans (Coe and Coe 1996: 84). Cacao continued to be used in economic transactions for several decades after the arrival of the Spaniards (Gibson 1964: 348–349, 358; Hicks 1994: 99).

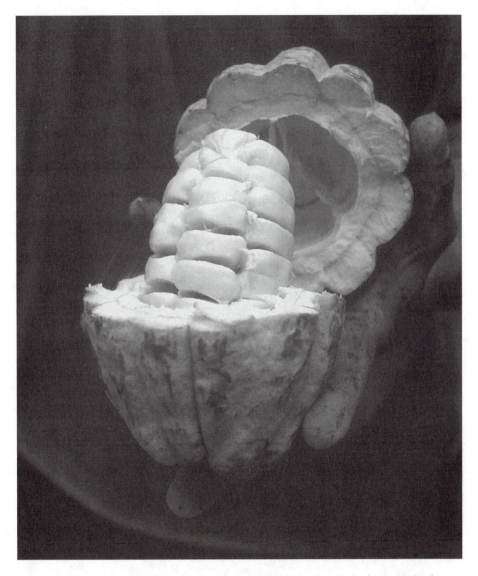

A man holds open a freshly harvested cacao pod, showing the seeds that provide the raw material for chocolate. (Bill White/Instructional Resources Corp.)

Just like our society, Aztec society had its fair share of counterfeiters. People would sometimes remove the chocolate from the outer husk and replace it with either sand or ground up avocado stones (Berdan 2002: 43).

Early colonial documents indicate that cacao beans continued to be used after the arrival of the Spanish. In those days, one cacao bean would get you one large tomato, a turkey egg would go for three beans, thirty cacao beans bought you a small rabbit. A more pricey sum of 200 cacao beans was required for a turkey (Berdan 2002: 43). Cotton cloaks represented greater economic value. Cloaks

Aztec merchants on the canal in Tenochtitlan before the Spanish conquest. Hand-colored woodcut. (North Wind Picture Archives)

would range in value from 65 to 300 cacao beans. Documents indicate that twenty cloaks (of undetermined quality) could support a commoner for an entire year (Berdan 2002: 43). Other items that approached the status of currency included quills filled with gold dust and small copper axes (Hassig 1993: 69).

Transport

Goods were most often transported on people's backs or in canoes. Human carriers—*tlamemes*—used woven-cane containers. These were often attached to wooden frames supported by tumplines (Hassig 1993: 28). This mode of transportation is still used in rural areas today.

Early colonial documents refer to the load that these carriers would transport. It has been reported that a carrier would transport a load of around 23 kg (roughly 50 lbs) over a distance of 21–28 km (13–18 miles). Although this is one of the instances where such figures are provided, we do not know if this is a reliable measure of what *tlamemes* did all over the empire (Hassig 1993: 32). It stands to reason that the load carried and distances covered were subject to the terrain a carrier had to negotiate. Changes in elevation, ground cover (dense jungle versus plains), and local topography all affected the carrier's ability to deliver (Hassig 1993: 33). It appears that *tlamemes* most frequently carried goods from their own cabecera, or capital town, to that of the neighboring district, rather than from border to border within their own districts (Hassig 1993: 35). Exceptions to this rule included (1) carrying tribute from the provincial centers to Tenochtitlan, (2) transporting war supplies, (3) assisting in *pochteca* trade, and (4) engaging in some public works (Hassig 1993: 36).

This form of transporting goods across the empire was subject to serious restrictions. Because professional porters had to be paid, some researchers have calculated that the minimum cost to carry maize to the market amounted to 30 percent of the value of the load per day's distance from the market (Hassig 1993: 128).

Aside from carriers the Aztecs also used canoes to transport goods. This was especially true for the Valley of Mexico and the capital Tenochtitlan. Because of its location on an island, and because of the presence of canals criss-crossing the city, canoe transportation was a highly efficient means of moving people and goods. Canoes moved at roughly the same speed as *tlamemes,* yet they propelled about 1 ton of cargo per person. This ratio was about forty times more efficient than that of transporting goods with *tlamemes* (Hassig 1993: 133). Although canoes were able to deliver more goods to the markets, especially at Tenochtitlan, they did not outperform carriers as far as speed is concerned. In most cases, canoes and *tlamemes* brought goods to cities in roughly the same timeframe (Hassig 1993: 134). Needless to say, this comparison can only be made for those cities that could be accessed by water; landlocked communities do not enter in this equation.

Roads

The Aztec road system was well developed within the cities and to some extent between the major cities of the empire. Other than that, the Aztec road system was limited in its extent and quality. We can identify between the following types of roads (Hassig 1993: 31):

- *Ohtli,* a general term for road
- *Ochpantli,* or main road (often with holes, muddy spots, and curves)
- *Ohpitzactli,* or trails (often with the connotation of being straight and narrow as opposed to other roads that curve)
- *Ixtlapalohtli,* or shortcut (with the same connotation of being straight)

- *Icxiohtli,* or footpath (small, narrow, and seldom traveled)
- *Ohquetzalli,* or new road
- *Ohcolli,* or old road

Because foot travel was the main mode of getting from point A to B, Aztec roads were often not concerned with gradients or with sharp turns.

Economics and Politics

The Role of Markets

A hotly disputed aspect of Aztec economy is the role that markets played in the early Aztec period. Some have argued that the roots of a regional Aztec market system can be traced back to this early period (Blanton 1996). Others (Minc, Hodge, and Blackman 1994) disagree. This is a topic that relates to another one discussed in this chapter: the archaeology of trade.

Settlement pattern studies and the dispersal—in an apparently regular fashion—of markets across the landscape can be interpreted in different ways. Blanton has argued that this regular spacing implies that the decision to implant a community was to a large extent determined by economic considerations (Blanton 1996: 82). Others have argued that the location of Aztec settlements was determined by historical accident and favorable ecological conditions (Brumfiel 1983: 270; Evans 1980; Hassig 1993).

Nucleated versus Dispersed Craft Production

Another related topic of debate has been the nature of the organization of craft production. One can identify two schools of thought: those who consider Aztec craft production as nucleated and those who see it as dispersed (Nichols 1994).

The Aztec capital provides the best example of a nucleated craft production pattern. This terminology refers to a concentration of craftsmen within certain areas of cities or towns. This concentration may have occurred because of reasons of efficiency (Sanders 1956; Trigger 1972: 578–579); conversely, these specialists could have been forced by city rulers to live and work in certain neighborhoods. Such a concentration would make it easier to exert control over production (Nichols 1994: 176).

Another model of craft production is that in which specialists are scattered—or dispersed—throughout a settlement, rather than living in what would be the equivalent of a neighborhood. This pattern of craft production could reflect household production (i.e., for consumption by the household itself) rather than workshop production (i.e., for consumption by a group of people outside the household of the manufacturers).

These two models do not necessarily exclude each other. A consensus exists that Tenochtitlan, and its evidence for nucleated production modes, was an exception. Moreover, investigations at provincial centers in the Aztec realm have yielded data that support the coexistence of both kinds of manufacturing inside the same city (Nichols 1994; Otis Charlton 1994).

Gift Giving

Even though Aztecs often engaged in barter trade to obtain necessities, they also practiced gift giving. The latter played an important role in the development of personal relationships and alliances. In this context, the exchange entails obligations on the part of those who receive toward those who give. The more one can give, the more indebted the other party becomes (Hicks 1991; 1994: 102). Although gift giving provided the framework for the development of ever tighter political and economic obligations, there is also evidence of direct interference into economic transactions by the elite.

Economic Decisions Made by the Ruling Elite for Political Reasons

We know that the elite were instrumental in establishing a new market venue at Tepeacac (Durán 1967, 2: 62; Blanton 1996: 52). The political establishment also took advantage of the aftermath of conflict to relocate markets at the expense of the defeated. For example, Cuauhtitlan used to be the market to trade slaves; it lost that privilege to Azcapotzalco after being defeated on the battlefield (Anales de Cuauhtitlan 1975: 42–43; Blanton 1996: 52, 75). In some cases, military defeats led to a physical destruction of the market. For example, after the defeat of Cuauhtitlan at the hands of Azcapotzalco, in 1428, the market ceased to exist as a physical space. It was planted with maguey (Anales de Cuauhtitlan 1945: 43–44; Blanton 1996: 78). The same happened at Culhuacan, where the Aztecs destroyed the market after a military conflict (Blanton 1996: 78).

Most often, after a defeat, a community would lose the right to sell higher-value goods on its market, rather than be stripped of the right to hold a market all together (Hassig 1993: 112). In some cases, however, a city would be allowed to continue selling special commodities even after a defeat. Azcapotzalco is a good illustration of this. After it was subjugated by the Triple Alliance, the city managed to retain its primacy as a slave market for more than a century (Hassig 1993: 111).

Local rulers also enacted taxes and regulations on local market activities going on within their own political sphere of influence (Anderson, Berdan, and Lockhart 1976; Blanton 1996: 52). As indicated earlier, access to and control over the distribution of goods at the local markets would have given local rulers a power base. The ruling elite in Tenochtitlan frequently made decisions that were economic in nature, and which were aimed at undercutting this power base. For example, in several cases, the decision was made to build causeways to connect the capital to the mainland; however, in some cases, these highways, which were important economic arteries, bypassed certain cities in favor of others. In other cases, especially after military defeats, the Aztecs would strip the local elite of its landholdings with the intention to reduce the economic base that the local elite might rely on to one day challenge Tenochtitlan again (Blanton 1996: 78).

Interregional Trade Fostered by Political Decisions

The Aztec emperors promoted trade within their empire by insisting that provincial towns pay tribute in nonlocal goods. The items typically requested as tribute were luxury items (Berdan 1996: 125). This forced people in some regions to trade with those in areas that did have the required items so that they could be obtained and then sent on to Tenochtitlan. Although the intent of fostering interregional trade might not have been there, the effect of making such a requirement was still to foster interregional trade (Berdan 1994: 306–307; Blanton 1996: 52; Smith 1996: 56). We should also note that some cities or provinces had resources that were not requested by Tenochtitlan, even though similar resources in other provinces might have been part of tribute payment to the capital (Berdan 1996: 129).

Market Size, Artisanal Production, and the Power of the Elite

The presence of a thriving market, the availability of exotic goods, and the presence of craftsmen who could transform these goods all contributed to an increase in importance of the ruling families. We know that the artisans were fully aware of this. In some cases, craftsmen might be tempted to jump ship and relocate to a city that had a bigger and more diversified market. Local rulers controlling less important markets would provide their craftspeople with inducements to stay. At Xochimilco, for example, the craftsmen would receive land and cloth, and they would be feasted twice a year (Blanton 1996: 83; Carrasco 1977: 237, 248).

The Archaeology of Trade

Trade represents action. Archaeologists, by definition, are interested in recovering the material evidence of human behavior. Trade is a prime example of such an activity, yet we are confronted with the limitations of the data available. How can we reconstruct activity based on the static evidence left behind in the archaeological record? In other words, are there any types of sources that we can access to improve our understanding of the trade that went on in Aztec days? There are ways, fortunately, to make this static picture come back to life.

Settlement patterns allow us to retrace the dispersal across the landscape of human settlement. We can date when such features as markets appeared and disappeared. We can also trace the distribution through time and space of various nonperishable commodities, such as ceramics, obsidian, and stone. These studies ideally should encompass multiple commodities, as well as the full length of time of Aztec history. In reality, time and especially financial constraints have conspired to limit studies in the range of objects studied as well as the length of time considered.

Archaeologists look for workshops to identify areas of specialized production. A workshop is typically defined as a location producing "in excess of the needs of the producer's household" (Nichols 1994: 179). Such spikes in distribution patterns of objects can be identified after systematic surface collections have been made (Otis Charlton 1994: 197).

Trace element analysis (e.g., of obsidian or ceramics) is a productive approach to reconstruct economic activities. The clay that is used to produce ceramics contains trace elements. Analysis of these elements can help us to deter-

Two plates, a tripod platter, and a water pitcher of the Aztec era are in the process of being restored. Subway construction workers and archaeologists joined forces in a race against time to preserve the legacy of the Aztecs. (Bettmann/Corbis)

mine whether ceramics were made from clay coming from a single source, or whether several sources of clay were mined to produce ceramics (Minc, Hodge, and Blackman 1994: 148). This type of analysis will identify the chemical composition of the clay, which may have elements in it introduced by the pottery maker, as well as naturally occurring elements. (For more literature on that subject, see: Rice 1987: 406–411, 418–419; Neff et al. 1988, 1989; Elam et al. 1992; Minc, Hodge, and Blackman 1994: 166, n. 5).

A study of various early Aztec pottery types found within the Basin of Mexico mapped their distribution in the Basin. It also compared this distribution with the assumed political boundaries that existed in that time period. This allowed the researchers to assess the role political boundaries might have played in restricting trade. Overall, it appeared that "political boundaries between confederations played a major constraint on exchange" (Minc, Hodge, and Blackman 1994: 159). This study of the distribution of ceramic types did not support the notion that during that period an integrative market system existed. In other words, there does not seem to have been a free-flowing Basinwide exchange of goods; instead, the picture that arose was one in which the early Aztecs and surrounding cities conducted trade mostly within the boundaries of their city–states, and occasionally just beyond those confines (Minc, Hodge, and Blackman 1994: 161).

Obsidian trace element analysis requires sampling obsidian outcrops or sources and performing a trace element analysis on those samples. The result provides the framework within which samples from unknown provenience will be retraced to their point of origin. Putting together such a comparative database requires the input of many people, and the investment of lots of time and money. This is an ongoing project (Boksenbaum et al. 1987; Charlton et al. 1978; Darras and Nelson 1987; Ericson and Kimberlin 1977; Ferriz 1985; Nelson et al. 1977; Trombold et al. 1993). The pay-off is considerable, though, because such a database will help us to identify from where obsidian came.

LONG-DISTANCE TRADE

As mentioned earlier, some people have suggested that the Aztecs possessed a regional market network, and that it dated back to the early Aztec period (Blanton 1996). Various institutions and groups of individuals played an important role here.

Pochteca: Long-Distance Businessmen

The Aztecs were not the first Mesoamerican people to engage in long-distance trade. There is ample evidence that long-distance traders existed long before the Aztecs were on the scene (Simons and Sullivan 1971: 203). Most of what we know about the Aztec pochteca comes from Sahagún (Sahagún 1959: bk. 9). Because of his book on the pochteca we are left with the impression that the pochteca specialized in long-distance trade of elite goods to and from foreign markets. This, it appears, is an oversimplification of their role. There is ample evidence of pochteca trading state goods on behalf of their rulers, bringing them from the Aztec capital to foreign capitals. In such contexts, the pochteca act as nothing more than agents for the emperor. We also know that on some of these official "state business trips," the pochteca brought along personal goods with the intent of selling them. The goods that they would have brought with them ranged from luxury items, such as obsidian earplugs for the elite, to rabbit furs and obsidian blades for the less fortunate (Berdan 2000: 192; Hassig 1993: 116–118). In this context, the pochteca acted as private entrepreneurs. Although the exchange of the royal goods may have taken place in a special context, there are good reasons to believe that the sale of items to nonroyal elite and common people occurred in the context of the regularly held markets. Payment for the goods would often include cacao beans. Sahagún (1950–1982: bk. 19, 27, 30) mentions how the returning pochteca would have cacao beans in their inventory. There is one thing that these pochteca items intended for private sale had in common: they were high-value, low-bulk items. We learn through Sahagún that the pochteca community was a very close-knit one.

We know that the pochteca lived in their own neighborhoods in the capital and very likely in other Aztec cities as well (Hassig 1993: 113, 117–118). We know that twelve cities in the Valley of Mexico had professional merchants such as the pochteca. These communities were Azcapotzalco, Chalco Atenco, Coatlichan, Cuauhtitlan, Huexotla, Huitzilopochco, Mixcocac, Otumba, Tenochtitlan, Texcoco, Tlatelolco, and Xochimilco (Hassig 1993: 121–122). Only the pochtecta from Tenochtitlan and Tlatelolco were allowed to trade goods for and from the emperor (Berdan 2000: 192).

Their organization is often compared with that of a guild—a tight community with restricted membership (Hassig 1993: 113). The occupation of a pochteca was primarily hereditary, meaning that one had to be born into a pochteca family to be allowed to become one. It seems that an intervention on the part of the ruler could also elevate an individual to the rank of pochteca (Simons and Sullivan 1972: 204).

The pochteca were led by two principal merchants. They had their own courts and laws (Hassig 1993: 118). For all practical purposes, the pochteca formed their own social class. Although they were not part of the aristocracy, they were allowed to wear outfits that were normally off-limits to commoners. Moreover, they provided neither personal service nor war service; however, they did give tribute to the ruler (Hassig 1993: 118).

Pochteca traders would often begin their careers by entering the guild at a low level of expenditure, trading in such commodities as salt, chili, and other inexpensive commodities. They would sell these door to door or in the markets of smaller communities (Hassig 1993: 118). They would eventually rise in the ranks and start trading more exotic goods. Pochteca from the Basin of Mexico would travel throughout the realm and sell manufactured goods and return with raw materials. Some of the manufactured goods included cotton capes, obsidian earplugs, and razors. Raw materials such as feathers, turquoise, amber, and animal skins would be traded to artisans (Hassig 1993: 120).

Most pochteca appear to have traded within the borders of the Aztec empire. As the empire expanded, so did their operating area; as it shrank, the pochteca likewise readjusted their activities (Hassig 1993: 114). It appears that only the pochteca from the Valley of Mexico were allowed to enter foreign territory (Hassig 1993: 120).

Traders had their own patron god, Yacatecuhtli. He was considered to have been the one who started commerce among Prehispanic peoples. People venerated this god in many different ways. One was to cover his statue with paper strips. They would sometimes burn copal in front of a bundle of sticks, which they considered represented Yacatecuhtli (Bandelier 1932: 41).

Extracurricular Pochteca Activities

Pochteca sometimes acted in realms outside that of trade. We know, for example, that the pochteca would occasionally cross the borders of the Aztec-controlled lands and engage in espionage. A special category of pochteca, the *nahualoztomeca*, acted both as vanguards and spies. We know that in at least one case pochteca were sent in as spies on the orders of emperor Ahuizotl (Hassig 1993: 121). Spying operations (i.e., the gathering of information abroad) tended to mean collecting information in the market. The pochteca, disguised as regular traders, were the best-suited individuals to keep their ears open in such environments (Berdan 2002: 43). Pochteca sometimes acted as warriors and conquered cities (Hassig 1993: 121).

This career aspect was wrought with danger. Any pochteca caught spying would face execution. In Sahagún's words:

> [before entering a foreign land] . . . they [would] first learn the language of these people; they adopt the mode of dress so they might not be taken for strangers, but for people of that same country. It often happened that the enemy recognized them, capturing and killing them. (Bandelier 1932: 42)

On the other hand, any execution of a pochteca invited Aztec military retaliation. In a sense, the presence of Aztec pochteca in certain foreign markets was a prelude to conquest. We should remember, however, that these cloak-and-dagger operations were not the pochteca's primary concern (Hassig 1993: 125).

REGIONAL AND LOCAL-LEVEL TRADE

Aside from the pochteca, there were a myriad of other merchants active throughout the empire. They have been described as nonguild merchant middlemen, or *tlanecuilo*, by the Aztec themselves. This term can be translated as "retailer" or "merchant" (Berdan 2000: 196). These were the people who brought in the necessities of life rather than the glitzy luxury items. We therefore find them bringing cacao, maize, chili, wheat, sandals, cotton, palm-fiber cloaks, painted gourd bowls, cane-carrying baskets, turkey, and salt to the local markets (Sahagún 1958–1982: Book 10, 65–94; Berdan 2000: 196).

As we have seen, the pochteca traded both in elite goods and more mundane goods sold for general consumption. They were not the only traders who worked with the Aztec empire, however. Aside from the pochteca, we can distinguish among the following types of Aztec merchants (Hassig 1993: 117):

> *Oztomecah*, vanguard merchants
> *Nahualoztomeca*, disguised mechants
> *Teyalualoanimeh*, spying merchants
> *Tecoanimeh*, slave dealers
> *Tealtianimeh*, slave bathers
> *Tlacohcohualnamacaqueh*, peddlers
> *Tlanamacanimeh*, peddlers
> *Tiamicqueh*, traders, dealers

AZTEC SUBSISTENCE METHODS: HOW DID THE AZTEC FEED THEMSELVES?

Aztec Soil and Land Use Classifications

Prehispanic people were very aware of the different soil types at their disposal and the use to which these soils could be put. The Aztecs were no exception to this. They identified seven different soil types. These included (Hassig 1993: 14):

Precolumbian people throughout Mesoamerica were used to carrying loads on their backs using a tumpline. This tradition continues today, as illustrated here by a Tojolabal Maya girl living in the state of Chiapas, Mexico. (D.Donne Bryant/DDB Stock Photo)

> *Atoctli,* or fertile alluvial soil
> *Cuauhtlalli,* or humus (i.e., soil enriched by decayed trees)
> *Tlalcoztli,* or fine, fertile yellow-reddish soil
> *Xalatoctli,* or sandy alluvial soil
> *Tlahzollalli,* or sand enriched by decayed matter
> *Xallalli,* or infertile sandy soil
> *Tezoquitl,* or firm, dark clayey soil

The Aztecs also distinguished between various land uses (Hassig 1993: 15), such as:

> *Tlalcolhualli,* or land that is bought or sold
> *Tlalmantli,* or flatland (land that is neither hilly nor hollowed)
> *Tlalhuitectli,* or land that is worked down, or packed
> *Tlalahuiac,* or land to which fertilizer is added
> *Atlalli,* land that is irrigated

Extensive Agricultural Methods: Slash-and-Burn System and the Infield–Outfield Method

The term *extensive* stands in opposition to *intensive* when referring to methods of producing food. We will discuss two closely related extensive agricultural methods.

Slash-and-Burn System

The slash-and-burn system is one in which the soil nutrients are not replenished. A section of land is cleared of its vegetation. This is done by cutting down the trees, and allowing them to dry for a short time period of a few weeks. The vegetation is subsequently burned. The ash fertilizes the crops planted over a period of roughly 2–3 years. No additional fertilizer is applied. After the period just mentioned, the soil has become completely devoid of nutrients, and crops returns are minimal. At that point, farmers select another area for clearance and the cycle is repeated. The land farmed during the preceding years is allowed to lay fallow for an extended period of time. It will eventually be cleared and planted again.

Infield–Outfield Method

Very similar to the slash-and-burn approach, the difference lies in the length of time a piece of land is allowed to lay fallow. With the infield–outfield method, this period is considerably shorter than it is with the slash-and-burn approach. Population pressure and growing lack of appropriate lands to clear usually lead to a shortening of the fallow period (Hassig 1993: 17).

Population pressure is thought to have brought about a shift from nonintensive to intensive agricultural methods. As populations grow and the land becomes a premium to live on, people will shift to a more labor intensive way of producing food (see Boserup 1973).

Intensive Agricultural Methods

A common aspect of the methods just reviewed is the use of naturally available nutrients (in the form of ash) rather than the use of additional fertilizer. The application of such additional nutrients did occur to some extent in the intensive agricultural methods discussed below. One should note, however, that Precolumbian farmers did not have large domesticated animals that could produce enough manure. The main Prehispanic source of fertilizer was night soil (Hassig 1993: 47).

Hillside Terracing

Aztec farmers worked the land wherever they could. In hilly terrains, this required taking measures to prevent soil loss through runoff. Archaeologists have excavated two kinds of stones terraces: contour terraces on hillsides and cross-channel terraces in ravines (Price and Smith 1992; Smith 1994: 331; Smith and Heath-Smith 1994: 351–352, 356). Although it is relatively easy to identify these types of walls, it is very difficult to date the construction of these terraces. Quite often, archaeologists look for potsherds or for stratigraphic associations with others part of the site that can be dated. Because the latter approach cannot always be taken, most archaeologists are limited to reporting the presence of these improvements, but often cannot date them.

Excavations of Aztec-period agricultural features at the sites of Capilco and Cuexcomate in Morelos, Mexico, have provided new data on the construction, function, and significance of agricultural terraces in Late Postclassic Central Mexico. Stratigraphic and chemical analyses of alluvial deposits associated with cross-channel terraces ("check-dams") have revealed that these features very likely served an agricultural function. Terrace walls were built in small increments, and associated sediments were created by alluvial deposition of eroding topsoil. These findings, together with demographic and social data from nearby excavated houses, suggest that Aztec-period agricultural intensification was a household-level response to population pressure (Smith and Price 1994).

Irrigation Agriculture

Irrigation agriculture was one of the most efficient ways of producing food. It remains so today; however, it could only be practiced in areas with access to rivers and lakes. The Aztecs undertook the most massive irrigation projects of the entire Precolumbian history of the Basin of Mexico during the Late Aztec period (Blanton 1996: 57). From early colonial accounts we may surmise that irrigation was also practiced on a wide scale in Morelos in Aztec days (Smith 1994: 327).

Raised Fields Agriculture

Chinampas, or floating gardens, formed an integral part of Aztec subsistence techniques. Food production of this nature was prevalent in the southern portion of the Valley of Mexico and in the area of the Chalco and Xochimilco lakes.

Reliance on these types of gardens started in the Early Aztec period; it peaked during the Late Aztec period (Blanton 1996: 57; Parsons et al. 1982).

These fields are described as "raised" or "floating" because of their appearance and the way they were built. A *chinampa* would be built in a lake environment. The Aztecs would start by driving wooden stakes into the lake. Vines and branches were then woven around these stakes to form an enclosure. Soil would be dumped inside these enclosures to build artificially raised surfaces. Trees were planted along the edges of these enclosures to provide additional strength to the construction (Hassig 1993: 47). The soil to fill up the enclosure tended to be taken from the areas in between the raised platforms. This approach served two purposes: the soil is extremely fertile, and its removal on a regular basis helped to maintain these canals. Maintenance of these canals resulted in dumping more of the very fertile mud on top of the *chinampa* surface (Hassig 1993: 47).

Irrigation of *chinampa* crops was taken care of by nature because the surface of these fields would rarely be more than 1 m above the water level. Combined with the high fertility of these fields, this made it possible to grow up to four crops per year. It appears that a brief fallow period of less than 3 months every 3–4 years was sufficient to rejuvenate the soil (Hassig 1993: 47).

Chinampa farmers had one more trick up their sleeves to increase the yield of their fields. This was the use of seedbeds. Aztec farmers would cover a bed of lake weeds with mud from the lake. This was allowed to harden over a period of several days. The mud and seaweed was then cut into small blocks into which seeds were then planted. The seeds were covered up with manure. To protect against the occasional frost, these young seedlings were covered with reeds. These seedlings were eventually transplanted from these rectangular blocks into the *chinampas*. This allowed the farmers to speed up the harvest cycle: once a crop was harvested, a new crop, already well on its way, would be planted. Moreover, by using these small mud blocks with seedlings, Aztec farmers could select which plants to transplant into the raised field by favoring the seedlings that had grown the most. Among the crops grown on *chinampas* were maize, chile, fruit, tomatoes, amaranth, beans, and flowers (Hassig 1993: 49).

Most of the *chinampas* were constructed in Lakes Xochimilco and Chalco, whereas they were rare to nonexistent in other lakes in the Basin of Mexico. This is primarily because of the brackishness of the water. Even though estimating the total surface dedicated to raised field agriculture is always subject to revision, current estimates range from 9,000 to 9,500 hectares (Hassig 1993: 50). Estimating what the annual yield of these fields might have been in Precolumbian days is completely impossible (Hassig 1993: 51).

House-Lot Gardens (Calmil)

House-lot gardens were associated with individual households (Smith 1996: 78). These gardens were small, and would have been used to grow such crops as tomatoes, chiles, herbs, and flowers for household use (Evans 1992: 105).

Food Provisions as Part of Tribute

One of the key aspects of the Aztec economy was that the heartland supplied craft goods to the outlying areas, from where, in return, foodstuffs were sent to the capital (Blanton 1996: 48; Parsons 1980; Sanders, Parsons, and Santley 1979: 180). How important was this flow of food items to the major political centers? How much did the people at the center of the realm rely on these shipments to survive?

Answering questions like these is not an easy proposition. Estimates of the importance vary widely. For example, Calnek (1978) suggests that food sent as tribute would have fed anywhere from 25 to 33 percent of the population of Tenochtitlan. Others believe that this flow of food items might have fed up to half of the capital's population (Parsons 1976). The city of Texcoco might have been able to feed about 20,000 of its inhabitants with food tribute (Offner 1983: 48).

Plant and Animal Domestication and the Aztec Diet

The Aztecs were the beneficiaries of millennia of efforts and experimentation in the area of plant and animal domestication in their part of the world. With regard to domestication, there are three points that need to be made: What does this term mean? When did it take place? Why did people start domesticating plants and animals?

Plant and Animal Domestication—Definition and Context

The term *domestication* can be translated as "bringing into the house(hold)." In other words, humans manage to establish a strong bond with plants and animals, so much so that these organisms are brought "into orbit" with us. This bond that humans have forged is typically one that took a long time to establish. Nobody wakes up one morning thinking, "Today I am going to start working in a field." Instead, all the available evidence points to a long sequence of experiments, spanning multiple generations, whereby—through trial and error—people produced what we call today a domesticated plant or animal.

With regard to the second and third points just mentioned, humans all over the world experimented with domestication, and they most often did so independently from each other. Mesoamerica was one of those areas where certain crops and animals were domesticated first. As to the reason why, the answer is less easy to provide. Given that it took multiple human generations to go from wild ancestral forms of plants and animals to fully domesticated ones, the people who started this process could not and did not foresee the outcome of their intervention. As humans became more and more successful in their attempts to control plant and animal life around them, however, they also became increasingly more and more dependent on these fruits of their labor for survival.

Agriculture especially allows larger communities to thrive. As production becomes more efficient, fewer and fewer people are required to produce enough food to support the population. As a result, others are free to pursue

Aztec manuscript depicting daily life. (Bettmann/Corbis)

different activities, including such specialties as manufacturing goods or occupying positions of leadership in a growing complex political system. A good
example of where such developments can lead is our society today. If it were
not for very efficient and productive means of generating food, our society
would not survive for very long. Take away the food producers in our midst

and you would quickly see mayhem and total chaos emerge, accompanied by an astronomical drop in population figures.

To return to the question of why people messed with domestication, perhaps the most honest answer would be that they did not know where this would lead, and that we, now that we know, cannot afford to go back. We are stuck, and so were the Aztecs.

Evidence of Domestication in the Material Record

What exactly does domestication entail and how can we as archaeologists identify the remains of domesticated plants and animals? As a result of human intervention, plants and animals tend to become increasingly dependent upon us for their survival. As far as plants are concerned, this typically means that humans ensure that the seeds are propagated. With regard to animals, people are often the ones who decide which animals reproduce and when. This human intervention in the reproductive cycle of other organisms is guided by our desire to obtain traits that we like and to do away with those we do not.

If we are to answer the question of when plants (and to some extent animals) were domesticated in Mesoamerica, we first have to be able to identify the telltale traits of such a state. Archaeologists have to be able to look at seeds or animal bones and be able to say with a high degree of certainty whether something was domesticated. With regard to plants, we will need to look for changes that have occurred in the seed-release mechanisms. For example, wild grasses will easily disperse. It is to their advantage that seeds are readily dispersed by wind or animals hitting the seed stalks. On the other hand, humans would have selected in favor of those seeds that did not release easily. (In nature, those seeds would never have a chance to germinate; however, their odds improve dramatically with human intervention.) Wild grasses have seeds where the connection between the seed and the rest of the plant breaks off easily, producing a clean break—something that we can observe under a microscope. This connection is much tougher with seeds of domesticated plants, and any break created here will require more force to be applied. It will also create a break area with rough and jagged edges.

Another feature that commonly appears is an increase in size of the seeds or fruits. Wild ancestral forms of plants will produce smaller seeds, whereas domesticated varieties yield larger seeds or fruits.

Observable traits of domestication among animals include shape changes, often a reduction in size of the animals, as well as a change in ratio of males versus females found in association with human settlement. Size reduction, it is argued, is sometimes the result of humans stepping in and separating animals when they start fighting, such as during the rutting season. Whereas in nature brawn would usually carry the day, thereby ensuring that the genes of the larger and more powerful animal are present in the next generation, with human intervention the smaller animals might also have a chance to reproduce. The more aggressive animal might sometimes even be considered a nuisance and be disposed of, thus guaranteeing that the genes of the smaller-sized individual are transferred to the offspring. When comparing overall stature of animals over time, and especially of those bones found in association with human presence, we can detect such a size change.

Another insight that the material record can provide us is the ratio of bones from females versus males and young versus older animals that we might find in garbage dumps. With a herd of domesticated animals, humans will select against males because only a few are necessary to procreate. As a result, the recovery of more bones of young males might indicate human intervention, and thus possibly reflect efforts to domesticate a species. Representations of animals in art rather than the physical remains of the animals occasionally might betray that they were domesticated. For example, among cattle the appearance of multicolored hides, or brindle as it is known, is said to be characteristic of domesticated animals; wild cattle do not display such a trait.

The Aztec Palate: What Did They Eat and How Do We Know?

Our information on what was on the Aztec menu is derived from the retrieval of the physical remains of their meals, as well as references in the literature of the time. Interest in the Aztec diet is something that was not a primary concern until fairly recently, and that is reflected in the following.

It is sometimes said that archaeologists like to go through other people's garbage. In the case of the Aztecs, and other long-gone civilizations, the garbage dumps are referred to as "middens." Middens tend to be closely associated with dwellings, a difference with our society, where our trash gets collected and disposed of outside the community. When sifting through an Aztec family's garbage, we will find broken pottery, broken or worn out tools, and remnants of meals. The latter quite often includes animal bones. Analyzing animal bones is the job of zooarchaeologists. They can identify the animals from which the bones came, which, in turn, can give us a good impression of what was eaten.

Plant remains are more difficult to collect. Sites in very dry environments will occasionally yield plant remains that have been preserved in a state of dehydration. This type of environment is not very typical for a lot of known Aztec sites, so we rely on the recovery of plant materials in two other ways: flotation and pollen analysis. Flotation involves dissolving soil that is surmised to contain plant remains into a liquid (part water, part detergent). This process leads to plant remains floating to the surface, where they can be collected with a scoop. These plant remains can then be identified under a microscope. Researchers also use very powerful microscopes to identify plant pollen. As any allergy sufferer knows, pollen are virtually indestructible parts of the plant. They can survive extreme heat, and long periods of submersion in water. These microscopically small plant remains can be collected and identified.

With a few exceptions, especially Sahagún, most writers are woefully brief in mentioning anything on the topic of food. This lack has been attributed to the fact that, at least among colonial-period writers, there were only men who chronicled events, and they had other things on their minds (Coe 1994: 5). Let us now go back in time and take a look at the Aztec menu.

Aztec Food Items

Plant Food

Maize is central to Mesoamerican culture. Sahagún mentions eight different kinds of maize: white maize, yellow maize, reddish maize, tawny maize, flower maize (white grain striped with color), blue-husked maize, black maize, and the black fly-speck maize (Coe 1994: 88–89; Sahagún 1950–1982, II: 279). Tribute lists mention three additional grains: beans, chía seeds, and *huauhtli*. The latter has most often been interpreted as amaranth seeds (Coe 1994: 89–90).

Beans were very often mixed with corn as part of a daily meal. This is still the case today. Chía seeds were mixed with water to concoct a drink. The *huauhtli* figured prominently in dishes related to religious ceremonies (Coe 1994: 90–91). Squash completed the triad of corn and beans. Aztecs ate both the flesh and the seeds (Coe 1994: 92).

Mexican cuisine today inherited these three ingredients, as well as others. Chiles and tomatoes were part of Aztec dishes and they remain so today. We know that the Aztecs taunted their Spanish foe that they might end up as part of a dish together with tomatoes and chiles (Coe 1994: 92). Sahagún lists the varieties of chiles and tomatoes and the range of appreciation the Aztecs had for them (Coe 1994: 93):

> The chile seller . . . sells mild red chiles, broad chiles, hot green chiles, yellow chiles, cuit-lachilli, tempilchilli, chichioachilli. He sells water chiles, conchilli; he sells smoked chiles, small chiles, tree chiles, thin chiles, those like beetles. He sells hot chiles, sharp-pointed red chiles, a late variety, those from Atzitziuacan, Tochmiclo, Huaxtepec, Michoacán, Anauac, the Huaxteca, the Chichimeca. Separately he sells strings of chiles, chiles cooked in an olla, fish chiles, white fish chiles.
>
> The bad chile seller sells chile [that is] stinking, sharp to the taste, evil-smelling, spoiled; waste from the chiles, late-formed chiles, chaff from the chiles. He sells chiles from the wet country, incapable of burning, insipid to the taste; unformed, not yet firm, immature; those which have formed as droplets, as buds.
>
> The tomato seller sells large tomatoes, small tomatoes, leaf tomatoes, thin tomatoes, sweet tomatoes, large serpent tomatoes, nipple-shaped tomatoes, serpent tomatoes. He also sells coyote tomatoes, sand tomatoes, those which are yellow, very yellow, quite yellow, red, very red, quite ruddy, ruddy, bright red, reddish, rosy dawn colored.
>
> The bad tomato seller sells spoiled tomatoes, bruised tomatoes, those which cause diarrhea; the sour, the very sour. Also he sells the green, the hard ones, those which scratch one's throat, which disturb—trouble one; which make one's saliva smack, make one's saliva flow; the harsh ones, those which burn the throat.

Aside from green herbs, the Aztecs also ate roots and other plants. One root that was commonly consumed was the *chayotli*, or chayote; another was the jícama root. Sweet potatoes and manioc were present on Aztec plates, but they were never of great importance (Coe 1994: 93).

Mushrooms occasionally served as a hallucinogen, as we shall see shortly, but they were also eaten. According to Sahagún's informants, there were at least six edible varieties of mushrooms. All had to be thoroughly cooked, lest they be lethal (Coe 1994: 94). The *huitlacoche*, a fungus that grew on maize (it still affects maize today) was related to these.

The agave plant provided raw materials for textiles, fuel, building materials, and even sewing equipment (the spines were sometimes used as needles). It also was a food source. Mesoamerican people tapped the agave to produce syrup, sugar, wine, and vinegar. Parts of it were eaten as well, again after they were thoroughly cooked (Coe 1994: 94). The Aztecs also ate at least thirteen different varieties of cacti (Coe 1994: 95).

The Aztecs differentiated between two kinds of fruits: those that tasted sour (*xocotl*) and those that were sweet (*tzapotl*). The Aztec dictionary also abounds with various terms for stages of ripeness, ranging from almost ripe to rotten (Coe 1994: 95).

Perhaps the best known and most widely appreciated contribution of Mesoamerica to the world's food items is chocolate. The Aztecs cannot claim to have been the first to consume chocolate. The Olmec, the earliest known complex society in Mesoamerica, are known to have savored the drink (Coe and Coe 1996: 39). Our word *chocolate*, however, may very well have been derived from the Aztec expressions "xoco" and "atl" meaning "bitter" and "water," respectively (Lopez 2002). Nahuatl-speaking informants told a Spanish naturalist, Francisco Hernandez, that the general term for cacao tree was *cacahuacuauhuitl*. This compound word combines *cacahuatl*, or "chocolate," and *cuauhuitl*, or "tree" (Coe and Coe 1996: 81). Cacao, on the other hand, may derive from the Mixe-Zoquean word "kakawa" (Coe and Coe 1996: 39).

Among the Aztec, consumption of chocolate was limited mostly to the upper crust of society. The emperor consumed it, as did those who were among the elite and who had the means to procure it (Coe 1994: 102). There were exceptions, however. Aside from royalty and members of the Aztec elite, the pochteca and soldiers on the march were also allowed to consume this "food of the gods" (Coe and Coe 1996: 93–94). For those who were allowed to partake in chocolate, especially during elaborate dinners in elite circles, it was only offered toward the end of the meal. A meal would be rounded off with chocolate and tubes of tobacco being offered to the guests, just as a glass of cognac and cigars would be offered in our society (Coe and Coe 1996: 94). It is of interest that even though the rich and famous would drink their chocolate—the most traditional way of consuming chocolate—soldiers would be issued chocolate in hard form. Military rations would include chocolate made into wafers or pellets (Coe and Coe 1996: 96).

Aztec society also made allowance for chocolate to be consumed by one other category of people. A special mixture of chocolate and water was occasionally given to those who were about to be sacrificed. As part of the myriad of religious festivals in the capital, a slave would be chosen to impersonate the god Quetzalcoatl. Over a period of 40 days he would be treated as a god. On the eve of his sacrifice he would be given warning and asked that he perform a ritual.

This commodity did not grow naturally in the Aztec heartland. It had to be brought in, usually as part of tribute payment, from an area called "Xoconochco," located along the Pacific coast of the present-day Mexican state of Chiapas and adjacent Guatemala. Cacao formed part of the tribute payments for eight out of nine tributary towns listed for this region (Smith and Berdan 1996: 278–279, 316).

Four varieties of cacao were identified at the time of Spanish incursion (Coe and Coe 1996: 81). Three out of these four were used as currency, and the fourth was consumed. Most people tend to associate cacao with a drink, but consumption of cacao also occurred in the form of eating the roasted seeds. There occasionally may have been cacao in a solid state that was eaten as well that was very similar, in consistency at least, to our chocolate bars (Coe 1994: 103). Among Mesoamerican people, Aztecs included, drinking cacao was the primary way of savoring cacao.

Like our society today, Aztec chocolate consumers were faced with chocolate of differing quality. This is implied in the Nahuatl term *tlaquetzalli,* meaning "precious thing," another way to refer to chocolate of the highest quality (Coe and Coe 1996: 87). High quality was sometimes mixed with other ingredients, thus leading to a lower quality product. Ingredients included corn and seeds (Coe and Coe 1996: 87).

Preparing cacao for drinking purposes was a laborious process. It involved grinding the beans, letting them ferment, and then toasting them (Coe 1994: 103). The resulting cacao "powder" was then mixed with tepid water. In some cases, the Aztec would also add ground maize and other ingredients. There are some depictions showing people pouring the liquid mixture from one vessel into another. A scene on a Maya cylindrical vase, now at the Princeton Art Museum, shows a woman standing up and pouring cacao out of a cylindrical vessel into a vessel placed on the floor in front of her. Such actions helped to aerate the cacao (i.e., to introduce air bubbles into it). This generated a foam head, always appreciated as a sure sign of quality cacao. Failure of such a foam head forming would have implied inferior cacao being used (Coe 1994: 103).

One should remember that there were a myriad of applications for chocolate among Mesoamerican people. Although primarily consumed in liquid form, Precolumbian chocolate was also a component of drinks, gruels, porridges, and powders. Modern chocolate scholars do not rule out the existence of solid chocolate in the days before the arrival of the Europeans (Coe and Coe 1996: 51).

In addition to maize, among the ingredients mixed in with the water and the cacao were chile water, hallucinogenic flowers, vanilla, bee honey, and powdered aromatic flowers (Coe 1994: 104–105). A misconception is that in Precolumbian days chocolate and cinnamon were mixed (Coe 1994: 105). Still, with all the added materials and the inherent qualities of the cacao, it was said that chocolate gladdens one, refreshes one, consoles one, invigorates one, and, yes, fattens one (Coe 1994: 105).

Domesticated Animals

Precolumbian people in general and the Aztec in particular did not stand out by the great variety of domesticated animals, yet there were some. The Aztec had five domesticated animals, including the turkey, the Muscovy duck, the dog, the bee, and the cochineal insect.

The turkey was the only true domesticated fowl in Mesoamerica. Other feathered creatures were eaten as well, but they were wild. Sahagún was very much taken by the taste of turkey, informing his readership, "I eat the wing tips of a turkey; I am given them. [I]t leads the meats; it is the master. It is tasty, fat, savory" (Coe 1994: 96; Sahagún 1950–1982, II: 53, 56). Demand for turkeys was apparently great. One market, at Tepeyac, apparently sold 8,000 gobblers every 5 days. The Aztec appetite for dogs is well known. Contrary to popular belief, they did not cook Chihuahuas, but rather selected a larger hairless variety of dog to join them as dinner. It appears that the Spanish also acquired a taste for dog, and incorporated huge numbers of them as ship stores. Even Cortés, in one of his letters to emperor Charles V, could not help mentioning that they were "very tasty" (Coe 1994: 96).

Game and Fish

Aside from wild fowl, the Aztecs added game and fish to their menu. Deer, peccary, rabbits, jackrabbits, mice, armadillos, snakes, gophers, possums, and iguanas were among these delicacies. The Aztec apparently considered a stew made out of snake meat and pulque, an alcoholic beverage, to be very wholesome for the elderly (Coe 1994: 99).

The lakes in Central Mexico both provided abundant amounts of fish and were also the home of other edibles. We find the Aztecs collecting water bugs, which they called *axayacatl,* as well as the eggs of the same bugs. These were called "water amaranth," or *ahuauhtli,* referring to their granular texture. They were turned into tortillas and occasionally wrapped in maize husks and roasted (Coe 1994: 99; Hassig 1993: 129). Another food item foreign to the Western palate were the *izcahuitli.* These were tiny worms living in lakes. They were prepared with salt and chile. Those who consumed them said that the end product had the consistency of crushed bread (Coe 1994: 99).

The Aztec also caught various kinds of lake shrimp and frogs. The tadpoles were also consumed. A very peculiar breed of salamander, the *axolotol,* still lives in the lakes in Mexico. It, too, was eaten by the Aztecs (Coe 1994: 100). Bones from reptiles are occasionally found as well (Smith and Heath-Smith 1994: 354).

Perhaps the most unusual food item retrieved from the lakes was *tecuicatl.* This was a green slimy substance (*Spirulina geitlerii*), harvested at certain times from the waters of Lake Texcoco. The Aztecs would go out onto the lake in their canoes and harvest the algae with their nets. Once their canoes were filled with these algae, they would return to shore and spread out the algae on the ground and allow them to dry. They would wait until it had formed into a loaf or cake about 1.5 in. thick. These loaves were then cut into bricks. This is how the *tecuicatl* was consumed. Those Spanish who tried it found it to be very salty, hardly a surprise given that the waters of Lake Texcoco were very salty as well. Because of this there is little doubt that it had a shelf life of about 1 year (Ortiz de Montellano 1990: 102–104). Despite its unusual nature, *tecuicatl* may have been a crucial item on the Aztec diet. Aside from its storability, other critical characteristics include abundance, rapid growth rate, and its high protein value. Researchers have estimated that 70 percent of *Spirulina*, by weight, is protein. Moreover, eight essential amino acids are present as well. Given that during Aztec times population density in the Basin was very high, the importance of this green slimy substance in maintaining these high numbers should not be underestimated (Sanders et al. 1979: 291).

It is remarkable that despite the thumbs-down given by the Spanish to this food item, they must have brought it to the Old World at one point. We know that people living along the shores of Lake Chad in Central West Africa consume the same kind of algae. Moreover, they do so after sun-drying them and then eating them with a sauce made of tomatoes and chili peppers. Ortiz de Montellano (1990: 105) suggests that all these ingredients must have been brought over by the Spanish after the conquest of Mexico.

Despite their appearance and salty taste, these algae were an ideal food in many ways. It is said to have a mix of proteins and amino acids similar to that of an egg, making it very nutritious. The algae are also very rich in vitamins and minerals, including niacin, which make *tecuicatl* an excellent supplement to corn. Moreover, the algae's cell walls are easily broken down in our digestive system.

Finally, the cochineal insect played an important role, but not as a direct source of food. These insects were used as a source to make red dye. As such they were very valuable (Coe 1994: 95).

Food Etiquette

On the occasion of a baptismal ceremony, the Aztecs would engage in lavish feasting. Before the guests started eating, the men would be offered smoking tubes, presumably ceramic, containing tobacco and fragrances. Food was served only after they had started smoking. The menu might have included a stew made with meat and fish, to which chile was added. Another dish would be a souplike liquid containing beans and toasted maize. The presence of chocolate and the preferred spice, *teunacaztli*, which was added to the beverage, was of utmost importance (Coe 1994: 78). This beverage was served at the end of the meal. Women did not receive chocolate; instead, they were served a type of gruel that included maize dough and water, a mixture that was occasionally cooked (Coe 1994: 77).

Sahagún's informants recounted a feast organized by a pochtecta, an event that was much rarer than a baptismal feast. The context here is much more than that of a meal among good friends; rather, the goal of a pochteca feast was to impress. To reach this goal, pomp and circumstance had to be observed, and certain rituals had to be incorporated into the event. Before dawn, long before the actual meal was served, guests would receive mushrooms. These were hallucinogenic rather than nutritional, and their consumption led to all kinds of visions that would later be shared among the guests after the effects of the mushrooms had worn off. The menu included fowl and maize, as well as a gruel made out of chía seeds (Coe 1994: 79–80). The prestige of the pochtecta host was greatly enhanced if he had been able to afford enough food to sustain his guests for 2 days in a row.

The overindulgence in *octli,* or pulque, as it is known today, occasionally would lead to drunkenness. This beverage was produced from the fermented sap of the agave plant. Its effect is said to be comparable to that of cider (Soustelle 1961: 156).

Social Position and Diet

Aztec rulers ate very well. Consider the description of the range of foods offered to the emperors on a daily basis, including hot tortillas, white tamales with beans forming a sea shell on top, red tamales, roll-shaped tortillas, sauces with turkeys, quails, venison, rabbit, hare, rat, lobster, fish, and sweet fruits. It is alleged that the upper crust of society, such as the emperor and his family, were offered 2,000 kinds of food each day (Berdan 2002: 44).

Aztec commoners were much more limited in their meals. A midday meal might consist of a maize gruel (called *atolli*), and a later meal could include tortillas with a chili sauce, beans, and vegetables. Meat was served only on very special occasions. The Aztec middle class, including the pochteca traders and luxury artisans, were wealthy enough and had sufficient privileges to have access to meats and fish (Berdan 2002: 44).

Nonfood Crops

The Aztec also grew a number of nonfood crops. One of them was maguey. It served many purposes. For example, its fibers were used to produce textiles and nets, and its needles were turned into sewing needles. Maguey sap was said to have medicinal powers (Berdan 2002: 41).

Aztec farmers also tended to the prickly-pear cactus. Even though this cactus could be eaten (as is still the case today), it also was home for small insects of great importance to the Aztec. These insects were the basis for producing red cochineal dyes (Berdan 2002: 41). These dyes were used to color textiles such as the cotton clothing that was common among the Aztec elite. Cotton was grown in its natural habitat; that of the lowland areas in Mesoamerica (Berdan 2002: 42).

The Aztec and Nutrition

We have just reviewed and discussed what was involved in food production, and detailed what was on the Aztec dinner table. One question that remains to be answered is: Did the Aztec have enough to eat, or were they subject to undernourishment or malnourishment?

There are two schools of thought regarding this question. One group of authors has suggested that before the Europeans set foot ashore, the Aztec did suffer from malnourishment and undernourishment. The arrival of the newcomers, this group of scholars argued, dramatically improved the native diet (Cook and Borah 1979). Two authors (Harner 1977 and Harris 1978) go further and claim that the Aztec, desperate for protein, had no choice but to resort to cannibalism.

An alternative view is supported by another group of scholars (Ortiz de Montellano 1990; Sanders et al. 1970; Santley and Rose 1979). In their opinion, the Aztec had access to superb food resources. This, combined with the presence of advanced agricultural systems (i.e., ridged gardens) allowed them to sustain population levels higher than today and with a diet that was superior to that of a large number of modern Mexicans (Ortiz de Montellano 1990: 73).

REFERENCES

Anales de Cuauhtitlan. 1945. *Códice Chimalpopoca: Anales de Cuauhtitlan y leyenda de los soles.* Translated by Primo Feliciano Velázquez. Mexico: Universidad Autónoma de Mexico, Instituto de Investigaciones Históricas.

———. 1975. In *Códice Chimalpopoca: Anales de Cuauhtitlan y leyenda de los soles.* Translated by Primo Feliciano Velázquez, pp.3–68. Mexico: Universidad Autónoma de México. (Reprint of 1945 edition)

Anderson, Arthur J. O., Frances F. Berdan, and James Lockhart. 1976. *Beyond the Codices: The Nahua View of Colonial Mexico.* Berkeley: University of California Press.

Bandelier, Fanny R. 1932. *A History of Ancient Mexico by Fray Bernardino de Sahagún.* Translated by Fanny R. Bandelier from the Spanish version of Carlos Maria de Bustamante. Nashville: Fisk University Press.

Berdan, Frances. 1975. *Trade, Tribute and Market in the Aztec Empire.* Unpublished Ph.D. dissertation. Austin: Department of Anthropology, University of Texas at Austin.

———. 1982. *The Aztecs of Central Mexico: An Imperial Society.* New York: Holt, Rinehart and Winston.

———. 1994. Economic Alternatives under Imperial Rule. The Eastern Aztec Empire. In *Economies and Polities in the Aztec Realm.* Edited by Mary G. Hodge and Michael E. Smith, pp. 291–312. (Studies on Culture and Society. Volume 6). Albany: Institute for Mesoamerican Studies.

———. 2000. Principles of Regional and Long-Distance Trade in the Aztec Empire. In *The Ancient Civilizations of Mesoamerica. A Reader.* Edited by Michael E. Smith and Marilyn A. Mason, pp. 191–203. Oxford: Blackwell Publishers.

Bernard, H. Russell and Salinas Pedraza, Jesús. 1989. *Native Ethnograhpy: A Mexican Indian Describes His Culture.* Newbury Park: Sage Publications.

Blanton, Richard E. 1996. The Basin of Mexico Market System and the Growth of Empire. In *Aztec Imperial Strategies.* Edited by Frances F. Berdan, Richard E. Blanton, Elizabeth H. Boone, Mary G. Hodge, Michael E. Smith, and Emily Umberger, pp. 47–84. Washington, D.C.: Dumbarton Oaks Research Library and Collection.

Blanton, Richard E., and Mary G. Hodge. 1996. Appendix 2. Data on market activities and production specializations in *Tlatoani* centers in the basin of Mexico and areas north of the basin (excluding Texcoco and Tenochtitlan-Tlatelolco). In *Aztec Imperial Strategies*. Edited by Frances F. Berdan, Richard E. Blanton, Elizabeth Hill Boone, Mary G. Hodge, Michael E. Smith, and Emily Umberger, pp. 243–246. Washington, D.C.: Dumbarton Oaks Research Library and Collection.

Boksenbaum, Martin, Paul Tolstoy, Garman Harbottle, J. Kimberlin, and Mary Neivens. 1987. Obsidian Industries and Cultural Evolution in the Basin of Mexico before 500 B.C. *Journal of Field Archaeology* 14: 65–75.

Boserup, Esther. 1973. *The Conditions of Agricultural Growth*. Chicago: Aldine.

Broda, Johanna. 1970. El tributo en trajes guerreros y la estructura del sistema tributario Mexica. In *Economía Política e Ideología Prehispánico*. Edited by Pedro Carrasco and Johanna Broda, pp. 115–174. Mexico City: UNAM.

Brumfiel, Elizabeth. 1983. Aztec State Making: Ecology, Structure and the Origin of the State. *American Anthropologist* 85: 261–284.

Calnek, Edward E. 1978. The City–State in the Basin of Mexico: Late Prehispanic Period. In *Urbanization in the Americas from its Beginnings to the Present*. Edited by Richard Schaedel et al., pp. 463–470. The Hague: Mouton.

Carrasco, Pedro. 1977. Los señores de Xochimilco en 1548. *Tlalocan* 7: 229–265.

Charlton, Thomas H., David C. Grove, and Philip K. Hopke. 1978. The Paredon, Mexico, Obsidian Source and Early Formative Exchange. *Science* 201: 807–809.

Coe, Sophie. 1994. *America's First Cuisines*. Austin: University of Texas Press.

Coe, Sophie, and Michael D. Coe. 1996. *The True History of Chocolate*. London: Thames and Hudson, Ltd.

Cook, S. F., and W. Borah. 1979. Indian Food Production and Consumption in Central Mexico before and after the Conquest (1500–1650). In *Essays in Population History: Mexico and California,* vol. 3, pp. 129–176. Los Angeles: University of California Press. (The authors argue that the Aztec diet before the arrival of the Spanish led to malnourishment and undernourishment. They suggest that the indigenous people had no choice but to resort to cannibalism.)

Dalton, George. 1971. *Economic Anthropology and Development: Essays on Tribal and Peasant Economies*. New York/London: Basic Books.

Darras, Véronique, and Fred W. Nelson. 1987. Nota informative primeros resultados de la caraterización química por medio de los elementos traza de los yacimientos de obsidiana en la región de Zináparo-Purpero, Michoacán. *Trace* 12: 76–79.

Durán, Fray Diego. 1967. *Historia de las Indias de Nueva España e Isles de la Tierra Firme*. Edited by Angel María Garibay. Mexico: Editorial Porrúa.

Ekholm, Gordon F. 1946. Wheeled Toys in Mexico. *American Antiquity* 11(4): 222–228.

Elam, J. Michael, Christopher Carr, Michael D. Glasscock, and Hector Neff. 1992. Utrasonic Disaggregation and INAA of Textural Fractions of Tucson Basin and Ohio Valley Pottery. In *Chemical Characterization of Ceramic Pastes in Archaeology*. Edited Hector Neff, pp. 93–111. Madison: Prehistory Press.

Ericson, J. E., and J. Kimberlin. 1977. Obsidian Sources, Chemical Characterization Hydration Rates in West Mexico. *Archaeometry* 19: 157–166.

Evans, Susan T. 1980. Spatial Analysis of Basin of Mexico Settlement Problems with the Use of the Central Place Model. *American Antiquity* 45: 866–875.

————. 1992. The Productivity of Maguey Terrace Agriculture in Central Mexico During the Aztec Period. In *Gardens of Prehistory. The Archaeology of Settlement Agriculture in Greater Mesoamerica.* Edited by Thomas W. Killion, pp. 92–115. Tuscaloosa: University of Alabama Press.

Ferriz, Horatio. 1985. Canlona, a Prehispanic Obsidian-Mining Center in Eastern Mexico? *Journal of Field Archaeology* 12:363-370.

Gibson, Charles. 1964. *The Aztecs under Spanish Rule: A History of the Indians of the Valley of Mexico, 1519–1810.* Stanford: Stanford University Press.

Harner, M. 1977. The Ecological Basis for Aztec Sacrifice. *American Ethnologist* 4: 117–135. (Harner argues that in Precolumbian times the Aztec diet was lacking in protein and that cannibalism was the only avenue available to compensate for this lack.)

Harris, M. 1978. The Cannibal Kingdom. In *Cannibals and Kings,* pp. 147–166. New York: Random House. (The author favors the absolute necessity of cannibalism as an answer to a diet insufficient in protein among the Prehispanic Aztecs.)

Hassig, Ross. 1982. Precolumbian Markets in Precolumbian Mexico. *American Antiquity* 47: 46–51.

————. 1993. *Trade, Tribute, and Transportation: The Sixteenth Century Political Economy of the Valley of Mexico.* Norman: University of Oklahoma Press.

Hicks, Frederic, 1978. Los calpixque de Nezahualcoyotl. *Estudios de Cultura Náhuatl* 13: 129–152.

————. 1984. Rotational Labor and Urban Development in Prehispanic Tetzcoco. In *Explorations in Ethnohistory:* Indians of Central Mexico in the Sixteenth Century. Edited by Herbert R. Harvey and Janns J. Prem, pp. 147-174. Albuquerque: University of New Mexico Press.

————. 1987. First Steps Toward a Market-Integrated Economy in Aztec Mexico. In *Early State Dynamics.* Edited by Henri J. M. Claessen and Pieter van de Velde, pp. 91–107. Leiden: E. J. Brill.

————. 1991. Gift and Tribute: Relations of Dependency in Aztec Mexico. In *Early State Economics.* Edited by Henri J. M. Claessen and Pieter van de Velde, pp. 197–212. New Brunswick, NJ: Transactions Publishers.

————. 1994. Cloth in the Political Economy of the Aztec State. In *Economies and Polities in the Aztec Realm.* Edited by Mary G. Hodge and Michael E. Smith, pp. 89–111. (Studies on Culture and Society, volume 6). Albany: Institute for Mesoamerican Studies.

Las Casas, Fray Bartolomé de. 1958. *Apologética historia sumaria.* Biblioteca de Autores Españoles, vol. 105. Madrid: Ediciones Atlas.

Lopez, Ruth. 2002. *Chocolate: The Nature of Indulgence Chocolate.* New York: Harry N. Abrams.

Medina, Andrés, and Naomi Quezada. 1975. *Panorama de las Artesanías Otomíes del Valle del Mezquital.* Mexico City: Universidad Nacional Autónoma de México, Instituto de Investigaciones Antropológicas.

Minc, Leah, Mary Hodge, and James Blackman. 1994. Stylistic and Spatial Variability in Early Aztec Ceramics. In *Economies and Polities in the Aztec Realm.* Edited by Mary G. Hodge and Michael E. Smith, pp. 133–173. (Studies on Culture and Society, volume 6) Albany: Institute for Mesoamerican Studies.

Molíns Fábregas, N. 1952–1953. El Códice Mendocino y la economía de Tencochtitlan. *Revista Mexicana de Estudios Antropológicos*, xiii, pp. 2–3, 315.

Neff, Hector, Ronald L. Bishop, and Edward V. Sayre. 1988. A Simulation Approach to the Problem of Tempering in Composition Studies of Archaeological Ceramics. *Journal of Archaeological Science* 15: 159–172.

———. 1989. More Observations on the Problem of Tempering in Compositional Studies of Archaeological Ceramics. *Journal of Archaeological Science* 16: 57–69.

Nelson, Fred W., K. Nielson, N. Mangelson, M. Hill, and Ray T. Matheny. 1977. Preliminary Studies of Analysis of Obsidian Artifacts from Northern Campeche, Mexico. *American Antiquity* 42: 209–226.

Nichols, Deborah L. 1994. The Organization of Provincial Craft Production and the Aztec City–State of Otumba. In *Economies and Polities in the Aztec Realm*. Edited by Mary G. Hodge and Michael E. Smith, pp. 175–193. (Studies on Culture and Society, volume 6) Albany: Institute for Mesoamerican Studies.

Offner, Jerome. 1983. On the Inapplicability of "Oriental Despotism" and the "Asiatic Mode of Production" to the Aztecs of Texcoco. *American Antiquity* 46: 43–61.

Ortiz de Montellano, Bernard R. 1990. *Aztec Medicine, Health, and Nutrition.* New Brunswick: Rutgers University Press. (The author reviews Aztec diet, the Aztec way of diagnosing and explaining illnesses, and how they attempted to cure them. De Montellano rejects the notion that Aztec cannibalism was practiced on a large scale to offset a perceived lack of protein in the diet.)

Otis Charlton, Cynthia. 1994. Plebeians and Patricians. Contrasting Patterns of Production and Distribution in the Aztec Figurine and Lapidary Industries. In *Economies and Polities in the Aztec Realm*. Edited by Mary G. Hodge and Michael E. Smith, pp. 195–219. (Studies on Culture and Society, volume 6), Albany: Institute for Mesoamerican Studies.

Parsons, Jeffrey R. 1976. The Role of Chinampa Agriculture in the Food Supply of Aztec Tenochtitlan. In *Cultural Change and Continuity: Essays in Honor of James B. Griffin.* Edited by Charles E. Cleland, pp. 233–262. New York: Academic Press.

———. 1980. Comment of Brumfiel, Specialization, Exchange and the Aztec State. *Current Anthropology* 21: 471–472.

Parsons, Jeffrey R., and Mary H. Parsons. 1990. *Maguey Utilization in Highland Central Mexico.* Ann Arbor: Anthropological Papers, Museum of Anthropology, University of Michigan.

Parsons, Jeffrey R., Elizabeth S. Brumfiel, Mary H. Parsons, and David J. Wilson. 1982. *Prehistoric Settlement Patterns in the Southern Valley of Mexico: The Chalco-Xochimilco Regions.* Ann Arbor: Memoirs of the Museum of Anthropology, University of Michigan, No. 14.

Pasztory, Esther. 1998. *Aztec Art.* Norman: University of Oklahoma Press.

Price, T. Jeffrey, and Michael E. Smith. 1992. Agricultural Terraces. In *Archaeological Research at Aztec-Period Rural Sites in Morelos, Mexico. Volume I: Excavations and Architecture.* Edited by Michael Smith, pp. 267–291. Monographs in Latin American Archaeology No. 4. Pittsburgh: University of Pittsburgh.

Rice, Prudence M. 1987. *Pottery Analysis: A Sourcebook.* Chicago: University of Chicago Press.

Sahagún, Fray Bernardino de. 1950–1982. *Florentine Codex: General History of the Things of New Spain*. Translated and edited by Arthur J. O. Anderson and Charles E. Dibble, 12 books. Santa Fe and Salt Lake City: School of American Research and the University of Utah Press.

Sanders, William T. 1956. The Central Mexican Symbiotic Region. In *Prehistoric Settlement Patterns in the New World*. Edited by Gordon R. Willey, pp. 115–127. New York: Viking Fund Publications in Anthropology No. 23. Wenner-Gren Foundation for Anthropological Research.

Sanders, William T. A. Kovar, T. Charlton, and R. A. Diehl. 1970. *The Natural Environment, Contemporary Occupation and Sixteenth Century Population of the Valley (Teotihuacan Valley Project Final Report)*. University Park: Pennsylvania State University. (Sanders and his colleagues spent enormous amounts of energy studying the ecology and settlement patterns in the Valley of Teotihuacan, which is part of the Valley of Mexico.)

Sanders, William T., and Robert S. Santley. 1983. A Tale of Three Cities: Energetics and Urbanization in Prehispanic Central Mexico. In *Prehistoric Settlement Patterns: Essays in Honor of Gordon R. Willey*. Edited by Evon Z. Vogt and Richard M. Leventhal, pp. 243–291. Albuquerque: University of New Mexico Press.

Sanders, William T., and David Webster. 1988. The Mesoamerican Urban Tradition. *American Anthropologist* 90: 521–546.

Sanders, William T., Jeffrey R. Parsons, and Robert S. Santley. 1979. *The Basin of Mexico: Ecological Processes in the Evolution of a Civilization*. New York: Academic Press.

Santley, R. S., and E. K. Rose. 1979. Diet, Nutrition and Population Dynamics in the Basin of Mexico. *World Archaeology* 1(2): 185–207. (The authors reject the notion that the Aztec resorted to cannibalism to offset an alleged lack of protein in their diet.)

Simons, Bente Bittmann, and Thelma D. Sullivan. 1972. The Pochteca. *Atti del XL Congresso Internazionale degli Americanisti* 4: 203–212.

Smith, Michael. 1994. Economies and Polities in Aztec-Period Morelos. In *Economies and Polities in the Aztec Realm*. Edited by Mary G. Hodge and Michael E. Smith, pp. 313–348. (Studies on Culture and Society, volume 6) Albany: Institute for Mesoamerican Studies.

Smith, Michael, and Frances Berdan. 1996. Province Descriptions. In *Aztec Imperial Strategies*. Edited by Frances Berdan, Richard Blanton, Elizabeth Hill Boone, Mary Hodge, Michael Smith, and Emily Umberger, pp. 265–349. Washington, D.C.: Dumbarton Oaks.

Smith. Michael E., and Mary G. Hodge. 1994. An Introduction to Late Postclassic Economies and Polities. In *Economies and Polities in the Aztec Realm*. Edited by Mary G. Hodge and Michael E. Smith, pp. 1–42. (Studies on Culture and Society, volume 6) Albany: Institute for Mesoamerican Studies.

Smith, Michael, and Cynthia Heath-Smith. 1994. Rural Economy on Late Postclassic Morelos. An archaeological Study. In *Economies and Polities in the Aztec Realm*. Edited by Mary G. Hodge and Michael E. Smith, pp. 349–376. (Studies on Culture and Society, volume 6), Albany: Institute for Mesoamerican Studies.

Smith, Michael E., and T. Jeffrey Price. 1994. Aztec-Period Agricultural Terraces in Morelos, Mexico: Evidence for Household-Level Agricultural Intensification. *Journal of Field Archaeology* 21 (1994): 169–179.

Soustelle, Jacques. 1961. *Daily Life of the Aztecs on the Eve of the Spanish Conquest.* Stanford: Stanford University Press.

Stross, Fred H., Thomas R. Hester, Robert F. Heizer, and Robert N. Jack. 1976. Chemical and Archaeological Studies of Mesoamerican and Californian Obsidians. In *Advances in Obsidian Glass Studies: Archaeological and Geochemical Perspectives.* Edited by R. E. Taylor, pp. 240–258. Park Ridge, New Jersey: Noyess Press.

Suárez de Peralta, Joan. 1878. *Noticias históricas de la Nueva España.* Edited by Justo Zaragoza. Madrid: Imprenta de Manuel G. Hernández.

Thomas, Hugh 1995. *Conquest: Montezuma, Cortés, and the Fall of Old Mexico.* New York: Touchstone.

Torquemada, Fray Juan de. 1975. *Monarquía Indiana.* 3 vols. Mexico City: Editorial Porrúa.

Trigger, Bruce G. 1972. Determinants of Urban Growth in Preindustrial Societies. In *Man, Settlement and Urbanism.* Edited by Peter J. Ucko, Ruth Tringham, and G. W. Dimbleby, pp. 575–599. Cambridge: Schenkman.

Trombold, Charles D., James F. Luhr, Toshiaki Hasenaka, and Michael D. Glasscock. 1993. Chemical Characteristics of Obsidians from Archaeological Sites in Western Mexico and the Tequila Source Area: Implications for Regional and Pan-Regional Interaction within the Northern Mesoamerican Periphery. *Ancient Mesoamerica* 4: 255–270.

VI

CHAPTER 6

Social Organization and Social Structure

AZTEC SOCIAL ORGANIZATION

When the Aztecs settled in the Valley of Mexico, they shaped their world after an already existing template: that of Late Postclassic Mesoamerica. At the core of the political organization of that era was the city–state, or *altepetl*, as it was called in Central Mexico.

An *altepetl* was a community with its own laws and well-defined boundaries. Its population was spread out over a central town and the surrounding tlahtoani countryside. A *tlatoani*, or king, ruled the *altepetl*. There were some fifty *altepetls* in the Valley of Mexico in 1519 (Smith 1996: 163).

There were several levels of division and subdivisions within each city. The capital Tenochtitlan was divided into four sectors, and these quarters were further split into eighty units that were known as *calpulli*. The term *calpulli* referred to a group of people as well as to the ward or temple with which they were associated. The calpulli as a whole owned land, and had its own patron deity, a temple, and a school. The members of a particular calpulli also practiced the same trade. The calpulli also served as a center for tax collection and military conscription (Berdan 2002: 39).

Social Stratification

Aztec society was divided into two large groups: the *pipiltin* and the *macehualtin*. The *pipiltin* were the people in power. As we shall see, their ranks were made up of those who controlled civil, religious, military, and economic aspects of society. The bulk of the population, the people who received orders, was called the *macehualtin*.

The nobility had wide-ranging privileges. These included private ownership of land, being favored for public positions, an exemption from working the land and paying tribute, being judged in their own court system, permission to have more than one wife, permission to wear insignia, and access to a special school, the calmecac (Matos Moctezuma 2003: 23).

Aztec society was divided in well-defined social layers. The emperor was at the top of the social pyramid. The ruler of a city or of a province was called a *tlahtoani*. A tlahtoani was sometimes subordinate to a higher tlahtoani. In that case, he is referred to as a *teuctlahtoh*. A tlahtoani was supported by tribute from commoners, subject towns, and the income from lands attached to the of-

This mural depicts the various social classes in Aztec society. Note the tlameme, or carrier, using a tumpline to move a load on his back. (Gianni Dagli Orti/Corbis)

fice of the ruler (Hassig 1988: 28–29). A *tlahtoani* was elected from among the nobility; his position was not hereditary (Matos Moctezuma 2003: 22). The term *tlahtoani* means "he who speaks." In addition to governing his people, his duties were to enlarge the temple dedicated to Huitzilopochtli and to expand the power of the empire (Matos Moctezuma 2003: 22).

Below the tlahtohqueh were the *teteuctin (sing. teuctli).* These were lords in charge of a *teuccalli,* or Lord's house. They were supported by the tribute paid by the commoners attached to the Lord's house, as well as by income from lands that they had inherited (Hassig 1988: 29).

The *tlahtoani* and the *teteuctin* made up the actual ruling class. Below them were the *pipiltin,* the offspring of these two groups. The pipiltin were considered to be hereditary nobles. They could hold important government positions, such as ambassador or minister of justice. The Aztecs identified several ranks with the pipiltin class. The highest ranking was the *tlahtohcapilli,* a son of a tlahtoani. Second in rank was a *tecpilli* or *teucpilli,* son of a teuctli. Next, they recognized a *tlazohpilli*, a son of a legitimate wife. Finally, there was a *calpanpilli*, or son of a concubine. The revenue generated by lands worked by commoners would support all the pipiltin. These lands, however, did not belong to the pipiltin; rather, they were considered to be part of the Lord's house holdings (Hassig 1988: 29).

Below all these people we encounter the *cuauhpipiltin*; commoners who had distinguished themselves on the battlefield. With this new station in life came advantages. They did not have to pay tribute. They also received lands to support them. They were allowed to take part in the war councils conducted by warriors of noble rank. There were constant reminders, however, of their original lower status: they were not allowed to have tenants on their lands and they were not allowed to sell their land to commoners. Certain positions seem to have been reserved for them: executioners, keepers of the arms, and military trainers (Hassig 1988: 29).

The highest-ranking commoners were the heads of the calpulli, the *calpolehqueh*. These ward headmen represented the members of their ward before the government. The office was theoretically an elected one, but proved in practice to be a hereditary one (Hassig 1988: 29). These calpullis are often compared with a type of "clan," which made up that particular ward or neighborhood in a city (Matos Moctezuma 2003: 23).

Calpulli owned their own land. They were also a unit of organization called upon to provide men for communal work inside the city, as well as warriors when war was imminent (Matos Moctezuma 2003: 23).

Below the *calpolehqueh* was the bulk of the Aztec population, the *macehualtin* (sing. *macehualli*). These people were organized in calpulli and were laborers. They were required to pay tribute in goods and labor until they were 52 years old. *Macehualtin* were also called upon to serve in the army. In fact, because the Aztecs did not have a standing army, the *macehualtin* made up the army whenever it was needed. A group of lower-ranking people were the carriers, or *tlamemehqueh*. They formed a separate segment of the population, and were probably trained from childhood to engage in this activity (Hassig 1993: 30). It seems to have been easy to become a member of the tlamemes; it was much more difficult to leave the ranks (Hassig 1993: 30–31).

The *mayequeh*, or *tlalmaitin*, another group of commoners, were laborers permanently employed on the lands of the nobility. This was a hereditary position. They did not have to pay tribute, but might be required to serve in the army (Hassig 1988: 29–30).

At the bottom of the social ladder there were the slaves, or *tlatlacohtin*. They could own property, buy their liberty, and even marry a free person. The ranks of the *tlatlacohtin* were filled with commoners who had been convicted of crimes, or those who had not paid their taxes. Some became slaves because they bet on a ball game and lost. Anyone guilty of murder or robbery would become the slave of the victim or his family (Matos Moctezuma 2003: 23). Families would sometimes sell a family member into slavery to obtain food. Some slaves were prisoners who were slated for sacrifice. People sometimes decided to become slaves themselves so that they could escape the responsibilities of normal life (Thomas 1995: 35). One could escape slavery by paying off one's debt or by taking refuge in a temple. If a slave managed to escape and make it to the royal palace, then he, too, would be set free (Hassig 1988: 30; Thomas 1995: 35).

We also know that a female slave became a free woman when the master took her as his wife (Matos Moctezuma 2003: 24). The children of slaves were always born free.

Expressions of Social Stratification

The status of Aztec aristocrats or warriors was reflected in the costumes they were allowed to wear. The Codex Mendoza illustrates the types of costumes warriors were allowed to wear, a ranking that was based on the number of captives that they had taken (Hassig 1988: 37–39; Pasztory 1998: 279). The higher the number of prisoners of war taken, the more elaborate the outfit would be.

The emperor received a warrior who had captured one prisoner unaided and provided him with a special outfit to be worn during peacetime. According to the Codex Mendoza, this consisted of a mantle with a flower design (Hassig 1988: 37). A warrior who had captured two prisoners would receive a mantle with a red trim. For taking three captives, a warrior could wear a mantle with the "wind twisted jewel" motif. At this stage he was entitled to become a leader of youths in the *telpochcalli*, or neighborhood school. Taking four prisoners entitled the warrior to a mantle with a design of two stripes of black and orange with a border. He was allowed to sport a special haircut, indicating his status as a veteran warrior. He also received special honorific titles indicating the same (Hassig 1988: 39).

The award ceremony during which these outfits were handed out and titles conveyed took place during the "Feast of Flaying of Men," or *Tlacaxipehualitzli*. This feast was held during the second of the 18 months of the solar calendar (Hassig 1988: 40).

We know of at least twenty outfits that Aztec rulers and upper levels of aristocracy were allowed to wear. Documents also refer to another twenty outfits that lower-level nobility could wear (Seler 1902–1923, II: 509–619). The costumes would often be made in five colors associated with the four cardinal directions and the center associated with the Aztec universe.

The emperor wore unique garments. His peacetime outfit would include a blue and white mantle, called the *xiuhtilmahtli*. Warrior costumes made for the Aztec emperor would represent Xipe Totec, the flayed god. The emperor would wear a helmet and royal insignia on his mantle (Hassig 1988: 40–41).

Social Mobility

Opportunities for social mobility were limited. A strict segregation existed between nobility and commoners. Rights and privileges were inherited, making it very difficult to move up the ladder. There were some exceptions, however. Throughout most of Aztec history, an Aztec commoner had three pathways that guaranteed upward social mobility: commerce, the priesthood, and a successful career in the military.

Aztec statue. (Gianni Dagli Orti/Corbis)

Commerce

Among the Aztec traders, there were the long-distance traders, or pochteca. Although their main job was to conduct commerce throughout the Aztec realm and in the adjacent areas, they also served as spies and sometimes even as warriors. Because of the dangers involved in the latter aspects of their role, they would receive great compensation from the emperor (Hassig 1988: 50).

Priesthood

Those who entered the *calmecac* were destined to become priests or warriors (Hassig 1988: 34). They would occasionally be joined by promising youth from

Aztec incense burner. (Werner Forman/Corbis)

the ranks of the commoners. They would all spend about 1 year being an apprentice, during which they would be referred to as *tlamacazton,* or "little priests" (Smith 1996: 220). The most accomplished of these trainees would eventually become priests, or *tlamacazqui,* meaning "giver of things."

Full priests would be entrusted with the performance of rituals. This entailed keeping the sacred fires burning, playing music, and making offerings to the gods. They would burn incense using a long-handled incense burner, resembling a frying pan, while performing these rituals. Priests would also be in charge of administration and caretaking. They were responsible for keeping track of the construction, personnel, and provisions of the temple compounds. Daily maintenance, such as sweeping and maintaining overall cleanliness, was also important. Finally, the priests were also involved in education. Full priests taught at the *calmecac,* supervised the novice priests, or *tlamacazton,* and kept the sacred books (Smith 1996: 220).

There were two more groups of priests. The *tlenamacac,* or "fire priests," were high-ranking priests. They were the ones who performed human sacrifice. The top echelon of priesthood was occupied by two priests, known as *quetzalcoatl.* They presided over the Tlaloc and Huitzilopochtli temples in the Sacred Precinct at Tenochtitlan (Smith 1996: 220).

Military Achievements

There were two types of schools that offered military training, the *telpochcalli* and the *calmecac.* The former took in primarily commoners and lower-ranking nobility associated with the *calpulli.* The *calmecac* counted the children of the higher-ranking nobility, including the emperor, among its students (Hassig 1988: 34).

During the reign of Motecuhzuma Ilhuicamina I (1440–1468), a new order was created, that of *quauhpilli,* or eagle lord (Smith 1996: 52). The emperor wanted to reward commoners who had conducted themselves exceptionally well on the battlefield by allowing them to move up socially. This proved to be a popular decision; however, it did not last very long. Under his great-grandson, Moctecuhzuma Xocoyotzin (1502–1520), the order of *quauhpilli* was abolished and this avenue for social promotion was closed.

Another opportunity for social mobility was the *calmecac,* or the temple school. Although primarily servicing the children of the nobility, these *calmecac* would accept promising commoner children. This would allow them eventually to serve in the priesthood. Moctecuhzuma Xocoyotzin also closed this door by restricting access to the *calmecac* to the children of the highest nobility (Thomas 1995: 33).

At the same time that emperor Motecuhzuma Ilhuicamina I provided an opportunity to move up the ladder, he also promulgated edicts that solidified the differences between the different social classes. His rules of conduct clearly outlined what each segment of society was allowed to do. For example, the nobility was allowed to wear embroidered cotton cloaks and loincloths. Ordinary people could not. They had to wear clothes made out of maguey fiber (Thomas 1995: 33). Furthermore, commoners were not allowed to wear sandals in the presence of higher-ranking individuals. Only the nobility could build houses with two stories, and only the nobility was allowed to consume chocolate. Aristocrats were given the right to eat out of painted or glazed ceramics, whereas the commoners were limited to earthenware (Anawalt 1980: 33–43; Thomas 1995: 33).

AZTEC LIFE CYCLE

Aztec parents, like parents anywhere, were concerned with the well-being of their children. They desired nothing but the best, and tried to ascertain as much as possible what the future would hold for their family.

Aztec oral tradition, later written down during colonial times, refers to a father addressing his daughter, and counseling about her destiny on earth (León-Portilla 2002: 70). Notice how this exchange typifies Aztec society in different ways. It betrays a fatalistic perception of life that Aztecs had, and it does so in a format often used in Aztec society: that of a poem.

> *Here you are, my little girl, my necklace of precious stones,*
> *my plumage. You are my blood, my color, my image [. . .]*
> *Here on earth is the place of much wailing, the place where*
> *our strength is worn out, where we are all well-acquainted with*
> *bitterness and discouragement. A wind blows, sharp as*
> *obsidian it blows over us. They say that we are burned*
> *by the force of the sun and the wind. This is the way*
> *here on earth [. . .]*

> *But the elders have also said: So that we should not go*
> *always moaning, that we should not be filled with sadness,*
> *the one who is near and close has given us laughter, sleep,*
> *food, our strength and fortitude and also the act by which*
> *we propagate.*
> *All this sweetens life on earth so that we are not always*
> *moaning. But even though it be like this, though it be true*
> *that there is only suffering, and this were the way things*
> *are on earth, even so, should we always be afraid? Should*
> *we always be fearful? Must we live weeping?*

Although there were clear-cut differences between the Aztec social classes, the upbringing of Aztec children was very similar, regardless of the social stratum that they belonged to. The Codex Mendoza is perhaps the best source on the Aztec life cycle.

Birth

Giving birth was accompanied by ritual as well as the expert help of a midwife. Aztecs attached great importance to this event and compared giving birth with fighting on the battlefield. If a woman died while giving birth it was said that she would go straight to the same heaven as warriors who had fallen on the battlefield.

The events that occurred during the first days after birth are described in the Codex Mendoza (Smith 1996: 135). Four days after a child was born, the midwife carried the child into the courtyard of the house. In this courtyard, there was a ceramic tub filled with water. The child received its first bath in that tub. This bathing ceremony also served as a name-giving event. The midwife would choose a name for the child. She would ask three boys to recite the child's name loudly after the bath was over. The ceremony also involved the use of gender-specific objects, symbolizing the life this child would lead. Boys would be given tools similar to what their fathers used; it reinforced that they, too, would be following in their father's footsteps. A girl would receive tools presaging the domestic chores she would engage in during her adult life. A final act in the ceremony involved the ritual disposal of the umbilical cord. A boy's umbilical cord was buried on a battlefield, together with a small shield and arrows—another reference to the boy serving as a soldier later on in life. A girl's umbilical cord was buried under a metate, a flat stone used for grinding corn.

With regard to baptism, the Aztec elite carefully noted the day and time a baby was born. Armed with that information, they would consult the astrologers and ask them what good or bad luck might be in store for the newborn. If the reply was favorable, then a baby would be baptized immediately; if it was not, then arrangements were made to adjust the date so that bad luck might be reversed and the baby baptized.

The baptism would take place at the house of the parents when the sun rose. Family and friends were invited to attend. Children from the same ward were welcome as well. A midwife performed the baptism (Bandelier 1932: 70).

Childhood

A child's identity was set early in life. Boys and girls were given the symbols of what was expected of them later in life. Moreover, Aztec children were put to work at an early age. Boys would be asked to carry light loads when they were as young as 5 years old. Girls of the same age were taught the beginnings of spinning yarn (Smith 1996: 136). Only 2 years later, at age 7, boys would be sent out to go fishing and girls would be spinning cotton.

Correct behavior was strictly enforced, and the means to achieve that goal would strike us as excessive, as illustrated in the Codex Mendoza (Smith 1996: 137). In order for their children to behave, the Aztecs had developed a series of age-specific punishments. For example, an 8-year-old boy caught being deceitful would be punished by having his body pierced with maguey spikes. If, by the age of 10, they still had not learned their lesson, parents would resort to beating them with sticks and dangling other threats over their heads. For the children who were really hard of hearing, Aztec parents would make them inhale chile smoke to drive home the point of obedience.

Somewhere between 10 and 20 years of age, children would attend school. The Aztecs had two different school systems. The most commonly available was the neighborhood school, the *telpochcalli*. Such schools were present in every town and city throughout the empire. Boys and girls would attend school separately, with the boys living at the *telpochcalli*. We do not know if girls also lived behind their school walls. Both sexes received instructions in singing, dancing, and playing music (Smith 1996: 137).

At the *telpochcalli*, boys would be tasked with civics projects, such as working on repairing infrastructure and temple buildings. The most important aspect of *telpochcalli* instruction was that of martial arts. Seasoned warriors would provide basic instruction, after which the boys would be sent off to war (Smith 1996: 137–138). These novices would not be thrown into battle right away. First, they would be involved in logistics, such as carrying the baggage and equipment of seasoned warriors. Later, they would graduate to combat and be allowed to participate in a battle (Smith 1996: 138).

In addition to the *telpochcalli* was the *calmecac*. The *calmecac* were temple schools. These were the training grounds for the future elite, with instructions provided in government, the priesthood, and warfare (Smith 1996: 138). This involved learning how to read Aztec manuscripts, including those devoted to astronomy. It also included training to become elite warriors.

When nobility wanted their child to attend the calmecac, they would organize a feast. They invited the priests who served in the calmecac as well as older prominent leaders of the neighborhood to attend. When the meal was finished these older men would exhort the priests to consider the youth as a potential future student in the calmecac, stating, "When he reaches the required age (. . .) may he enter and live in the house of our lord" (Bandelier 1932: 199).

Tradition demanded that the priests replied to this entreaty with much humility. They usually remarked that it was not to them that this request should be made, but rather to the god whose servants they were. The boy would then be taken to the calmecac, where the parents offered gifts to the statue of Quetzalcoatl. The boy's body would be painted and decorated with beads. They would also pierce his ears to extract blood, which would then be offered to the statue of Quetzalcoatl. After the conclusion of this ceremony, the family and boy would return to their home, having made their intentions clear to all parties involved. Finally, when the youth had reached the appropriate age, they would take him to the calmecac again and leave him there to start his education (Bandelier 1932: 200).

Life within the calmecac was subject to an extensive set of rules. These stated that all those who were priests or ministered to the gods had to spend the night in the calmecac. The students were also required to get up at 4:00 A.M. to sweep and clean the building. Older students had to go out and collect maguey spines. Still older students were tasked to collect firewood. This was used to keep the fires alight at night. At daybreak, in case any construction work was required, they all left the building together. This work might have included building walls, or digging canals or irrigation ditches, as well as tilling the fields. They would stop work "somewhat early," according to Sahagún, in order to return to the school and start penance and prayers. Before they would start these activities, however, they had to bathe. When the sun set, they prepared for their tasks later in the night. They would all eventually leave the school and set off in the forest, by themselves and carrying the maguey spines. They would deposit these spines in a ball of hay and leave them in a special place in the forest, whereupon they would return to the school building. Another rule stipulated that two priests could never share one blanket when sleeping.

Food was considered communal property. It was either prepared at the school, or, if food was brought in from home, it was shared. At midnight, all were supposed to get up and pray. Those who were asleep were rudely awakened with painful jabs from the sharp thorns of the maguey. Students were generally told not to be overbearing, and not to offend one another. Customs and rules were to be obeyed; any offense, such as public drunkenness, was punished by death. (The latter was accomplished by garroting the offender, by burning him alive, or by shooting him with arrows.) The boys would be punished by having their ears pierced or by whipping them with nettles for any presumably lesser offense. The priests were required to take a bath in a pond, and they had to do so at midnight (given the location of Tenochtitlan, such requirement did undoubtedly test the resolve of the heartiest among the priests, especially during the winter months). All were supposed to adhere to the rules when it came to fasting. Furthermore, proper etiquette was strongly encouraged. This included the art of speaking eloquently, the ability to recognize when to bow, and courtesy. Again, maguey spines were close at hand to reinforce these rules. The students were also required to sing all the songs that were said to have been written down in "their books by signs." They were taught astrology, the interpretation of dreams, and the calendar. Finally, the priests had to abstain from sexual relations, to eat abstemiously, not to tell lies, and to live in a devout way (Bandelier 1932: 201–202).

Adulthood: Marriage and Death

An Aztec did not have the same life expectancy as we have today, so it should not surprise us that certain milestones in life, such as marriage, came at a much earlier time in Aztec society than it does in ours. Just as in many other cultures, however, marriage was surrounded by customs and ceremonies. Girls could be married at the age of 10, whereas boys might get married when they were in their late teens or early twenties.

Romantic love did not seem to have featured heavily in traditional Aztec society. When the parents of a boy had decided that he had become old enough to get married, they would try to select an appropriate bride. They would consult with a wide array of people for this, including relatives and the boy's teachers (Smith 1996: 138). With regard to the teachers, the parents would inform the principal of their son's school of their intention to have their son married. The parents would ask the principal to approve of this plan. To this end, the parents would invite the teacher and all of his students and provide them with food and drink. The parents would make a speech and place a hatchet intended for cutting down trees in front of him. This symbolized him taking leave of his companions (Bandelier 1932: 70).

The boy's parents would also engage the services of a matchmaker, who would act as a go-between with the girl's family. If the ensuing negotiations were successful, then it was time to ask a soothsayer to set the date. Here, again, we find an example of how deterministic Aztec society was: the Aztecs believed that a marriage was doomed to failure if it was celebrated on an unlucky day (Smith 1996: 138).

A young man studying in the telpochcalli occasionally might decide that he wanted to get married. This would entail leaving the school. To obtain permission from the teachers to do so, these youths would donate ten to twelve large blankets called *quachtli*. In other words, they bribed the teachers into allowing them to leave the school, an approach open only to the wealthy (Bandelier 1932: 198).

Once a date was set, the wedding ceremony proceeded along well-defined procedures. The all-day feast would begin at the bride's house. Guests would be fed an abundance of tamales, which the bride's female relatives would have been preparing for days. Aside from food and drinks, the guests would also receive gifts of flowers and tobacco. Both pulque and cacao were among the drinks offered.

When the sun set, the bride would be bathed and provided with a special dress. The elders from the groom's family then proceeded to lecture the bride-to-be (Smith 1996: 139):

> *Forever now leave childishness, girlishness; no longer art thou to be like a child . . . Be most considerate of one; regard one with respect, speak well, greet one well. By night look to, take care of the sweeping, the laying of the fire. Arise in the deep of night [to begin domestic tasks].*

The groom's relatives would then carry the bride to the groom's house, and the second part of the wedding ceremony would begin. It was getting darker

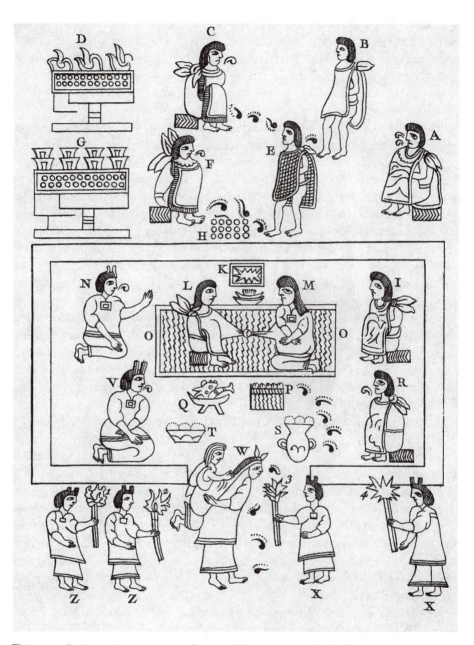

This scene depicts various steps in an Aztec wedding ceremony. In the foreground we see how the bride is carried to the ceremony. Inside the building we see the newlyweds seated on a mat. (Bettmann/Corbis)

while she was being carried, and relatives of the bride and groom would accompany the procession with torches (Smith 1996: 139).

The ceremony at the groom's house is described in the Codex Mendoza (Smith 1996: 139):

> *And when they arrived at the groom's house, the groom's parents led her to the patio of the house to receive her, and they put her in a room or house where the groom was waiting. And the bride and bridegroom sat on a mat with its seats, next to a burning hearth, and they tied their clothes together, and offered copal incense to their gods. And then two old men and two old women, who were present as witnesses, gave food to the bride and bridegroom, and then the elders ate.*

Four days later, another celebration took place, involving food and dance. The two families exchanged gifts at that point as well. This was the start of married life for the newlyweds.

From then on, both husband and wife took on their responsibilities. Commoners most often tilled the soil as farmers, and that was considered man's work. Women were tasked with maintaining a clean house, preparing food, and going to the market. At the market, she would buy the necessary supplies for her family and sell some of the textiles that she had woven. A noble woman also was expected to weave, even though she would not have had the many other concerns that her commoner counterpart had to face on a daily basis (Smith 1996: 140–141).

Royal Marriages

Aztec rulers and their nobility practiced polygyny, meaning they were allowed to marry multiple wives. These wives had different rank, depending on their status at birth and the type of marriage contracted. The highest rank was given to women who were of high status at birth and who were married in a public ceremony after a process of petitioning. High-status women, known as *tlazopilli*, frequently brought a retinue of other noblewomen or servants with them. These women in turn sometimes became wives or concubines. Sisters could become joint wives (Carrasco 1984: 44).

The ranks of the wives in turn defined the rank of their children. Children of wives of high rank received the high status of their mother, whereas those born to concubines were of lower status (Carrasco 1984: 44).

Special rules applied when a king died. A royal widow could only marry a man of the same rank as her deceased husband. Because of this rule, most royal widows did not remarry (Carrasco 1984: 45).

Historians have identified two types of marriages that were in place among the Aztec upper crust. They are, in predictable fashion, referred to with Greek names: interdynastic hypogamy and hypergamy.

In some cases members of two dynasties of unequal rank enter into marriage. For example, a higher-ranking ruler may give his daughter in marriage to a subordinate king or another ruler of lower status. This type of marriage is called interdynastic hypogamy and was practiced by the rulers of Texcoco and those of Teotihuacan (Carrasco 1984: 47).

In the case of interdynastic hypergamy, the ruler takes a wife of lower rank. The first Aztec ruler, Acamapichtli, took wives from all the leading families. The Aztec nobility descended from them (Carrasco 1984: 54). Later Aztec rulers continued the tradition. For example, Moctecuhzuma Xocoyotzin married one of the daughters of the king of Tlacopan. When sons were born out of these unions, they were usually not selected to be the next king. They became part of the lesser nobility. Sons born out of interdynastic hypogamy, in which the woman was of higher rank than the husband, were slated to succeed their fathers (Carrasco 1984: 55).

Funerals

Funeral rites were well defined. Early colonial sources reveal how this worked (Smith 1996: 142):

Some people were buried in the fields; others, in the courtyards of their own homes; others were taken to the shrines in the woods; others were cremated and their ashes buried in the temples. No one was interred without being dressed in his mantles, loincloths, and fine stones. In sum, none of his possessions were left behind; and if he was cremated, the jar which received his ashes was filled with his jewelry and stones, no matter how costly. Dirges similar to our responses were chanted and the dead were mourned, great ceremonies taking place in their honor. At these funerals people ate and drank; and if the deceased had been a person of quality, lengths of cloth were presented to those who had attended the funeral. The dead man was laid out in a room for four days until mourners arrived from the places where he had friends. Gifts were brought to the dead man; and if the deceased was a king or chieftain of a town, slaves were killed in his honor to serve him in the afterlife. The funeral rites lasted for ten days filled with sorrowful, tearful chants.

The Aztecs firmly believed that the manner in which one died determined the destination the deceased would reach in the afterworld. For example, soldiers who had perished in battle and sacrificial victims were thought to accompany the rising sun from then on. Women who died in childbirth would accompany the sun during its setting. Those who drowned would end up in Tlalocan, a paradise associated with the god of rain, Tlaloc. Most people, however, were thought to be destined to go to one of the nine levels of the underworld (Smith 1996: 141–142).

Daily Routine

Aside from the events that mark the various stages of an individual outlined earlier, there is also the topic of what daily life in an Aztec commoner family would have looked like. Sahagún provides us with some insights.

In many ways, there are many similarities between the daily routine an ancient Aztec family would have gone through and that which applies to their modern-day descendants. In rural areas of modern Mexico, people still rise before the sun comes up, and go to sleep not long after sunset. The Aztecs living in the Basin of Mexico would have woken up when the ambient temperature would still have been on the chilly side. Preparing breakfast then was very likely the domain of women, as it still is today. They would have fanned the fire that would have smoldered overnight between the traditional three hearth stones. Breakfast would have included corn tortillas, which they referred to as *tlaxcalli*. The *massa,* or dough, necessary to make these pancake-sized breakfast items would have been prepared from cornmeal produced by manually grinding corn on a stone surface.

In the rural areas, most of the men would set out to work their fields. This would entail lengthy trips along pathways or paddling along the many lakes and canals. Men would stay in the field all day long, so they would carry their lunch with them in a bag.

The routine and the setting of waking up in the morning would be different in the cities. People tended to live in higher-quality buildings, usually made out of sun-dried brick. Most modest buildings would only have one room, with the kitchen being in a separate structure in the backyard (Soustelle 1962: 121). Greater family wealth allowed for more rooms. A typical Aztec dwelling would have included a kitchen, a room where the entire family slept, and a small domestic shrine. The family would use a *temezcalli,* or steam bath, which would have been located away from the house.

Furniture in most houses, from the simple huts built with sticks in the rural areas to the more spacious mud-brick dwellings in the cities, would be considered Spartan today. The Aztec would sleep on a mat, or *petatl,* laid out on the floor. These mats would be used as seats during the day. Although most Aztecs would have sat on the floor during the day, there was a more evolved form of seating furniture: a low chair without feet that they called *icpalli.*

It would have been common for the mother to wake the other members of the family in the early morning hours. She then encouraged all of them to go place their offerings to the gods in the family home's oratories. These offerings would have included copal, or resin, which was burned (Bandelier 1932: 157).

The Aztec marked midnight with loud banging on kettles and drums. They would apparently wake up everyone who was not awake at that time by throwing water at them (Bandelier 1932: 162). It is not clear if this behavior was tied to a specific religious observance or whether this was a "daily" routine.

SETTLEMENT PATTERNS: AZTEC CITIES AND FARMS

Cities

The picture we can draw of Aztec cities is heavily influenced by two factors. First, the overwhelming majority of Spanish-written information pertains to the capital. Our knowledge of conquest-period Aztec cities outside the capital is much more limited. Although archaeological research could be counted upon to remedy that shortcoming, this is where the second factor appears. In the Basin of Mexico, most of the Aztec cities are buried under modern communities. Archaeological research is very difficult to undertake. Digs outside the Valley of Mexico could help redress this imbalance. Investigations in Morelos,

Puebla, and the Toluca Valley have unfortunately been relatively few (Smith 1992, 1997).

Furthermore, in our evaluation of Aztec urbanism, we might be tempted to project the image we have of the Aztec capital across the Aztec landscape and imagine a world of cities just like Tenochtitlan, only smaller in size. This is an oversimplification, partly created by the preponderance of data having been derived from descriptions of the capital. Research carried out in the rest of the Aztec realm fortunately has generated data that are offsetting this skewed view.

The growth of a city is determined by various factors. These include the availability of sufficient amounts of food that can be brought into the community. That, in turn, depends in general terms on the existence of enough land to work and produce the food. Moreover, access to water will allow more intensive and thus more productive methods to be used, whereas proximity of these fields to the community will also determine the cost to bring the food to market.

In practical terms this often meant that only those Aztec communities that had access to reliable sources of water nearby were able to sustain growth because they would increase the production of their fields by multicropping, irrigation, and fertilization (Hassig 1993: 21–23).

Distribution Across the Landscape

The study of the distribution of sites across the landscape is also known as *settlement pattern studies*. Such studies entail mapping and surface collecting large areas in order to evaluate where people once lived and when. Surface collections tend to produce pottery sherds and construction materials, indications that help us identify where humans were once present. The pottery frequently allows archaeologists to date the site preliminarily.

These data (i.e., location of sites and their chronological frameworks) are then plotted on regional maps. It allows us to look for patterns to evaluate if, for example, there was a shift from one preferred location to another over time. These determinations will then help archaeologists select sites for further investigation.

The Basin of Mexico has been the target of some very extensive settlement pattern surveys (Sanders 1956; Sanders et al. 1979). Early Aztec period communities generally appear to have been new settlements, without prior existing presence. They tended to congregate around the lakeshore. During the Late Aztec period, there is continuity in the location of the settlements, as well as growth (Smith and Hodge 1994: 10–11). Another trend that was identified was that settlement was nucleated in the central part of the Basin of Mexico, and that settlement was more dispersed in the southeastern part of the same Basin (Parsons 1971; Parsons et al. 1982; Sanders et al. 1979; Smith and Hodge 1994: 11).

With the exception of Tenochtitlan, Aztec cities were relatively small, with populations estimated to be in the range of 30,000 or less. The growth of these cities depended upon the hinterland that they could draw upon to sustain their inhabitants. In Mesoamerica this hinterland was relatively small, partly because of the lack of draft animals and wheeled vehicles. The absence of these two features effectively reduced the area from whence goods could be brought to a city. Conditions such as these in turn mean a smaller population. In practical terms, we find that cities were distributed across the landscape at 21–28 km intervals. This picture is especially true in the Central Mexican plateau (Hassig 1993: 40, 145).

Layout

The founding of a new city–state tended to start with the construction of three core elements: the royal palace, the temple pyramid, and the market (Smith 1996: 163). As a city grew, these three components would also see major renovations to reflect the more powerful status of the *altepetl*.

Tenochtitlan's Layout

The layout of Tenochtitlan is the best known of all Aztec cities. Cortés, in his second letter to Emperor Charles V, reports that the city "is built on the salt lake, and no matter by what road you travel there are two leagues from the main body of the city to the mainland. There are four artificial causeways leading to it, and each is as wide as two cavalry lances. The city itself is as big as Seville or Cordoba" (Cortés 1986: 102).

On a map published in 1524 in Nürenberg, we can clearly see how the city was organized in five sections and how the causeways all converged on the ceremonial center of the city. One could trace this division back to the guidelines left by Huitzilopochtli, when they finally arrived at the spot where an eagle was devouring a snake while perched on top of a cactus. According to these divine exhortations, there was to be a central area in the city devoted to a "house" for Huitzilopochtli to rest, and, surrounding that core, four main wards (Carrasco 1999: 37). This order was eventually transformed into reality. The Aztec elite, involved in organizing the construction of the city, referred to these four wards as "Nauhcampa," meaning "Four Directions of the Wind" (Carrasco 1999: 37).

These four causeways had great symbolic value to the city because they converged at the foot of the shrine dedicated to Huitzilopochtli. They also served a very practical purpose: to act as gigantic and reliable levees to protect the city from floodwaters of the lake (Carrasco 1999: 37).

The four-way division of the city into wards was also replicated on the ward level. Colonial-period maps and archaeological investigations point to each of these wards being organized around its own center, where the ward's temple complex, marketplace, and administrative buildings could be found. This spatial organization around a center was present at even lower levels, within these four wards. Each neighborhood within the four wards had its own small-scale ceremonial precinct, as well as its own market and school (Carrasco 1999: 39).

The core of the city consisted of a sacred precinct. Scholars originally believed that the precinct was surrounded by a *coatepantli*, or serpent wall. The excavations at the Templo Mayor have shown that this was not the case (Matos Moctezuma 1988; Carrasco 1999: 237, n. 55).

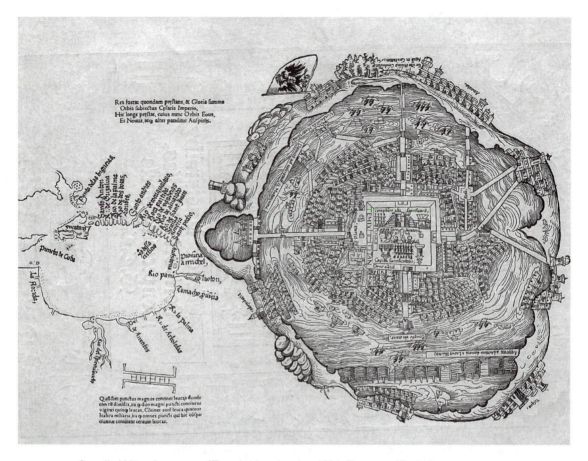

So-called Nürenberg map of Tenochtitlan, dated to 1524. (Bettmann/Corbis)

There were residential zones surrounding this ceremonial center. The imperial palaces were built close to the temple complex; the residences of well-off citizens formed the next set of neighborhoods. As one approached the edge of the island city, the quality of the architecture and the size of the structures involved diminished. Townspeople living in the margins in both senses of the word were farmers who would have worked in the *chinampa* gardens.

The city was linked to the mainland by means of a series of causeways. These causeways extended into broad avenues, which at one point in history gave Tenochtitlan's street pattern an appearance similar to that of many American cities: a perfect grid; however, there was one typical Aztec variation on this theme. Aside from many surface roads, the Aztec capital also counted on numerous waterways to move people and goods in and out of the city. The existence of both canals and floating gardens strongly affected the city's ultimate grid pattern layout. Floating gardens, or *chinampas,* were laid out in rectangular shapes, divided by canals. This was the most efficient way of constructing these gardens. Efficiency of use also affected the layout of the canals

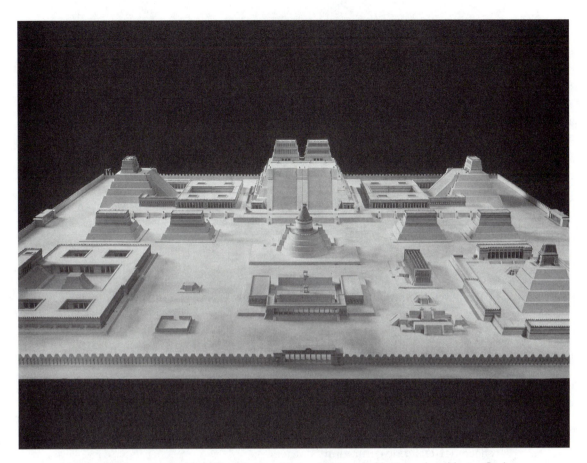

Model of the Aztec capital city of Tenochtitlan. (National Museum of Anthropology, Mexico City) (Gianni Dagli Orti/Corbis)

in the city. Since thousands of canoes entered the city on a daily basis, having straight canals rather than meandering ones was the best solution (Hassig 1993: 60).

As we have seen, Tenochtitlan annexed Tlatelolco during the reign of Axayacatl. The newly created urban agglomeration covered some 2,500 acres. Rome within the Aurelian walls covered 3,423 acres (Soustelle 1962: 6). The other cities in the Aztec sphere of influence were much smaller than Tenochtitlan. Tenochtitlan may have had as many as 250,000 inhabitants (Smith and Hodge 1994: 9); the second-largest city in the Basin of Mexico was Texcoco. It had about 30,000 citizens. Most other Aztec cities had between 10,000 and 20,000 inhabitants (Sanders et al., 1979: 154; Hodge 1994: 55).

Aztec Regional Political Hierarchy

Early colonial documents allow for the reconstruction of the hierarchy that existed among cities in the Basin of Mexico. Five categories and related ranks of cities have been identified (Table 6.1).

TABLE 6.1. Political Ranking of Aztec Communities in the Basin of Mexico, ca. AD 1500

Rank	Category	Definition
1	Imperial Capital	Tenochtitlan
2	Regional State Capital	Founding member, Triple Alliance
3	City State Center	Tlahtoani subordinate to ruler of regional state capital
4	Dependent City State Center	Tlahtoani subordinate to ruler of level 3 city-state
5	Administered City State Center	Tlahtoani removed. City administered by Triple Alliance administrator

SOURCE: Hodge 1994: 54, Table 2.1.

In general, the ranking also reflects the overall population size of the cities involved. This is especially true for cities ranked 1 and 2. Communities in levels 3 and 4 sometimes have overlapping population numbers, which is seen as evidence that the differences between these levels were not all that great (Hodge 1994: 54).

The exercise of ranking Aztec communities raises another question: How does one delineate the boundaries of any Aztec community so that we can compare them in size? If we are ranking communities, and are linking size of settlement, among other things, to membership in a particular rank, how do archaeologists define community borders?

To answer this question is also to illustrate how one has to involve specialists from many different fields, ranging from colonial document specialists to ceramic specialists and surveyors. It also entails working with colonial and modern-day maps.

Colonial documents quite often mention the names of city–states and their dependencies. The names mentioned in these early Spanish documents are frequently still in existence today, and they can be located on a modern map. Archaeological data play a secondary role in this case because they can be used to provide additional verification of a border between communities. In those cases where communities are not listed on colonial maps, however, or where there are no early maps available for a given area, we have to resort to archaeological information. This is where archaeological surveys play an important role. They can delineate communities based on the distribution patterns of ceramics and architecture across the landscape (Hodge 1994: 47).

Based on information gathered with the methods just described, it appears that the territory occupied by Aztec-period city–states was fairly small. In one particular study, carried out on fifteen Late Aztec city–states in the Basin of Mexico, archaeologists determined that the average distance between the city center and the farthest dependent community was 7.1 km (about 5.5 miles) (Hodge 1994: 59). In practical terms, this means that most of the citizens of a city–state, even the ones living in the rural "hinterlands," were never very far away from the political center of their world. Most rulers of city–states, the *tlahtoani*, did not feel the need, therefore, to construct more than one administrative and political center in their sphere of influence (Hodge 1994: 59–60).

Aside from colonial-era maps, there might be other documents available from that time period that one might be tempted to use. Examples of such ostensibly useful sources would be parochial documents outlining the extent of a parish, or even Precolumbian Aztec tax records. One would be ill-served to resort to these materials in both cases. We can often establish that there is very little overlap between colonial civil boundaries and church territories (Gerhard 1970: 31; Hodge 1994: 45). Moreover, tax documents, even though they date to the Prehispanic period, also do not reflect political boundaries (Hodge 1994: 63).

Rural Communities

Rural surveys are of great importance in reconstructing the dispersal of settlement across the terrain. Surveys allow us to gather information on where people lived in the rural areas. Because most of our nonsurvey data typically deals with city folk, rural surveys provide the additional benefit of offsetting the imbalance in our information favoring city dwellers. As mentioned before, the written sources that are at our disposal favor the large cities. The ruins of the major monuments in these cities continue to attract the attention of archaeologists.

Archaeological surveys conducted in the Valley of Mexico identified two types of rural communities. In the southeastern portion of the Valley, where we know that the people often had a serflike, or *mayeque,* status, villages were often very small. A community would have just a few houses, all of them often similar in size and layout. In contrast, the villages in the northeastern part of the Valley were larger and showed greater internal variation in the size and layout of their buildings (Evans 1991: 64). Archaeologists have suggested that these larger villages were inhabited by the *macehualtin.* Even though making very general statements like these is always dangerous, one could argue that in this case they might actually be based on reality. A village occupied by serfs who work on the estates of the local nobility would show less internal variation in building size than a village in which the occupants worked on their own land and produced goods and tribute (Evans 1991: 64). These latter villages were the building blocks of the political system, in which tribute and access to land was organized by neighborhood, the *calpulli.*

The administrator of the *calpulli* would occupy the position of "elite" in these larger villages. It appears that these *calpulli* administrators were "elected by the members of the ward." This typically boiled down to them being "sons or kinsmen of their predecessors" (Evans 1991: 64). These *calpulli* leaders would be the village's *teuctli,* or chief. These leaders would have maintained a residence to which they called heads of households for village meetings. This residence we call *tecpan,* and it served as the center of power in the community.

The *calpulli* leader was responsible for the community's goods, its labor force, and for sending on tribute to the capital. The *teuctli* was equally responsible for organizing work details for projects of all kinds: local work that would benefit the community or projects for the regional or confederation powers. It was ultimately the *teuctli* who had to bring together the workers. Part of the *teuctli's* responsibility was to entertain his guests whenever there was a meeting at the *tecpan*. We know that meetings were held several times a year, and that the *calpulli* leader had to provide food and drink for his guests (Evans 1991: 66). This aspect of the job could prove to be very expensive for the elder.

The *tecpan* also served as the place where the village documents were kept, where the items collected as tribute were first kept, and where the leader's family and his servants would live (Evans 1991: 67). The layouts of these dwellings varied, but they had one thing in common: there was a large gathering place in the form of a patio by the entrance of the building. A number of rooms would surround this courtyard. This pattern is found in both the palaces of the rulers of Texcoco and the much more humble abodes of the *teuctli* in rural areas (Evans 1991: 68–69).

Research in Rural Communities: An Example

How did people in Central Mexico live during the Late Postclassic period? What was the role the elite played in their lives? Who were the elite? How did people sustain themselves economically? What was life like before and after Aztec conquest? Questions such as these were at the core of the research design developed for the communities of Capilco and Cuexcomate in the state of Morelos (Smith 1992; Smith et al. 1989).

Both sites were occupied for about 300–350 years, with occupation starting around AD 1200 at the earliest and ending early in the Spanish colonial period, around AD 1550 (Smith and Heath-Smith 2000: 218). Both sites experienced substantial growth throughout their occupation. Population estimates for Capilco in the early stages of its existence peg the nonelite population at twenty-eight. By the end of the site's history, that figure had increased to 116. (See later for a discussion of how archaeologists arrive at population estimates.) Cuexcomate was a larger community, one in which both elite and nonelite residences were present. The total population estimate for this village early in its existence was 237 and 803 by the time the Spanish had taken over (Smith and Heath-Smith 2000: 220, Table 11.1).

Local resources included soils sufficiently productive to support agricultural production. The clays were also suitable for ceramic production. Low-grade chert was available for stone tool production, as were wild fig trees. The bark of the latter served as the basis for paper production. Basalt used in the production of grinding equipment was present about 5 km away from Cuexcomate (Smith and Heath-Smith 2000: 219).

The diet in both locations consisted primarily of plant food, with agricultural products making up the bulk of the food items. Animal protein was present in the form of turkey, dog, and rabbit bones; however, because of their low occurrence, it is clear that the people ate very little meat. We find maize, tomato, squash, avocado, and several tree fruits among the domesticated plants. The presence of cotton was implied through the recovery of cotton-spinning artifacts (Smith and Heath-Smith 2000: 222).

The hills that surround Cuexcomate were dotted with contour terraces and cross-channel terraces. Excavations made it clear that some of the terrace walls had been subject to water erosion. Damages appeared to have been repaired. The carrying capacity of the land (i.e., the ability of the land to produce enough food in relation to the population in the area) appears to have been more than sufficient. The fields in the terraced areas very likely did produce enough food to sustain the inhabitants of Capilco and Cuexcomate, and allowed a surplus to meet regional and even imperial tribute requirements (Smith and Heath-Smith 2000: 222).

Excavations of individual residences in these two communities led to the retrieval of evidence of craft production. Spindle whorls were found in both elite and nonelite contexts; stone tools, including bark beaters, were found in 70 percent of the houses with large samples of excavated middens. This suggests that paper making was widespread among households (Smith and Heath-Smith 2000: 223, Table 11.2, 224). The latter tool is typically used in the production of paper. Bark beaters are rectangular grooved stones, about the size of a bar of soap. They were used to beat the fibers in the bark into a pulp, which was eventually transformed into a form of paper. The spindle whorls reflect the importance of textile production, most likely with the intent to export. These two communities were occupied late enough also to have copper and bronze artifacts, including needles, chisels, and awls (Smith and Heath-Smith 2000: 224).

One particular kind of material was found primarily in elite context: mineral paint pigments. Three colors seem to have been used: red (hematite), yellow (limonite), and black (graphite). These colors were very likely used to paint manuscripts that were produced locally, as implied by the presence of bark beaters.

Farms

Documentary evidence such as exists for city–states is extremely rare for peasant communities. When these documents do exist (e.g., in the case of Tepetlaoztoc, a village in the eastern portion of the Basin of Mexico), we can use them as a tool to measure the rate of preservation of the archaeological remains. In this particular case, the documents attest to the existence of 169 farms in the community; unfortunately, but predictably, archaeologists could only find surface evidence for a small number of these dwellings (Williams 1994: 73–78).

Components

A farm usually had three components: a dwelling, a house garden close to the residence, and a field further removed from the house. In documents, the dwellings tend to be represented by a glyph, which shows either a flat-roofed house or a thatch-roofed house. The location of the dwelling was very often determined by the location of the most fertile land available to the family. In turn, that also determined the development of the house garden. The farmers would take good care of these house gardens, planting fruit trees, herbs, and vegetables. They would also cultivate what is called a milpa. Fields that were further removed from the farmstead received less maintenance. Crops such as corn, squash, beans, and maguey would be grown there (Williams 1994: 80).

DEMOGRAPHIC ESTIMATES: HOW MANY AZTECS WERE THERE?

As mentioned in the discussion of settlement pattern studies, we can point to a sharp rise in population going from the Early Aztec into the Late Aztec periods. Various factors may have contributed toward facilitating or even encouraging population growth (Smith and Hodge 1994: 17). First, the stage was set during the Early Aztec period for later population growth because of the Aztec colonization of large areas inside the Basin of Mexico. The Aztecs were experiencing a period during which there was plenty of land, but not enough people to work it. Such a situation may favor demographic growth (Polgar 1975; White 1973). A second factor that might have promoted population growth is the political competition that we know existed among various city–states. Rulers stood to benefit from larger populations because they would help till ever-larger territories and would also help man armies to fend off enemy attacks (Brumfiel 1983). Finally, as agricultural techniques improved, the carrying capacity of the land (i.e., the ability of the land to support a given number of people) would have allowed population growth as well.

There is general consensus that there was a population increase, and that there were many Aztecs at the time of contact (Sanders et al. 1979: 184). The questions remain: exactly how many, and how do we establish these numbers?

How Do Archaeologists Estimate Population Numbers?

The Ideal World

In very general terms, archaeologists try to compute population numbers based on the extent of the material remains they have uncovered. This is an approach wrought with pitfalls and shortcomings, but it is the only way to proceed when working with archaeological data.

In an ideal world, an archaeologist should be able to excavate all the structures at a given site. Moreover, this same archaeologist should also have no problem identifying which structures within the site were used as dwellings, and which were used as public spaces. The same investigator should also be able to determine which of the dwellings were occupied at any given time and which had been abandoned. This will help to assess how many people lived in the settlement at any particular time period. The archaeologists should also be able to ascertain the average number of people that would have lived in an average dwelling.

The Real World: Archaeological Information and Written Documents

In the real world archaeologists seldom have the chance to excavate a site completely. Separating buildings into the category of domestic versus public space is not an easy task. Some of the houses were so simple and the materials used so perishable that they did not leave any trace. We therefore risk underestimating the number of people that would have lived at a site.

The issue of which dwellings were occupied and which ones had been abandoned in the time period that we are trying to compute demographics for further complicates the picture. It is clear that reliance on purely material evidence will not solve the problem. We need other sources to bypass these obstacles. We need access to descriptions that refer to population sizes and to the extent of settlements. Few fortunately have some of these documents, but they will only help shed light on the last portion of Aztec history.

Early Spanish sources discuss the extent of cities and also (and perhaps more importantly) the size of Native American armies that opposed the European invasion. There is no doubt that the Spanish were incredibly outnumbered on the battlefield, especially so in the very early days of their march on Tenochtitlan; however, the Spanish chroniclers were not unfamiliar with the concept of embellishing reports to impress the reader at home. Compare how Cortés reported that a Tlaxcaltecan army numbered 100,000 soldiers, whereas one of his subordinates, eyeballing the same army, reported that there were about 40,000 soldiers opposing the Spanish (Smith 1996: 60).

With this cautionary tale we will proceed to discuss specific cases, such as the extent of the population in the Aztec capital, Tenochtitlan.

CASE STUDY: POPULATION ESTIMATES FOR TENOCHTITLAN

Tenochtitlan's population in 1519 is estimated to have been between 150,000 and 250,000 people (Calnek 1976: 288, 1978: 316; Hassig 1988: 59; Sanders, Parsons, and Santley 1979: 154; Hodge 1994: 45). While acknowledging that the available data to reconstruct population figures are very scant, some historians proceed to estimate Tenochtitlan's population as ranging between 500,000 and 1 million (Soustelle 1962: 9). It is likely that this enormous figure might approximate the number of people who lived in all the communities in and around the southern lake system at the time of the conquest. Cortés notes that the lakeshore communities in the vicinity of Tenochtitlan extended into the lake. This seems to indicate that they were expanding, and doing so in the same way Tenochtitlan had been: by building onto the water (Soustelle 1962: 9).

Although we may never know the exact number of Tenochtitlan's inhabitants, the early Spanish chroniclers have left enough references to the awe they felt seeing the city. They were impressed by both the quality of the architecture and the layout of the city, as well as by the number of inhabitants. With regard to the latter, some of these early writers made the point that, if it were not for the canals and the role these played in daily people traffic, "no one could move about the streets nor come out of their houses" (Soustelle 1962: 12). In other words, it seems that the number of citizens during the early morning "commute" to work was sufficiently large to create crowded streets. The canals were more efficient means to move people than were the street, and they probably acted as more efficient people movers, much like public transportation in our modern cities.

As we have seen earlier, our ability to reconstruct population figures is heavily dependent upon our ability to identify and count houses and then multiply that number of dwellings with a figure representing the number of inhabitants. Family size and household composition are difficult to reconstruct. Archaeologists assume that among commoners, an average household consisted of five to seven persons. It is also very likely that a dwelling was home for more than one married couple. The assumptions regarding the size of an elite household suggest a much greater number of people per dwelling. The nobility, by virtue of the fact that they could afford to support multiple wives, did have multiple spouses. Documents relate how some of these elite dwellings were home for up to thirty-five people, not the five to seven cited earlier. Although elite houses would be more spacious, the notion that the number of inhabitants in any Aztec building could range that considerably should give us pause when we read population estimates (Evans 1991: 77).

A detailed colonial-era population census does exist for the Basin of Mexico; unfortunately, this census dates to 1568, at a time when the impact of European diseases had dramatically reduced the number of indigenous people. This census reports how in 1568 the number of non-Spanish people in the Valley of Mexico was 410,000 and 970,000 in Central Mexico (Smith 1996: 61). Modern researchers have been tempted to apply statistics to these numbers to project a population number for the Aztec world just before the arrival of the Spanish. Because of the uncertainties outlined earlier and different formulas being applied, the population estimates for Aztec Central Mexico that these researchers have come up with range from 3.3 to 6.4 million people (Smith 1996: 61–62). These are figures that apply to the year 1519, just before the Spanish arrived.

REFERENCES

Anawalt, Patricia. 1980. Custom and Control: Aztec Sumptuary Laws. *Archaeology* 33(1): 33–43.

Bandelier, Fanny R. 1932. *A History of Ancient Mexico by Fray Bernardino de Sahagún.* Translated by Fanny R. Bandelier from the Spanish version of Carlos Maria de Bustamante. Nashville: Fisk University Press.

Berdan, Frances. 2002. Aztec Society: Economy, Tribute and Warfare. In *Aztecs.* Edited by Eduardo Matos Moctezuma and Felipe Solis Olguín, pp. 38–47. London: Royal Academy of Arts.

Brumfiel, Elizabeth M. 1983. Aztec State Making: Ecology, Structure, and the Origin of the State. *American Anthropologist* 85: 261–284.

Calnek, Edward, 1976. The Internal Structure of Tenochtitlan. In *The Valley of Mexico.* Edited by Eric Wolf. Albuquerque: University of New Mexico Press.

———. 1978. The Internal Structure of Cities in America: Pre-Columbian Cities; the Case of Tenochtitlan. In *Urbanization in the Americas from its Beginnings to the Present.* Edited by Schaedel, Richard, Jorge Hardoy, and Nora Scott Kinzer. The Hague: Mouton Publishers.

Carrasco, Pedro. 1984. Royal Marriages in Ancient Mexico. In *Explorations in Ethnohistory: Indians of Central Mexico in the Sixteenth Century.* Edited by Herbert R. Harvey and Hanns J. Prem, pp. 41-81. Albuquerque: University of New Mexico Press.

Cortés, Hernan. 1986. *Letters from Mexico.* Translated and edited by Anthony Pagden. New Haven: Yale University Press.

Evans, Susan T. 1991. Architecture and Authority in an Aztec Village: Form and Function of the Tecpan. In *Land and Politics in the Valley of Mexico. A Two Thousand Years Perspective.* Edited by H. R. Harvey, pp. 63–92. Albuquerque: University of New Mexico Press. (Provides information on the dwellings in which rural elite lived. Provides a counterbalance to the data favoring the big cities.)

Gerhard, Peter. 1970. A Method for Reconstructing Political Boundaries in Central Mexico. *Journal de la Société des Américanistes* n.s. 59: 27–41.

Hassig, Ross. 1993. *Trade, Tribute, and Transportation: The Sixteenth Century Political Economy of the Valley of Mexico.* Norman: University of Oklahoma Press.

Hodge, Mary G. 1994. Polities Composing the Aztec Empire's Core. In *Economies and Polities in the Aztec Realm.* Edited by Mary G. Hodge and Michael E. Smith, pp. 43–71. (Studies on Culture and Society, volume 6) Albany: Institute for Mesoamerican Studies.

Parsons, Jeffrey R. 1971. *Prehistoric Settlement Patterns in the Texcoco Region, Mexico.* Memoirs No. 3. Museum of Anthropology, University of Michigan, Ann Arbor.

Parsons, Jeffrey R., Elizabeth M. Brumfiel, Mary H. Parsons, and David Wilson. 1982. *Prehispanic Settlement Patterns in the Southern Valley of Mexico: The Chalco-Xochimilco Region.* Ann Arbor: Memoirs No. 14, Museum of Anthropology, University of Michigan.

Pasztory, Esther. 1998. *Aztec Art.* Norman: University of Oklahoma Press.

Polgar, Steven. 1975. Population, Evolution, and Theoretical Paradigms. In *Population, Ecology, and Social Evolution.* Edited by Steven Polgar, pp. 1–26. The Hague: Mouton.

Sanders, William T., Jeffrey R. Parsons, and Robert S. Santley. 1979. *The Basin of Mexico: Ecological Processes in the Evolution of a Civilization.* New York: Academic Press.

Seler, Eduard. 1902–1923. *Gesammelte Abhandlungen zur Amerikanischen Sprach- und Atertumskunde.* 5 volumes. Berlin: A. Asher. (Reprinted Graz, Austria, 1960)

Smith, Michael E. 1992. *Archaeological Research at Aztec-Period Rural Sites in Morelos, Mexico. Volume 1, Excavations and Architecture.* Investigaciones Arqueológicas en Sitios Rurales de la Epoca Azteca en Morelos, Tomo 1, Excavaciones y Arquitectura. University of Pittsburgh Memoirs in Latin American Archaeology 4. Pittsburgh: University of Pittsburgh.

———. 1997. Life in the Provinces of the Aztec Empire. *Scientific American* September: 76–83.

Smith, Michael E., Patricia Aguirre, Cynthia Heath-Smith, Kathryn Hirst, Scott O'Mack, and Jeffrey Price. 1989. Architectural Patterns at Three Aztec-Period Sites in Morelos, Mexico. *Journal of Field Archaeology* 16: 185–203.

Smith, Michael E., and Mary G. Hodge. 1994. An Introduction to Late Postclassic Economies and Polities. In *Economies and Polities in the Aztec Realm.* Edited by Mary G. Hodge and Michael E. Smith, pp. 1–42. (Studies on Culture and Society, volume 6) Albany: Institute for Mesoamerican Studies.

Smith, Michael E., and Cynthia Heath-Smith. 2000. Rural Economy in Late Postclassic Morelos. An Archaeological Study. In *The Ancient Civilizations of Mesoamerica. A Reader.* Edited by Michael E. Smith and Marilyn A. Mason, pp. 217–235. Oxford: Blackwell Publishers.

Soustelle, Jacques. 1962. *Daily Life of the Aztecs on the Eve of the Spanish Conquest.* Translated from the French by Patrick O'Brian. Stanford: Stanford University Press.

Thomas, Hugh 1995. *Conquest: Montezuma, Cortés, and the Fall of Old Mexico.* New York: Touchstone.

White, Benjamin. 1973. Demand for Labor and Population Growth in Colonial Java. *Human Ecology* 1: 217–236.

Williams, Barbara J. 1994. The Archaeological Signature of Local Level Polities in Tepetlaoztoc. In *Economies and Polities in the Aztec Realm.* Edited by Mary G. Hodge and Michael E. Smith, pp. 73–87. (Studies on Culture and Society, volume 6) Albany: Institute for Mesoamerican Studies.

VII

CHAPTER 7

Politics

THE ARCHAEOLOGICAL RECORD
AND ANCIENT POLITICAL SYSTEMS

Archaeologists are interested in reconstructing human behavior. They do so by working with as many sources as possible, and these include the material record and written sources. Because most of our history occurred in a prehistoric context and because the written record is most often very patchy for those cultures that are considered historic, we must often rely on material remains of human activity to reconstruct how a culture worked. This reconstruction of what people did in the past is sometimes very straightforward. For example, the recovery of grinding stones and cooking vessels will easily allow us to identify how people processed and ate their food. If we are lucky, the presence of preserved food remains will even tell us what they were eating.

Things get trickier when it comes to human behavior that does not leave behind a lot of material remains. For example, take abstract thought, philosophy, or mathematics. How does one ascertain what level or kind of abstract thought existed in a given culture in the past? This becomes a daunting, if not impossible, task to accomplish unless we have written sources.

Ancient political systems are also difficult to identify immediately in the archaeological record. Some activities related to political structure and organization have material reflections; others do not. A modern government meets in a building, and the remains of that building can be found. The problem is how to identify it as, for example, the Capitol, rather than as a large church or a large building with an unidentified purpose. In the case of the Capitol in Washington, we can rely on written sources that help us clearly identify the function of the building.

How can we tease from the material record enough information to reconstruct the way a society was organized? When faced with the task of defining what constitutes a state-level society, the participants in a seminar on archaic states organized by the School of American Research came up with the following suggestions (Marcus and Feinman 1998: 6–7):

1. The existence of a settlement hierarchy that includes at least four levels.
2. The existence of a decision-making hierarchy that involves at least three levels.
3. The presence of an ideology of stratification and descent. Rulers are considered to rule by divine right whereas commoners have a nondivine origin.

4. The presence of two endogamous social strata, dividing society into two segments.
5. The presence of a palace as the ruler's residence.
6. The existence of a government that exercised a monopoly in the use of deadly force, while denying that same right to its citizens.
7. The presence of governmental laws and the ability to enforce them.

It should have become obvious to the reader that recognizing these aspects from the material record alone would be very difficult and that the additional assistance of written sources is highly desirable. Evidence for the presence of these traits in the Aztec world does exist in the material and written record. Their presence constitutes the basis for the chapters of this book because there would be nothing to write about without them.

THE CONCEPT OF AZTEC RULERSHIP

The Tlahtoani

Political legitimacy of an Aztec ruler was directly linked to his genealogical connection with the ruling dynasty at Tula. The Aztec referred to this genealogical link as *tlatocayotl.* This desire to establish this link was so strong that the Mexica, upon their arrival in the Valley of Mexico, endeavored to have their ruler marry a princess from Culhuacan. Because her family did claim a direct genealogical link to the Toltec dynasty, this union ensured that subsequent Aztec rulers could claim the same. In other words, the requirement of *tlatocayotl* had been met (Smith 2003c: 149).

The Aztecs had a precise idea of what traits represented a good *tlahtoani* (Smith 1996: 164):

> The good ruler is a protector—one who carries his subjects on his arms, who unites them, and who brings them together. He rules, he takes responsibilities, and he assumes burdens. He carries his subjects in his cape; he bears them in his arms. He governs; he is obeyed. To him as shelter, as refuge, there is recourse.

IMPERIAL SUCCESSION

As we saw in Chapter 3, Aztec imperial succession tended to be a family affair. Our colonial sources inform us that the emperor was selected in a large meeting attended by nobility. This council of *tetecuhtin* consisted specifically of male kin of the deceased ruler. They were the ones who deliberated to select a successor. The question is: Who had a chance to become the new emperor?

We are told that these male relatives of the deceased emperor could cast votes for all the princes who were sons of lords. This means that, in theory at least, more than one individual stood a chance of becoming the next emperor.

We are told, for example, that in one particular case, a speaker at the meeting announced twenty sons of three of the previous emperors were eligible candidates to become the next emperor. Reality was different. The appearance of a plurality of candidates was just that—an appearance. It tended to happen that a major dignitary at the meeting would advance the name of only one candidate. Such a "suggestion," it appears, was never refused (Rounds 1982: 75).

A Spanish chronicler, Motolinia, made the following cynical observation about the election process:

> If it could be called an election, it was among the sons and brothers of the deceased ruler, and although for this election many great and minor lords gathered, there were no votes nor election by balloting, but already they had looked to whom the kingdom belonged, and if in him there were no faults that would render him incapable, and if there were diverse opinions, the elections depended upon the ruler who had the right of confirmation, who was already well resolved and informed of to whom the lordship belonged, and without contradiction that was accepted by all. (Motolinia 1971: 338)

Although this critical comment exposes the reality of choosing a leader, it does not provide us with all the necessary information to determine who in practical terms appointed the new emperor. Motolinia mentions that "the elections depended upon the ruler who had the right of confirmation," without telling us to which ruler he is referring. There are three theoretical possibilities: he must be referring to the group of three rulers in charge of the Triple Alliance. Of these three rulers, we have seen that the ruler of Tenochtitlan had the greatest power. It is fair to assume then that the "ruler who had the right of confirmation" was the emperor residing in Tenochtitlan (Rounds 1982: 76). In this decision-making process, the three ruling figures of the Alliance were assisted by the cihuacoatl and the members of the Council of Four.

The Council of Four was made up of the four closest advisors to the ruler of Tenochtitlan. The two highest Aztec military officers, the *tlacateccatl* and the *tlacochcalcatl*, were among these four men. Rounds (1982: 77) identifies these two individuals as close male relatives of the king. They were men who were appointed by the ruler into their position of authority within the military command. It appears that holding one of these two positions was part of the career track for an Aztec emperor (Rounds 1982: 77).

Once a decision was made with regard to succession, the stage was set for elaborate ceremonies. These ceremonies primarily served the purpose of validating the new ruler as a worthy representative of the god Tezcatlipoca. In the words of de Durand-Forest (1996):

> Without being a god himself, the king was the ixiptla (the image, the representative) of the gods. When he was elected as a tlatoani, he was imbued with a part of their divine nature.

An Aztec ruler proved his worth by first standing naked in front of a statue of the god Huitzilopchtli and presenting offerings. He then retreated with the *tetecuhtin* for a 4-day period of fasting and penance. After this retreat the future

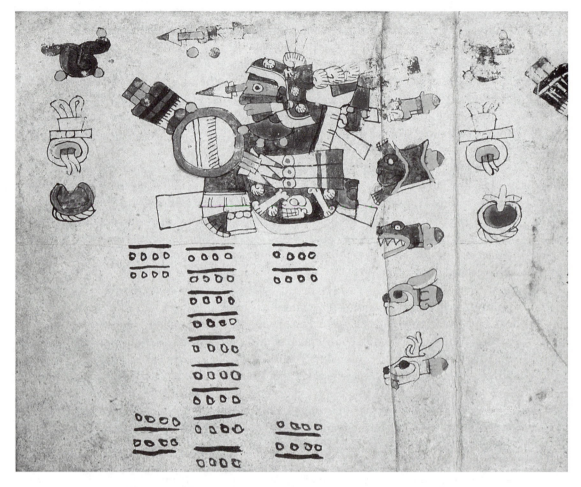

A detail of the Codex Cospi, an Aztec divinatory calendar, showing the god Tezcatlipoca in his black aspect, representing the god of the north and the night sky. (Werner Forman/Corbis)

tlahtoani was required to lead troops into battle; he had to capture warriors to be sacrificed during the inauguration.

The inauguration ceremony was a grand spectacle that served many purposes. It was intended to awe and impress the guests. Among the latter were rulers and nobility from neighboring kingdoms, the citizenry of the capital, and, in some cases, even the rulers of enemy territories. With regard to the latter, the Aztecs hoped to instill respect and fear through the grandeur of the ceremonies and the scale of human sacrifice (Hodge 1996: 28). These festivities also served to underline the link between the new king and Tezcatlipoca (Smith 2003c: 149).

The Role of Women in Imperial Succession

The role played by women in imperial succession was limited. We know that a male's status was derived from both parents. Moreover, a man's rights to rank and privilege were determined by the status of his mother and that of his wife.

Sixteenth-century engraving showing a sacrificial ceremony. (Stapleton Collection/Corbis)

Succession practices varied as a result. A son could succeed his father; occasionally, it could be a grandson (a son's son *or* a daughter's son) acceding to the throne. The son of a high-ranking wife was always looked upon favorably (Carrasco 1984: 43).

Most often, this is where the role of women in imperial succession ended; however, in a few cases we know of a woman who held office or title. For example, in Chalco, a woman by the name of Xiuhtoztzin is said to have received the title of *tlailotlacteuctli*, and as being a *cihuapiltlahtohuani* or "queen" (Carrasco 1984: 43–44). In Tenochtitlan, there are reports that the daughter of Moctecuhzuma Ilhuicamina, a woman by the name of Atotoztli, may have succeeded her father (Carrasco 1984: 44).

DANGERS INHERENT IN THE SYSTEM OF UNCERTAIN SUCCESSION

The system described herein was one that allowed for a period of uncertainty between two rulers. After the death of an emperor, the throne was vacant while the close-knit group of people referred to earlier decided on who should be the next ruler. As a result of this so-called interregnum, or period between two reigns, there was always the danger of internal strife erupting, as well as conflict with external powers. These dangers became even greater at times of problematic successions (Rounds 1982: 78). Because of these tendencies on the part of internal political factions or external enemies to test the strength of the opposition, a military campaign to restore order became the standard thing to do for the new Aztec emperors.

The way the Aztecs attempted to deal with this period of uncertainty was through a political institution of a stand-in person called *cihuacoatl*. This referred to a person who took over the reign in times of potential instability, especially during a period between rulers. The *cihuacoatl* had only one very important duty: keeping the realm together. To achieve this goal, he must have had complete administrative control (Rounds 1982: 79). This control also included, as we just saw, a role in the election process of the new emperor.

The term *cihuacoatl* refers to the name of the patron deity of the city of Colhuacan. We assume that the role of stand-in for the next emperor originally belonged to the chief priest of this goddess. It appears that the term eventually stuck to the office, without the holder of the office having to be a priest.

ADMINISTRATION IN THE CAPITAL

Once a new ruler had been inaugurated, he started exercising control over the state. He was assisted in this by a council of nobles and bureaucrats. The king acted as the supreme military leader. As indicated earlier, he is a protector. As such he was in charge of military campaigns, as well as supervising the defense of the city. The *tlahtoani* was also called upon to act as a supreme judge. He had to settle cases that lower-ranking judges had been unable to resolve (Smith 2003c: 149).

The second-most important political office belonged to the *cihuacoatl*. We have just seen how this person acted as a stabilizing force during the period of transition between emperors. Even though those responsibilities of the *cihuacoatl* ended with the election of a new emperor, other political duties continued for the *cihuacoatl*. Colonial sources mention how the *cihuacoatl* acted as a prime minister or viceroy. When the emperor was away from the city, the *cihuacoatl* would act as his representative.

Aside from the *tlahtoani* and the *cihuacoatl*, the administration in the capital included a council of nobles and a cadre of lower-ranking bureaucrats who participated in the administration of the community.

PROVINCIAL ADMINISTRATION

Prior to the emergence of Tenochtitlan, political power in the Valley of Mexico was divided among roughly forty city–states. With the expansion of Aztec political power, most of these entities were absorbed into the Aztec realm. The need to administer these regions gave rise to the development of a provincial administration. This administration was responsible in matters of tribute collection, military affairs, and meeting political obligations (Hodge 1996: 23).

After the successful conclusion of a military campaign, the Aztec army most often withdrew and left the local rulers in place. As discussed in Chapter 4, the Aztecs preferred indirect rule rather than leaving Aztec governors behind to rule the new territory (Hassig 1988: 17; Berdan 1994: 291; Berdan 1996: 122).

Those who have studied Aztec rule identify three different kinds of "provinces," or territories (Berdan 1996; Smith 1996; Umberger 1996). These include tributary provinces, strategic provinces, and outer provinces. Their borders did not always overlap (Hodge 1996: 25).

The tributary provinces tended to be areas that were incorporated by the Aztec by the end of the fifteenth century, before the reign of Moctecuhzuma II (Berdan 1996: 135). These provinces, although part of the realm, were typically still allowed to retain their own rulers. As mentioned in Chapter 5, ties between the ruling local elite and the Aztec political class were solidified through marriage alliances, gift exchanges, and participation in ceremonies (Berdan 1994: 299; Berdan 1996: 122). The victorious Aztecs replaced the local rulers with one of their own people only in a few cases (Hassig 1993: 104). Because of the practice of Aztec noblemen marrying into the local elite after one generation, the new rulers were both de facto and de jure Aztec rulers (Hassig 1993: 105). Within the borders of these provinces, individuals who had shown their prowess as warriors on the battlefield were granted commissions as tribute collectors (Hodge 1996: 23).

The presence of the provincial administration was also required at political rituals in the capital, especially those rituals performed by the emperor himself (Hodge 1996: 28). These rulers were also expected to host banquets for rituals in Tenochtitlan. For example, during the festival of *Huey tecuilhuitl* held in the capital, a number of provinces acted as hosts (Hodge 1996: 28):

> [F]or 10 days there was eating and banqueting in the city of Mexico. Each one of the nearby provinces was obliged to contribute and feed the lords. The Chalcas provided on the first day, the Tepanecs on the second, others on the third. Thus, each had its turn, providing splendid, rich foods and drinks—chocolate, pinole, great quantities of pulque—with all striving to give the best.

The Aztec did install tribute collectors (see Chapter 5), and, occasionally, military garrisons. The latter were usually intended to protect the province's borders. This Aztec military presence, however, did not guarantee peace within the borders of a given province. We know that Aztec provincial towns would sometimes continue hostilities with traditional enemies, even if those enemies themselves had become incorporated into the Aztec world (Berdan 1996: 122).

RURAL POLITICAL ORGANIZATION

Our understanding of rural political organization is lacking compared with that of the larger metropolitan areas. Still, thanks to early colonial-period litigation between the Spanish nobility and the inhabitants of the Prehispanic communities, we have some notion on the political structure of the Aztec countryside. Local claims of land ownership were typically backed up with pictorial manuscripts dating back to Precolumbian times.

We know from ethnohistorical descriptions that city–states traditionally kept detailed records of population size and land ownership. These documents would have been stored in the palace. Like their modern counterparts, these documents were probably updated on a regular basis. These census documents and cadastral records were made in the form of pictorial manuscripts. Only two of these pictorial manuscripts are known to have survived, and both of them are from the community of Tepetlaoztoc.

Barbara Williams undertook a study of the territorial and political organization of rural settlements as they existed shortly after the conquest (Williams 1991). It is in this context of rural organization that the term *tlaxilacalli* was used. Early colonial documents used in court proceedings inform us about the external boundaries of the *tlaxilacalli* (Williams 1991: 189–190). A detailed pictorial representation of households and landholdings informs us about the internal territorial organization of Tepetlaoztoc. It appears that this *tlaxilacalli* consisted of twelve localities. These localities, comprising small villages and hamlets, had a total population of 1,324 people (Williams 1991: 194). These documents tell us clearly that this territorial unit called *tlaxilacalli* was composed of discreet individual rural settlements. There was a hierarchy of these settlements within this territory, ranging from small to large communities. Moreover, the territorial boundaries were very well defined, and within them we find both agricultural and nonagricultural lands. It also appears that access to agricultural lands was unevenly distributed within the *tlaxilacalli*. This is seen as reflecting social and economic stratification within the communities. In other words, even at the lowest level of social and economic organization within the Aztec world, there was a limited form of inequality, with some people having greater access to wealth and resources than others (Williams 1991: 206).

In terms of political organization, Williams determined that the *tlaxilacalli* was part of a larger political unit during the early colonial era (Williams 1991: 206). It is assumed that this situation echoed one that existed before the Spanish arrived. Officials who were part of the larger political unit outside the *tlaxilacalli* seem to have had a supervisory role when lands within the *tlaxilacalli* were allocated: they authorized and confirmed transfer of land ownership.

WARFARE

The Aztec reputation for being fearsome warriors is widespread. We will discuss elsewhere that this was not the only field in which they excelled. They were accomplished thinkers and builders as well. The Aztec's martial aspects were most often the result of early colonial sources. Scribes would recapitulate Aztec conquests and thereby contribute to this reputation. Archaeological remains are more scant. Mesoamerican people did not have the custom to build large-scale fortifications along the lines medieval European people would. Furthermore, one can only imagine the difficulties involved in finding and recognizing a Precolumbian battlefield.

Written Documents

There are references in Aztec texts to warfare. We saw how emperor Tizoc ordered a stone carved in which he was represented as a successful warrior. Early colonial documents also carried references to conflict. The historic section of the Codex Mendoza, for example, depicts various temple buildings with their roofs upended while smoke and fire are escaping from the edifice. This scene refers to "conquest" because capturing the temple in an enemy city often led to the enemy laying down his arms.

Archaeological Evidence

Fortifications—settlement locations in easily defensible areas—are material indications of the prevalence of warfare. There is good material evidence of such traits. The border area between the Aztec and Tarascan cultures were dotted with strongholds and no-man's-land. Archaeologists have turned their attention to this region, and studied some of the fortifications (Gorenstein 1985).

Although fortifications and hilltop locations are easily recognizable material traits of the incidence of warfare, there are other forms of conflict where archaeological evidence might be more difficult to encounter. For example, flower wars were (ostensibly) not intended to capture territory, only sacrificial victims. We know that the Aztec and their opponents met on previously designated battlefields, yet even in this context we might not have material evidence of where a battle took place. Two carved stone monuments have been found in the southwestern portion of the modern Mexican state of Puebla. These monuments represent an eagle perched on the shoulder of a jaguar. The jaguar is dressed as a warrior, with a shield on its back, and with a spear thrower, or *atlatl,* and darts to one side of the shield. A heart can be seen on the other shoulder of the jaguar. A dart pierces it. The second monument represents a feathered serpent. A liquid from its body flows.

The carved decoration on these two stones refers to the flower war. The heart is thought to represent human sacrifice, an interpretation underscored by the dart going through it. The eagle and jaguar very likely correspond to the two warrior orders. The feathered serpent could stand for Mixcoatl, the Cloud Serpent, who required sacrificial blood (Plunket and Uruñuela 1994: 439–441).

OVERALL ASPECTS OF AZTEC WARFARE

What Constituted a *Casus Belli* for the Aztecs?

The terminology *casus belli* comes to us from the Romans. One could translate that in plain English as, "For what reason would the Aztecs declare war?" There are several answers to this question. In some cases they would feel that they had been slighted and war was inevitable. The Aztecs would sometimes have been the instigators, without any provocations on the part of the opposite side. War was sometimes initiated after consultation with the enemy regarding time and place to start the conflict.

The Aztecs entertained the concept of a "just" war. If Aztecs or allied merchants had been killed in another city, then war could be declared (Hassig 1993: 120–121). While discussing the role of the pochteca earlier (see Chapter 5), a special category of pochteca was identified: the *naualoztomeca*. They acted as spies and vanguards for Aztec forces. Their capture and execution did constitute a *casus belli* for the Triple Alliance (de Durand-Forest 1996).

The Aztecs made further distinctions against their enemy, depending on a number of factors. If a town had rebelled, and it used to be a tribute-paying community, then war was justified; however, the retaliation depended on whether or not the entire population had engaged in rebellion, or only the nobility. In the case where the entire population had risen, the Aztecs would first attempt to avoid conflict by sending messengers asking that they resume paying tribute. If the nobility were at fault, then the army would be sent to capture them. They would be tried in public (Hassig 1988: 8).

The Aztecs were master provocateurs. They would send ambassadors to independent cities to request that they start paying tribute, and that they accept the Aztec gods. If these requests were not honored, and especially if the ambassadors had been harmed in the process, then war would follow (Hassig 1988: 8).

Once the Aztecs had decided that war was likely, they would first send three groups of envoys: one to the ruler of the target city, one to the nobility of that community, and one to the general public. These envoys would announce that the Aztecs felt that they had been wronged and that they demanded satisfaction (Hassig 1988: 8). This behavior on the part of the Aztecs reminds us of the Spanish promulgating a "requerimiento" document on the battlefield.

Religion played an important role in the declaration and conduct of hostilities. Once the Aztecs had decided that war was inevitable, they would rely on signs from the gods to start hostilities. The gods were the ones who would let the Aztecs know when it was auspicious to start a war, who would win, and what the Aztecs needed to do to please the gods (Hassig 1988: 8–9). Before the troops would march off, they would receive weapons at the main temples. There they would also engage in autosacrifice, offering their own blood to the gods to ensure a successful outcome of combat. Priests and sorcerers would remain extra vigilant at home during a campaign, but they would also accompany the army in the field (Hassig 1988: 9).

The Chain of Command: The Military Hierarchy

The emperor was commander in chief, and would join his troops in battle. A supreme council consisting of four trusted officers always surrounded him. These officers would always be high-ranking noblemen. Aside from this retinue, the emperor would also stand out because of his outfit. Although this made him easily recognizable among his own troops, it also made him a readily identifiable target.

For example, in the battle between Texcoco and Huexotzinco, the king of Huexotzinco expressed great interest in knowing the type of insignia worn by the king of Texcoco. His intentions were clear: find out where the enemy leader was during the battle, and have him killed; however, the king of Texcoco somehow learned of these intentions and transferred his arms to a nobleman in his army, allegedly to honor him. The nobleman perished, the king survived (Hassig 1988: 42).

Military costumes worn by high-ranking Aztec officers stood out because of the colorful feather work. They also restricted body movements, making fighting more difficult. This would include escaping the intentions of the opposing side, which zeroed in on them because their outfit betrayed their ranking (Pasztory 1998: 279).

Leadership positions in combat were usually reserved for experienced fighters, men who tended to come from the ranks of the nobility. They had received a long and rigorous training in the *calmecac*, as we saw in Chapter 6. The Aztecs developed an elaborate system of body adornments and grooming methods to indicate the position that a person had attained as a warrior.

When a boy entered the school, his hair would be completely cut. At the age of 10, a small tuft of hair would be allowed to grow on the back of the head. By the time he turned 15, this hair would be long and indicate that he had not yet taken any prisoners. If in war he was able to capture a prisoner without any help, the tuft of hair would be cut; however, if the capture happened with the help of others, then only the left side of the tuft would be shaved off, the right side was left long. This was a sign that he still needed to capture a man unaided before he would be considered a true warrior (Hassig 1988: 36).

An unsuccessful warrior who had failed to capture anyone after three battles would be called a "youth with a baby's lock," a *cuexpalchicacpol*. If he continued to be unsuccessful, his status would be made very obvious for all to see: his head would be pasted with feathers. Those who could not even get a captive with the assistance of others would have the crown of their head shaved (Hassig 1988: 36).

Successful warriors would signal their status in various ways. Warriors painted their face and bodies according to their achievements. When a warrior took a prisoner, his face was painted red and yellow (Hassig 1988: 41). As outlined in Chapter 6, military garb also reflected the number of prisoners taken. Membership in military orders brought with it specific outfits and body decoration. Some warriors had half of their heads painted blue and the other half painted red or yellow (Hassig 1988: 41).

Membership in a military order, such as the order of the eagle or that of the jaguar, was based upon prowess in the battlefield. Men who had taken more than four prisoners would be allowed to join. There were no restrictions based on one's social background. Thus, warriors from the commoner class who were able to capture more than four prisoners would find themselves rising in the ranks. This could in theory be interpreted as a great social equalizer. In reality, most of the members of military orders came from the ranks of the aristocracy. They were the ones who had received better training and, when going

An Aztec warrior of Moctecuhzuma's army. (Bettmann/Corbis)

Life-size ceramic figure found in the House of the Eagles in Tenochtitlan. Originally interpreted as representing an Eagle Warrior, this statue is now thought to represent the sun at dawn. Traces of white paint may have depicted feathers. (Danny Lehman/Corbis)

into their first battle, they were the ones benefiting from the protection of veteran warriors. The sons of noblemen stood a much better chance of surviving and eventually capturing the necessary quota of prisoners to be allowed to join a military order (Hassig 1988: 45).

In addition to the jaguar and eagle orders, the Aztec had two more levels of military orders. These were reserved for men who had taken five or six prisoners. These warriors would receive special insignia, such as a "net device staff," and a shield decorated with the "nose moon device." They wore their hair bound in a tassel with a red ribbon (Hassig 1988: 45–46).

The Role of Military Intelligence

The adage that the best defense is a good offense certainly applies to the Aztecs. As noted earlier, the Aztecs were not interested in conquering territory and leaving garrisons behind, nor were they keen on building elaborate border fortifications. Given these situations, they left themselves vulnerable to attack, which meant that good intelligence on enemy intentions was of premium value (Hassig 1988: 49–50). The Aztecs had four different channels through which they gathered information on "the other side." These channels included long-distance traders, or *pochteca*, formal ambassadors, messengers, and spies (Hassig 1988: 49).

The Role of Long-Distance Traders, or *Pochteca*

Pochteca were long-distance traders who would travel throughout the Aztec realm and beyond to engage in trade and, occasionally, intelligence gathering. This would most often entail reporting to the emperor what they had observed while traveling through certain areas, and how the inhabitants of other parts of Mesoamerica had treated them. In some cases, however, the emperors would entrust them with specific missions. This would result in these traders using disguises and changing their appearance in an attempt to pass themselves off as locals.

These traders would sometimes travel fully armed, sending a clear signal that their job was more than making commercial exchanges. The killing of *pochtecatl* or their mistreatment would invariably lead to war. The role played by these traders was of great importance to the defense of the Aztec heartland. Because the Aztecs lacked systematic border fortifications in most areas, these traders acted as trip wires. Any pent-up hostility among neighboring tribes would be unleashed first upon the *pochtecatl*, alerting the capital that an attack was possible (Hassig 1988: 49–50).

Ambassadors

The office of an ambassador was surrounded by less cloak-and-dagger stuff than that of the *pochteca*. Among Mesoamerican cultures, ambassadors were usually treated with great respect. Their office was deemed inviolable. They would even be allowed into enemy cities. They were supposed to be immune from attacks as long as they stayed on the main roads. The Aztecs would often send ambassadors to independent cities and request that they become a tributary of the Aztec state. Not everyone acceded to this request. Needless to say, any attack on an ambassador would bring swift retaliation (Hassig 1988: 50–51).

Messengers

Aztec runners were responsible for communicating news to the emperor in a timely fashion. They would also convey his messages throughout the realm and sometimes beyond. Aztec runners were stationed along roads at regular intervals, about 4 km apart (Hassig 1993: 32). Groups of runners were able to cover a total of about 400 km a day. Although runners were used most often to convey messages, it is alleged that the emperors could eat fresh fish from the Gulf of Mexico brought to them by a Prehispanic version of "same day delivery" (Hassig 1993: 32).

In times of war, messengers would be sent out to alert allies to start mobilizing their troops and to request that supplies be made available by those towns that were in the direct line of approach of the Aztec army. As mentioned, these messages would usually reach their intended audience fairly quickly. Just like the office of the *pochteca* and that of ambassadors, that of messengers was supposed to be sacrosanct (Hassig 1988: 51).

Spies

Once war was decided upon, but before mobilization had been declared, the Aztecs would send spies into enemy territory. They would usually disguise themselves as the local population. They would travel most often by night. Their job was to observe enemy strongholds, troop concentrations, and movements. They would sometimes bribe people to get information. This was a dangerous job, which would lead to immediate execution upon one's discovery (Hassig 1988: 50–51).

Types of Arms and Armor

Warriors would go into battle carrying both offensive and defensive weapons. Offensive weaponry included bows and arrows, spear throwers and darts, spears, slings, swords, and clubs. The soldiers would protect themselves by means of body armor, helmets, and shields.

Offensive Weapons

Projectile Weapons. Among the first weapons to be used on a Mesoamerican battlefield, and probably on most battlefields, are those that can hit the enemy from a distance. In Mesoamerica that meant the use of *atlatls,* bows and arrows, and slings.

Atlatls, or spear throwers, acted as extensions of the arm. These weapons took the shape of a stick, often elaborately decorated. These sticks had two distinctive features. At one end there was a hook while at the opposite end there were grips, in the shapes of circles carved out of the wood. It should be noted that not all *atlatls* had such grip features. This spear thrower would hold a sturdy dart, placed in a groove carved along the length of the spear thrower. The hook at the end of the instrument would hold the dart and move it forward as the *atlatl* was moved forward. Before the dart could be released, the warrior had to hold the *atlatl* in a horizontal plane above his left or right shoulder. By placing two fingers through the carved holes just mentioned, he could move the *atlatl* from a horizontal plane to a vertical plane, releasing the dart at the appropriate moment to propel it over a great distance.

Whereas most spear throwers had one groove, and therefore were used to fire one dart, there is one known example of an *atlatl* with two grooves, ostensibly meant to fire two darts at once. The darts were made mostly of oak and

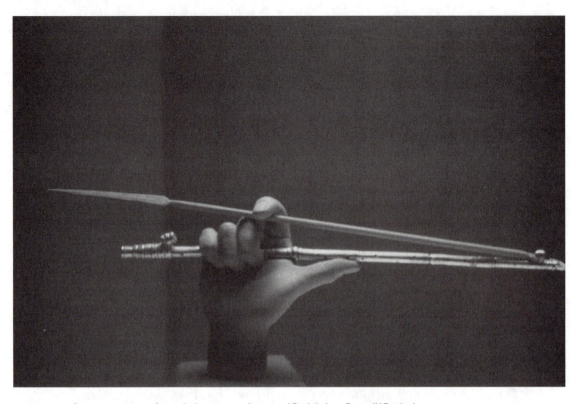

Reconstruction of an atlatl, or spear thrower. (Carl & Ann Purcell/Corbis)

had feathered ends. They were single pointed, and quite often fire hardened. Aside from these fire-hardened points, the Aztecs also used two-, and even three-pronged darts. Obisidian, flint, and copper were materials of choice to manufacture the points (Hassig 1988: 79).

This was a powerful weapon, one that even the Spaniards came to respect. According to Spanish sources, darts propelled by an *atlatl* could, and did, penetrate armor (Díaz del Castillo 1908–1916, 1: 285 [bk 4, ch. 78], 1: 238 [bk 4, ch. 65]; Hassig 1988: 79). Few *atlatls* have survived and very little data about the effective range of this weapon are available. It is thought, however, using information from other similar weapons from other parts of the world, that a spear thrower maintained great accuracy and penetrating force up to more than 40 m (or about 150 ft). The advantage of an *atlatl* over a spear thrown without the aid of such an instrument was that it provided additional thrust, and thereby increased the range and power with which the dart was thrown. Moreover, *atlatl* darts had greater penetrating power than arrows, even when hitting targets at the same distance (Hassig 1988: 79).

Aztec bows were simple bows rather than composite bows. This meant that they were produced out of a single piece of wood rather than a mixture of different materials. These bows could be up to 1.5 m (or 5 ft) long. An archer would use arrows with obsidian, flint, or even fishbone tips. During battle these arrows were kept in a quiver, with a total of probably twenty arrows per quiver. We do not know of any poison-tipped arrows that were in use in Mesoamerica, but we do have evidence that burning arrows were used in sieges to set fires to structures inside the fortifications (Hassig 1988: 79). The arrows were made out of reeds and were all of the same length. Arrows featured prominently on Aztec tribute lists. The advantage of having arrows of similar length was that archers would be able to deliver their arrows in the same target area by using the same bow pull, without having to adjust their pull effort (Hassig 1988: 80).

An arrow could penetrate Mesoamerican quilted cotton armor. Some communities specialized in archery, to the extent that they were sought after as archers to serve in the Aztec armies. For example, the archers from Teohuacan could fire two or three arrows during the same time that less-skilled archers could fire one.

Comparative data coming from firing similar North American Indian bows have indicated that archers could hit targets as far away as 90 and up to 180 m (from 300 to 600 ft). Obsidian tips were very effective in penetrating tissue, and were known to have inflicted widespread damage.

A final set of projectiles used by the Aztecs were pebbles fired from slings. These slings were made from maguey fiber. Aztec slingers would select their stones ahead of time, favoring hand-shaped rounded stones. In a few cases such stones were requested by the Aztecs as part of the tribute. Slingers could hurl their stones about 200 m away (roughly 660 ft).

Because of the distance that their weapons could reach, slingers and archers would often operate together. Once they had exhausted their supply of projectiles, they would withdraw, and allow warriors carrying shock weapons to step forward.

Shock Weapons. Aztec shock weapons included thrusting spears, swords, and clubs. These weapons were intended to be used in close-quarter combat. The Aztec thrusting spear, or *tepoztopilli*, was used to slash and thrust (Hassig 1988: 81). The cutting edge of these spears was made up of a series of very sharp obsidian blades set into a groove along the edge of the wood. This made for a very effective cutting surface, as the Spanish attested. In one case, a blow by such a spear apparently cut through the armor of one of the Conquistadors, only to be stopped by the cotton underpadding (Hassig 1988: 83). The length of these spears is estimated to have been equal to that of a man. The working end of the spear was triangular or ovoid in shape. That is where the obsidian blades were inserted into the groove. Although these spears were not intended to be thrown, they could be if so required (Hassig 1988: 83). One example of an Aztec thrusting spear survived in the Royal Armory in Madrid until 1884, when it was destroyed in a fire.

The Aztecs also made good use of wooden swords, or *macuahuitl*, which had cutting edges made out of obsidian blades. Two varieties were employed on the battlefield: a one-handed and a two-handed version. The former was more than 1 m long (about 3.5 ft) and about 7–20 cm wide (or 3–4 in.). A two-handed *macuahuitl* was longer, up to the length of a man, and 10 cm wide (or 4 in.). The cutting edge of these swords was present on both sides of the weapon. The Aztecs inflicted considerable damage upon their opponents by both slashing and cutting with these swords. Spanish eyewitness accounts relate how one well-placed blow by such a sword cut off a horse's head (Hassig 1988: 83). An example of an Aztec sword survived in Madrid, side by side with the thrusting spear. It, too, was lost in the same fire that destroyed the spear.

Finally, the Aztecs also employed clubs. Some of these were made completely out of wood; others had a stone blade. One variant consisted of a wooden club with a ball at the end (Hassig 1988: 85). A club was sometimes equipped with a knob at its end, and four spikes on its four sides, making it very similar to a European mace of medieval times (Hassig 1988: 85).

Defensive Weapons.   On the battlefield, the Aztecs would protect themselves with shields, and by donning helmets, quilted vests, and full body armor. Although the shields came in a wide range of sizes, and with various materials being used, the majority of them were either made of hide or plaited palm leaves. One exceptional type of shield, described by the Spanish, was apparently flexible enough to be rolled up when not in use, but could be unrolled to cover the body from head to toe when needed (Hassig 1988: 85).

In Chapter 5 we discussed how feather working was a full-time craft specialization. Among the objects produced were shields decorated with feathers. One of these is preserved in the Museum für Völkerkunde in Vienna, Austria, and two more are in a museum in Stuttgart, Germany. One might be tempted to think that these shields served no real defensive purpose and had only been manufactured for esthetic reasons, but Spanish chroniclers tell us differently. The fire-hardened wood used as backing for the feathers was apparently so sturdy that it would completely stop arrows. Only a bolt from a crossbow would penetrate it (Hassig 1988: 86).

Armor usually consisted of layers of quilted cotton. Cotton was indigenous to Mesoamerica, and most soldiers wore a heavy cotton quilted vest, or *ichcahuipilli,* for protection (Pohl and McBride 1991: 9). Only the military leaders wore body armor. Unspun cotton would be stitched between two layers of cloth. That combination would then be sewn to a leather border. The finished armor was one and a half to two fingers thick, which was sufficient to stop an arrow or *atlatl* dart from penetrating it. Cotton armor was part of the tribute sent in by some communities. The sizes and styles varied greatly. Elite warriors would also have a war suit, or *tlahuiztli,* worn over their armor (Hassig 1988: 88). Most of these consisted of feathers attached to textile. Warriors from lower social classes would wear a mantle made out of maguey fiber, or sometimes only a breech cloth and body paint (Hassig 1988: 40).

Fortifications

Fortified sites, once considered a rare phenomenon in Mesoamerica, are now known to have been widespread (Armillas 1951). This is especially true for the Maya region, but we are increasingly becoming aware of Aztec-era fortifications.

Map of the Aztec capital, Tenochtitlan. (Gianni Dagli Orti/Corbis)

Tenochtitlan, in the Aztec heartland, was not girded by European-style defensive works. Still, the city enjoyed a good defensive position because it was surrounded by water on all sides. We also know that the causeways linking the capital to the mainland had gaps in them. Although this was ostensibly to allow waters from the various lakes to flow through, it also allowed the Aztecs to return the city quickly to its island status by removing the timber bridges that covered those gaps. We also know of one isolated example of a defensive structure in the city: the Aztecs controlled traffic on their causeways both by means of removable bridges and by means of a two-towered fortification that dominated the juncture of two causeways. This strong point was ringed by a crenellated wall 12 ft wide (Hassig 1988: 52). The Spanish accounts of the final battles in the capital do not mention the existence of any strong points in the city, other than the temple precinct (Gorenstein 1966: 53).

The Aztecs did fortify some of their settlements, especially those close to disputed border areas. A very good example of such a disputed border area was that between the Aztecs and the Tarascans. We are aware of a string of fortified Aztec sites in that region (Hassig 1993: 296, n. 10). We should not envision Maginot Line–style fortification when considering Aztec or Tarascan fortifications. Most of these sites were strongholds that acted more as a refuge for a civilian population rather than a fortification occupied by troops only. Such refuge sites tend to be located on hilltops, with garrisons only present during times of war.

We are reminded that the Aztecs did not have a standing army. Like other Mesoamerican civilizations, the Aztecs lacked the logistics to maintain a permanent military presence in the field. We also know that in most cases the troops that were used to man these fortifications were provided by the local rulers, as part of their tribute requirements to the Aztec emperor (Hassig 1993: 96–97).

Even though the Aztecs might not have extensively fortified their communities, they were familiar with the concept of building camps during military campaigns. When the armies reached the intended battlefield, they would construct a camp nearby. This protected the troops while preparing for battle, while also providing a safe haven to retreat to after battle (Hassig 1988: 72).

Types of Warfare

Coronation Wars

Aztec rule was not universally accepted. Aztec rule was also never enforced in an enduring way by, for example, the systematic disposition of garrisons throughout the realm. These aspects, combined with resentments against the tax burden imposed on communities that had been incorporated by the Aztecs, guaranteed that there would always be a temptation to go it alone during a period of transition of power in Tenochtitlan. Such unrest, or even uprisings, meant that the emperors quite often had to engage in hostilities shortly after they had been crowned. They needed to campaign, both to protect their tax base and to set an example. Failure to do so would set a dangerous precedent.

Wars with Neighboring Cultures

The Aztecs fought two kinds of wars with neighboring cultures. Some were bloody battles intent on subjugating or even destroying the opposite side. Such wars took place, for example, between the Aztec and the Purepecha (better known as the Tarascans). Other battles were fought for the sole purpose of obtaining sacrificial victims rather than conquering and occupying territory. Those wars are known as "flower wars." They were fought between the Aztec and some of the communities just outside the Valley of Mexico, such as Cholula, Huexotzinco, Atlixco, and Tliliuhquitepec (Thomas 1995: 37). We shall look first at those wars I will call wars of attrition.

Wars of Attrition

With wars of attrition one should understand that the Aztecs set out in these types of wars to reduce the enemy immediately by physically eliminating the opposing forces on the battlefield. These kinds of wars sometimes also included the total destruction of the enemy infrastructure, including their cities. One should note, however, that a flower war, to be discussed next, also amounted to a war of attrition (Isaac 1983: 125), except in this case the enemy was subjected to attrition over a longer time period. Moreover, with flower wars, ritual played a greater role than in this first category of warfare.

As the Aztecs grew in power and as they began to wield influence outside the Valley of Mexico, they encountered two determined foes: the Tarascans and the Tlaxcalans. The Aztec were not successful in subjugating either one of these opponents.

With regard to the Tlaxcalans, the Aztecs instituted a policy of encirclement. They established client states around the Tlaxcala area, and proceeded slowly to reduce their power by cutting of their external trade routes, and by engaging in wars of attrition (Smith and Hodge 1994: 14). The relations between Aztecs and the Tarascans were very different than those between the Aztecs and the Tlaxcalans. The Tarascans were a powerful people. Their realm did rival that of the Aztecs in wealth and military prowess (Gorenstein 1985; Pollard 1982; Smith and Hodge 1994: 14).

The border area between the Aztec and Tarascan realms was one defined by the construction of strongholds on both sides, the remnants of which have been mapped and to some extent excavated (Gorenstein 1985).

As discussed in Chapter 3, Moctecuhzuma Ilhuicamina I launched a brutal and costly, but ultimately successful, campaign against Chalco. By 1465, the Chalcan federation at the southern end of the lakes in the Basin of Mexico had been routed (Isaac 1983: 124). The same emperor also waged war in Veracruz, along the Gulf Coast. Among his opponents were the Huaxtecs, who were caught in an Aztec ambush whereupon the Aztec army

> *annihilated them. Not one of the Huaxtecs escaped; all were killed or taken prisoner . . . After this the Aztecs entered the city, sacked and burned the temple and killed old and young. All this was done with . . . the determination to remove all trace of the Huaxtecs from the face of the earth.* (Durán 1964: 108, Ch. XIX; Isaac 1983: 124)

Motecuhzuma proved to be a very mercurial Aztec leader, engaging in hostilities in what is now the state of Oaxaca in Mexico. It appears that some pochteca had been killed in Coaixtlahuaca. That triggered a massive Aztec army of 200,000 warriors accompanied by 100,000 porters to invade the region (Isaac 1983: 124). In a series of wars, in which the Aztecs were not always victorious, they ended up defeating the Mixtec and Zapotec armies. The Oaxacans had apparently begged for mercy when things started to go awry, but the Aztecs

> *turned on them, making such a cruel slaughter that blood ran down the mountains, paths and roads, leaving such a multitude of dead that the animals of the mountains and the birds of prey had food for many days, because almost all of the natives [Mixtecs] of Oaxaca died; only the Zapotecs were taken prisoner . . . .* (Tezozomoc 1878: 359–360, Ch. XXXVIII; Isaac 1983: 124)

Under emperors Axayacatl and Tizoc, the tables were turned on the Aztecs twice. In 1478 Axayacatl launched a war against Michoacan, an independent kingdom located to the west of the Aztec heartland. Although sources differ in the numbers they mention, they do agree that the Aztecs were outnumbered by Michoacan's troops and suffered a defeat. Very few Aztec warriors returned home (Isaac 1983: 125).

Under emperor Ahuizotl, the Aztec armies stayed away from the two enemies that had inflicted such heavy losses on them under the previous ruler, instead concentrating on Tlaxacala, Huexotzinco, and Cholula. The sources again mention executions of the beaten enemy forces in the field, rather than captives being marched to the capital to be sacrificed later (Isaac 1983: 126).

The same approach was taken under emperor Moctecuhzuma Xocoyotzin. Aztec troops marched against the Otomí in the present state of Mexico, as well as against enemies in Oaxaca. In Oaxaca, the Aztecs proved themselves capable of storming the fortified city of Tototepec and taking it. All the adult inhabitants and most of the younger people were killed; children 8 years and younger were spared (Isaac 1983: 127).

Flower War or *Xochiyaoyotl*

Flower wars are special kinds of wars of attrition. Hassig (1988: 225) refers to flower wars as "an effective means of continuing a conflict that was too costly to conclude immediately." In those cases where the Aztecs still encountered opposition and steep losses had occurred repeatedly, they reverted to another tactic: slowly chip away at the manpower available to your opponent, and isolate them from their allies by encircling them (Plunket and Uruñuela 1994: 443). The immediate aim of flower wars was to obtain sacrificial victims and ostensibly not the occupation of enemy territory. The ultimate aim, however, was the same as any war: the obliteration of any opposition to Aztec rule and the incorporation of their territory into Aztec territory as a tribute-paying region. This custom may have started as early as 1375, when the Aztecs fought a flower war against Chalco. It survived until 1518 (Thomas 1995: 37).

It is interesting to note that these conflicts took place on a preset date at a preselected place (Hassig 1988: 10). There is reason to believe that these preset locations to engage in flower wars might have been marked by specially carved stones (Plunket and Uruñuela 1994: 439).

Some communities, who had the misfortune of existing along the natural communication routes between the Aztecs and their enemies, had to take the brunt of Aztec warfare on their territory. For example, in the Valley of Atlixco, located to the southeast of the Valley of Mexico, was the venue for many a flower war between the Aztecs and their traditional enemies, the Tlaxcalans (Plunket and Uruñuela 1994: 435).

Seasonality of Warfare and Logistics

Mesoamerican cultures, the Aztecs included, were limited in their capacity to wage war by a number of factors. Some of these, like the agricultural cycle and the advents of the rains, would determine when wars could be fought.

Another factor was distance, which determined whether a conflict could take place, even if the weather and the harvest cycles were propitious. Logistical concerns could nix any desire to wage war if the distances involved were too great.

In the highlands, the cultivation and harvesting cycles took up most of the spring and late summer/early fall. The heavy rains would last from May to September. The timing of these two factors resulted in large-scale warfare being conducted mainly from the late fall through early spring (Hassig 1988: 53–54). It should be noted that small-scale conflicts, such as raids and flower wars, could take place at any time. The Aztecs' ability to engage in long-lasting campaigns at great marching distances away from the Basin of Mexico was severely limited by their ability to provision those troops. Food was an essential item in this regard. Because the Aztecs relied on porters to carry the food that the army would consume, one could almost calculate to the day when an army that had left Tenochtitlan would be forced to stop its progress, having run through all its supplies.

We know that the Aztec employed an additional tactic to enable the troops to extend their reach. Messengers would be sent out, well ahead of the army columns, to request that local communities prove their loyalty to the Aztec emperor by providing supplies for the approaching army. Those that refused to do so clearly opened themselves up to attack, so very few ever did. In addition, the construction of royal granaries throughout the realm enabled the army to conserve its supplies by accessing locally available reserves first (Hassig 1993: 97). The types of specific supplies that were requested are related by a colonial source (Hodge 1996: 25):

> *Motecuhzuma and Tlacael then began to prepare their men for war, and sent messengers to the neighboring cities to obtain great quantities of toasted maize cakes, toasted grains of corn, and maize flour. They also obtained great quantities of bean flour, salt, and chili, pumpkin seeds, together with pots, plates, grinding stones, and mats in order to make tents and huts in the field.*

Finally, the Aztecs were expert in shifting the burden of logistics away from themselves and onto the shoulders of their allies. The messengers sent out ahead of the Aztec army, as it set out from Tenochtitlan, would not only request that supplies be made available, but also that the allies ready their own armed men to join the Aztec army when it marched through. In doing so, it was not necessary to carry provisions for the entire army. Because some of them joined along the way, the army grew in size slowly, and its supplies came from a combination of sources, including local ones (Hassig 1993: 99).

The Aztecs were well aware of the importance of logistics. Whenever an army took to the field, two high-ranking military officials would remain in the capital. Their job was to send supplies and reinforcements, if necessary (Hassig 1988: 58).

Aside from nature dictating when wars could be fought, the supernatural also played an important role. Just like the Romans, who would sacrifice an animal and have a soothsayer predict the future by reading the entrails of the animal, the Aztecs also consulted soothsayers when they wanted to go to war. Moreover, once a campaign was started, Aztec priests kept a vigilant eye on supernatural signs that might announce a change in fortune. We know, for example, that during a campaign against Tlaxcala, Huexotzinco, and Atlixco, astrologers of the Triple Alliance sent word to the emperor to cease fighting. The emperor heeded the admonition and stopped his advance (Hassig 1988: 9).

Army Composition and Size

Both nobility and commoners made up the army ranks. Among the commoners, it was the macehualtin class who provided most of the muscle. Other commoners' ranks, such as the artisans and the middle class, were not as heavily affected by military requirements (Hassig 1993: 94).

Because the macehualtin made up the bulk of army, it should be no surprise that the basic army units were based on the calpulli, or wards (Hassig 1993: 95). In case a city had more than one calpulli, the army units leaving for war would march off under the leadership of one officer, a tlahtoani. Even though sources are lacking in this regard, it is generally assumed that the army was organized in units of 8,000 men (called *xiquipilli*). These units would be called up until an army had been constituted that was deemed to be large enough to deal with the enemy. In some cases, like the war between Tenochtitlan and Coaixtlahuacan, 200,000 warriors were sent into the field (Hassig 1988: 56).

There would be numerous smaller units within each *xiquipilli*. Most of these would have a mix of experienced warriors and new recruits. The veterans were placed among these newcomers. They watched over the well-being of their less-experienced comrades in arms, and would only intervene when a veteran enemy warrior threatened them (Hassig 1988: 56).

Aztec Battle Order

How did the Aztec army engage in battle? How did they fight? Regardless of the type of warfare they had in mind, Aztec armies and their opponents would apply the following tactics.

Opposing forces would approach each other until they were well in range of the archers and slingers. According to descriptions, the lines would converge on each other until they were 50–60 m apart. At that point, the archers and slingers would unleash volleys of arrows and pebbles. This initial barrage was intended to cause maximum disruption in the opposite ranks. It never lasted very long, since an archer would deplete his arrow supply in probably 3 minutes. A slinger probably went through his supplies of projectiles even faster.

Once the long-range projectiles had been fired, the battle formations would close in until they reached the range of *atlatl* darts, and another volley of projectiles was sent off. That episode would not have lasted very long either. Archers were extremely vulnerable during these initial hostilities. Because they were using both hands to fire, they could not protect themselves with a shield. There are a few reports of shieldmen protecting the archers against incoming projectiles (Hassig 1988: 98).

Once the troops came in reach of each others shock weapons, the archers and slingers withdrew to the rear. They were too vulnerable to participate in the fight. As is true in many preindustrial societies, when the first clash occurred, armies would employ their elite warriors, usually characters who would refuse to leave the battlefield. They would either have to be killed or else kill everyone else before they would withdraw. This was true with the Aztecs. The Aztec equivalent of these troops were called the *cuahchic* warriors. They fought in pairs and swore never to retreat, not even in the face of overwhelming odds (Hassig 1988: 100).

These *cuahchiqueh* warriors would be followed by additional troops, arraigned on the battlefield according to their experience, with the most experienced troops committed to battle first. Young warriors who had never been tested in battle formed the rear. They had veteran warriors in their ranks to teach them and watch over them.

Battle tactics varied, but Mesoamerican armies generally tried to present a solid front, deep enough to prevent the enemy from breaking through the ranks. Aztecs would achieve victory by breaching the enemy's center, by turning an enemy flank, or through double envelopment (Pohl and McBride 1991: 10). These kinds of battlefield maneuvers depended on an ability to communicate troop movements effectively in the heat of battle. Timing and coordination in these movements was pursued through the use of conch shells and drums. The brightly colored and highly visible outfits worn by elite warriors and unit commanders provided very visible beacons for the other troops to follow. This combination of signals, both audible and visible, contributed to Aztec success over their opponents. (The elaborate racks worn by elite warriors, however, also impeded their mobility and made them obvious targets.)

Hand-to-hand combat occurred only between frontline troops. Because the Aztecs tended to have numerical superiority on the battlefield, they used this to their advantage by extending the battle line as much as possible, thus forcing their opponents to do the same. This tactic forced the enemy's line to become very thin, and thus easier to breach (Hassig 1988: 101). Because hand-to-hand combat was very exhausting, troops were said to have been rotated on 15-minute intervals (Pohl and McBride 1991: 12). If this is true, then the Aztecs possessed an unknown means of calculating time with that precision (Hassig 2001: 32).

The Aztecs had a few tricks that they employed. They were very cunning in drawing their opponents into ambushes. This would sometimes involve feigning a retreat, thus enticing pursuit by the enemy into a new location where additional Aztec troops lay in waiting. One ruse stands out: during a campaign against Tehuantepec, emperor Axayacatl drew his enemy into an area where his troops were hidden in foxholes. The Aztecs jumped out and ambushed the Tehuantepec warriors, totally annihilating them (Hassig 1988: 103). The same emperor and some of his generals once hid in foxholes themselves, during hostilities with the people of Toluca. While they were in hiding, they allowed the Tolucan army to march by. The emperor and his generals then jumped out and attacked and killed the Tolucan lords. The ensuing confusion led to the disintegration and rout of the Tolucans. The Aztecs were fully aware that "neutraliz-ing" the opposing leadership could mean shortening of the war and ultimate victory (Hassig 1988: 103).

Another tactic employed by the Aztec was to envelop the enemy almost completely while leaving one route open for them to flee. This tactic allowed the Aztecs to induce panic among the fleeing enemy. This approach was pre-ferred over completely cutting off an enemy because in that case, the oppo-nents would face annihilation and fight with extreme determination (Pohl and McBride 1991: 13).

Reinforcements were introduced on a regular basis. This seems to have been a general practice by most Mesoamerican armies. The Aztecs had a policy by which they left behind two generals in the capital. Their duty was to send rein-forcements when needed. Such a provision would be most effective in case the hostilities occurred very close to Tenochtitlan for the reinforcements to make a difference on the battlefield. We know of one instance, however, in which rein-forcements were sent from the capital after 20 days of combat (Hassig 1988: 105).

CESSATION OF HOSTILITIES

Fighting could end in many ways. One of the warring sides might break off the engagement and withdraw. An army, realizing that defeat was imminent, sometimes might lay down its arms. If combat entailed attacking a city, the fighting would usually end by burning the temple. Looting usually ensued as one way to compensate the victorious army (Hassig 1988: 107–113).

In the case of hostilities involving a city, the destruction of a temple was suf-ficient to put an end to all armed resistance on the part of the defenders. We find references to this custom in the various codices that deal with the subject of conquest. In the Codex Mendoza, for example, on the well-known first page of the document, there are two place glyphs with an associated representation of a temple. The roof of the temple is tipped in both cases, and scrolls repre-senting smoke can be seen escaping from the building. This imagery is clear to all, even non-Nahuatl speakers: these two communities have been conquered (Carrasco 1999: 25).

If an Aztec army had been defeated, news of this event was usually accom-panied by the priests of all the temples weeping over the lost souls. The sur-viving warriors would also enter the city while weeping. They would proceed to the temple of Huitzilopochtli, they would speak to the emperor, and then burn their weapons and insignia. A victorious Aztec army awaited a different reception. The access roads into the city would be lined with well wishers. People would play drums and trumpets, and food and gifts would be sent to the capital. Those who had captured enemy warriors would be honored. The families of those who had died received gifts as well. Social rank determined the nature of these gifts: families of slain commoner-rank warriors received clothing, whereas the relatives of noblemen who had died would also be given jewels and feather work (Hassig 1988: 118). If hostilities had taken place close enough to the capital, then the bodies of the slain warriors would be brought home. Most of them would be cremated, although some of the commoners might be buried with their insignia (Hassig 1988: 118).

REFERENCES

Armillas, Pedro. 1951. Mesoamerican Fortifications. *Antiquity* 25: 77–86.

Berdan, Frances. 1994. Economic Alternatives Under Imperial Rule. The Eastern Aztec Empire. In *Economies and Polities in the Aztec Realm.* Edited by Mary G. Hodge and Michael E. Smith, pp. 291–312. (Studies on Culture and Society, volume 6) Albany: Institute for Mesoamerican Studies.

———. 1996. The Tributary Provinces. In *Aztec Imperial Strategies.* Edited by Frances F. Berdan, Richard E. Blanton, Elizabeth H. Boone, Mary G. Hodge, Michael E. Smith, and Emily Umberger, pp. 115–135. Washington, D.C.: Dumbarton Oaks.

Carrasco, Pedro. 1984. Royal Marriages in Ancient Mexico. In *Explorations in Ethnohistory: Indians of Central Mexico in the Sixteenth Century.* Edited by Herbert R. Harvey and Hanns J. Prem, pp. 41-81. Albuquerque: University of New Mexico Press.

Carrasco, David. 1999. *City of Sacrifice. The Aztec Empire and the Role of Violence in Civilization.* Boston: Beacon Press.

de Durand-Forest, Jacqueline. 1996. Response from Jacqueline de Durand-Forest. *Nahua Newsletter,* November.

Díaz del Castillo, Bernal. 1908–1916. *The True History of the Conquest of New Spain.* Translated by Alfred Percival Maudslay. Five vols. London: Hakluyt Society.

Durán, Diego. 1964. *The Aztecs: The History of the Indies of New Spain.* Translated by D. Heyden and F. Horcasitas. Norman: University of Oklahoma. (Original written in 1581)

Durán, Diego. 1994. *The History of the Indies of New Spain.* Translated by Doris Heyden. Norman: University of Oklahoma Press.

Gorenstein, Shirley. 1966. The Differential Development of New World Empires. *Revista Mexicana de Estudios Antropologicos* XX: 41–67.

———. 1985. *Acambaro: Frontier Settlement on the Trascan-Aztec Border.* Vanderbilt University Publications in Anthropology, No. 32. Nashville: Vanderbilt University.

Hassig, Ross. 1988. *Aztec Warfare. Imperial Expansion and Political Control.* Norman: University of Oklahoma Press.

———. 2001. *Time, History, and Belief in Aztec and Colonial Mexico.* Austin: University of Texas Press.

Isaac, Barry. 1983. Aztec Warfare: Goals and Battlefield Comportment. *Ethnology* XXII, 2: 121–131.

Marcus, Joyce and Gary M. Feinman. 1998. Introduction. In *Archaic States.* Edited by Gary M. Feinman and Joyce Marcus, pp. 3-13. Santa Fe: School of American Research Advanced Seminar Series.

Motolinia, Fray Torribio de Benavente o. 1971. *Memoriales o Libro de las Cosas de la Nueva España y de los Naturales de Ella.* Mexico City: Universidad Nacional Autónoma de México.

Pasztory, Esther. 1998. *Aztec Art.* Norman: University of Oklahoma Press.

Plunket Nagoda, Patricia and Uruñuela, Gabriela. 1994. Impact of the Xochiyaoyotl in Southwestern Puebla. *In Economies and Polities in the Aztec Realm.* Edited by M.

Hodge and M. Smith, pp. 433-446. *Studies on Culture and Society, 6.* Albany: State University of New York at Albany, Institute for Mesoamerican Studies.

Pohl, John. MD., and Angus McBride. 1991. *Aztec, Mixtec and Zapotec Armies.* (Men-at-War Series) Oxford: Osprey Publishing.

Pollard, Helen Perlstein. 1982. Ecological Variation and Economic Exchange in the Tarascan State. *American Ethnologist* 9: 250–268.

Rounds, J. 1982. Dynastic Succession and the Centralization of Power in Tenochtitlan. In *The Inca and Aztec States 1400–1800.* Edited by George A. Collier, Renato I. Rosaldo, and John D. Wirth, pp. 63–89. New York: Academic Press. (Discusses the policy adopted by the Aztecs to guarantee a smooth succession from one emperor to the next. Includes a discussion on the position of *cihuacoatl,* or stand-in for the emperor during the interregnum.)

Smith, Michael E. 1996. The Strategic Provinces. In *Aztec Imperial Strategies.* Edited by Frances F. Berdan, Richard E. Blanton, Elizabeth H. Boone, Mary G. Hodge, Michael E. Smith, and Emily Umberger, pp. 137–150. Washington, D.C.: Dumbarton Oaks.

Smith, Michael E., and Mary G. Hodge. 1994. An Introduction to Late Postclassic Economies and Polities. In *Economies and Polities in the Aztec Realm.* Edited by Mary G. Hodge and Michael E. Smith, pp. 1–42. (Studies on Culture and Society, volume 6) Albany: Institute for Mesoamerican Studies.

Smith, Michael E. 2003c. *The Aztecs,* 2nd Ed. Malden: Blackwell Publishing.

Tezozomoc, Hernando Alvarado. 1878. *Crónica Mexicana.* Bibliotéca Mexicana. Edited by J. M. Vigil, pp. 223–701. Mexico City. (Originally written in 1598)

Thomas, Hugh. 1975. *Conquest. Montezuma, Cortés, and the Fall of Old Mexico.* New York: Simon and Schuster.

Umberger, Emily. 1996. Aztec Presence and Material Remains in the Outer Provinces. In *Aztec Imperial Strategies.* Edited by Frances F. Berdan, Richard E. Blanton, Elizabeth H. Boone, Mary G. Hodge, Michael E. Smith, and Emily Umberger, pp. 151–179. Washington, D.C.: Dumbarton Oaks.

Williams, Barbara J. 1991. The Lands and Political Organization of a Rural Tlaxilacalli in Tepetlaoztoc, c. A.D. 1540. In *Land and Politics in the Valley of Mexico. A Two Thousand Year Perspective.* Edited by H. R. Harvey, pp. 187–208. Albuquerque: University of New Mexico Press.

VIII

CHAPTER 8

Religion and Ideology

THE CONCEPT OF TEOTL

When discussing the topic of religion with regard to a civilization of the past, the term *pantheon* is quite often used. This term, literally meaning "all gods," tends to conjure up images of anthropomorphic gods; that is, supernatural beings who have taken on the shape of a human being. On occasion, such as with Greek or Viking gods, there are more human aspects to them than just their shape. These gods have human as well as supernatural qualities: they quarrel, they fight, they are jealous.

Some of these features are present among the Aztecs, but the anthropomorphic part is not. There is a wide array of difficult-to-define supernatural entities, which we can call gods, or deities. Moreover, what the Aztecs did define was a concept, which they called *teotl*, which referred to a deity or sacred power (Smith 1996: 211).

This chapter will examine a wide array of these Aztec deities, as they have been described, catalogued, and categorized by contemporary scholars. We need to start out, however, by noting that the Aztecs saw binary oppositions in the world around them: hot and cold, wet and dry. This binary aspect is also present in their religious beliefs.

One effort to catalogue and classify Aztec deities listed no fewer than 200 (Nicholson 1971). Nicholson's work has been the standard for subsequent works on the Aztecs (Smith 1996: 213; Townsend 2000: 118–119). He identified three groupings of Aztec deities, with each group having "jurisdiction" over specific aspects of the universe. These three groupings include (Nicholson 1971: Table 3):

- Group I: Gods of celestial creativity and divine paternalism
- Group II: Gods of rain, moisture, and agricultural fertility
- Group III: Gods of war, sacrifice, and blood nourishment of the Sun and Earth

The most important deity was *Ometeotl* because this dual entity was the force that created all the other deities. This duality of character is reflected in that *Ometeotl* was perceived as incorporating both a male and female principle. These were referred to, respectively, as *Ometecuhtli* and *Omecihuatl*. As we shall see later in this chapter, *Ometeotl* was thought to live in the uppermost of the thirteen levels of heaven, underscoring the greatest importance this deity had; however, *Ometeotl* remained a rather abstract notion. We do not know of any formal cult associated with *Ometeotl* (Smith 1996: 214).

TABLE 8.1   The Aztec Gods: a Synopsis

Group ID	Deity's name	Meaning	Principal role(s)
Group I	Ometeotl	Two-God	Creator, parents of gods
	Ometecuhtli Omecihuatl	Two-Lord Two-Lady	
	Tezcatlipoca	Smoking Mirror	Omnipotent (often malevolent) universal power
	Xiuhtecuhtli	Turquoise Lord	Fire, paternalism
Group II	Tlaloc	(Uncertain)	Rain
	Chalchiuhtlicue	Jade her skirt	Water
	Centeotl	Maize cob Lord	Maize
	Xochipilli	Flower Prince	Solar warmth, flowers, feasting, pleasure
	Ometochtli	Two-Rabbit	Fertility
	Teteoinnan	Mother of Gods	Patroness of curers, midwives
	Xipe Totec	Our Lord with the flayed skin	Agricultural fertility, patron of the goldsmiths
Group III	Tonatiuh	Sun	Sun
	Huitzilopochtli	Hummingbird left	War, sacrifice, patron of the Mexica
	Mixcoatl	Cloud serpent	War, sacrifice, hunting
	Mictlantecuhtli	Lord of Mictlan	Death, underworld, darkness
Other deities	Quetzalcoatl	Quetzal Feathered Serpent	Creativity, fertility, Venus, patron of priesthood
	Yacatecuhtli	Nose Lord	Commerce, patron of merchants

SOURCE: Nicholson 1971: Table 3

Tezcatlipoca struck fear and trepidation into the hearts of the Aztecs. He could see anything that took place in the world. Any wrongdoers would soon experience *Tezcatlipoca's* wrath through his darts. It should not surprise us that a deity with these traits was the patron god of kings (Smith 1996: 214–215).

A panel from the Codex Fejervary-Mayer showing the god Tezcatlipoca. (Werner Forman/Corbis)

Sacred fires were maintained in temples throughout the empire. *Xiuhtecuhtli* was the patron of fire and life. One of his manifestations was *Huehueteotl*, "the Old God," whose domain included the domestic fires (Smith 1996: 215).

Tlaloc, the rain god, can be traced back to Teotihuacan. He was seen as the purveyor of nourishing rains that helped the crops grow, especially maize (Smith 1996: 215). *Centeotl*, the maize god, was closely associated with *Tlaloc*. Because maize was one of the staple foods in Mesoamerica, this deity figured prominently on the minds of the Aztecs (Smith 1996: 215).

Ometochtli was perhaps equally important, at least to some Aztecs. *Ometochtli*, Two Rabbit, was a deity whose domain included the alcoholic beverage *pulque* (Smith 1996: 215). *Teteoinnan* encompassed various earth deities associated with agricultural and sexual fertility. A well-known goddess in this group was *Xochiquetzal*, or Flower-Quetzal Feather. She stood for sexual desire, flowers, feasting, and pleasure (Smith 1996: 215–216). A related goddess in this regard

Representation of the head of Tlaloc, the goggle-eyed rain god. (Danny Lehman/Corbis)

was *Tlazolteotl,* goddess of, among other things, childbirth (Smith 1996: 216–217).

One of the recurring images that most people have about the Aztec is their predilection for human sacrifice. The deity of sacrifice wears the appropriate title of *Xipe Totec,* or "our lord with the flayed skin." This title refers to the custom priests had to wear the skin of a sacrificial victim, once it had been removed from the unlucky individual (Smith 1996: 217).

There was a direct link between human sacrifice, bloodletting, and warfare. The Aztecs believed that some deities needed to be nourished with blood,

Image from the Codex Borbonicus depicting the gods Quetzalcóatl and Tezcatlipoca. (Bill White/Instructional Resources Corp.)

either through human sacrifice or through self-sacrifice. The sun god, *Tonatiuh*, was one of the gods who needed blood sacrifice. *Tonatiuh* had both a benevolent and a malevolent aspect. As sun god, he was a creative god, providing warmth and fertility to make the crops grow. On the other hand, *Tonatiuh* was also the patron of warriors, whose duty it was to capture as many victims as possible to sacrifice in honor of their god. Another deity who required an endless supply of sacrificial victims was *Huitzilopchtli*. The Earth Lord, or *Mictlantecuhtli*, was among the most feared of all, being associated with death and the underworld (Smith 1996: 218–219).

Finally, the Feathered Serpent, *Quetzalcoatl*, is probably the best-known Aztec deity. His job description included many fields: creator, affiliations with the wind god, *Ehecatl*, and rain god, *Tlaloc*. As patron of the elite *calmecac* schools, *Quetzalcoatl* was a god of learning and knowledge (Smith 1996: 219).

The Aztecs had a well-developed religious system that incorporated a multitude of deities in all their aspects. It was a system that was taught in various degrees in the school systems, and one with which the Aztecs probably felt very comfortable. This latter feeling rose to the surface in a discourse that was held by Aztec priests in 1524. Their intended audience was made up of

Spanish Friars, who had already worked very hard to relegate Aztec religion to the past; however, they are also addressing us. Through the writings of Sahagún, we can partake in this final frank expression of Aztec religious beliefs by its practitioners, the *tlamatinime,* or wise men (León-Portilla 1990: 63–67). While acknowledging defeat, the wise men chided the Spanish for imposing their own religious beliefs. After reviewing the origins of their own religious beliefs, the wise men continued to admonish the Spanish, stating, "We cannot be tranquil, and yet we certainly do not believe; we do not accept your teachings as the truth, even though this may offend you."

AZTEC CREATION STORIES

Aztecs believed that the world had gone through four incarnations, and they were living in a fifth one. Each of these incarnations of the world they referred to as "suns," a stage in which the world was inhabited by a different race of people and ruled by different gods. Each of these worlds was characterized by a symbol that also presaged the way in which that world would come to an end.

The beginning of the world, the first sun, was presided over by *Tezcatlipoca.* The world then was inhabited by a race of giants. The end came when these giants were devoured by jaguars. *Quetzalcoatl* ruled over the second sun, or creation. This time around, the world's population was made up of humans who ate acorns. Hurricanes destroyed this world: water rose and those people who survived by rushing into trees were transformed into monkeys. The third sun saw a world dominated by water. It should not come as a surprise, then, that the overseeing deity was *Tlaloc.* He ruled over a race of people who ate aquatic seeds. *Tlaloc's* sun came to an end through fiery rain. The aquatic seed-eating people were replaced with dogs, turkeys, and butterflies. The fourth sun was ruled by *Chalchiuthtlicue.* The earth's inhabitants were people who ate wild seeds. A great flood brought that creation to an end, as all people were transformed into fish.

That brings us to the Aztec world, the fifth sun, in which they lived, and in which we also live. *Tonatiuh,* the sun god, is the ruling deity. The earth is populated with maize eaters. The sign for this world is *Ollin,* or movement. It predicts that this world too will come to an end, very likely through earthquakes ("movement") (Smith 1996: 205).

BELIEF IN HEAVENS AND UNDERWORLD

The Aztecs accepted that the universe was divided into three planes, one of them being the heavens, one the world in which we live, and finally the underworld. These three planes were connected to each other through a nexus, a central axis, or navel.

The Aztecs believed in thirteen heavens, all separated from one another by what we could conceive of as floors, or passages between heavens. Various Nahuatl documents relate how these thirteen heavens were stacked on top of each other (León-Portilla 1990: 49).

The lowest heaven, the one that we all can see, is the heaven through which the moon travels and from which the clouds are suspended. The second heaven, *Citalco,* was the place of the stars. The stars were thought of as a luminous skirt wrapped around the feminine aspect of *Ometeotl.* They were divided into two groups: "four hundred" (Aztec parlance for "countless") stars of the North and "four hundred" stars of the South (León-Portilla 1990: 49–50). The third level of the heavens was called *Ilhuicatl Tonatiuh,* or the Heaven of the Sun. This was the heaven through which the sun traveled on its daily trek from east to west. The fourth heaven was the realm of Venus, and was called *Ilhuicatl huitzlan* (León-Portilla 1990: 51). The fifth heaven was home to the comets. According to some traditions, only the colors green and blue could be seen in the sixth and seventh heavens. Other versions relate how only black and blue could be seen in those two levels, possibly referring to night and day. The eighth heaven was associated with storms. The three subsequent heavens each had a color assigned to them: white, yellow, and red. The gods resided in these levels. Levels twelve and thirteen were the most important. They constituted *Omeyocan,* the place of duality and the primordial dwelling place of *Ometeotl* (León-Portilla 1990: 52).

The underworld consisted of nine different levels, the lowest of which was known as Mictlan. In one of the early colonial Aztec codices, the so-called Ríos Codex, an entire section is devoted to the fate of those who descend into Mictlan (León-Portilla 2002: 65). A series of trials awaited the dead in Mictlan. They lasted 4 years, and only then could complete rest be attained (León-Portilla 1990: 59).

The world in which we all live, Tlalticpac, was seen as a great disk located in the center of the universe. This earth was surrounded by an immense body of water, *teo-atl,* which merges with the surrounding celestial water where they both meet on the horizon. Because of this configuration, the Aztecs referred to our physical world as *"cemanahuac,"* or "that which is entirely surrounded by water" (León-Portilla 1990: 57).

The Aztec believed that upon death, body and soul would separate. Whereas the body or ashes would remain in the earth, the soul, or *teyolia,* would travel to the place intended for it (Matos Moctezuma 1995: 30). Depending on the nature of the death and the kind of burial given to an individual, his or her soul could go to three distinct places.

The souls of those people who had met their death in the battlefield, or as the result of being sacrifices, as well as women who had died in childbirth, were destined to go to the house of the sun. There, the souls of the warriors would accompany the sun across the sky from sunrise until noon. The souls of women who had died in childbirth would then take over and continue traveling with the sun until sunset. The souls of the warriors would eventually enter life after death. The Aztecs believed that these warriors' souls would be transformed into beautiful birds after 4 years (Matos Moctezuma 1995: 30).

A second destination was conceived as a place that was always green, with plants and fruits, a place where it was always summer. This was known as Tlalocan, a place associated with the god *Tlaloc.* The souls of those whose death was somehow related to water would end up here (Matos Moctezuma 1995: 31).

A third and final place was known as Mictlan. This was the destination for the souls of those who had died a natural death; however, before they would reach Mictlan, the souls would have to cross a series of obstacles. These included, according to Sahagún, two colliding mountains, a path guarded by a snake, a place of the green lizard, eight cold and windy plains and eight hills, a place with extremely cold wind, and a place where the river Chicunauhapan was crossed before arriving in Mictlan (Matos Moctezuma 1995: 31). This was the place where the gods of death, *Mictlantecuhtli* and *Mictecacihuatl,* lived (Matos Moctezuma 2003: 34).

CONFESSION

When the Spanish set out to convert people, they were very confused by the realization that the notion of confession for past sins already existed among Precolumbian people, including the Aztecs.

There are two interesting aspects pertaining to the act of confession. Prehispanic people believed in confessing sins, and that once a confession was made regarding a past sin, then all would be forgiven. They also believed, however, that if the same sins were repeated, forgiveness would no longer be available (Bandelier 1932: 32). As a result, Sahagún informs us that "confessions of great sins, such as adultery, were only made by old men" (Bandelier 1932: 32). He adds, "It is said that the old men confessed their great sins of the flesh from which fact we may deduce that they probably had greatly sinned in their youth but did not confess until they were old, but that they would continue sinning while young, for it was their belief that once confessed they could not sin again" (Bandelier 1932: 33).

SACRIFICE

Even though the Aztecs might just as well be characterized as accomplished architects and creative poets, it is human sacrifice that is their legacy today. Most people probably have never heard of Aztec poetry, but they are certainly eager to learn more about human blood being spilled. It is ironic that the Spanish heavily emphasized the brutality of Aztec religion, yet the impact of the arrival of Europeans caused the death of a much greater number of indigenous people than any of the previous egregious acts on the part of any of the local civilizations (Arnold 1999: xvii).

Types of Sacrifice

We can distinguish between two categories of sacrifice: those that involved humans and those that did not. The most common animal sacrifice was the decapitation of quail (Carrasco 1999: 83).

The Aztecs also spilled both their own blood through self-sacrifice and that of others through human sacrifice. Self-sacrifice involved using sharp maguey spines as needles to pierce various body parts, such as ears, tongue, arms, thighs, chest, and even genitals.

Priests typically engaged in this type of bloodletting. They would bathe and purify themselves. Then, at night, they would burn incense and carry out the sacrifice in a secluded spot. Through Sahagún we know of four kinds of self-sacrifice: "the drawing of straws," "the offering of thorns," "the bloodying," and "the cutting of the ears" (Smith 1996: 221).

Human sacrifice usually meant heart sacrifice. It was performed by a special group of priests, known as the *Tlenamacac,* or "fire priests." Human sacrifice took on many forms. The sacrificial victims were carefully chosen to conform to the requirements of the god to whom they would be sacrificed.

Most often, captured warriors would be sacrificed. Some gods apparently were content with slaves. Others required women or children to be killed. In all cases, the sacrificial victim would take on the persona of the god to whom he or she would be sacrificed, a concept referred to as *ixiptla.* Preparations for a sacrifice would very often take a long time, up to 1 year. During that time period the *ixiptla* would be housed, fed, and dressed. Those in contact with this person would treat him or her as the representative of the god to whom they would be sacrificed.

When the day of sacrifice was at hand, there would be special ceremonies and activities. These included fasting, dancing, and music making. For example, during the festival of *Panquetzaliztli,* victims were asked to sing and dance the night before their sacrifice. The dance they engaged in was that of the serpent. The slaves sacrificed at this festival were obtained in the market at Azcapotzalco, close to Tenochtitlan. The sacrificial victims were selected to "be without blemish of body and free of disease of any kind" (Bandelier 1932: 43). After they had been purchased, the slaves would be bathed and given an abundance of food. Their ultimate destiny was not only to be sacrificed, but also to be eaten (Bandelier 1932: 43). The dancing and music making served to make the victims tired, although Sahagún was careful to point out that "they did in no way fear or mind the sort of death awaiting them" (Bandelier 1932: 43).

There occasionally were ways to escape being sacrificed. For example, if a slave appeared to be a good prospect as a servant (i.e., someone "quick and intelligent in serving"), or if a female slave was willing and able to prepare food and drink, then they could be bought by the elite and thus avoid being killed (Bandelier 1932: 43).

At the festival of Xilonen, during the eighth month of the year, a woman was sacrificed. The preceding night men and women would stay up all night singing hymns to the goddess. Nobody closed their eyes. At daybreak they would start dancing (Duverger 1993: 119–120). Offerings were made to *Tlaloc,* the god of rain, on the first day of the month: Atl Cahualo. Children, selected for favorable signs (e.g., having two cowlicks in their hair and with the correct day signs), were dressed in dark green, black striped with chili red and light blue. They were sacrificed in seven different locations. The Aztecs believed that the children's tears would ensure rain (Carrasco 1999: 85).

Rank was important as well: the higher the rank of a captive warrior, for example, the greater the honor to his captor (Smith 1996: 224).

Most sacrifices would take place on top of the pyramid. Sahagún described a heart sacrifice (Smith 1996: 222–223):

> *Thus was performed the sacrificial slaying of men, when captives and slaves died, who were called "those who have died for the god."*
>
> *Thus they took [the captive] up [to the pyramid temple] before the devil, [the priests] going holding him by his hands. And he who was known as the arranger [of captives], this one laid him out upon the sacrificial stone.*
>
> *And when he had laid him upon it, four men stretched him out, [grasping] his arms and legs. And already in the hand of the fire priests lay the [sacrificial] knife, with which he was to slash open the breast of the ceremonially bathed [captive].*
>
> *And then, when he had split open his breast, he at once seized his heart. And he whose breast he laid open was quite alive. And when [the priest] had seized his heart, he dedicated it to the sun.*

After the heart was removed, the body of the victim was rolled down the steps of the pyramid. A priest cut off the head and placed it on a *tzompantli,* or skull rack, next to the pyramid.

Not all human sacrifices took place on top of the pyramid. The god *Xipe Totec* required specific ceremonies during which victims were to be sacrificed. Two such ceremonies are known. In some cases, an exceptionally brave captured warrior would be tied to a large circular stone. He would be issued a sword, whose obsidian blades had been replaced with feathers, and then forced to engage in combat with a warrior who did have real weaponry. The outcome was predictable. In another form of sacrifice, a victim would be tied by hands and legs to a wooden frame and then killed with arrows (Smith 1996: 225).

Although Sahagún's informants claimed that the sacrificial victims climbed the steps of the pyramids with dignity and pride (Smith 1996: 225), there is reason to believe that the Aztecs resorted to means other than tradition to make sure that victims went "willingly" to their death. For example, the fact that the victims were kept awake up to 4 days before the sacrifice by means of music and dance must have made them exhausted. In addition, the sacrificial victims were given *teooctli* to drink, an inebriating concoction that must have clouded their perception of reality even more. The same effect was obtained by making these people inhale the fumes of aromatic herbs and perfumes. If you add to all this the requirement that they danced and sang, it is easy to see how sacrificial victims might have gone up the stairs without fully realizing what was about to happen (Duverger 1993: 120).

Explanation of Aztec Sacrifice

Human sacrifice served several purposes. The Aztecs shared with other Mesoamerican peoples the belief that sacrifice to the gods was necessary to ensure the continued existence of the universe. Even though Aztec onlookers must have felt chills going up their spines as they watched people being sacri-

Aztec heart sacrifice as shown in the Florentine Codex. (Bettmann/Corbis)

A stone representation of the Tzompantli or skull rack. This Tzompantli was found during excavations in the Templo Mayor Precinct in Tenochtitlan/Mexico City. (Keith Dannemiller/Corbis)

ficed, it was also very likely that in their minds they had come to terms with it. Without these gruesome ceremonies, they feared an even greater evil: the end of the world as they knew it.

The Aztecs stand out in that we know they practiced human sacrifice quite often. Either Aztec gods were insatiable in their thirst for human blood, or these sacrifices also played another role. Modern scholars of Aztec religion are convinced that the frequency with which these sacrifices occurred had the additional aspect of propaganda. Those intended to receive the message were both Aztec citizens and foreign leaders. The message to them was simple: don't mess with Aztec rule. Enemy rulers would occasionally be invited to attend important ceremonies in the capital. There, these rulers would be witness to the sacrifice of countless human beings, including their own captured warriors. The skull rack adjacent to the pyramids served as a more permanent reminder of the awesome power of the Aztecs (Smith 1996: 226–227).

The chronicler Durán relates how these visits to the capital by foreign and sometimes enemy rulers were organized by the Aztecs (Carrasco 1999: 81):

> *This was done so those lords might secretly enter the city of Tenochtitlan together and to give them certain instructions so they would not be recognized . . . Their customary garments*

were changed in favor of those of the Aztecs and, in order to disguise them further, they were made to hold flowers, branches, and rushes, as though they were men who were coming to adorn the temple and the royal house [. . .] All the lords from the provinces and all the enemies were watching from within bowers that had been built for this occasion. Prisoners from the lines began to mount the steps [of the Great Temple] and the four lords, assisted by the priest who held the wretches about to die by their feet and hands, began to kill.

One theory about Aztec sacrifice belongs to the realm of the fantasy. It entails the notion that the Aztecs engaged in human sacrifice because they were cannibals. This will be discussed in Chapter 11.

POLITICS AND RELIGION

There was a very tight link between religion and politics. The Aztecs did not practice separation of church and state. The Aztec emperors were important political and religious leaders. This linkage becomes clear when we consider some of the evidence excavated in the heart of Mexico City since 1978.

The Archaeology of Religion and Ideology

The Sacred Precinct in Tenochtitlan

Templo Mayor Excavations. As mentioned in Chapter 3, there has been substantial archaeological research conducted inside the boundaries of the Ceremonial Precinct. A period of very intense excavations lasted from 1978 through 1982. These investigations have been continued ever since. As a result of this work, there "is more written, pictorial, and archaeological evidence about the Templo Mayor than about any other single building in Mesoamerica" (Carrasco 1999: 241, n. 14).

The construction of twin temples, rather than a single temple, on top of the main pyramid in the Sacred Precinct is considered to be an Aztec innovation. More important, the presence of a temple dedicated to *Tlaloc* indicates an Aztec preoccupation to legitimize their rule and their history through the incorporation of well-known symbols from earlier civilizations. *Tlaloc* is one of these symbols.

Tlaloc was part of the great pre-Aztec civilizations in Central Mexico. According to Aztec tradition, *Tlaloc* had also been the one who had given the Aztecs permission to settle in the lake area. By adopting *Tlaloc* into their belief system, the Aztecs were making both a religious statement and a political one. In the temple of *Tlaloc* we can see a religious symbol that also validated their political hold on the region (Carrasco 1999: 71–72).

We know that the Sacred Precinct was the center of the Aztec world, both in terms of politics and religion. This will be elaborated on more fully in Chapter 9. The Sacred Precinct also presents us with another dichotomy: the incredible architecture formed the backdrop for gruesome ceremonies, not the least of which was human sacrifice. We seem here to be facing a seemingly unexplainable juxtaposition of creative and destructive forces. The Aztecs were great builders and they excelled in the arts, and yet they were also engaged in bloody rituals at very regular intervals. How can one explain this coexistence of this two opposite ends of human behavior?

Modern scholars have argued that the Sacred Precinct represented the way in which the Aztec saw their world. The layout of this inner sanctum in the center of their capital reflected their interpretation of how things had come to be. The Templo Mayor, through its size and quality of construction, affirmed to the Aztecs that they were the center of the universe; the bloody rituals that took place on top of the pyramid platform also served to impress upon all the spectators, especially those from the peripheries of the empire and beyond, that the Aztecs were to be feared (Carrasco 1999: 51–53).

Religious Architecture in the Hinterlands

Because our knowledge of rural sites is still rather limited compared with what we know of larger Aztec cities, our understanding of these smaller communities is limited as well. Still, investigations carried out at the site of Cuexcomate (Morelos) has revealed the presence of a small temple. At the site of Calixtlahuaca, located north of Toluca in the modern state of Mexico, there is a circular temple. Temples of this shape are said to be dedicated to *Ehecatl*, god of the wind (Smith et al. 2003c: 39).

Domestic Rituals

A little-known aspect of Aztec culture, as indeed with most other Mesoamerican cultures as well, pertains to domestic rituals. When we approach this topic from an archaeologist's point of view, what would the material evidence be for domestic rituals? One could imagine small altars, statues of deities, evidence of incense burners, and perhaps mural paintings displaying religious iconography. An abundance of clay figurines found in excavations is traditionally linked to such kinds of rituals.

AZTEC RELIGIOUS CEREMONIES

Monthly Ceremonies

The Aztec calendar had 18 months of 20 days each. A particular ceremony was celebrated during each of these months. Most of the ceremonies pertained to agricultural fertility. Food production was then, as it is now, of utmost importance. Two early colonial chroniclers, Durán and Sahagún, left descriptions of the ceremonies that took place during each of these Aztec months.

The month of Toxcatl coincided with the height of the dry season (May 4–24). Farmers were anxious to ensure that rain would return to assure a bountiful crop. Because of this concern, the ceremonies during Toxcatl were dedicated to the god *Tezcatlipoca*. As we saw earlier in this chapter, a victim would be selected and prepared to be sacrificed up to 1 year before the ceremony. This victim would take on the persona of the god, and would be referred to as an *ixiptla*. In this case, the *ixiptla* of *Tezcatlipoca* had to be a young man of physical perfection, as described by Sahagún (Smith 1996: 236):

For he who was chosen was of fair countenance, of good understanding and quick, of clean body—slender like a reed; long and thin like a stout cane; well built.

This *ixiptla* received training in flute playing, speech, and flower carrying. He was given an entourage, including the company of four women, and they would roam the streets of the capital for 1 year. The women were treated as goddesses, the *ixiptla* as the symbol for *Tezcatlipoca*. When the *ixiptla* was eventually sacrificed, that moment was considered the symbolic end to the dry season (Smith 1996: 237).

During the month of Panquetzaliztli, a foot race was held in the capital. This race, called Ipaina Huitzilopochtli, or the swiftness of *Huitzilopochtli*, was intended to celebrate the pursuit of the 400 gods by *Huitzilopochtli* (Carrasco 1999: 64–65). The sacrificial victims who climbed the stairs to be killed were symbolic of these 400 gods who attempted to kill the Mother of all Gods.

The New Fire Ceremony

Every 52-year period something astonishing happened throughout the entire Aztec empire. All fires would be extinguished and one new fire would be kindled by Aztec priests on Citlaltepec mountain close to Tenochtitlan. This is the traditional view of what transpired in the Aztec timekeeping traditions. The idea that this ceremony traditionally always took place on Citlaltepec mountain is under review. Hassig (2001: 45–46) argues that this hill may have been the location for the New Fire ceremony only once in Aztec history. Aztec manuscripts refer to eight New Fire ceremonies throughout Aztec history: 1143, 1195, 1247, 1299, 1351, 1403, 1455, and 1507. Tenochtitlan's control over the mountain was not complete until the very last New Fire ceremony, that of 1507. Previous ceremonies were thought to have taken place in Tenochtitlan (Hassig 2001: 47). The first four of these ceremonies took place before the city existed, so the location of the New Fire ceremonies held in 1143, 1195, 1247, and 1299 is completely unknown.

This 52-year period resulted of the combination of the 260-day ritual calendar with the 365-day annual calendar. That produced a calendar cycle of 18,980 days, or 52 years. The end of each of these 52-year calendar cycles was of great importance to the Aztecs. As described earlier, in their cosmovision, there had been four creations, or "suns." Each of these four creations had come to a violent end on the last day of this 52-year cycle. It stands to reason, then, that the Aztecs approached the end of such a 52-year cycle with great apprehension.

In preparation for the end of their creation, the fifth sun, the Aztecs embarked on a thorough housecleaning. All household idols were discarded; cooking implements, clothing, and mats were thrown out. The house itself and the adjacent yard were swept. Word went out during the last 5 days of the 52-year cycle to extinguish all fires. Women would close up granaries to prevent them from being transformed into fiery beasts that would devour all human beings. Pregnant women donned masks made out of maguey leaves, and parents kept their children awake for fear that they would be turned into mice

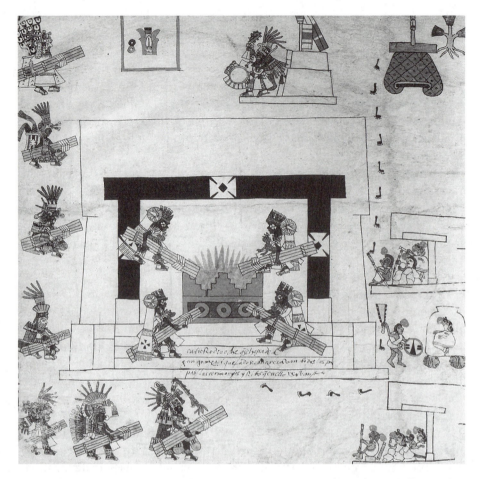

Early colonial representation of the New Fire ceremony. (Biblitheque de L'Assemblee Nationale, Paris, France/Foto Marburg/Art Resource/NY)

(Carrasco 1999: 96). People climbed up on the roof of their houses and awaited the possible end of their world (Smith 1996: 238).

On the last day of the 52-year cycle, after sunset, Aztec priests accompanied a sacrificial victim to Citlaltepec mountain near the capital. From the top of this mountain they would observe a star constellation they called Tianquiztli, or Marketplace. We know it as the Pleiades constellation (Carrasco 1999: 97). If they saw it crossing the zenith (as it had done in previous cycles), then the priests knew that the creation would last at least another cycle of 52 years. They had to perform one more important ceremony: they had to kindle a fire with a fire drill that was placed on the chest of the sacrificial victim. This was a moment of great tension (Smith 1996: 238):

> *All were frightened and filled with dread [. . .] It was claimed that if fire could not be drawn, then the [sun] would be destroyed forever; all would be ended; there would evermore be night.*

Once the fire was started, the victim was killed, and his heart thrown into the new fire. This new fire was built up to be large enough so as to be visible from the neighboring mountains (Carrasco 1999: 101). From that mountain location the new fire was then transported to the temple of *Huitzilopochtli* in the capital (Carrasco 2003: 134–135). There, it was placed in the fire holder of the statue of the god. In a scene that must have resembled the passing of the Olympic torch, runners carried torches to bring the new fire to every community in the realm. As the fires were lit in the temples, people would come and get new embers to start their own fires at home. A new cycle had started, the creation was safe for another 52 years, and "all were quieted in their hearts (Carrasco 2003: 135).

This New Fire ceremony was also called Toxiuhmolpillia, or "Binding of the Years." It is said that this ceremony started under emperor Moctecuhzuma. He issued an order to find among the captive warriors an individual whose name included the term *xihuitl,* meaning turquoise, grass, or comet, a symbolic name connoting precious time (Carrasco 2003: 135).

Michael Smith and his team excavated a ritual dump of pottery and other household goods at the rural community of Cuexcomate (Smith 1992). There they found two shallow pits in residential courtyards. They contained sherds of pottery vessels. The pits were capped with a layer of rocks. The archaeologists were able to reconstruct the pots from the sherds they recovered. In other words, these were very likely pots broken on purpose to be deposited in these pits. These were not ordinary refuse pits, but rather pits that contained the results of the ritual smashing of all pots at the end of a 52-year period (Smith 1996: 238–239). Smith and his colleagues have argued that this ritual may have been widespread in Central Mexico throughout the Postclassic period, and that the Aztecs very astutely appropriated what was already there into their own ritual calendar as a way to legitimize and facilitate their control over these areas (Elson and Smith 2001).

Sahagún relates what happened next, once the new fire was lit and the continued existence of the universe appeared assured (at least for another 52 years) (Carrasco 1999: 102):

> *Then, at this time, all renewed their household goods, the men's array, and the women's array, the mats—the mats of large fat reeds—and the seats. All was new which was spread about, as well as the hearth stones and the pestles. Also, at this time (the men) were newly dressed and wrapped in capes. A woman (such as she) dressed newly in their skirts and shifts.*

With tongue in cheek Smith surmises that every 52-year cycle was anticipated with great joy by pottery makers, obsidian knappers, mat and idol makers, and other artisans because everyone was about to purchase a completely new outfit of clothes and sets of domestic wares (Smith 1996: 238).

The Mesoamerican Ball Game

Perhaps one of the most fascinating aspects of Mesoamerican culture is the ball game. Its origins are murky, its rules not always understood, and its ultimate role within the various societies that played hotly debated. Ask anyone about the ball game as it was played, however, and most people will tell you "didn't they kill the winning team after the game was over?" The interest is there, but the exact details may be missing.

From what little we do know, the origins of the game may go back to Olmec times. The Olmec lived in the Gulf Coast area of modern Mexico around the first half of the first millennium BC. They are considered the mother culture of all other Mesoamerican culture. A recent discovery of balls made out of natural rubber in a swamp close to the Olmec heartland implies that this game was already played at these early times.

The use of natural rubber is also reflected in one of the many names that were given to the game: "Ulama," which is a word that finds its root in the Spanish word "ule," meaning rubber. In the present-day Mexican state of Sinaloa there are still people to be found who play a version of this game, making Ulama one of the oldest known continuously played games in human history. Aside from Ulama, other labels applied as well. The Aztec called it "tlatchli," and the Maya "Pok ta pok." The Maya terminology very likely resembles the sound the ball made as it was bounced around the playing field.

When we refer to "the ball game" we should clarify that in all probability there were many different kinds of ball games played. It is similar to referring to "the ball game" as it is played in North America. There are several, not just one, that can be found in our culture.

These games share in common the fact that a rubber ball was used and that the way in which the ball could be touched seemed to have been well defined. The ball could not be touched with one's hands, although some scholars have not ruled out that the ball was occasionally kicked.

The ball game was played in a variety of settings. Perhaps the best known of these settings is the cut-stone masonry ballcourts found at various Maya sites, including the city of Chichen Itza in the northern part of the Yucatan Peninsula. These courts, laid out in the shape of a capital letter "I," sometimes had sloping walls flanking what has been called the ballcourt playing alley (similar to the court in a basketball arena). The end portions of these courts were often open. Spectators were probably seated along the edges of the alley rather than at the end zones. The purpose of the game seems to have been to bounce rubber balls through large stone hoops that were placed in the walls along the alley. The opening of the hoops faced sideways, opposite to the way a basketball hoop opens in our sports arenas.

Not all ball games were played in an I-shaped court. Mural paintings at the megasite of Teotihuacan represent people playing with a ball. They are holding a curved stick, reminiscent in shape to a field hockey stick. The paintings do not show any ballcourt. It is tempting to assume that perhaps the game at Teotihuacan was played in similar ways to how it is still played today in the state of Sinaloa.

In modern Sinaloa, Mexico, men occasionally gather to play a game of Ulama. This involves wearing leather loincloths, a solid rubber ball, and the drawing of a long straight line on a dirt surface. The players then line up along the line, not on either side of it, and proceed to play ball (Leyenaar 1979, 1980).

One of the defining traits of Mesoamerica is the presence of ball games. Mesoamerican-style ball games – without human sacrifice – are still played today in remote areas of Mexico. (Suzanne Murphy-Larronde/DDB Stock)

We know that the ancient Mesoamerican ball game played an important religious role and perhaps also one in the world of politics and warfare. There are references to a ball game in the Maya creation story known as the Popol Vuh, in which the main protagonists of the story, known as the Hero Twins, engage in a ballgame. There is also a possibility that a ballcourt rather than a battlefield may have been chosen to settle differences between opposing groups. What, then, do we know about the ball game in the Aztec world?

The Aztecs and the Ball Game

The ritual ball game was one of the traits that the Aztecs shared with other Mesoamerican people. The presence of ballcourts, and therefore the playing of the game within the Aztec realm and during Aztec times, is well attested (Nicholson and Keber 1991).

Politics, religion, and entertainment come together in the ball game *tlachtli*. The game had a high degree of religious symbolism attached to it. The rubber ball bouncing up and down the court represented the sun that passed through the underworld. The teams stood for a variety of opposing notions, such as the sun and the planet Venus, or the gods of youth and those of old age. Certain predictions for the future were sometimes assigned to the teams. The outcome of the game was seen as an omen, with the prediction assigned to the winning team seen as the most likely path the future would take. Death was also associated with the game, as the ball was often also compared with a human skull.

The Aztec elite and their contemporaries in allied towns often used the ball game to increase their power, prestige, and wealth. The latter was often affected directly by the enormous sums that the nobility bet on the outcome of the game. We have several examples of Aztec emperors engaging in tremendous wagers. Emperor Axayacatl, for example, entered into a wager against the ruler of Xochimilco. Axayacatl bet his entire annual tributary income against that coming to the ruler of Xochimilco. Axayacatl lost the bet. This outcome, however, proved to be most nefarious for the ruler of Xochimilco, as he was assassinated on the orders of the Aztec emperor (Santley et al. 1991: 14). In a related story, Maxtla, the ruler of the Azcapotzalco, is said to have lost a wager, and, as a result, his kingdom as well (Santley et al. 1991: 15).

This close link between the ballgame and politics has been interpreted to mean that the ball game served as a substitute for warfare. According to Theodore Stern, who came up with this notion (Stern 1950: 96–97):

> It is no accident that strong parallels exist between warfare patterns and those of the competitive ball game [. . .] The pitting of teams from two communities against each other in a game in which hard-driving, dexterous actions wins high stakes, frequently though not everywhere, at the risk of injury or death, all lead to the occasional substitution of the game for overt warfare [. . .] Not only may games of this type be consciously employed on occasion to secure ends usually attained by fighting, but it may also function as a safety valve to relieve suppressed intercommunity conflicts, thus operating to sublimate belligerent tendencies and directing them into harmless action.

Santley and his colleagues (Santley et al. 1991) used Stern's idea to propose an explanation for the distribution of ballcourts across the landscape and through time in Central Mexico. Thinking through Stern's logic, they suggested that highly centralized political systems (e.g., the late Aztec history) should lack ballcourts, whereas we can expect to find ballcourts in most communities in a decentralized political system. They think that the data available supports this hypothesis. For example, the episode in which emperor Axayacatl placed a wager dates to the early part of Aztec history, when their political system was not quite as centralized as it would be a century later (Santley et al. 1991: 16–17).

AZTEC RELIGION AND IDEOLOGY:
SOME FINAL THOUGHTS

The Aztec shared a desire to make order out of chaos with all other human beings. They sought to provide themselves and future generations with an explanatory framework that would both make sense out of what they observed as well as provide a justification for their actions. Even though the Aztecs were around for only a relatively short amount of time, they did manage to create one of the most complex religious frameworks known in the Americas. In this achievement they find themselves equal to other advanced societies.

REFERENCES

Arnold, Philip. 1999. *Eating Landscape. Aztec and European Occupation of Tlalocan.* Boulder: University Press of Colorado.

Duverger, Christian. 1993. *La Flor Letal. Economía del Sacrificio Azteca.* Mexico: Fondo de Cultura Económica.

Elson, Christina M. and Michael E. Smith. 2001. Archaeological deposits from the Aztec new fire ceremony. *Ancient Mesoamerica* 12(2): 157–174.

León-Portilla, Miguel. 2002. Aztec codices, literature and philosophy. In *Aztecs.* Edited by Moctezuma, Eduardo Matos, and Felipe Solis Olguín, pp. 64–71. London: Royal Academy of Arts.

Leyenaar, Ted. 1979. *Ulama: The Perpetuation in Mexico of the Pre-Spanish Ball Game Ullamaliztli.* Leiden: E. J. Brill.

———. 1980. Ulama: The Survival of the Pre-Columbian Ball Game in Mexico. *Méxicon* 2(3): 35–37.

Matos Moctezuma, Eduardo. 1995. *Life and Death in the Templo Mayor.* (Translated by Bernard R. Ortiz de Montellano and Thelma Ortiz de Montellano). Niwot: University Press of Colorado.

Nicholson, Henry, and Eloise Quiñones Keber. 1991. Ballcourt Images in Central Mexican Native Tradition Pictorial Manuscripts. In *The Mesoamerican Ballgame.* Edited by Gerard van Bussel, Paul van Dongen and Ted Leyenaar, pp. 119–133. (Leiden: Mededelingen van het Rijksmuseum voor Volkenkunde, No. 26.)

Santley, Robert, Michael Berman, and Rani Alexander. 1991. The politicization of the Mesoamerican ballgame and its implications for the interpretation of the distribution of ballcourts in central Mexico. In *The Mesoamerican Ballgame.* Edited by Vernon J. Scarborough and David Wilcox, pp. 3–24. Tucson: University of Arizona Press.

Smith, Michael. 1992. *Archaeological Research at Aztec-Period Rural Sites in Morelos, Mexico. Volume 1, Excavations and Architecture.* Pittsburgh: University of Pittsburgh Monographs of Latin American Archaeology, no. 4.

Stern, Theodore. 1950. *Rubber-Ball Games of the Americas.* New York: J. J. Augustin.

IX

Material Culture

SOURCES

When archaeologists talk among each other the expression *material culture* is often part of the conversation. This means nothing less than the tangible remains of what the Aztecs (or anyone else for that matter) have left behind. Remember, archaeologists are people who try to reconstruct human behavior using the material remains from these past cultures. Perhaps the most impressive material Aztec culture is made up of is the ruins of their cities. In addition to ruined cities, Aztec material culture is also comprised of what you and I have in our homes: cups and plates, perhaps a scrap of paper, utensils, and the like.

What we know of Aztec cities is derived from their city maps as well as from what we have excavated. These maps allowed them to keep track of landownership and of their tax base. We know that at the level of the *calpulli* such documents were generated to illustrate the distribution of families across the neighborhood (Soustelle 1962: 13); unfortunately only one small map fragment of the capital was preserved. It is known as the *Papel de Maguey*, named after the material (maguey fiber) from which it was crafted. It dates to the early colonial period (Soustelle 1962: 14).

Aside from depictions, made both before and shortly after the European conquest of the area, there are material remains of the buildings and other structures for us to consider. Because the Aztec capital was razed during the bloody fighting of 1520 and 1521, indications of all but the largest structures disappeared. Add to this picture that a new city arose on top of the rubble of Prehispanic buildings, and one can appreciate the problem confronting anyone who attempts to describe Aztec material culture.

ARCHITECTURE

The Aztecs were accomplished architects. When the Conquistadors arrived in the Valley of Mexico, they were awed by what they saw. One of them, Bernal Díaz del Castillo, left the following eyewitness account (Carrasco 1999: 49–50):

During the morning we arrived at a broad causeway and continued our march toward Iztapalapa and when we saw so many cities and villages built in the water and other towns on dry land and that straight and level causeway going toward Mexico, we were amazed and said that it was like the enchantments they tell of in the legend of Amadis, on account of the great towers and cues and buildings rising from the water, and all built of masonry. And some of the soldiers even asked whether the things they saw were not a dream. Gazing on such wonderful sights, we did not know what to say . . . and the lake itself was crowded with canoes and in the causeway there were many bridges at intervals and in front of us stood the great City of Mexico . . .we went to the orchard and garden, which was such a wonderful thing to see and walk in, that I never tired of looking at the diversity of the trees, and noting the scent which each one had, and the paths full of roses and flowers, and the many fruit trees and native roses and the pond of fresh water . . . and all was cemented and very splendid with many kinds of stone (monuments) with pictures on them, which gave me much to think about.

Public Buildings

Palaces in the Capital

Close to the center of the capital, in the immediate vicinity of the Sacred Precinct, lived the emperors. Their palaces were more than just residences. These royal compounds also included courthouses, warrior's council chambers, tribute storage rooms, armories, rooms for bureaucrats and visiting dignitaries, a library, an aviary, and a zoo, as well as courtyards, gardens, and ponds (Berdan 2002: 44). Such compounds were huge. We know that the palace for Netzahualcoyotl, ruler of the city of Texcoco, covered more than 200 acres (Berdan 2002: 44).

Palaces in the Hinterlands

Around the beginning of the fifteenth century, an aristocratic family occupied a large residence at the site of Cuexcomate, in the present-day state of Morelos. Excavations conducted in 1985 and 1986 uncovered the remains of this rather large dwelling, dubbed "the palace of a rural noble" by its excavator Michael Smith (Smith 1992).

A series of unassuming mounds turned out to be the ruins of a series of interconnected low platforms. These platforms were arranged around a patio; each one of these platforms consisted of rooms, passages, and shrines. The platforms were made of stone and covered with a layer of plaster lime painted red.

The identification of these ruins as a palace was based upon several factors. Its size is about twenty-five times as large as the average other structures. The surface of this compound was 540 sq. m (or slightly more than 5,800 sq. ft); the surface area of the smaller structures was 20 sq. m (or 215 sq. ft). Aside from the size difference, the quality of the construction material was also higher in this larger structure than it was in the smaller ones. These smaller houses, identified as commoner houses, also tended to be built on the ground instead of on a platform. The trash found associated with these two ranges of buildings yielded domestic pottery, such as cookpots, serving bowls, and obsidian cutting blades. The trash generated by the palace included a greater proportion of fancy imported items than did the deposits next to the commoner houses.

The palace seems to have been occupied long enough to have gone through at least four different construction stages. It was abandoned in the 1430s or 1440s.

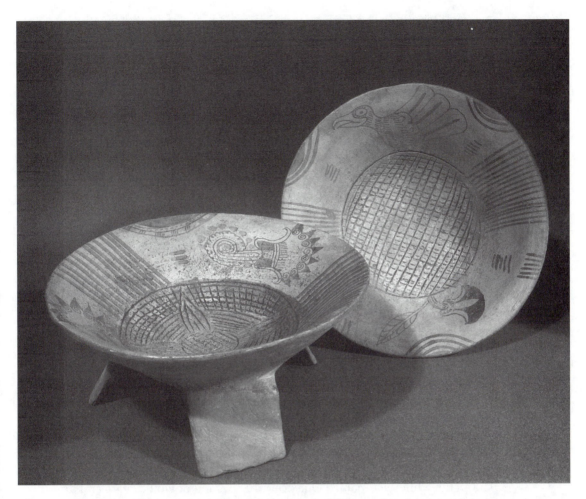

Aztec pottery. The Aztec did not use the potters wheel. It is possible that these plates were used to grind chiles. (Werner Forman/Corbis)

Temples in the Capital

The value of the contributions of early colonial-period chroniclers comes to light with Sahagún's detailed listing of no less than seventy-eight structures that once stood inside the Great Temple Complex of Tenochtitlan. It appears that all towers or pyramids faced west (Bandelier 1932: 148). The following is an overview of these buildings as provided by Sahagún.

The main temple was located in the center of the enclosure. It was dedicated to the god *Huitzilopochtli*. Sahagún shares how "this tower was divided at its top so that it looked like two. It had two chapels or altars at the top, each one topped by its spire. [. . .] In one of those chapels, the principal one, stood the statue of *Huitzilopochtli*, [. . .] in the other one the image of the god *Tlaloc*" (Bandelier 1932: 147–148; Matos Moctezuma 2002: 49). Located in front of these statues was a round stone, called *texcatl*, which is where they would sacrifice people to the gods (Bandelier 1932; 148).

A second temple, called Epcoatl, was dedicated to the gods of the water, or *tlaloques*. This was the place where the priests would fast for 40 days prior to the festival of the gods. Anyone serving in the compound and found wanting in their devotion or the execution of their service would be punished during the festival. This punishment entailed being dunked in mud and water (Bandelier 1932: 148).

A third temple, known as Mocuicalli, served as backdrop for the execution of foreign enemy spies. As soon as a spy was identified, they were brought to this temple and dismembered (Bandelier 1932: 148).

A fourth temple was called Tecuxcalli. This temple contained many statues. The ruler would retire to this spot for a period of 4 days and do penance at the time of great and solemn festivals. A number of captives would be executed in honor of the gods (Bandelier 1932: 148).

A fifth temple was called Poiauhtla. During the Etzalqualiztli festival, this is where the priests would fast for 4 days while burning incense to the statues of the gods. They would also sacrifice captives in honor of the gods (Bandelier 1932: 148).

They called the sixth structure Mixcopantezonpantli. This formed the backdrop for the gruesome display of the severed heads of those who had been sacrificed to the god *Mixcoatl*. The heads were skewered on a massive system of poles and cross-bars. According to some Spanish eyewitness accounts, on one given day there were 136,000 heads thus displayed—and the Europeans claimed that that figure was only part of what they saw. The Spanish also observed how these heads faced south (Bandelier 1932: 148–149).

A seventh building was called Tlalxico, dedicated to the god of hell. Ceremonies were held every year during the month of Tititl to honor this god. Part of the festival included the execution of a prisoner (Bandelier 1932: 149).

The eighth edifice was named Quaxicalco. The emperor would retire and do penance in honor of the sun god in this building. They would do so every 200 days. They would fast and also sacrifice six prisoners, two of whom they would refer to as the image of the sun and the moon (Bandelier 1932: 149).

The ninth building was called Tochinco, a low square temple with stairways on all four sides. The Tochinco was dedicated to *Umetochtli*, the god of wine. Every year, during the festival honoring this god, a captive, dressed up to represent this deity, was killed (Bandelier 1932: 149).

The tenth location was not a real building, but resembled a grove. It was called Teutlalpan, a term meaning "craggy land." The Aztec had constructed a representation of a craggy landscape by hand. On top of this landscape they had planted shrubs. This complex was walled on all four sides. Each year, during the month of Quecholli, the Aztec went around the Teutlalpan in a procession. Upon completing this procession, they would immediately proceed to the slopes of a mountain chain called Cacatepec, where they continued with the ceremonies (Bandelier 1932: 149).

They called the eleventh location Tlilapan, meaning "black water." Just like Teutlalpan, this was not a structure; rather, it was a very deep pond filled with black-colored water. Four times a month, before the beginning of a religious

Modern rendering of the temple of Huitzilopochtli in the Templo Mayor Precinct in Tenochtitlan/Mexico City. (Charles & Josette Lenars/Corbis)

ceremony, priests would come to this body of water and bathe themselves. After this ritual bath, they would burn incense in the temple of *Mizcoatl* and then retire to their monastery (Bandelier 1932: 149).

A twelfth building was the Tlilancalmecac, which served as an oratory (Bandelier 1932: 149–150).

The thirteenth structure was called the Mexicocalmecac. This is where the priests serving the god *Tlaloc* lived and performed rituals. The fourteenth building was named the Quaucalli, which acted as a "prison" for the statues of the gods that the Aztec armies had brought back with them. The fifteenth structure was the Quauchxicalco, a round temple. This temple, small in size, was dedicated to the god Titlacaoan. It had no roof. The priests serving here would burn incense to honor the four cardinal directions of the world. An individual slated to be sacrificed to this god would play flute in this location as often as he wanted (Bandelier 1932: 150).

The sixteenth edifice was called the Quauchxicalco the second. It was a virtual copy of the building with the same name just mentioned. The Aztecs had planted a tree in front of this structure, and had decorated it with strips of paper. On top of this temple, a person dressed as a clown would occasionally dance (Bandelier 1932: 150).

Human sacrifice on a massive scale would occur at the seventeenth building, the Teccalco. The Aztec would throw a great number of captives into a fire lit on the occasion of the festival called Teutleco (Bandelier 1932: 150).

The eighteenth structure was the infamous Tzompantli or skull rack. This consisted of a series of upright wooden beams, supporting several horizontal shafts over which human heads were skewered and put on public display (Bandelier 1932: 150).

The nineteenth building was called the Huitznaoacteucalli. Each year during the festival of Panquetzalitztli, images of gods as well as live captives would be sacrificed in this location (Bandelier 1932: 150).

The twentieth building was the Texcacalco. This served as an oratory containing statues called the *omacama* (Bandelier 1932: 150). The twenty-first building was a house called the Tlacochcalco. This served as an armory, for within it the Aztec stored a large quantity of darts. The Aztec would also dispatch prisoners of war there, whenever they felt like it (according to Sahagún), rather than have those sacrifices coincide with any particular festival (Bandelier 1932: 151).

The twenty-second building was called the Teccizcalco. In this temple they kept the images of the god Tmacatl and of other deities. Captives would occasionally be sacrificed here as well. The twenty-third building was the Huitztepecalco, that was described as a corral, or a space surrounded with four walls. This is where the priests would dispose of the maguey spines after they had used them in bloodletting rituals. Blood-soaked strips of cane were also deposited in this location (Bandelier 1932: 151). The twenty-fourth building was a monastery inhabited by the priests devoted to the god Huitznaoac. A third version of the Quauchxicalco made up the twenty-fifth edifice. It was built like the other two already mentioned. This round temple formed the backdrop against which the Tzompantli was placed. This temple had a wooden statue in it, called the Umactl. Whenever captives were killed in this location, the Aztec would smear their blood over the statue's mouth, so as to let it taste it (Bandelier 1932: 151).

The twenty-sixth building was called the Macuileipactli and Teupan. This was a large religious structure built in honor of *Macuilcipactli*. The Aztec would also sacrifice people in this structure in honor of the god (Bandelier 1932: 151).

The twenty-seventh edifice was the Tetlanmancalmecac, a monastery inhabited by priests dedicated to the goddess *Chantico*. The twenty-eighth building was the Iztaccinteutliteupan, a temple dedicated to the goddess *Cinteotl*. In this temple, the Aztec killed their leprous captives, whose flesh they did not eat (the addition of the latter detail implies that this was customary behavior otherwise) (Bandelier 1932: 151). The twenty-ninth building was called Tetlanma. This was the temple dedicated to a goddess called *Quoxototlcantico* (Bandelier 1932: 151). The thirtieth structure was called Chicomecatl and Teupan, a temple devoted to the god *Chicomecatl*, where human sacrifices were practiced as well (Bandelier 1932: 151–152).

The thirty-first location was a pond called Tezcaapan. This is where those who had vowed to do penance would come to bathe. Because people were wont to do penance throughout the year and for periods of undetermined length, there would always be bathers in this pond (Bandelier 1932: 152). The thirty-second building was a ballcourt, the Tezcatalcho, located in between temples. The Aztecs would sometimes sacrifice people here. The thirty-third edifice was a Tzompantli, or skull rack. This was presumably second to the skull rack already mentioned. This skull rack served to display the severed heads of those killed in honor of the gods called *Omacama* (Bandelier 1932: 152). The thirty-fourth building was the Tlamatzinco. It was a temple dedicated to the god *Tlamatzincatl*. Every year, during the festival of Quecholli, captives were sacrificed in honor of this god. The priests who served in this temple lived in the thirty-fifth structure, called the Tlamatzinco Calmecac (Bandelier 1932: 152).

The thirty-sixth building was called the Quauaxicalco. This was a small temple where they would burn the paper they used in making promises. The thirty-seventh building, called Mizcoateupan, was a temple dedicated to the god *Mizcoatl*. This is where the Aztecs celebrated the festival called the Quechollitlami. The thirty-eighth building was the Netlatiloia. A cave at the foot of this temple served as storage place for the skins of the human victims they had flayed during the festival of Tlacaxipeualiztli (Bandelier 1932: 152).

The thirty-ninth spot was a ballcourt, the Teutlachco. This is where captives called Amapanme were sacrificed during the festival of Panquetzaliztli. The fortieth location was called Hilhuicatitlan. It consisted of a tall column, on top of which the morning star was painted. On top of this column, another one made out of straw was erected. Each year captives were sacrificed in front of this column, when the morning star appeared in the sky (Bandelier 1932: 152).

The forty-first building was called the Veitzompantli. This was a skull rack placed in front of the temple of Huitzilopochtli—it displayed the heads of the victims killed in that temple during the festival of Panquetzaliztli (Bandelier 1932: 152–153). The forty-second building was called the Mecatlan. This is where those who attended to the statues of gods learned to play the horn. The forty-third building was called the Cinteupan, a temple dedicated to the goddess *Chicomecoatl*. They would sacrifice a woman who was said to resemble the goddess. The forty-fourth building was called the Centzontotochtiniteupan, dedicated to the gods of wine. They killed three captives every year during the festival of Tepeilhuitl (Bandelier 1932: 153).

The forty-fifth edifice was named the Cinteupan. This temple contained a statue of the god of the corn fields. Once a year an individual personifying this god was killed in this temple. The forty-sixth location was called Netotiloian, part of the temple precinct, where captives and slaves danced before they were sacrificed during the festival of Xilomaniztli. The forty-seventh structure was a temple known as Chililico. This is where slaves were sacrificed during the Atlcaoalo festival. These were slaves given by lords only. The forty-eighth location, Cocoaapan, was another pond. This was the bathing area for the priest who served in the temple of Coatlan. No other person was allowed to enter this body of water. The forty-ninth building was a temple devoted to the god of merchants, Yiacatecutli. Priests were said to have served night and day in this building (Bandelier 1932: 153).

The fiftieth building, a temple called Yopioco, was the setting for the sacrifice of massive numbers of captives. This happened every year during the ceremonies surrounding the festival of Tlacaxipeualiztli. The fifty-first building was a monastery, called Atlahauhco. It was the residence of the priests who served in the temple dedicated to the goddess *Huitzilinquatec* (Bandelier 1932: 153). The fifty-second building was called Xiacatecutli. It was a temple dedicated to the god of merchants. They would sacrifice a person representing the god during the festival of Tititl (Bandelier 1932: 153–154).

The fifty-third structure was called the Huitzilinquate and Teupan. In this temple, they would sacrifice a woman representing the goddess. This was done every year during the festival of Tititl. The fifty-fourth building was the Yopico Calmecac. This monastery was the locale for the mass execution of prisoners every year during the festival of Tlacaxipeualiztli. The fifty-fifth location was yet another skull rack, the Yopico Tzompantli. This is where the heads of those killed during the previously mentioned festival of Tlacaxipeoaliztli would be displayed. The fifty-sixth structure was a skull rack as well, a Tzompantli. This one was used to display the heads of those sacrificed during the festival of *Yiacatecutli,* the god of merchants (Bandelier 1932: 154).

The fifty-seventh structure was known as Macuilmalinaliteupan. This temple housed two statues: one of *Macuilmalinatl* and the other of *Topantlacaqui*. They celebrated a festival in this temple every 203 days. The fifty-eighth structure was an oratory where offerings were made to the goddess known as *Civapipilti*. The fifty-ninth spot was called Netlatiloian. This was a cave where the skins of the people flayed during the festival of Ochpaniztli would be deposited (Bandelier 1932: 154).

The sixtieth building was the Atlaulico. This was a temple dedicated to the goddess *Civateutl*. Every year a woman, said to represent this goddess, was killed in her honor. This sacrifice happened in the temple called Coatlan, located near this structure. This sacrifice took place during the festival of Ochpaniztli. The sixty-first building was the Tzonmolcocalmecac. This was a very important temple to the Aztecs: this is where the priests of the god *Xiuhtecutli* would build and distribute the new fire every year. This would take place during the festival of Oauhquiltamas (Bandelier 1932: 154). [**Note:** The reader is invited to compare Sahagún's statement with that of the description of the New Fire ceremony in Chapter 8.]

The sixty-second feature was the Temalacatl, a large circular stone with a hole in the middle. This was the famous stone to which slaves who were scheduled to be executed were tied and then made to fight. The captives would be tied in such a way that they could walk around the stone. They received weapons with which to fight. A priest would accompany these sacrificial victims to the stone, tie them, and provide them with weapons. Once a captive had been killed, the dead person would then be turned over to another priest who would proceed to tear out the heart (Bandelier 1932: 154–155).

The sixty-third building was a structure called the Nappatecutliyteupan. In this temple, dedicated to the god *Nappatecutli,* they would sacrifice a person representing the god. This happened every year during the festival of Tepeilhuitl. The sixty-fourth temple was that called Tezonmolco. It was dedicated to the god of fire, *Xiuhtecutli.* They would kill a large number of people here every year, during the god's festival. Four of these were men, who were dressed to represent the god. The victims would also include two women who were sacrificed on a platform at the foot of the pyramid stairs (Bandelier 1932: 155).

The sixty-fifth building was a temple called Coatlan. This is where people representing certain gods would be sacrificed. These sacrifices would also take place during the festival of Quecholli and when they started the New Fire ceremony (Bandelier 1932: 155). The sixty-sixth building was called Xuchicalco. This temple served the gods known as *Tlatlauhquicinteutl* and the goddess called *Atlatonan.* Every year, during the festival of Ochpaniztli, the Aztec would sacrifice a woman representing this goddess. The sacrifice would take place at night. The next morning, a priest who had dressed up in her skin would dance in this temple (Bandelier 1932: 155).

The sixty-seventh structure was Xochipalco; it served as a lodging facility for visiting dignitaries. The sixty-eight location was Tozpalatl. This was a spring from which the general audience of the religious festivals was allowed to drink. The sixty-ninth structure was called Tlachcalco, Quahquiaxaoac. This temple housed a statue of the god *Macuiltotec.* Captives were sacrificed here in honor of the god during the festival of Panquetzaliztli (Bandelier 1932: 155–156).

The seventieth building, Tulnoac, was the place where the captives were killed in honor of the god Tezcatlipoca. The seventy-first building was Xilocan. This is where the dough was produced that was used in the manufacture of the statue of *Huitzilopochtli.* The seventy-second structure was Itepeioc. This was the location where the dough was brought to be made into the image of *Huitzilopochtli.* The seventy-third edifice was called Huitznaoaccalpulli. This is where the Aztecs made the images of *Tlacavepancuexcotzin,* the companion of *Huitzilopochtli* (Bandelier 1932: 156).

The seventy-fourth house was Atempan. Children and lepers who were about to be sacrificed would be gathered in this location first. The seventy-fifth building was called the Tezcacoactlacochcalco. This temple functioned as an armory, being a repository of darts. Slaves were sometimes killed here. The seventy-sixth building was Acatlayiacapan Veicalpulli. This was the gathering point for the slaves destined to be killed in honor of the *tlaloques*. They would be dismembered and cooked as soon as they were executed. This "food" was later served to the lords only; it was not offered to commoners (Bandelier 1932: 156).

The seventy-seventh building was the Techielli. This was a small temple structure. The Aztec would sometimes make offerings here of a type of cane that they called Acxolate (Bandelier 1932: 156). The seventy-eighth building was the Calpulli. This name refers to a small cluster of buildings that surrounded the entire Sacred Precinct on the inside of the wall. This is where visiting lords would come to do penance (Bandelier 1932: 157).

Archaeology in the Sacred Precinct

Even though the description left to us by Sahagún appears to be very detailed, we do not have enough archaeological materials to back up the existence of all these features and structures. In 1978 workers for the Mexican electric company were working behind the National Cathedral in Mexico City. As they were digging they came across an image of an Aztec goddess carved in an oval stone more than 10 ft in diameter. It was in perfect condition and showed the goddess *Coyolxauhqui*, sister of *Huitzilopochtli*. This discovery marked the beginning of uninterrupted and intensive excavation efforts that lasted until 1982. They have continued at a lesser pace until today.

These excavations clearly showed that the Templo Mayor was the material embodiment of Aztec religious beliefs. A divine Aztec tradition relates how *Huitzilopochtli* was born in a place called Coatepec, or Snake Mountain. It all started when the Mother of Gods, Lady of the Serpent Skirt, was sweeping the temple on Coatepec mountain. She was known as the mother of the 400 gods of the south, of whom *Coyolxauhqui* was one. According to the story, some plumage then fell on her. These feathers stood for divine semen, which caused the Mother of the Gods to become pregnant. When the 400 gods of the south learned that their mother had become pregnant, they became very angry and set out to kill her. The unborn inside the Mother of Gods was *Huitzilopochtli*. While still in the womb, he talked to his mother and calmed her. As the 400 gods reached the peak of Coatepec mountain, with *Coyolxauhqui* leading them, *Huitzilopochtli* was born fully grown. He quickly put on military gear and promptly killed his sister, *Coyolxauhqui,* by dismembering her. The story notes how her body parts rolled down the hill. *Huitzilopochtli* then proceeded to chase and totally annihilate his 400 siblings (Carrasco 1999: 60–62).

The Sacred Precinct at Tenochtitlan, we now know, reconstructed that sacred environment. The pyramid supporting the temples of *Tlaloc* and *Huitzilopochtli* was referred to as Coatepec. The carved representation of *Coyolxauhqui*, showing her disarticulated body, was found at the foot of the stairs leading up to the temple of *Huitzilopochtli*. As human sacrifices were performed on the platform

A current view of the Templo Mayor Precinct in Mexico City. (Corel Corporation)

on top of the pyramid, the bodies of these victims were thrown down the steps, where they very likely came to rest close to or on top of the stone carving of *Coyolxauhqui.* In other words, we appear to have had a constant ritual reenactment of this divine story (Carrasco 1999: 62).

Caches, or ceremonially buried items, reveal the extent to which this pyramid was also considered to represent *Tlaloc*'s realm of mountains, paradise, caves, and seas. For example, among the items included in these caches were fish remains. If we stopped our commentary here, the reader might be tempted to infer that the fish remains in the caches represent food offered to the gods. A detailed analysis of these fishes, however, points us in a different direction.

With the exception of a Pacific Ocean grouper, all the identified specimens came from the Gulf of Mexico. Very few fish came from the lake system in Central Mexico. Among the identified species of fish that are present in these ceremonial deposits, only about 30 percent of them are considered edible, the remaining 70 percent are considered poisonous. Moreover, it seems that the Aztecs deposited mostly the heads and scales of the fish, rather than the meatier parts (Carrasco 1999: 245, n. 42). One could argue that the head and scales are the parts that preserve best and that fish bones are so intrinsically fragile that they could have turned to dust before the archaeologists found them. Still, it is clear that the Aztecs had special rules to select certain fishes and perhaps prepare them before they were added to the caches.

Aside from animal remains, the Aztecs also took great pains to incorporate symbols from civilizations past, such as masks from Teotihuacan and the Olmec culture (Carrasco 1999: 71). With regard to Teotihuacan, we know that the Aztec emperors would undertake regular pilgrimages to this gigantic ruined city. While they were there, they must have undertaken some of the earliest excavations. Some of the Teotihuacan objects thus retrieved were reburied, but in an Aztec temple instead. Among these mementos brought down from Teotihuacan were masks, figurines, and recipients made out of green stone or pottery. In all, forty-one of these Teotihuacan-era objects have been found during excavations in the Templo Mayor area (León-Portilla 1992: 92).

In December 2003, during excavations carried out in the Chapultepec section of Mexico City, archaeologists came across evidence of a Teotihuacan settlement. The remains included funerary urns and portions of a building (Camila Castellanos, The Associated Press, Jan. 29, 2004). This discovery, will, when verified and elaborated upon, considerably refocus our understanding of the history of human presence in the Mexico City area.

Another example of a symbol from the past being incorporated were the Chacmool figures. These stone figures, showing a backward reclining person, predate Aztec civilization. We find them in Tula, a Central Mexican site revered by the Aztecs. Their inclusion into the Templo Mayor architecture reflects Aztec concern to "bring the superior cultural past into their mighty present" (Carrasco 1999: 73).

In all, more than 7,000 artifacts have been found in the caches associated with the Great Temple. The majority of these pieces were of non-Aztec origin, specifically from southern Mexico. Their incorporation into these offerings is the result of either strong economic ties between Tenochtitlan and southern Mexico or tribute requirements being fulfilled by rulers in southern Mexico (Matos Moctezuma 1990: 217).

Aside from the religious and political connotations of the Templo Mayor, there was also its sheer size. That meant that anyone standing on the top had a breathtaking view of the surrounding area. Consider this description left by Bernal Díaz del Castillo (Carrasco 1999: 57):

> We stood looking about us, for that huge and cursed temple stood so high that from it one could see over everything very well, and we saw the three causeways which led into Mexico, that is the causeway of Iztapalapa by which we had entered the city 4 days before, and that of Tacuba, and that of Tepeaquilla, and we saw the fresh water that comes from Chapultepec, which supplies the city, and we saw the bridges on the three causeways which were built at certain distances apart through which the water of the lake flowed in and out from one side to the other, and we beheld on that great lake a great multitude of canoes, some coming with supplies of food and others returning with cargoes of merchandise; and we saw that from every house of that great city and all of the other cities that were built in the water it was impossible to pass from house to house, except by drawbridges which were made of wood or in canoes; and we saw in those cities Cues and oratories like towers and fortresses and all gleaming white, and it was a wonderful thing to behold; then the houses with flat roofs, and on the causeways other small towns and oratories which were like fortresses.

The sheer size of the main temple was a result of a continuous process of enlarging this structure. Whenever a new emperor ascended to the throne, one of his first acts was to make arrangements to enlarge the temple (Matos Moctezuma 2003: 82). Procuring such building materials as wood, stone, earth, and lime was relatively easy for the Aztecs. The burden was shifted to the sub-jugated people, who had to provide these materials to fulfill their tribute re-quirements (Matos Moctezuma 2003: 82).

A series of structures of great importance, some of them of incredible size, constructed with the participation of labor gangs from both within Tenochtitlan and beyond, all added up to one thing: they were intended to convey Aztec might.

Tradition holds that the first temple was built in 1325, when the Aztecs set-tled in the area. A series of expansions and renovations took place over the next two centuries. In 1520, the temple was eventually probably 45 m high. In the following years, it was destroyed and razed by the Spanish and their allies (Matos Moctezuma 2002: 54).

When the Great Temple was built, laborers came in from all over the region. Their affiliation is sometimes known and it appears that specific portions of the temple were constructed by labor gangs from specific regions. For exam-ple, when the Great Temple was being enlarged during the reign of Moctecuhzuma Ilhuicamina I, laborers from the regional state of Texcoco built the façade. Workers from the Tlacopan were involved in raising the back of the structure. Crews from Chalco helped with the left side, and others from Xochimilco with the right side of the temple. Sand used in construction was furnished by the Otomí and lime was brought in from lower-lying areas. The rulers from Tlacopan and Texcoco personally supervised the crews from their province (Hodge 1996: 26).

Temples in the Hinterlands

All major cities and towns in the Aztec hinterlands would have had their own temples. These formed the backdrop for the celebration of ceremonies that were part of a very busy religious calendar.

Perhaps the most important ceremony these lesser temples participated in was to serve as distribution points for new fire at the beginning of a 52-year cy-cle. As we saw in Chapter 8, the New Fire ceremony was extremely important in the Aztec world. Once a new fire had been drilled by the priests and after it was brought to the capital, runners were enlisted to bring it to all the commu-nities in the realm. Sahagún describes how the torches were relayed and the role played by the temples in the hinterlands (Carrasco 1999: 98):

This same all the village fire priests did. That is, they carried the fire and made it hasten. Much did they goad [the runners] and make them hurry, so that they might speedily bring it to their homes. They hurried to give it to one another and take it from one another; in this way they went alternating with one another. Without delay, with ease, in a short time they caused it to come and made it flare up. In a short time everywhere fires burst forth and flared up quickly. Also, there they first carried and brought it direct to their temples, their priests, houses and each of the calpullis. Later it was divided and spread among all everywhere in each neighborhood and in the houses.

A painting showing Tenochtitlan and one of the wide causeways linking it to the mainland. (Charles & Josette Lenars/Corbis)

PUBLIC WORKS

Dikes

Flooding was a problem that threatened Tenochtitlan regularly. After prolonged rains, the level of the lakes in the Valley would rise dramatically and cause extensive flooding. To help alleviate this situation, the Aztecs built a dike in 1440 under the rule of emperors Montezuma I and Netzahualcoyotl. The dike was reinforced later during the rule of emperor Ahuitzotl (Gibson 1964: 236). This dike extended over about 15 km on the east side of the city and protected the city from the flood waters of Lake Texcoco (Gibson 1964: 532, n. 88).

Causeways

Three causeways, or raised roads, linked the capital to the mainland. One causeway went north to Tepeyacac, another went west to Tlacopan, and the third road extended south to Ixtapalapa and Coyoacan (Hassig 1993: 57). They were of different length, ranging from 6,000 to 8,000 m, but of uniform dimensions: each one of these raised roads was 7 m wide and 5 m high (Hassig 1993: 57).

These three causeways, which could easily be seen from the top of the main temple in the capital, had bridges at regular intervals. These bridges spanned gaps in these causeways through which water would flow from one part of the lake to the other. These bridges were razed during the conquest, effectively transforming Tenochtitlan into an island fortress (Soustelle 1961: 10).

Aqueducts

One aspect of construction in which the Aztecs excelled was providing the entire city of Tenochtitlan with clean drinking water. This was achieved by constructing aqueducts linking springs on the mainland to the island city. These aqueducts, we are told, ran along one of the causeways that connected the island to the shore. They were of considerable width and depth (two paces wide and 6 ft deep) to allow for a considerable amount of water to reach the metropolis. Moreover, the Aztecs showed signs of forward thinking: they had built two such aqueducts, one carrying water with the other remaining empty. The latter was kept in reserve and put to use when the former needed cleaning (Ortiz de Montellano 1990: 127). Under emperor Ahuizotl, a second aqueduct was constructed. It appears that the city had outgrown the capacity of the existing system, so a greater flow of water was achieved by adding another aqueduct (Ortiz de Montellano 1990: 128).

Roads

The streets in Tenochtitlan were wide and straight. Cortés has left us a good description:

> *The principal streets are very wide and very straight. Some of these and all the smaller streets are made as to the one half of earth while the other is a canal by which the Indians travel in boats. And all these streets, from one end of the town to the other, are opened in such a way that the water can completely cross them. All these openings—and some are very wide—are spanned by bridges made of very solid and well-worked beams, so that across many of them ten horsemen can ride abreast.* (Cortés, as quoted in Soustelle 1962: 12)

DOMESTIC BUILDINGS

Houses in the Cities

The size and layout of Aztec houses in the cities was determined by one's social and economic status. Most Aztec houses were single storied, low, rectangular, and flat roofed. Exceptions were the houses that belonged to the elite, who had both the economic clout and the political connections to build a house with a second story.

As a general rule, the dwellings of the elite were located close to the city or town center. This is where the main religious structures tended to be, as well as the palace of the local ruler. The choicest real estate, therefore, was picked up by those who could afford it (Soustelle 1961: 11, 121). The choice of building materials reflects this fact because elite dwellings often used cut-stone masonry. As we move out from the city center, the quality of the construction material as well as the size of the dwelling diminishes. We ultimately encounter simple houses made out of wattle and daub, a mud-and-stick construction, covered by a thatched roof. These simpler dwellings were sometimes constructed on a raised platform.

The layout of a house reflected an inward focus. The exterior walls were often windowless. In the case of a larger dwelling, multiple rooms would all be opened up onto a courtyard. This open area no doubt provided space and light for weaving, pottery making, and food preparation. Smaller houses would not have had this layout, as they might have been restricted to one or two rooms. Wealth brought more rooms, and some of them were set aside for special purposes. For example, there tended to be rooms reserved for women in larger dwellings. If a steam bath was present, that, too, was built separately (Soustelle 1961: 121).

House furnishings were modest compared with our taste. Aztec beds were no more than mats (*petlatl*) laid down on the floor. The only difference here would have been that more affluent people could afford several mats of finer quality than poorer people. These sleeping areas in elite houses and palaces had a type of bed-curtain set up over them (Soustelle 1961: 121). In most houses, and especially in the dwellings of the poorer people, these sleeping mats did double duty: a bed at night and a seat during the day (Soustelle 1961: 122). In some cases, there were *icpalli;* chairs made out of wicker and lacking feet. They had a back support that leaned back somewhat and extended higher than the head of the seated person. Furniture to store belongings did exist. These were usually wickerwork baskets (referred to as *petlacalli*).

The walls in most houses were probably undecorated, or, at most, whitewashed. In contrast, the walls of the elite houses and palaces were decorated with mural paintings and carved-stone monuments (Soustelle 1961: 123). Heating was provided by burning wood in a hearth, or charcoal in a brazier. Indoor lighting was provided by lighting resinous torches made out of pine wood (*ocotl*) (Soustelle 1961: 123).

The hearth that provided warmth at night also served as the place to cook. In typical Mesoamerican fashion, the hearth incorporated three stones. These stones served as supports for pots, while firewood was placed between them (Soustelle 1961: 123).

The confines of a city environment also dictated the spatial interval at which these houses were built. City houses were typically built close together, and arranged along a gridlike street and canal pattern. This is different from what we find in rural areas.

Houses in the Rural Areas

Houses in rural areas were more dispersed across the landscape than were those in urban environments. Aside from this difference, rural farmsteads would have been built in the same simple fashion as the dwellings of the lower social classes in the cities. Their construction involved wooden frames, wattle-and-daub walls, and a thatched roof. Wall foundations and floors were occasionally made out of stone. These are most often the only remains that archaeologists find. It is remarkable, or perhaps not, the care that these alleged simple folk took in maintaining a clean residence. The area in front of their dwellings was kept very clean. People instead threw out their trash to the side and behind the building (Smith 1992). The accumulation of such garbage, reflecting as it does the daily routine of production and consumption, is called a "midden." It represents a gold mine for archaeologists interested in reconstructing Aztec behavior.

CERAMICS

Aztecs were accomplished pottery makers. Pottery is by far the most abundant category of artifacts recovered at archaeological sites. This reflects the widespread use that this type of material had through Aztec society. We know from excavations and eyewitness accounts that Aztec houses had a wide variety of pots in them. These were used for storing, preparing, cooking, and serving food. Water was stored in large water jars. The mainstay of the Aztec diet, the tortilla, was cooked on a *comalli,* a griddle that was a relatively thin circular ceramic object resembling our pizza dishes in size. In an Aztec kitchen there would also have been a pot to soak corn in, a tripod bowl with a rough bottom used to grind chiles and tomatoes, a salt jar, and various plates, bowls, and cups in which to serve the meals.

Most of the ceramics produced were utilitarian. They did not serve an aesthetic purpose, but were geared to daily use; however, we do occasionally encounter beautifully crafted ceramic vessels. The thing that stands out with all these ceramic pots is that they were all made without the benefit of a potter's wheel. The Aztecs would either make a pot by hand or use a mold to craft it. A European-style potter's wheel was absent from the potter's workshop.

From Sahagún we learn that there were at least two types of pottery makers: those who made a wide range of ceramic vessels, and those who specialized in griddles. Sahagún also shares that sometimes it was the potter who would take his or her wares to the market. We do not know with any certainty of Aztec kilns (Smith 1996: 111). Investigations into Aztec ceramic production still have to produce answers to such question as: Who produced ceramics? Did a small number of ceramic workshops produce all the pots the Aztecs needed, or are we to assume that most communities had their own potters? If we assume that pottery workshops were dispersed throughout most Aztec communities, then were these people full-time specialists, or part-time producers? What was the extent of their ceramic workshops?

STONE TOOL PRODUCTION

When we marvel at the Teotihuacan pyramids, or try to decipher Maya hieroglyphs, there is one aspect of which we risk losing track. With few exceptions, and the Aztecs were one of them, Mesoamerican cultures were not familiar with metallurgy. They relied on stone tools to shape their world. In brief, they were a Stone Age culture.

The Aztecs relied heavily on one particular kind of so-called lithic material: volcanic glass. This material, also known as obsidian, is the second-most abundant artifact category retrieved from Aztec archaeological sites (the most abundant category is made up of ceramics).

It should not come as a surprise that obsidian is found throughout the Valley of Mexico, wherever volcanoes are present. This material is by nature very brittle, but in the hands of an expert tool maker, obsidian can be turned into a tool with the sharpest known edge of any implement. It is said that obsidian cutting implements generate sharper cuts with cleaner and straighter edges that those made by surgical steel. The Aztec took advantage of this property to manufacture a wide variety of tools.

The most commonly manufactured obsidian item was a prismatic blade. Blades are rectangular pieces (in this case of obsidian) with two cutting edges. Their cross-section has a prism shape, hence the technical term "prismatic blade." The Aztecs used these blades as knives as well as sickles and razors (Smith 1996: 86). A single blade was sometimes used, and sometimes several of them were incorporated in what we call a composite tool. Perhaps the best known Aztec composite "tool" that included obsidian blades was the *macuahuitl,* or sword. It consisted of a wooden shaft in which a series of obsidian blades would be set along the edges. It was a frightfully effective cutting machine in the hands of an experienced Aztec warrior, as we have seen earlier.

Another category of obsidian artifacts includes the ear spools and lip plugs. These items of personal adornment represent a high degree of craftsmanship. We have to remember that they had to create these cylindrical ear spools without the benefit of our array of highly sophisticated tools.

The manufacturing process of obsidian tools is one that included many steps. The first one took place at the mines where obsidian was extracted. Archaeologists have found evidence of initial shaping flakes in direct association with obsidian mines. This seems to indicate that excess material was removed from these nodules before they were taken to the obsidian workshops (Smith 1996: 88).

Once the obsidian chunks arrived at the workshops, the specialists applied one of two technologies: biface production or prismatic blade production. The term *biface* refers to the "two faces" or sides that a stone tool can have. By definition, a bifacial tool is one that has had material removed from both its upper and lower surfaces. In contrast, prismatic blade production results in the rectangularly shaped flakes that have a cutting edge on both of its long sides. Prismatic blades were "peeled" off from a more or less cylindrically shaped core. By applying the right of pressure, specialists were capable of peeling off a large number of blades (up to 200) from such cores, before they reached a stage when they could no longer do so (Smith 1996: 88). At that point a core is said to be "exhausted." Because we lack eyewitness accounts of how the Aztecs made their obsidian tools, and because the Aztecs themselves did not leave any description behind, we have to rely on experimental archaeology to retrace the various stages in the manufacturing process. As we do so, we have come to appreciate the high degree of artisanship displayed by these Aztec specialists. It is assumed that some of these people were part-time specialists. Farmers may have developed the necessary skills to manufacture their tools. It is also likely that full-time specialists made obsidian tools all day long in certain areas (Smith 1996: 88–89).

THE ARTS

Mural Paintings

We know of only a small number of Aztec mural paintings. Most of these examples come from the excavations of the Templo Mayor in Mexico City. The temple of *Tlaloc* has pillars with the *Tlaloc*'s eyes painted on them. The same pillars also have several bands of colors, as well as a representation of a human walking over a current of water (Matos Moctezuma 2003: 62). Other examples of mural painting were found in the so-called red temples located on both sides of the Great Temple. These walls were completely painted with red, ocher, blue, white, and black designs. Paintings were also present in the Eagle Warrior Precinct. In some of these murals, we can see miniature representations of humans, reminiscent of codex representations (Matos Moctezuma 2003: 62).

In 1964 a shrine was found north of the Great Temple. On one of its sloping surfaces, archaeologists encountered representations of *Tlaloc* masks. These masks showed three white teeth framed by the characteristic mustache of *Tlaloc*. The colors were still very vibrant, with blue, orange, white, and black being present (Matos Moctezuma 2003: 62).

Excavations carried out in the 1960s in the city of Tlatelolco also revealed mural paintings. Other than attesting to their presence, we cannot present a description because these murals still await study. Murals discovered in 1989 in Tlatelolco's cylindrical temple depict an old man and a woman. It is possible that they represent the primordial pair, *Cipactonal* and *Oxomoco* (Matos Moctezuma 2003: 62, 64). There are various day glyphs in the upper portion of the mural (Matos Moctezuma 2003: 64).

The site of Malinalco, located some 80 km outside Mexico City, also has remnants of mural painting. One of these depicted a procession of warriors, a not altogether surprising theme given that Malinalco was the place where eagle warriors went for training (Matos Moctezuma 2003: 64). A palace at Yautepec, a site even further removed from the Aztec capital, was also decorated with elaborate polychrome murals (Smith 1996: 158).

Stone Sculpture

One of the best-known Aztec objects is the famous calendar stone. It is also one of the best illustrations of an area in which Aztec artists excelled: stone sculpture. Whereas other Mesoamerican cultures also produced stone sculpture, the Aztec seem to have taken it further than anyone else. In their stone works of art, they display the ability to represent realism, as in a sculpture of the goddess *Tlazolteotl* giving birth, as well as the ability to represent microscopically small objects, as in a sculpture of a flea.

Aztec stone sculptors loved portraying animals, especially snakes and jaguars. Some of the snake representations were extremely naturalistic, but others were more stylized, especially when referencing *Quetzalcoatl*. Carved stone boxes, bowls, and panels were also common. The talent to carve such objects was present throughout the empire, as illustrated by stone sculptures retrieved from provincial centers (Smith 1996: 265).

Aztec calendar stone. (Danny Lehman/Corbis)

The art of stone carving underwent a major change after the establishment of the Triple Alliance. Tenochtitlan became the focus of a new school of monumental imperial stone carving. Artists were put to work to convey to the world the might and legitimacy of the empire by means of stone sculptures.

One of the monuments that conveyed this message is the so-called Temple of Sacred Warfare. It is a stone model of a temple-pyramid, decorated with relief carvings on all sides (Smith 1996: 267–268). The themes developed in these carvings relate to warfare, human sacrifice, death, self-sacrifice, the sun, and the founding of Tenochtitlan. Through these images, the message was conveyed that war and sacrifice were inseparable and necessary to ensure the continued rising of the sun and the continuing glory of the Aztec capital (Smith 1996: 268).

The so-called Aztec calendar stone alluded to earlier was a colossal stone sculpture, measuring 3.6 m in diameter and weighing more than 25 tons. The image on this monument referred to creation stories that prevailed in the Aztec world, and linked them to a date with political importance, 13 Acatl. This date marked both the creation of the fifth sun, the world we still share with the Aztecs, as well as the ascension to the throne of emperor Itzcoatl (Smith 1996:

Aztec carving representing a serpent head. (Stan Honda/AFP/Getty Images)

268–269). To those who saw it and were familiar with the symbols, this calendar stone conveyed a simple and powerful message: the Aztec empire covers the whole earth; it is founded upon the sacred principles of time, directionality, and divine warfare, and it is sanctioned by the gods (Smith 1996: 270).

Metallurgy

The ability to produce metal tools was very much in its infancy when the Spanish arrived. It is generally assumed that the technical knowledge was introduced to Mesoamerica by people, probably traders, from South America. The earliest evidence of metal objects comes from western Mexico, along the Pacific coast (Smith and Heath-Smith 1994: 359).

Traders from South America appear to have introduced Mesoamerica to metallurgy at two different time periods. They brought the techniques of copper tool manufacturing around AD 700, and knowledge of how to manufacture bronze tools reached Mexico around AD 1200. The latter requires greater skill and the ability to attain and maintain higher temperatures. West Mexico was the primary region of bronze production during Aztec times. The archaeological record has revealed a wide array of objects made from either copper or bronze. These objects included bells, rings, and tweezers, as well as sewing needles, chisels, awls, axes, and fishhooks (Smith 1996: 97; Smith and Heath-Smith 1994: 359).

It appears that Precolumbian metalsmiths controlled the composition of two bronzes: copper-arsenic and copper-tin. Low concentrations of tin or arsenic (2–5 percent) resulted in greater hardness and strength, while avoiding brittleness. Higher concentration of these components (10–20 percent) resulted in the objects taking on desired silver and gold colors (Smith 1996: 98).

We should remember that it was the Tarascans who excelled in metallurgy in Northern Mesoamerica. Further south, the Mixtecs also proved to be very accomplished metalsmiths. The Aztecs in the Valley of Mexico never adopted the technology themselves, although they did avail themselves of the metal objects that were available through trade or conquest. We know that bronze objects were available for purchase at the Tlatelolco market. Provincial centers seem to have acquired some of these tools, and they seem to have been able to perform local repairs or modifications. It is still believed that the ultimate source of bronze tools within the Aztec realm was western Mexico (Smith 1996: 98).

It is possible that the Aztecs might eventually have been swayed to start producing bronze tools themselves and even experiment with other metals. We know that they never got to this stage independently because they were introduced to iron and steel in a rather brutal fashion by the Spanish Conquistadors.

REFERENCES

Bandelier, Fanny R. 1932. *A History of Ancient Mexico by Fray Bernardino de Sahagún.* Translated by Fanny R. Bandelier from the Spanish version of Carlos Maria de Bustamante. Nashville: Fisk University Press.

Berdan, Frances. 2002. Aztec Society: Economy, Tribute and Warfare. In *Aztecs.* Edited by Eduardo Matos Moctezuma and Felipe Solis Olguín, pp. 38–47. London: Royal Academy of Arts.

Carrasco, Davíd. 1999. *City of Sacrifice. The Aztec Empire and the Role of Violence in Civilization.* Boston: Beacon Press.

Gibson, Charles. 1964. *The Aztecs under Spanish Rule. A History of the Indians of the Valley of Mexico, 1519–1810.* Stanford: Stanford University Press.

Hodge, Mary. 1996. Political Organization of the Central Provinces. In *Aztec Imperial Strategies.* Edited by Frances F. Berdan, Richard E. Blanton, Elizabeth H. Boone, Mary G. Hodge, Michael E. Smith, and Emily Umberger, pp. 17–45. Washington, D.C.: Dumbarton Oaks.

León-Portilla, Miguel. 1992. Pasado de los Aztecas. In *Azteca. Mexica. Las Culturas del México Antiguo.* Edited by José Alcina Franch, Miguel León-Portilla, and Eduardo Matos Moctezuma, pp. 87–98. Madrid: Lunwerg Editores.

Matos Moctezuma, Eduardo, 1990. Imperial Tenochtitlan. In *Mexico. Splendors of Thirty Centuries,* pp. 212–234. New York: Metropolitan Museum of Art.

———. 2002. The Templo Mayor, the Great Temple of the Aztecs. In Eduardo Matos Moctezuma, and Felipe Solis Olguín, pp. 48–55. London: Royal Academy of Arts.

Smith, Michael, and Cynthia Heath-Smith. 1994. Rural Economy on Late Postclassic Morelos. An Archaeological Study. In *Economies and Polities in the Aztec Realm*. Edited by Mary G. Hodge and Michael E. Smith, pp. 349–376. (Studies on Culture and Society, volume 6) Albany: Institute for Mesoamerican Studies.

X Intellectual Accomplishments

MATHEMATICS

The Aztec numerical system differs from ours in many ways. Our way of counting is called a decimal system—a system whereby we count in units of ten—whereas the Azecs employed a vigesimal system. Their way of counting relied on units of twenty. The roots of these approaches are believed to be the ten digits on our hands or all digits, on hands and feet. Moreover, the Aztec used a subset of units of five with their vigesimal system. Nahuatl number words clearly reflect this approach, where the Nahuatl word for "six" literally means "five plus one" (Payne and Closs 1986: 214–215). [Such an approach is not totally unheard of even in modern languages. For example, consider the French way of referring to "eighty" as "quatre-vingt," or "four times twenty," and "ninety" as "quatre-vingt dix," or "four times twenty plus ten."]

To refer to numbers larger than twenty, the Aztec employed a technique very similar to that of the French. For example, to refer to "thirty," they would use the expression "cempoalli ommatlactli," or "one score (i.e., twenty) plus ten" (Payne and Closs 1986: 216). As numerical values go up, they eventually will reach 400, or twenty times twenty. That number was called *"tzontli,"* meaning either "hair" or "growth of garden herbs," which are terms that refer to an abundance of things (Payne and Closs 1986: 216). The third power of twenty, or 8,000, was called *"cenxiquipilli."* The latter term contains the word "xiquipilli," or "bag of cacao beans" (Payne and Closs 1986: 217).

Writing Numbers: The Positional Notation System

The Aztec number system relied on a different positional notation than we do. In our system, numbers are written down along a horizontal line, with commas to refer to the order of magnitude of a number and a dot to indicate a decimal point. The Aztecs, like their Maya contemporaries, used a system in which numbers were "stacked"; that is, they were written down in a vertical rather than horizontal fashion. The location of a numerical symbol in this vertical stack determined the value of that symbol.

The Matrícula de Tributos or How the Aztec Used Numbers

It is ironic that tax records should be among the important sources of information on Aztec culture. The Matrícula de Tributos, a listing of taxes levied by the Aztecs throughout their realm, employs the Aztec numerical system, this time by means of notations. We know that a dot was used to refer to the quantity "one," a representation of a flag inferred the value "twenty." A symbol vaguely

TABLE 10.1. Nahuatl Number Words

Decimal System	Aztec Vigesimal System
One	Ce
Two	Ome
Three	Ei or yei
Four	Nahui
Five	Macuilli
Six ("five plus one")	Chicuace
Seven ("five plus two")	Chicome
Eight ("five plus three")	Chicuei
Nine ("five plus four")	Chiconahui
Ten	Matlactli
Eleven ("ten plus one")	Matlactli once
Twelve ("ten plus two")	Matlactli omome
Thirteen ("ten plus three")	Matlactli omei
Fourteen ("ten plus four")	Matlactli onnahui
Fifteen	Caxtolli
Sixteen ("fifteen plus one")	Caxtolli once
Seventeen ("fifteen plus two")	Caxtolli omome
Eighteen ("fifteen plus three")	Caxtolli omei
Nineteen ("fifteen plus four")	Caxtolli onnahui
Twenty ("one counted group")	Cempoalli

representing a feather stands for "400," and a bag (presumably holding cacao beans) should be read as meaning "8,000" (Payne and Closs 1986: 226, 228).

Notation of Area

The tax records mentioned earlier also show symbols used to refer to area. In some cases the Aztec drew a picture of a mantle. In addition to a symbol indicating the number of these they wished to receive in tax payment from a given community, they sometimes added another set of symbols that referred to the size of the mantles. For example, the appearance of two fingers on top of the mantle, flanking the symbol for quantity, signaled that the type of mantle requested was to be twice as wide as a normal mantle. These fingers are said to refer to two "brazas," a measurement of distance whose metric equivalent is still under scrutiny (Payne and Closs 1986: 228).

There are two early colonial-era documents from Texcocan context that shed light on how the Aztecs referred to area. One such document is the Códice de Santa María Asunción; the other is known as the Codex Vergara. Both documents contain a census by household and record landholdings for sixteen localities (Harvey and Williams 1986: 238–239).

The standard unit of linear measurement in the colonial period was called the *quahuitl*, approximately 2.5 m (Harvey and Williams 1986: 241). Colonial-period scribes would use lines and dots to indicate the length and width of fields in *quahuitl*. A dot is said to have meant "twenty," and a line "one"

(Harvey and Williams 1986: 241). It is assumed that the situation in place in the sixteenth and seventeenth centuries, both in terms of representing property and units of measurement, are identical to Prehispanic situations in the Basin of Mexico. One argument favors this assumption to be true. In Europe, chroniclers tended to focus on how much of a given crop a field could produce rather than indicate how big it was (Harvey and Williams 1986: 255). These two documents refer to linear measurements of the field rather than volume of harvest produced, so we may assume that these notations reflect an indigenous mind at work rather than that of a Spanish scribe.

Working with this notion of *quahuitl*, modern scholars have gone back through early documents and engaged in their own computations to establish the size of fields that are listed in tax records (See Harvey and Williams 1986: 247–249). There is good evidence that the Aztec employed a notion similar to our hectare. Their "hectare" was 400 sq. units (or twenty by twenty linear units). This does not mean that these 400 sq. units were equal in surface to our hectare. In one particular case, that of the community of Tepetlaoztoc, the "400 sq. units" would have been the equivalent of about a quarter of our hectare (Harvey and Williams 1986: 250).

CALENDAR

The Aztec calendar was based on two cycles. One cycle consisted of 260 days; the other comprised 365 days. Each of these two cycles also contained shorter cycles. A combination of both 260- and 365-day calendars resulted in a 52-year cycle.

The Sacred Calendar: *Tonalpohualli*

The term *Tonalpohualli,* or "counting of the days," refers to the calendar comprising 260 days. This cycle is made up by combining thirteen-day names with twenty-day signs, resulting in 260 different combinations. This 260-day calendar is not unique to the Aztecs. It can be found among other Mesoamerican civilizations, including the Maya (Sharer 1994: 560–562). The traditional sequence of the twenty-day signs in the Aztec *Tonalpohualli* calendar are listed in Table 10.2.

TABLE 10.2.   The Twenty-Day Signs in the Aztec *Tonalpohualli* Calendar

Cipactli (caiman)	Ozomahtli (monkey)
Ehecatl (wind)	Malinalli (grass)
Calli (House)	Acatl (reed)
Cuetzapalin (Lizard)	Ocelotl (jaguar)
Coatl (snake)	Cuauhtli (eagle)
Miquiztli (death)	Cozcacuauhtli (vulture)
Mazatl (deer)	Olin (earthquake)
Tochtli (rabbit)	Tepatl (flint)
Atl (water)	Quiahuitl (rain)
Itzcuintli (dog)	Xochitl (flower)

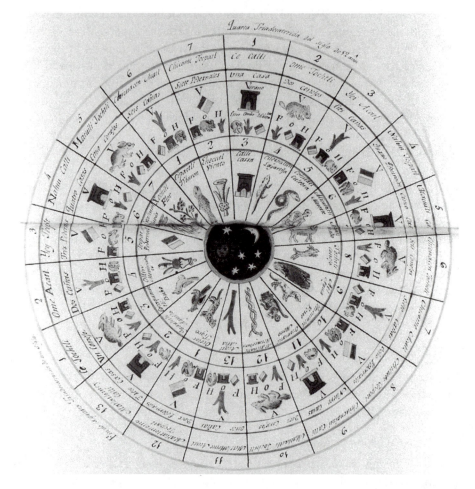

Representation of the calendar wheel as seen in an early nineteenth-century manuscript. (Corbis)

The thirteen-day names, or Lords of the day, were given the names listed in Table 10.3.

One of the purposes of the 260-day calendar appears to have been to organize the birthday festivals of the patron deities of the neighborhoods and local communities throughout the Aztec realm. This contrasts with the solar calendar, to be discussed next, which was used to mark the festivals of the prominent deities of agriculture, including sun, rain, and fertility (Carrasco 1999: 82).

The Tropical (Solar) Year Calendar: *Xihuitl*

The Aztec also identified a cycle of 365 days. It was made up of eighteen units (we tend to compare them with our months), each with twenty days in them. The Aztec added five extra days to complete the 365-day cycle of the year. These days were counted after the eighteen "months" of 20 days had run their course. The five extra days were referred to as *nemontemi* (Hassig 1993: 76).

TABLE 10.3.   The Thirteen-Day Names Used in the Aztec
Tonalpohualli **Calendar**

Xiuhteuctli (Turqoise-Lord)	Tlaloc (Land Lier)
Tlalteuctli (Earth-Lord)	Quetzalcoatl (Plumed Serpent)
Chalchiuhtlicue (Her Skirt is Jade)	Tezcatlipoca (Mirror that Smokes)
Tonatiuh (Sun)	Chalmecateuctli (Lord who Dwells in
Tlahzalteotl (Filth-Goddess)	Chalman)
Mictlan Teuctli (Lord of Mictlan)	Tlahuizcalpan Teuctli (Lord of Dawn)
Centeotl (Dried Ear of Maize God)	Citlalli Icue (Her Skirt is Stars)

A similar phenomenon of five extra days to complete the solar year existed among the ancient Maya (Sharer 1994: 562).

A listing of the 18 "months" is shown in Table 10.4 (Hassig 1993: 77; 2001: 14).

In our calendar we refer to specific years by assigning numbers to them. The Aztec identified years by the day name on which they began. The "months" as they are listed in the table are all named in honor of gods. This relationship highlights the link between calendar and events of great importance to the Aztec, such as when to sow crops or when to harvest them, as well as when to start a war. This link was elaborated upon by Sahagún, who described them as follows (Matos Moctezuma 1995: 21–22):

Atlcahualo—Started on February 2. It was dedicated to the *tlatoques* (Rain God helpers); to *Chalchiuhtlicue*, the goddess of water, and to *Quetzalcoatl*. During this month, the Aztecs sacrificed many children, and they did so on top of mountains. By tearing out their hearts and offering them to the gods of rain, they hoped for abundant rain later in the year. The tears of the

TABLE 10.4.   Names of the Eighteen Months used in the Tropical (Solar)
Year Calendar, or *Xihuitl*

Atlcahualo (Water is Abandoned)	Huei Miccailhuitl (It is the Great Festival
Tlacaxipeualiztli (It is the	of the Dead)
Flaying of Men)	Ochpaniztli (It is the Road-Sweeping
Tozoztontli (It is the Short Vigil)	Action)
Huei Tozoztli (It is the Long Vigil)	Pachtontli (It is the Little Spanish Moss)
Toxcatl (It is a Drought)	Huei Pachtli (It is the Great Spanish Moss)
Etzalcualiztli (It is the Eating of the Bean	Quecholli (Macaw)
Porridge)	Panquetzaliztli (It is the Flag Raising)
Tecuilhuitontli (It is the Little Festival of	Atemoztli (It is the Decent in the Form of
the Lords)	Water)
Huei Tecuilhuitl (It is the Great Festival of	Tititl (It is a Shrunken Thing)
the Lords)	Izcalli (It is a Sprout)
Miccailhuitontli (It is the Little Festival of	
the Dead)	

A detail of the Codex Cospi, an Aztec divinatory calendar. (Werner Forman/Corbis)

children were considered good omens—the more tears, the more rain they could expect (Bandelier 1932: 51).

Tlacaxipeualiztli—Started February 22. It was dedicated to *Xipe Totec*. Sacrificial victims were flayed in what is interpreted to be a ritual of renewal. Slaves and war captives both were sacrificed. Their bodies would be rolled down the steps of the pyramid after the act of sacrifice was complete. From there the bodies were taken to the various calpullis, where they would be cut into pieces and eaten (Bandelier 1932: 52).

Tozoztontli—Lasted during parts of March and April. Dedicated to *Tlaloc*, with the intent to attract rain, considering that this period is the end of the dry season. During this month they would sacrifice children again, with the same intent as before: to guarantee abundant rains. Others, wearing the skins of the flayed sacrificial victims killed the month before, would go to place them in a cave (Bandelier 1932: 53).

Huei Tozoztli—Dedicated to the goddess of corn, *Centeotl,* and to *Chicomecoatl.* During this month people would honor the Goddess of Corn by performing acts of self-sacrifice. They would sprinkle their houses with blood from their ears and shin bones. Stalks from young corn plants were brought back from the fields and placed inside the houses in front of statues representing their gods (Bandelier 1932: 54).

Toxcatl—Dedicated to *Tezcatlipoca.* During this time period a young man representing the god was sacrificed. He was considered without any physical blemish. Moreover, he had been "kept in the delights of life for a whole year, being instructed to play musical instruments, to sing, and to speak" (Bandelier 1932: 54). As soon as the young man was sacrificed, another one would be selected to be killed the following year. This was considered the most important festival of the entire year (Bandelier 1932: 54).

Etzalcualiztli—Dedicated to *Tlaloc* and the *tlatoques.* Slaves wearing an outfit representing this god were sacrificed during this time. As part of the celebrations this month, priests would also go to a location called Citlaltepec to cut down cypress trees. On their way back to the capital they were given the liberty to accost anyone who dared show himself on the road. The priests were allowed to strip these unfortunate souls of all their belongings, even clothes. If they happened to come across an imperial tax collector, even he would be fair game (Bandelier 1932: 55).

Tecuilhuitontli—Corresponded to a portion of June. It was dedicated to *Uixtocihuatl,* sister of the *tlatoques.* In her honor the Aztec would sacrifice a woman dressed in the outfit of the goddess. She was killed in a ceremony together with a large number of prisoners of war (Bandelier 1932: 56).

Huei Tecuilhuitl—This month was dedicated to *Xilonen,* goddess of the green corn, which grew in this month. During the festival, for 8 days straight, the poor, the old, and the young were fed in honor of the goddess.

Tlaxochimaco/Miccailhuiltontli—Corresponded to part of July. In honor of *Huitzilopochtli,* god of war, and to other deities of death. This month was also known as *Miccailhuiltontli,* or small feast of the dead. During this month the first flowers of the year were offered to statues of *Huitzilopochtli.* After the statues had been adorned, the Aztecs would consume large quantities of food, including fowl and dogs. Singing and dancing would end the evening (Bandelier 1932: 58).

Xocotl Huetzi—Dedicated to the god of fire, *Xiuhtecuhtli.* Another term for this month was *Huei Miccailhuitl,* or great feast of the dead. As part of the celebrations for the fire god, the Aztec would tie prisoners by their hands and feet and then throw them into a fire. Before they were dead, they would pull them out and then proceed to extract their hearts in front of the statue of *Xiuhtecuhtli* (Bandelier 1932: 58).

Ochpaniztli—Corresponded to portions of August and September. It was dedicated to *Toci*, mother of the gods. Also honored were *Huitzilopochtli* and neophyte warriors. On the first day of this month, a festival was held in honor of the goddess. People would dance in silence. In silence they would also sacrifice a woman dressed in the manner of the goddess (Bandelier 1932: 59).

Teotleco—Also known as *Pachtontli*. It corresponded to the last 20 days of September. It was dedicated to the arrival of all the gods. Altars dedicated to the gods were decorated with flowers on the fifteenth day of this month. The Aztecs believed that the first of their gods would arrive for the festival on the eighteenth day. On the last day of this month they assumed that all gods had made it back, and a big festival in their honor was held. In order for the Aztecs to know that their gods had arrived, they placed a compact pile of corn on a straw mat. Priests would hold vigil all night, looking for a footprint of the gods as proof that they were present. As soon as this was observed, the sounds of horns and shells would mark the beginning of food offerings in the temples (Bandelier 1932: 60–61).

Tepeilhuitl—Also referred to as *Huei Pachtli*. This month corresponded to part of October. During this month, people honored hills, where the rain clouds were formed. In honor of the mountains, the Aztecs would fashion replicas. They would use wood for this, which they would cover with *tzoalli* (amaranth dough). On top of these mountains they placed a replica of a human head. The Aztec also sacrificed four women and a man in honor of the mountains. These victims were ultimately cut into pieces and eaten by the community (Bandelier 1932: 61–62).

Quecholli—This month corresponded to parts of October and November. It was dedicated to *Mixcoatl*. Spears and darts were made over a period of 5 days. These they would use in war and on their hunts. On the tenth day of the month, the Aztecs would go into the mountains and start a communal hunt the next day. They would kill captives and slaves afterward (Bandelier 1932: 62–63).

Panquetzaliztli—During this month, feasts took place to honor *Huitzilopochtli*, god of war. The priests who served in the temples dedicated to this god had gone through a 40-day fast prior to these ceremonies. As part of the ritual, the god—represented by one of his priests—would descend from the temple and proceed to a ballcourt, where he would dispatch four slaves. Additional slaves would subsequently be sacrificed (Bandelier 1932: 63–64).

Atemotzli—Most of this month corresponded to December. This marked the end of the dry season, and it was said that it began to thunder and "to show signs of rain." This month was dedicated to *Tlaloc* and the *tlatoques*. The Aztec would make images using dough, and then offer food to them. They would eventually end this ceremony with more food and drink (Bandelier 1932: 64).

Tititl—This month was dedicated to *Tona*. War-related ceremonies took place in the Templo Mayor. This festival involved the sacrifice of a woman. The Aztecs would celebrate in a more jovial mood on the following day: they would make pouches and attach rope to them, about the length of an arm. They filled these bags with something soft, like fur or wool, and hid them under their cloaks, or mantas. When encountering a woman in the street, they would hit her with these bags for fun (Bandelier 1932: 64–65).

Izcalli—This month corresponded to a portion of January. It was dedicated to *Xiuhtecutli*, god of fire. The new fire was lit in the middle of this month. The Aztecs would make an image of the god in his honor, one that appeared to have flames coming out of it. Every fourth year, they would celebrate this festival with the sacrifice of captives and slaves. They would also perforate the ears of children who had been born in these 4 years and provide them with godparents (Bandelier 1932: 66).

Nemontemi days—This followed Izcalli. This period lasted 5 days, which were considered to be unfortunate. Anyone born within this period was considered doomed to a life full of mishaps. Moreover, the Aztecs did not work these 5 days, and they did their best to abstain from quarreling among themselves. Stumbling on any of these unlucky days was equally considered bad luck (Bandelier 1932: 66).

Although these months have names that represent real tongue twisters for non-Nahuatl speakers, they do present us with a pattern that makes sense. These Aztec "months" start out during the dry season, so we see how Aztec ceremonial thought is centered on attracting rain during the first 3 months of their calendar. Rains would typically come during the fourth month. Corn, the staple food in Mesoamerica, would be growing during the subsequent 4 months. This is celebrated during the eighth month with the festival for *Xilonen*, the goddess of green corn. There would be time and opportunity (especially during the dry season–portion of this time period) for warfare once harvests had been finished. Thus, we see months 11, 14, 15, 17, and 18 dedicated to martial themes and war-related gods (Matos Moctezuma 1995: 23).

A Shorter Cycle of Counting Days: The Nine Lords of the Night

This short cycle of 9 days is thought to have run independently from the Tonalpohualli and the solar year cycle. It included the following 9-day names (Hassig 1993: 78).

TABLE 10.5. A Shorter Cycle of Counting Days:
The Nine Lords of the Night

Xiuhtecuhtli (Turquoise-Lord)	Chalchiuhtlicue (Her Skirt is Jade)
Iztli/Tecpatl (Obsidian/Flint)	Tlahzolteotl (Filth-Goddess)
Piltzinteuctli (Child-Lord)	Tepeyollohtli (Mountain Heart)
Centeotl (Dried Ear of Maize God)	Tlaloc (Land Lier)
Mictlan Teuctli (Lord of Mictlan)	

The 52-Year Cycle: The *Xiuhmolpilli*

The Aztec went beyond using the two calendrical systems just described. They combined both of these in a much larger cycle of 52 years, known as the *Xiuhmolpilli*. In this system, calendar dates would be identified by their assigned codes, found in either of the two shorter calendars. The combination of these two codes resulted in a system that would repeat itself every 52 years.

AZTEC COSMOVISION

The Aztecs shared a worldview with other Mesoamerican cultures that involved a universe divided into three levels. The central level, earth, was inhabited by humans. There were thirteen layers of skies above earth, and the last one these was called Omeyocan, or the place of duality. The underworld was below the earth plane, and it consisted of nine layers. The deepest layer of the underworld was called Mictlan, and it was ruled by two deities, *Mictlantecuhtli* and *Mictlancihuatl* (Matos Moctezuma 2002: 54).

The Aztecs also recognized four cardinal directions, each identified by a god, plant, color, and a glyph, as outlined in Table 10.6 (Matos Moctzuma 2002: 54–55).

The Great Temple stood at the center of this cosmovision. The Aztecs believed that the axis of the world went through this temple, connecting the present world with that of heaven and the underworld. In addition, the temple stood at the intersection of the four cardinal directions. In short, the Great Temple was the center of centers (Matos Moctezuma 2002: 55). This vision, rich in symbolism, found an expression in the great number of offerings that were included over the years as the temple was expanded. Some of the offerings included remains of felines (members of the cat family) and objects related to the god *Tlaloc*; others included human remains, stone sculpture, and green beads (Matos Moctezuma 2002: 53–55).

ASTRONOMY

Aztec priests were keen observers of celestial phenomena. They were able to follow the path of the planet Venus. They kept track of the movement of star

TABLE 10.6. Aztec Cosmovision

Cardinal Direction	Associated traits	Associated God	Associated Plant	Associated Color	Associated Glyph
North	Death, cold	Tezcatlipoca	Tree	Black, Yellow	Sacrificial knife
South	Dampness	Huitzilopochtli		Blue	Rabbit
East	Masculinity	Tezcatlipoca or Xipe Totec		Red	Reed
West	Femininity	Quetzalcoatl		White	House

constellations, such as the Pleiades, to mark important calendar events, such as the New Fire ceremony. They also referred to the rising and setting of the sun to align buildings. When archaeologists excavated the Great Temple in Mexico City, they came across evidence for seven renovations carried out over a 100-year period. Each of these seven building phases had an alignment of 7 degrees and 6 minutes south of a true east–west line. This alignment confirmed statements made by colonial writers that the Aztecs aligned their buildings such that they could register the sun and the equinox (Carrasco 1999: 112–113).

WRITING

Aztec Paper

The Aztecs would use various media on which to write, which is a trait they share with other Mesoamerican people. Perhaps the best-known medium is what they called *amate*, a term we translate as paper. This paper was produced through a laborious process from the fibers of the bark of the wild fig tree. During colonial periods and even today, communities in Morelos excelled in producing *amate*. The papermakers would strip the bark of the wild fig tree and immerse it in water to coagulate the sap. The sap was then scraped off and the bark was boiled in an alkaline solution. This helped loosen and separate the fibers. The artisans then arranged these wet fibers in various layers on a wooden drying board. They then applied stone bark beaters; usually rectangular pieces of basalt stone in which wide parallel grooves had been cut. By beating these fibers with these tools, the papermakers ensured that the fibers became both pliable and fused together. The sheets of *amate* thus produced were then cut to size and coated with white lime. This stiffened the paper and also produced a surface that could be painted (Smith 1996: 246).

Aztec Writing

In all, five different writing systems have been identified in Mesoamerica. They include the Aztec, Maya, Mixtec, Zapotec, and epi-Olmec systems (Smith 1996: 248). A common theme in all these systems, as far as we can tell, is that they are predominantly used to communicate information pertaining to ruling dynasties, elite affairs, rituals, and calendrics (Smith 1996: 249).

Picture

The Aztec writing system included two elements, pictures and glyphs. The pictures refer to events, places, people, and things. Because of their nature, these notations could very easily be understood by those who saw them. That meant that even non-Nahuatl speakers had no problems with that portion of Aztec writing (Smith 1996: 249–250). One could compare these pictures with the universally understood signs encountered at airports or other places through which large groups of people tend to pass.

Hieroglyphs

Hieroglyphs, a term borrowed from Greek meaning "sacred writing," are signs that stand for a specific word, sound, or concept in a particular language (Smith 1996: 250). Several hundred glyphs were used in Aztec writing. We can distinguish three types of hieroglyphs, each with an increasing complexity and degree of abstraction. They are pictographs, ideographs, and phonetic elements (Smith 1996: 250).

Pictographs

- Pictographs were the most common hieroglyph in Aztec writing. They show objects and people, and thus convey meaning. Pictographs were often used to refer to place names. For example, *Tochtepec* ("on the hill of the rabbit") was depicted as a rabbit on a hill (Smith 1996: 252).

Ideographs

- Ideographs are more difficult to understand and require a certain familiarity with the culture. As we have seen in the discussion of warfare, a city was considered taken when enemy forces put fire to the main temple. An ideograph showing a burning temple was used by the Aztecs to connote "the city was taken" (Smith 1996: 253).

Phonetic Elements

- With phonetic elements we have arrived at the most complex level of Aztec writing. The rebus principle is often employed at this level. This often meant that words that were difficult to depict with pictographs and ideographs were represented with signs that sounded alike. For example, the place name "Coatlan" (meaning "where there are many snakes") was written using a combination of a pictograph showing a snake and a depiction of teeth (which are pronounced "tlantli") to arrive

Aztec scribes were among the educated elite in their society. Here a scribe is preparing to work on a large scroll. We do not know if scribes ever signed their masterpieces. (Gianni Dagli Orti/Corbis)

at the portion "-tlan" in the place name. The teeth themselves had nothing to do with the locality, but the sound of the word for teeth was borrowed to arrive at the correct pronunciation of the word "Coatlan" (Smith 1996: 253).

Who Could Write—The Profession of the Scribe

The importance of writing and words in Aztec society is illustrated by the fact that Nahuatl terms for ruler, scribe, chronicler, poet, and ambassador were all derived from the term *tlatoa*, meaning "to speak" (Marcus 1992: 48). The Aztecs' own perception of a scribe was written down in the early sixteenth century by Sahagún (Marcus 1992: 49):

THE SCRIBE
The scribe: writings, ink are his special skills. He is a craftsman,
an artist, a user of charcoal, a drawer with charcoal; a painter who
dissolves colors, grinds pigments, uses colors.

The good scribe is honest, circumspect, far-sighted, pensive; a judge
of colors, an applier of the colors, who makes shadows, forms feet,
face, hair. He paints, applies color, makes shadows, draws gardens,
paints flowers, creates works of art.
  The bad scribe is dull, detestable, irritating—a fraud, a cheat. He
paints without luster, ruins colors, blurs them, paints askew—acts
impetuously, hastily, without reflection.

The profession of scribe, or tlacuilo, was inherited from father to son. Scribes were quite often members of the nobility. In virtually all of the known depictions of Aztec scribes they are males; however, there is one exception: a female scribe is depicted in one of the codices. She is said to have worked for the emperor Huitzilihuitl (Marcus 1992: 49).

Who Could Read—The Role of the Calmecac

As we saw in Chapter 6, those who attended the temple schools, or calmecac, were given instructions on how to read. We also know that an overwhelming majority of those who attended came from the ranks of the nobility. Only a select few students came from the ranks of commoners. As a result, with the exception of a lucky few, Aztec commoners could not read or write.

This is very different from our society, where literacy is much more widespread. Although we are inundated with texts both at home and on the street, this was not the case in Aztec cities. Meaning was conveyed in ways other than texts. Art, especially monumental stone sculptures, played an important role in this regard. One could compare this situation in the Aztec world with that which we would have encountered in Medieval Europe. In the latter, literacy was limited to a few as well, and instructions were conveyed by means of art, especially monumental stone sculptures (i.e., in the churches to illustrate bible passages).

Rewriting of Aztec History

The Aztecs were fully aware of the power of written documents and the role they played in perpetuating the memory of Aztec society for later generations. It should not come as a surprise then that the Aztecs engaged in rewriting history. A good example of massive rewriting occurred during the reign of Itzcoatl. One of our sources relates (Marcus 1992: 146):

They preserved their history, but it was burned at the time that
Itzcoatl reigned in Mexico. The Aztecs decided it, saying, "It is most
wise that all the people should know the paintings." The commoners would
be driven to ruin and there would be trouble, because these paintings
contain many lies, for many in the pictures have been hailed as gods.

Verbal Arts

In a society where writing was an art limited to a few, as was the ability to read the written word, there was high emphasis on the spoken word. Nahuatl was a highly formalized language, and one that Europeans came to appreciate as florid, elegant, and highly symbolic (Carrasco 2003: 136).

Aztec poetry, which was preserved in oral traditions well into the colonial period, and eventually written down, is said to compare favorably with Old World poetry from Classic cultures. This form of oral tradition included sacred hymns, and epic and lyric poetry (León-Portilla 2002: 67). Of all the forms of poetry just mentioned, the best preserved was lyric poetry. Lyric poetry can be upbeat, using repetition of ideas and expression of sentiments as its hallmarks. A device often used in this type of poetry is the uniting of two words that complement each other to evoke a third idea. An example of this technique includes "flower and song" meaning poetry, "arrow and shield" standing for war, and "seat and mat" implying power (León-Portilla 2002: 68).

Although Aztec society, in most people's minds, evokes imagery of brutal warfare and human sacrifice, it should be remembered that the Aztecs were also, and perhaps more so, accomplished poets. They celebrated love and friendship, but they also lamented the evanescence of life. Consider this poem on friendship (León-Portilla 2002: 68):

> *Now, oh friends,*
> *listen to the words of a dream,*
> *each spring brings us life,*
> *the golden corn refreshes us,*
> *the pink corn becomes a necklace,*
> *At least we know,*
> *the hearts of our friends are true!*

Sentiments like the ones echoed in the poem were part of the education elite children received in the calmecac. There they would receive instructions in rhetorical skills from the tlamatinime. These men were experts in raising philosophical questions about human nature and its relationship to the ultimate truth. They were often described as a "stout torch that does not smoke," and considered ideal guides in human affairs. These men would be among the few who could read and write, and they would rely on these documents as they pondered the fragile and ephemeral condition of human existence (Carrasco 2003: 136).

The tlamatinime firmly believed that there was truth to be found in the realms beyond life, specifically "in the region of the gods above and in the region of the dead below." This is where they were convinced a stable reality existed, a condition that they contrasted with the transitory and vulnerable nature of our own human existence; yet, how could one get to this stable reality? The tlamatinime sought to achieve this goal by connecting human personality with the divine worlds by means of special verbal arts, which they called *in xochitl* or *in cuicatl* (flower or birdsongs).

Recitation of metaphorical speeches was not the unique domain of the tlamatinime. On specific ceremonial occasions, such as the coronation of a ruler, the entry of a youth into the calmecac, the delivery of a baby by a midwife, or a marriage ceremony, the Aztecs would resort to the Huehuetlatolli, or "the Ancient Word." These speeches would often have been imparted to the speaker as part of his or her formal education. Consider how the following speech uttered by a midwife after a baby is born links the human condition with the world of the divine (Carrasco 2003: 138):

> And when the baby had arrived on earth, then the midwife shouted: she gave war cries, which meant that the little woman had fought a good battle, had become a brave warrior, had taken a captive, had captured a baby . . .
>
> If it was a female, she said to it: "My beloved maiden, my youngest one, noblewoman, thou has suffered exhaustion, thou hast become fatigued. They beloved father, the master of the lord of the near, of the nigh, the creator of men, the maker of men, hath sent thee. . . .
>
> "My youngest one! Perhaps thou wilt live for a little while! Are thou our reward? Art thou our reward? Art thou our merit? Perhaps thou wilt know thy grandfather, thy grandmothers, thy kinsmen, thy lineage.
>
> "In what way have thy mother, they father Ometecuhtli, Omecihuatl, arrayed thee? In what manner have they endowed thee?"

Riddles were another form of verbal art. Although Nahuatl was a very formal language, it also lent itself to the creation of what has been called verbal pictures. Sahagún learned from his informants that riddles were part of daily life. Knowing the answers to riddles apparently indicated that the person came from a good family. Consider the following Nahuatl riddles (Carrasco 2003: 139):

> What is a little blue-green jar filled with popcorn? Someone is sure to guess our riddle; it is the sky.
>
> What is it that goes along the foothills of the mountain patting our tortillas with its hands? A butterfly.

Scholars have also identified the art of poetry of war within the realm of verbal arts. This type of poetry was closely tied to the court and to Aztec imperialism. This particular type of poetry was one that was tied to and patronized by the Aztec royal lineage in the various cities throughout the Aztec realm. These royal lineages would order poets to commemorate battles, heroes, sacrifices, and victories. These poems of war would then be recited in the context of the presentation of captive warriors. As we have seen elsewhere, these presentations ultimately led to the sacrifice of the captives.

Because of the high importance associated with these types of poems, the rulers wanted to ensure that there would always be enough poets at hand to commemorate the events just mentioned. In order to achieve this goal, the rulers would set up *cuicacalli,* or houses of song, throughout their cities. In these cuicacalli, specialists in poetic themes, music, and choreography would be at hand to provide the theatrical backdrop for important festivals.

Once composition of a war poem was completed, the people needed to learn and memorize it. Poets and dancers were sent to the various neighborhoods and a town crier would call the citizenry to a meeting so they could all learn the new poem. Considering the political circles patronizing such poems, this approach ensured that everyone was exposed to the ideology of the ruling circles. Expressing Aztec sentiments that might sound strange in our ears, the Aztec poets would refer to warriors as poets, not as powerful individuals. The Aztec poets transformed the battlefield into a garden of religious beauty, where warriors avoid the magical transformation of death (by killing or capturing their opponents first) (Carrasco 2003: 143).

THE AZTEC EDUCATION SYSTEM

The Tepochcalli

The Tepochcalli was a school associated with the wards, or *calpulli*. Commoners and lower-ranking nobility associated with the calpulli attended. A career in the military would start with years of preparation in the tepochcalli. Parents who wished that their child served in the army would take it to the tepochcalli at a very early age: 20 days after birth. The master of youths, the *tiachcauh*, would received gifts from the parents, hoping to ensure the child's entrance to the school at the appropriate age (Hassig 1988: 30–31). That age was 15, when the father relinquished responsibility to the tepochcalli to train the boy to become a warrior (Hassig 1988: 31). These schools would educate a sizeable group of students. In 1519, the estimated number of students attending the tepochcalli ranged from 8,380 to 11,180 (Hassig 1988: 31).

The training would entail duties inside the school building as well as participation in campaigns in a noncombatant role, such as shield-bearer. Tepochcalli students would eat at home, but would sleep at the school (Hassig 1988: 33). Weapons training included learning how to handle a bow and arrow, how to throw darts with a spear thrower, or atlatl, and how to handle a shield and sword (Hassig 1988: 33).

The Calmecac

As outlined in Chapter 6, the Calmecac provided religious, political, and military training primarily for children of the highest-ranking nobility. These students were destined to become priests or warriors. Some lower-ranking commoners were allowed to study at the calmecac and did so to become priests (Hassig 1988: 34). In this regard, the calmecac served its function as one of the avenues for upward social mobility.

Training at the calmecac generally began at a much earlier age than it did at the tepochcalli. The king's sons would enter the school at age 5, whereas the sons of high-ranking noblemen would enter as early as age 6 (Hassig 1988: 35). The training provided here was also more rigorous than it was at the tepochcalli. Students were taught reading and writing, the calendar, discourse, songs, and other aspects of Aztec life (Hassig 1988: 35). Weapons training started at age 15 (Hassig 1988: 36). This training was very thorough and tended to take place at the houses of the military orders that each of the students had pledged to join. These orders included that of the eagle order and that of the jaguar order.

AZTEC PHILOSOPHY

Colonial-period transcripts of preconquest oral traditions indicate that the Aztecs engaged in what we would call a philosophical discourse. One of the recurring themes in Aztec thinking was one that captivates minds today as well: the fleeting nature of our existence on earth. This theme is repeated in various poems and writings. The ruler of Texcoco, Netzahualcoyotl, is said to have put it this way (León-Portilla 2003: 69):

> "I, Netzahualcoyotl, ask this:
> Is it true that one lives on the earth?
> What is it that has roots here?
> Not forever on earth,
> Only a brief while here.
> Although it were jade,
> It will be broken;
> Although it were turquoise,
> It will be shattered
> As if it were just quetzal feather.
> Not forever on earth,
> Only a brief while here."

The Aztecs also broached the subject of what is usually associated with German philosophical thinking: How do we know that what we see is in fact reality and not a dream? We find the same question, however, expressed in an Aztec poem (León-Portilla 2002):

> Do we speak true words here, giver of life?
> We merely dream, we only rise from a dream,
> All is like a dream.
> No one speaks here of truth.

Philosophical thought involves a desire to the meaning and true value of things. A philosopher can be described as a person who "must experience the need to explain to himself why things happen as they do" (León-Portilla 1990: 4). Such a sentiment existed in Aztec culture. Poetry was the favorite medium to express these thoughts. Their quest to find a foundation for man and the universe was central to Aztec philosophical pursuits. They tackled such questions as "what is truth," as illustrated in the following poem (León-Portilla 1990: 7):

> Does man possess any truth?
> If not, our song is no longer true.

Is anything stable and lasting?
What reaches its aim?

These are age-old questions. In some cases, cultures develop religious doctrines to provide answers. The fact that the Aztecs had poems such as these strongly supports the notion that they were no longer satisfied with the answers provided by religion. Instead they pursued rational thinking as a way to find answers (León-Portilla 1990: 8–9).

Aztec philosophical teachings occurred in the context of the calmecac. Some of these instructions were written down in the early colonial period by Aztecs who had attended the calmecac. There are references to wise men, *tlamatini* or philosophers, in some of these documents (we shall see later in this chapter that the term *tlamatini* is also applied to doctors). These men are described as teachers, psychologists, moralists, examiners of the physical world, and men interested in things metaphysical (León-Portilla 1990: 15).

AZTEC LEGAL SYSTEM

The Aztec legal system has been the subject of a number of studies. Certain concepts, in legal terms known as *legalism, the reasonable man,* and *the role of precedent,* were in use in the Aztec legal system. The concept of legalism holds that rules are "the exclusive manifestation and source of law," and that they are also "the exclusive and concrete answers to particular disputes" (Pospisil 1971: 22; Offner 1977: 141). Another standard used is that of the "reasonable man." This entails using implied standards of behavior (i.e., that of a reasonable man) to be applied to the case by the judge (Offner 1977: 142).

Aztecs placed a premium on being a law-abiding citizen. Their term, *nahuatilpiani,* means exactly that: "he who keeps the law" (Offner 1977: 144). Laws were promulgated and obedience was strictly enforced. In Tenochtitlan, Moctecuhzuma changed the legal code, effectively widening the gap that existed between commoners and the aristocracy (Smith 1996: 52). The new laws also included stipulations as to what punishments should be handed out in certain cases. Among other things, these are some examples of what Moctecuhzuma proclaimed:

- The king must never appear in public except when the occasion is extremely important and unavoidable . . .
- Only the king and the prime-minister Tlacael may wear sandals within the palace . . .
- The great lords, who are twelve, may wear special [cotton] mantles of certain make and design, and the minor lords, according to their valor and accomplishments, may wear others . . .
- The commoners will not be allowed to wear cotton clothing, under pain of death, but can use only garments of maguey fiber . . .
- Only the great noblemen and valiant warriors are given license to build a house with a second story; for disobeying this law a person receives the death penalty.

- Only the great lords are to wear labrets (lip plugs), ear plugs, and nose plugs of gold and precious stones . . .
- All the neighborhoods (calpulli) will possess schools or monasteries for young men where they will learn religion and correct comportment.
- There is to be a rigorous law regarding adulterers. They are to be stoned and thrown into the rivers or to the buzzards.
- Thieves will be sold for the price of their theft, unless the theft be grave, having been committed many times. Such thieves will be punished by death.

In Texcoco, laws were drawn up against drunkenness, theft, and adultery. They meted out different punishments to offenders depending on their social class, occupation, age, and sex. Even the type of evidence and the number of previous offenses was taken into account (Offner 1977: 143; Berdan 2002: 47).

Provincial judges resided in the other capitals of the Triple Alliance. They were housed in the palaces of the local rulers. Their job was to hear cases arising out of those localities (Gibson 1971: 389).

Punishment

It seems that punishments were meted out based on the social status of the guilty party, as well as the circumstances in which a misdeed occurred. In general, it seems that offenses carried out in the public arena were treated more harshly than those that happened in private. Moreover, social status also determined where and how a person was punished.

For example, the students who attended the tepochcalli were not allowed to drink wine. If ever a youth was found drunk in public, or if he was found with wine in his possession, or if he was seen lying down in the street, or if he was observed singing in company of other drunkards, then swift punishment would follow. A student of commoner origin would be beaten to death, or even garroted in front of everyone. This was supposed to set an example. If the culprit was of noble birth, however, he would be spared this public spectacle; instead, he would be garroted in secret (Bandelier 1932: 198).

A priest who was found drunk met the same fate as the students; he was condemned to die. The same was true for any dignitary who would be found drunk in the palace of the ruler. A lesser punishment, such as the loss of office and title, would befall any official who managed to get caught drunk at home. The difference here compared with the preceding cases is that drunkenness at home presumably did not involve scandal. The law was more lenient for the lower social classes and their overindulgences of alcohol. Any regular citizen who had had a few too many would have their head shaved for their first offence. A second offence, however, would have the same severe consequences: death (Soustelle 1961: 157). It is interesting to note, however, that the enjoyment of octli was not completely forbidden. Old men and women were allowed to drink (Soustelle 1961: 157).

MEDICINE

If there is one aspect that stands out with regard to the European conquest of the Americas, it is not the violence that accompanied it; rather, it is the incredible loss of life that the indigenous populations suffered as a result of being exposed to unknown diseases. This brings up these questions: How healthy were the Aztecs before the arrival of the Spanish? What kind of medical knowledge did they possess? There is another question related to this: What do we know about the Aztec's understanding of illnesses and how to cure them?

Scholars generally agree that Precolumbian people were relatively free of disease. Various suggestions to explain this phenomenon have been put forward. One hypothesis has been that the traditional land route across the Bering Strait taken by the original settlers acted as a "cold filter." The idea here is that the cold would have killed those pathogens that spent part of their life cycle outside the human body, as well as any insects that would have been carried along on this trek.

Second, compared with the inhabitants of the Old World, Precolumbian people were not as exposed to animal-borne infections and parasites for the simple reason that they had fewer domesticated animals.

Finally, large urban agglomerations were a relatively late phenomenon in the New World. This meant that such crowd diseases as measles, smallpox, typhus, and cholera were absent. These diseases need large urban agglomerations to maintain themselves. Although Mesoamerica was home to some impressive urban centers, the time interval between the existence of these cities and the Spanish conquest was too short for these diseases to develop (Ortiz de Montellano 1990: 121). Once the Spanish had arrived, these diseases were introduced on the first day of contact.

There is an ongoing debate about the presence, before the arrival of the Spanish, of diseases such as syphilis and malaria. Some scholars have argued that syphilis could be the expression of an infectious disease called treponematosis. Among hunters and gatherers, the bacterium that causes the infection enters through the skin and causes a disease called yaws. The argument continues, however, that once people moved to cooler and drier climates and started living in urban environments, the bacterium changed its point of entry into our bodies from the skin to the mucous tissue of the mouth and genitalia. At that point we are dealing with syphilis (Ortiz de Montellano 1990: 122). Another theory holds that the yaws and syphilis both evolved out of a treponemal infection. This still leaves the question of where the disease evolved unanswered. Finally, evidence derived from skeletal material in the Americas suggests that syphilis originated in the New World (Ortiz de Montellano 1990: 122).

The question of where malaria arose is still being debated as well. It is assumed that the Anopheles mosquito had always been present in the Americas. What may have been missing, however, was the malaria parasite itself, Plasmodium. The Aztecs do refer to a condition they called atonahuitztli, or aquatic fever, and described it as an intermittent fever with episodes of chills

(Ortiz de Montellano 1990: 122). When we compare the distribution of the malaria parasite throughout the world, there is evidence to suggest that the parasite may have been a recent arrival in the Americas (i.e., that it was introduced when the Spanish arrived). In Africa and Asia, we find malaria in all mammals; in the Americas it exists only in humans and some cebid monkeys (Ortiz de Montellano 1990: 123). This more limited dispersal of the parasite reflects its more recent arrival and therefore lack of time to infect additional life forms. Another argument in favor of late introduction of malaria into the Americas comes from the eyewitness reports from early explorers, who relate finding thriving indigenous communities in those regions that today are infested by malaria. The apparent lack of disease-related problems, especially malaria-related stress, supports the notion that malaria was not indigenous, but rather was introduced from outside the Americas (Ortiz de Montellano 1990: 123).

Medical Knowledge Among the Aztecs

Scholars have researched what cures the Aztecs pursued and have also used the list of remedies as indications of the ailments that afflicted the Aztecs. This is a roundabout way of answering a question that our sources might not always provide a straightforward answer to: What diseases were prevalent among the Aztecs?

From lists of remedies thus complied (Ortiz de Montellano 1990: 125), it appears that infectious diseases were more prevalent in Mexico than they were in Europe. There are good indications that the Aztecs suffered from infections of the respiratory and gastrointestinal tracts, which are still leading causes of death in modern Mexico (Ortiz de Montellano 1990: 125). Diarrhea, dysentery, and fevers were prevalent.

Some scholars have suggested that the Aztecs had a very high birthrate and equally high childhood mortality. Archaeologists excavating Aztec cemeteries have determined that skeletons of children between ages 4 and 6 represented more than 10 percent of the sample. Indications are that the mortality rate of newborns was even higher. Even for those who survived the dangerous years of childhood, the average life span of an Aztec was 34–40 years. Although this is short compared with our standards, it compares well with an average life span in eighteenth-century France, where people on average lived to be 29 (Ortiz de Montellano 1990: 126).

The silver lining in all of this is that the Aztecs would not have suffered much from such chronic diseases as cancer, strokes, and cardiovascular problems because, simply put, they did not live long enough to be struck by these ailments, which typically appear at a much more advanced age. In addition, the Aztec diet, combined with strenuous daily exercise, would have kept incidences of cardiovascular problems low (Ortiz de Montellano 1990: 126).

The Aztecs were familiar with neurological afflictions, including epilepsy and paralysis. Convulsions traditionally were associated with deified women who had died in childbirth. Anyone who met with them was subject to epilepsy and paralysis (Ortiz de Montellano 1990: 126). It is said that dead men do not tell tales, but, in reality, they often do. Physical anthropologists have studied Aztec bones looking for evidence of disease and violent behavior. Many Aztec skeletons show evidence of fractured bones that had healed. Signs of arthritis and rheumatism were present. There are indications of micro- and macrocephaly among the stillborn or newborn babies. Achondroplastic dwarfism was present; we know that dwarfs were associated by the Aztecs with the supernatural realm. The imperial court was a place where dwarfs, hunchbacks, and albinos would often be seen (Ortiz de Montellano 1990: 127).

The advantage of breastfeeding, assuring the continued intake of sufficient amounts of calcium, becomes apparent in the total absence of rickets. Corn prepared with alkali and made into tortillas ensured that dietary calcium continued to be ingested during childhood and adulthood (Ortiz de Montellano 1990: 127).

Aspects of Public Health

In some aspects, the Aztecs in their capital were quite advanced in protecting public health. Access to clean drinking water plays an important role in maintaining good overall health. As we saw in Chapter 9, the Aztecs constructed two aqueducts connecting the city to springs on the mainland. To put things in perspective, one should know that the citizens of London relied on the polluted Thames as late as 1854 to supply themselves with water for all their needs (Ortiz de Montellano 1990: 127). The Aztecs also showed a degree of sophistication when it came to waste management. Although a drainage system was lacking and waste water eventually found its way into the lake system, the Aztecs did come up with a way to deal with human waste. Excrement was collected by canoe from both public places and private homes. The waste was either used as fertilizer in the *chinampas* or was sold in the markets to help tan animal hides. Urine was collected in pots and was used as a mordant for dyeing cloth (Ortiz de Montellano 1990: 128). The city itself had an army of public servants sweeping and watering the streets and maintaining overall cleanliness.

Aspects of Personal Health

In terms of personal hygiene, the Aztecs maintained practices very different from their contemporaries elsewhere in the world. Early colonial manuscripts abound with references to soaps, deodorants, toothpastes, and breath sweeteners. Contrary to European custom of the time, the Aztecs bathed very often (Ortiz de Montellano 1990: 128). In general, one could say that the Aztecs were healthy people, because of good nutrition, relative freedom of endemic diseases, and advanced public sanitation (Ortiz de Montellano 1990: 128).

Aztec Etiology: Sources of Illness

Aztecs had a holistic view to explain illness. They were convinced that the origins of illness were complex and that they could not be explained by pointing to one cause. The Aztecs therefore encapsulated elements from three realms into their diagnoses and explanations: the supernatural, the magical, and the natural (Ortiz de Montellano 1990: 130).

On the level of the supernatural, the Aztec feared the gods as a source of disease. One of the aspects of Tezcatlipoca was Titlacahuan. This supreme Aztec deity was capable of rewarding pious Aztecs as well as punishing them for breaking vows. When the entire population was guilty of committing a sin, then the punishment would sometimes affect the entire population. The presence of plagues was one example of what the Aztecs considered collective punishment. When the Spanish started their conquest and infectious diseases ran rampant through the native populations, the Aztecs were convinced that these afflictions came from Tezcatlipoca as punishment for a wrong committed by the entire population (Ortiz de Montellano 1990: 131).

People made up another source of illness. This is where we enter the realm of magic. In the Aztec mind, it was perfectly possible for a sorcerer to put a spell on an individual, who then fell ill. The most commonly used term for sorcerer was *tlacatecolotl*. Because this word is very similar to that meaning "owl" (*tecolotl*, or horned owl), the symbol used to refer to an Aztec sorcerer was quite often an owl (Ortiz de Montellano 1990: 133).

A sorcerer had the power to cast spells, sometimes leaving them behind in a physical form. For example, the Aztecs were convinced that an ailment could be left by the side of the road, where it would be picked up by the feet of the first person who walked by. This is how they often explained *xoxoalli*, an inflammation of the feet and ankles. Spells sometimes took on the form of ants, who would then convey it to their victims (Ortiz de Montellano 1990: 140).

Aztec sorcerers sometimes engaged in contact magic. They would try to ensure the outcome of a spell by performing certain acts, during which they would have certain objects or materials. They would later then bring these objects or materials in contact with the intended victim in the hope no doubt of transferring the spell onto the victim. For example, there was a sorcerer called a *tetlepanquetzqui* ("He who prepares fire for people"). He would try to kill people by first adorning a rod with funerary paper and then performing rituals associated with burial in front of it. Some of these rituals involved placing food in front of the rod for a period of 4 days, the customary period of mourning. On the fifth day, the victim would be offered some of that food, while the sorcerer kept wishing that person to die. In some cases, the sorcerer would go further and try to acquire some of that person's hair, so that it could be burned. This was seen as symbolically presaging the cremation of the corpse of the victim (Ortiz de Montellano 1990: 142).

Although knowing that someone out there might be casting spells and affecting your well-being as a result could be very disconcerting, the Aztecs did not stand idly by either. They took active measures to combat this type of magic. As a countermeasure, the Aztecs would try to destroy the magical powers of sorcerers by capturing them and then cutting the hair from the crown of their head, an approach that might remind some of us today of the story of Samson and Delilah. Once the hair had been cut, the Aztecs believed that the sorcerers would lose their magical powers and would eventually die (Ortiz de Montellano 1990: 140).

Cases of belief in sympathetic magic are also known. Anyone eating the seeds of a tree called *pochotl* was doomed in the Aztecs' mind to become as rotund as the tree trunk. Most of the examples of Aztec sympathetic magic seem to pertain to expectant mothers. Any action by the mother was believed to affect the unborn baby. A pregnant woman was not supposed to chew gum or tar. If she did, then the baby risked being born with swollen lips, a cleft palate, or the inability to suckle. If a mother burned corncobs, then she risked giving birth to a baby with pockmarks. A mother was not supposed to see anyone being hanged for fear that the baby would get entangled in the umbilical cord (Ortiz de Montellano 1990: 142).

Diagnosing and Explaining Illness

We know that the Aztecs approached illness from a holistic point of view. As noted, they believed that the causes of what afflicted a person could reside in three realms: the supernatural, the magic, and the natural realm. With regard to those ailments that had their origin in the supernatural and/or in the magic realm, the Aztecs resorted to specialists to diagnose and cure a person.

In order to cure someone afflicted by an ailment of supernatural origin, a specialist would be required to identify the deity that had been offended and suggest the appropriate rituals to appease him or her. The Aztecs clearly believed in proactive behavior and would engage in conciliatory rituals long before an ailment had struck and the services of specialists were required. Specialists would be required to travel to other worlds in order to divine what had gone wrong and how this situation could be rectified. Such travel to other realms involved partaking in hallucinogens. Those specialists who took "medicine" were known as *paini* ("he who drinks medicine").

The Aztecs resorted to various rituals to divine the future. In all cases described in the following the intent was to find out: Would the patient live or die? In one instance, a diviner would tie knots along a cord and then pull on the ends of the cord. The patient would recover if the knots untied or loosened; however, if the knots were further tightened by this action, then the patient was destined to die.

Most of the divinatory rituals involved corn, especially corn kernels. Corn kernels were sometimes tossed onto a piece of textile. The patient's future was divined by assessing how the kernels were arranged after they were thrown. If they scattered, the patient would die. If they had come down in piles or rows, there was hope for full recovery. Diviners would sometimes shape the kernels by biting off the points of the kernels. These kernels were then thrown onto a cloth. If they fell with the bitten end down, the patient would recover (Ortiz de Montellano 1990: 144–145). Kernels were sometimes thrown into a bowl of water. If they sank to the bottom, prognosis for recovery was good. If they floated, however, one's days were numbered (Ortiz de Montellano 1990: 146). Aztec diviners had ways of affecting the outcome of such rituals as throwing kernels into a bowl of water. They realized that fresh corn tends to sink in water, whereas older kernels will float. By selecting one or the other kind of kernel, a diviner could rig the prognosis (Ortiz de Montellano 1990: 148).

Aztec diagnosis and treatment of wounds caused by natural factors was relatively effective. In some cases modern medicine has come around to corroborate Aztec beliefs. For example, headaches were believed to be caused by an excess amount of blood in the head. Modern medicine has confirmed that some migraine headaches involve constriction of the blood vessels and subsequent increase in blood pressure and pain. As far as treatment of such conditions is concerned, there might not be as much support forthcoming from modern medicine. Consider the ways in which the Aztecs attempted to reduce the perceived excess blood in the cranium: they would induce bleeding, usually through the nose. The patient would be required to inhale specific kinds of herbs that were thought to produce nosebleeds. In some cases obsidian knives were used to cause the nosebleed or to draw blood from other areas of the head (Ortiz de Montellano 1990: 150).

Curing Illness

Curing illnesses was something that required a holistic approach. This is a logical extension of the Aztec holistic approach to diagnosing ailments. In the case where a person was deemed to have been afflicted by a disease that could be attributed to a god, rituals, offerings, confessions, and prayers to that god were aimed at curing the disease. For example, some skin and eye diseases were attributed to the god *Xipe Totec*. In order to obtain a cure, people with these symptoms would participate in *Xipe Totec* ceremonies. This entailed wearing the flayed skins of those people who had first impersonated the deity and were then sacrificed. In Aztec religion, these mortal impersonators had become the deity. By wearing the skin of these sacrificial victims, it was believed, the patients could be cured (Ortiz de Montellano 1990: 163).

The cure sometimes lay in confessing first, followed by ritual actions. Any illness brought about by sexual immorality required one to confess before the goddess *Tlazolteotl*. One aspect of this goddess was called *Tlaelquani*, or "filth eater." Confession would typically be followed by penance, including fasting and puncturing one's tongue with a sharp reed (Ortiz de Montellano 1990: 164).

Incantations were also used to heal. The Aztecs were masters in the use of flowery speech, the format often used to find a cure for an ailment. The healer would acquire additional powers by resorting to such incantations. Aztec patients would know and expect this; in their worldview, it was appropriate to use special words to divine the nature of the disease and to identify the cure. Today, such an approach might be dismissed as being nothing more than a placebo, affecting a psychological benefit rather than a "real" change in the disposition of the patient. In the Aztec world, however, incantations were not considered similar to a placebo. They were a necessary step that had to be taken to achieve a cure (Ortiz de Montellano 1990: 168–169).

In some cases the Aztec resorted to cures similar to ours. A bone fracture would be treated with a plaster called *poztecpatli* ("fracture medicine"), a

A statue of *Tlazolteotl*, Aztec goddess of childbirth. (Douglas Miller/Ropical Press Agency/Getty Images)

splint, and an incantation. The presence of the latter reinforces what we have seen earlier: diagnosing and curing an ailment required a holistic approach. In some cases, when a fractured bone failed to heal, the Aztecs resorted to a twenty-first-century medical technique. The fractured bone was exposed, and a very resinous stick was inserted within the bone. The cut was then covered with the fracture medicine just mentioned. This approach resembles what modern doctors call an intramedullary nail (Ortiz de Montellano 1990: 174). In a similar vein, Aztecs would lance a knee to relieve accumulated fluid by using a pointed thorn (Ortiz de Montellano 1990: 179).

Aside from setting bones and lancing knees, the Aztec also possessed extensive knowledge of accumulated herbal cures. These cures would be administered by *tlamatini*, referring to a wise man or a doctor. The Aztecs were fully aware that there were people who had true knowledge of nature and could heal people. They also knew that there were charlatans, who would only deceive their patients. Consider this passage (León-Portilla 1990: 26–27):

The true doctor.
He is a wise man;
> *he imparts life.*

A tried specialist,
He has worked with herbs, stones, trees, and roots.
His remedies have been tested;
> *he examines, he experiments,*
> *he alleviates sickness.*

He massages aches and sets broken bones.
He administers purges and potions;
> *he bleeds his patients;*
> *he cuts and he sews the wound;*
> *he brings about reactions;*
> *he stanches the bleeding with ashes.*

The false physician.
He ridicules and deceives the people;
> *he brings on indigestion;*
> *he makes illness worse;*
> *his medicines are fatal.*

He has dark secrets he will not reveal;
> *he is a sorcerer and a witch;*
> *he is familiar with the noxious herbs and possesses their seeds,*
> *he practices divination with knotted ropes.*

He makes sickness worse;
> *his herbs and seeds poison and his cures kill.*

Emperor Moctecuhzuma Illhuicamina I established a botanical garden in Tenochtitlan. Plants gathered from all over the Aztec realm were brought to the city and grown in this garden. Some of the plants were used for medicinal purposes. In what seems like a Precolumbian version of socialized medicine, the Aztecs gave plants with medicinal qualities to patients. This was done for free on the condition that the patients returned to report the results. After the conquest, the Spanish sources admiringly relate how Aztec doctors had been able to heal Spaniards who had long suffered from serious and chronic diseases (Ortiz de Montellano 1990: 181).

An area in which the Aztecs excelled over the Spanish was that of battlefield medicine. The European approach current at the time of conquest was to cauterize the wound with boiling oil, followed by the recitation of prayers. European doctors fully expected infection to set in; in fact, they were waiting for "laudable pus" to develop, which they saw as a sign that healing had begun. Because the Aztecs were often at war, their doctors had ample opportunity to engage in medicine. As a result, they had developed an array of effective techniques to treat wounds. Sahagún (Ortiz de Montellano 1990: 182) relates how:

First, the blood is quickly washed away with hot urine. And when it has been washed away,
then hot maguey sap is squeezed thereon. When it has been squeezed out on the place where

the head is wounded, then once again maguey sap, to which are added [the herb] called mat-
lalxihuitl and lampblack with salt stirred in, is placed on it. And when [this] has been placed
on, then it is quickly wrapped in order that the air will not enter there, and so it heals. And if
one's flesh is inflamed, this medicine which has been mentioned is placed on two or three
times. But if one's flesh is not inflamed, this medicine which has been mentioned is placed on
only once and for all.

Aztec doctors were also specialized in obstetrics. Midwives would visit the expectant mother around the seventh or eighth month of the pregnancy. They would examine the unborn baby by feeling around the mother's belly. When delivery was imminent, the midwife would wash and massage the mother who lay down in a steam bath. If needed, the midwife would turn the baby by external massage, in order to avoid a breech delivery. Giving birth was done by squatting rather than lying down. Contractions could be brought about by administering an oxytocic drug. This medicine, known as *cihuapatli,* continued to be used into the colonial period and even today in Mexico's rural areas (Ortiz de Montellano 1990: 185).

We know of other Aztec empirical cures. When an Aztec was bitten by a spider or a snake, treatment would involve making a cut into the wound, sucking out the poison, and rubbing ground-up tobacco into the wound (Ortiz de Montellano 1990: 187–188).

The use of obsidian scalpels may also have contributed to some of the medical success the Aztecs had. An obsidian scalpel has sharper edges than a scalpel made of surgical steel. Because of this sharpness, the cut made by an obsidian scalpel would result in less damage to the tissue, which in turn ensures faster healing (Ortiz de Montellano 1990: 188).

ART, MUSIC, AND DANCE

Art

An important aspect of Aztec art is that it was highly symbolic. Sculpture, painting, architecture, dance, and poetry all contain references to religious symbolism. Moreover, scholars have suggested that Aztec art, and Precolumbian art in general, begins and ends with myth (Matos Moctezuma 2003: 39).

For Westerners, art falls within the realm of the senses. In other words, art is supposed to be seen, or heard, in order to be appreciated. This was not the case for the Aztecs. Some of their art could not be seen, and was not intended to be seen. It existed, for example, in representations of *Tlaltecuhtli,* an earthly god. Statues representing this god were carved underneath, in places that could not be seen. This made perfect sense to the Aztecs, given the realm over which the gods ruled (Matos Moctezuma 2003: 41).

The Aztecs were accomplished artists, and the abundance of artwork that has survived is an eloquent testimony to this. Moreover, written documents also refer to the production of art, and the patronage of art by Aztec rulers. The Toltec city of Tula is often invoked as a place of origin for Aztec-period artistic endeavors and capabilities. We find the term *tolteca* referring to "prime official artist." The Toltec name also shows up in the term *toltecayotl*, which has been translated as meaning "artistic sensitivity" (Olguín 2002: 56).

Aztec-language documents also talk about the concept "artist," and do so by using various terms. *Yolteotl* can be translated as "god in his heart," and *tlayol-teuhuiani* means "he who puts the deified heart into objects." *Moyolnonotzani,* or "he who confers with his heart," reinforces the notion that seemed to have existed in Aztec minds that artists were special. This is undoubtedly also a notion supported by the fact that a lot of Aztec art was closely linked to political and religious topics (Olguín 2002: 56).

The Aztecs seem to have categorized artists into different ranks. They based this ranking on the perceived importance of the works. Among the most highly regarded artists were the *amantecas,* those who produced feather art, the *tlacuiloque,* or scribes, and the artisans who worked with such semi-precious stones as jade and turquoise. The gold- and silversmiths were also held in high regard; they too were referred to with the title of *tolteca,* or "prime official artist." These men were followed in the ranking of artists by such craftsmen as carpenters, bricklayers, whitewashers, potters, spinners, and weavers (Olguín 2002: 56).

The written record has left us only brief indications of how art was appreciated by the Aztecs, in particular by the Aztec elite. In one such example, we read about emperor Moctecuhzuma Ilhuicamina I's desire to perpetuate his memory by having scenes carved into Chapultepec hill. It seems that the emperor was very pleased with the results because the sculptors were rewarded with clothes described as "embroidered cloths" and "honorable garments" (Olguín 2002: 57).

It is hard for us to argue that the Aztecs had a concept of art for art's sake, although we should not necessarily deny them that sensibility. On the other hand, what we know of the context of Aztec art and the content of Aztec art does seem to point to a utilitarian purpose of art: it served religious, economic, and political purposes.

Feather Work

Feather works were produced by a special class of artisans, and consumed by the upper crust of Aztec society. You have already read that one way in which membership to a specific social class (especially higher social class) could be signaled to others was through the wearing of feather cloaks and shields decorated with feathers. We know from Aztec tribute requirements that fancy feathers from the tropical lowlands of Mesoamerica were very much in demand. In a few fortunate cases Aztec-period, or early colonial, feather works have survived. The collections of the Museum für Völkerkunde in Vienna have several of these objects. One of these is a feather headdress worn by Aztec priests in the early sixteenth century. It consists of 450 quetzal feathers, gold appliqué decorations, and fiber netting (Olguín 2002: 62). Perhaps one of the most famous Aztec feather-work objects is a shield. It is dated to about 1500. With a diameter of 70 cm (slightly more than 2 ft), it contains feathers, sheet

This shield may have been part of a Spanish shipment made in 1522. The animal in the center may represent a coyote, an animal associated with war. The speech scroll in front of the animal depicts water and fire, another reference to war. (Werner Forman/Corbis)

gold, agave paper, leather, and reed. The shield had two loops for carrying. The feathers used are those of scarlet macaws, blue cotingas, yellow orioles, and spoonbills. The shield carries an image of a coyote. These animals are associated with war. This connotation, plus the fact that coyote might also refer to a military order in Mesoamerica, leaves no doubt as to the function of the shield (Van Bussel 2002: 475).

Stone Sculpture

The Aztecs carved monumental art, as well as medium- and small-sized objects, out of a wide range of stone. The sculpting of monumental stone sculptures predates Aztec history. We find large stone columns in the shape of human figures at the sites of Teotihuacan and Tula, predating, in some cases, Aztec stone

Turqouise Aztec pectoral ornament in the shape of a double-headed serpent. (Werner Forman/Corbis)

monuments by 1,000 years. Aside from these so-called atlantes, the Aztecs also carved large calendar stones. An image often used in souvenir shops today is that of the Aztec Sun stone, one of many such circular calendars. Another example of such a stone is the so-called Tizoc's stone, discussed in Chapter 3. In general, monumental stone sculptures were put on public display during celebrations (Olguín 2002: 60).

Alabaster, mined in the present-day Mexican state of Puebla, was used to produce medium- to small-sized objects. Some of these were deer heads and rattle staffs. We know that alabaster was also used by the inhabitants of Teotihuacan to carve masks. We occasionally find such masks in the context of an Aztec building (Matos Moctezuma 1990: 219).

Other Art Forms

The Aztec elite commissioned the manufacture of turquoise mosaic masks, gold and silver jewelry, and jade and crystal-rock ornaments. A beautiful example of a turquoise work of art is a pectoral in the shape of a double-headed serpent. It dates back to the period of 1400–1521. The serpent was made out of wood decorated with a mosaic of small turquoise pieces. Cut-shell fragments were fashioned to represent the serpent's fangs (Olguín 2002: 57).

There are only a few examples of painting that have survived. Most of these have come from the excavations of the Great Temple. The pallet used a wide range of colors, including blue, orange, red, yellow, white, and black (Matos

Stone representation of an Aztec wooden drum. (Gianni Dagli Orti/Corbis)

Moctezuma 2003: 62). Mural paintings have also been found outside Tenochtitlan. At the ceremonial center of Malinalco, famous for its temple carved into the rock, a painting was found showing a procession of warriors. Because we already knew that Malinalco played an important role in the training of Eagle Warriors, this depiction does not come as a total surprise (Matos Moctezuma 2003: 64).

Musical Instruments

Very little is known of Aztec music because it was not written down. In the absence of Aztec sheet music, we are forced to rely on descriptions, depictions of instruments, and surviving instruments. Aztec musical instruments included both percussion and wind instruments. Vertical wooden drums, called *huehuetl*, were very popular.

They were made from tree trunks, and an example of such an upright drum was preserved in Malinalco. Its decoration was carved, depicting, among other things, the symbol for the present world-era, Nahui Ollin (four movement),

Aztec musicians playing shells, rattles, and drums. (Bettmann/Corbis)

and a series of warriors (Olguín 2002: 62). The Aztec also played on horizontal drums, or *teponaxtli*. These instruments would also be made out of wood and were decorated with scenes relating to the ceremonies in which the drums were used (Olguín 2002: 62).

Aztec musicians also played ceramic rattles and rasps. The latter were sometimes made out of human or animal bones. The omexicahuaztli was a special kind of rasp instrument that was fashioned out of a human femur, or thighbone. These were scraped with a shell (Olguín 2002: 62).

Sea shells and ceramic shells made to resemble sea shells functioned as trumpets. Ceramic whistles, sometimes used in human sacrifice, were also part of the repertoire of musical instruments (Olguín 2002: 62).

Art, dance, and music were important in the life of the Aztecs. This is illustrated by the fact that the god *Xochipilli-Macuilxochitl* (or "Flower-Prince-Five

Three Aztec men wearing long feathered headdresses perform a ceremonial dance at the Chehaw National Indian Festival in Chehaw Park, Albany, Georgia, May 22, 1995. (Kevin Fleming/Corbis)

Flower") was the god of music, song, and dance. We have seen earlier (see Chapter 6) that children attending the tepochcalli, or neighborhood schools, received instructions in singing, dancing, and playing music (Smith 1996: 137).

Dance

Of Aztec dancing, Jacques Soustelle (Soustelle 1961: 243) remarked: "Dancing was not only an amusement; it was not even only a rite; it was a way of deserving the favor of the gods 'by serving them and calling upon them with one's whole body.'"

People would dance on different occasions. A great and sacred dance was organized during the month of the year called Uey tecuilhuitl. Only army captains and battle-tested warriors were allowed to participate. This dance took place at night, in the light of a multitude of torches. These warriors would dance in pairs. Each pair was then joined by a woman (said to be the *auianime*, the companions of the unmarried soldiers). These women would dance with their hair loose, on their shoulders; they would have been dressed in a fringed, embroidered skirt (Soustelle 1961: 46). The dancers also wore jewels, used both as body ornaments and to signal their social position. This dance was apparently sufficiently important for the emperor to take part in it (Soustelle 1961: 47).

Another solemn dance would be performed during the month called Tlaxochimaco, which followed Uey tecuilhuitl, this time during the day. People would dance around noon in honor of Huitzilopochtli, and do so in front of his temple. Again, the participants would be warriors, who were organized according to their rank and achievements, as well as women (Soustelle 1961: 47).

Every 4 years, during the festival honoring the Aztec god of fire, the emperor and his chief ministers would engage in a "dance of the dignitaries." They would do so dressed up in their finest outfits (Soustelle 1961: 47).

Religious ceremonies were often accompanied by dances. In some cases, these dances must have appeared totally out of this world. For example, during the ceremony of the Tlacaxipeualiztli, the final act would consist of a dance performed by priests dressed up in human skins (Soustelle 1961: 146).

REFERENCES

Bandelier, Fanny R. 1932. *A History of Ancient Mexico by Fray Bernardino de Sahagún.* Translated by Fanny R. Bandelier from the Spanish version of Carlos Maria de Bustamante. Nashville: Fisk University Press.

Berdan, Frances. 2002. Aztec Society: Economy, Tribute and Warfare. In *Aztecs.* Edited by Eduardo Matos Moctezuma and Felipe Solis Olguín, pp. 38–47. London: Royal Academy of Arts.

Carrasco, Davíd. 1999. *City of Sacrifice. The Aztec Empire and the Role of Violence in Civilization.* Boston: Beacon Press.

Garcia Samper, Asuncion and Rossana Enrique. 2002. *El Santo Juan Diego el mensajero indigena de la Virgen de Guadalupe.* Mexico: Centro de Estudios Mesoamericanos.

Harvey, Herbert R., and Barbara J. Williams. 1986. Decipherment and Some Implications of Aztec Numerical Glyphs. In *Native American Mathematics.* Edited by Michael P. Closs, pp. 237–259. Austin: University of Texas Press.

Hassig, Ross. 1993. *Trade, Tribute, and Transportation: The Sixteenth Century Political Economy of the Valley of Mexico.* Norman: University of Oklahoma Press.

———. 2001. *Time, History and Belief in Aztec and Colonial Mexico.* Austin: University of Texas Press.

León-Portilla, Miguel. 1990. *Aztec Thought and Culture. A Study of the Ancient Nahuatl Mind.* (The Civilization of the American Indian Series) Translated by Jack Emory Davis. Norman: University of Oklahoma Press. (Paperback edition)

Leon-Portilla, Miguel. 2002. Aztec Codices, Literature and Philosophy. In *Aztecs.* Edited by Eduardo Matos Moctezuma and Felipe Solis Olguín, pp. 64-71. London: Royal Academy of Arts.

Marcus, Joyce. 1992. *Mesoamerican Writing Systems. Propaganda, Myth, and History in Four Ancient Civilizations.* Princeton: Princeton University Press.

Offner, Jerome A. 1982. Aztec Legal Process: the Case of Texcoco. In *The Art and Iconography of Late Post-Classic Central Mexico.* Edited by Elizabeth Hill Boone, pp. 141-158. Washington, DC.: Dumbarton Oaks Research Library and Collections.

Olguín, Felipe Solís. 2002. Art at the Time of the Aztecs. In *Aztecs*. Edited by Eduardo Matos Moctezuma and Felipe Solis Olguín, pp. 56–63. London: Royal Academy of Arts.

Ortiz de Montellano, Bernardo. 1990. *Aztec Medicine, Health, and Nutrition.* New Brunswick: Rutgers University Press.

Payne, Stanley E., and Michael P. Closs. 1986. A Survey of Aztec Numbers and Their Uses. In *Native American Mathematics*. Edited by Michael P. Closs, pp. 213–235. Austin: University of Texas Press.

Pospisil, Leopold. 1971 *Anthropology of Law: A Comparative Theory.* New York: Harper and Row.

Sharer, Robert J. 1994. *The Ancient Maya*, 5th ed. Stanford: Stanford University Press.

Soustelle, Jacques. 1961. *Daily Life of the Aztecs on the Eve of the Spanish Conquest* Translated from the French by Patrick O'Brian. Stanford: Stanford University Press.

Van Bussel, Gerard. 2002. Catalogue. Object 299. In *Aztecs*. Edited by Eduardo Matos Moctezuma, and Felipe Solis Olguín, p. 475. London: Royal Academy of Arts.

XI

The Aztecs: Bloodthirsty or People Like Us?

E ven though "only" 500 years or so separate us from the Prehispanic Aztec civilization, a great number of questions remain about them. True, we have access to the data generated by archaeological projects. That database is ever growing, and new questions are generated as old ones get answered. That is the nature of the beast with which we are dealing. We also have access to historical or written documents, some dating back to Prehispanic days, but with most coming to us from the colonial period. To return to a question posed near the beginning of this book: Who were these Aztecs? Are our preconceived notions of the Aztecs as highly efficient militaristic killing machines who engaged in human sacrifice and even human cannibalism correct? Another question that comes to mind is: What happened to Aztec culture and the people that were part of it after the Spanish conquest?

In the preceding pages you have been presented with an overview of what we currently know and the sources of that information. It is extremely important to realize that all of our sources of information, either archaeological data or historic texts, come with their inherent advantages and disadvantages. Some are more trustworthy than others.

Archaeological data—the material remains alluded to in the beginning with which we can work to reconstruct past human behavior—tend to be straightforward sources of information. A carved stone, a piece of pottery, remains of a building, and even skeletal remains all have a story to tell. Better still, in most cases we have the means to extract that story and add it to our understanding of who the Aztec were. In other words, material remains are trustworthy. Bones will not lie to you and pretend to be what they are not. A collection of pottery sherds cannot deceive you regarding the vessel type to which they belonged. Things are not so easy and straightforward when we deal with written sources.

Writing is meant to convey meaning. Writing exists because there is an audience to address. A potter who creates a new vessel does not think about the end user of his pot in the same way as a writer of a text thinks about the readership the text will receive. This is where the difference lies. Written documents, although they have the occasional advantage of being eyewitness accounts of the events in which we are interested, nevertheless present us with the conundrum of wanting to believe what we read and yet not being able to know what is true and what is not.

In this chapter we will visit, or in some cases revisit, topics that could be characterized as "unanswered questions." We will start with human sacrifice, especially its extent and purpose. We will end by considering another question: Whatever happened to the Aztec after their defeat by the Spanish?

HUMAN SACRIFICE

Aztec Human Sacrifice: Its Extent and Purpose

As discussed in Chapter 8, human sacrifice served two intertwined purposes. They occurred for religious and political reasons. The continued survival of the universe was at stake. In addition, as people were allowed to witness these sacrifices, they would receive an unmistakable message: do not challenge the power of the Aztec ruler.

One theory posits a third explanation: the Aztecs were forced to kill people on a massive scale because they would eat them (Harner 1977). They would be forced to eat human flesh because they allegedly did not have access to enough protein. Although the Aztecs did not in fact have access to a lot of animal protein, their diet did include a more than ample supply of protein through processed maize and beans (Smith 1996: 226–227).

Today, most scholars focus on the religious and political roles played by human sacrifice in Aztec society. Because the Aztecs were convinced that human sacrifice was of the utmost importance to ensure the survival of the universe, they would continue practicing it. Tenochtitlan was the center of their universe, and, in their mind, of the entire creation, so the capital formed the backdrop for a never-ending series of such sacrificial ceremonies. In the words of Davíd Carrasco, the Templo Mayor was "not only the axis of their universe, it was the *imago mundi* [italics his], the architectural image of their cosmic order and sense of political destiny" (Carrasco 1999: 52). It made sense, then, in the mind of the Aztec rulers that tribute should flow to the center and that human sacrifices would also be carried out in the center in numbers exceeding any other place in their universe.

We know that Aztec warriors who took a captive unaided were entitled to the body after sacrifice. When an Aztec warrior took a captive with the help of others, then specific rules of sharing applied. The actual captor would receive the body and the right thigh, the second warrior who had helped would get the left thigh, the third obtained the right upper arm, the fourth took the upper left arm, the fifth was given the right forearm, and the sixth the lower left arm (Hassig 1988: 36).

It appears, however, that the captor himself was not permitted to eat part of his captive because he himself could have been a captive as well. We know that the warrior who captured an enemy would utter the words, "Shall I perchance eat myself?" when the ritual meal of the warrior's remains was about to begin. Moreover, this sentiment is one that was shared between captor and captive. A warrior who had captured an enemy would say, "He is as my beloved son," and the captive would reply by referring to his captor as, "He is my beloved father" (Carrasco 1999: 145).

Illustration of Aztec human sacrifice. (Gianni Dagli Orti/Corbis)

When we consider that the Aztecs ate well-defined portions of their captives, rather than their entire bodies, the argument that the Aztec "had to eat other people" because they did not have enough protein in their diet becomes null and void. If they truly had the need to consume human flesh, one would expect them to eat the entire body, rather than just portions of it.

What Was the Extent of Aztec Human Sacrifice?

Aside from the flawed logic in eating humans for dietary needs, there is also the contentious issue of the extent of human sacrifice during Aztec times. The proponents cite a population figure of 25 million people in Precolumbian Central Mexico, and an estimated 250,000 human sacrifices in Central Mexico alone. Population estimates for Tenochtitlan put forward by proponents of cannibalism are in the range of 300,000, with an accompanying estimate of human sacrifice of 15,000 per year (Ortiz de Montellano 1990: 85–86). These estimates are rejected by Ortiz de Montellano (1990: 86). He argues that the population estimates for Central Mexico are much too high.

Sacrificing Children

Archaeologists uncovered the skeletal remains of children during their investigations at Tlatelolco. Some of these children tended to be small infants, and they were found as part of offerings that included copper rattles, shells, obsidian, wood, and bird bones (Román Berrelleza 1991: 11).

Several explanations have been offered to explain child sacrifice. One seems to be that children were considered pure. As such, they made the best possible messengers to the gods. In addition, some of the skeletal remains had clear signs of disease. So it has been suggested that the children who were sacrificed were selected at least partly because their physical health would not have allowed them to live much longer. To put it in what we would consider very crude terms, these children were about to die, and their premature death would upset the energy balance that the Aztecs perceived in the universe. So they decided to turn this situation to their benefit by sacrificing these infants (Román Berrelleza 1991: 14).

Self-Sacrifice

One recurring aspect of Aztec society is that of blood and gore. Blood played an intricate role in Aztec devotional behavior. Blood could come from the individuals performing the ritual, from other human beings who were sacrificed, or from animals who were slaughtered.

Autosacrifice, or the letting of blood by the person engaged in the prayer, involved the use of cutting or sticking implements. The Aztec often used obsidian knives or maguey thorns to achieve this goal. They would pierce their tongues and then pass a series of straws through this opening. The bloodied straws were then left in front of the statue of the gods to whom they were praying. The Aztec would also cut or pierce their arms, legs, and ear lobes. When sacrificing a slave, they would collect the blood in a cup and then add paper to the liquid. They would then take that blood-soaked paper and visit various shrines. They would use the paper to smear the faces of the statues (Bandelier 1932: 159).

WHAT HAPPENED TO AZTEC CULTURE AND ITS PEOPLE?

To argue that Aztec culture vanished overnight after their defeat at the hands of the Spanish is incorrect. It would be equally incorrect to argue the opposite and suggest that the Aztec retained political and economic control over their fate. It seems that the truth lies somewhere in the middle. We will now examine the fate that befell the Aztec survivors in the realms of landownership, politics, and religion.

Demographic Decline: Its Causes and Repercussions on Land Ownership

As we have seen, the clash between the two worlds resulted in a struggle that ultimately was won by the Spanish. This outcome was predictable given the technological superiority of the Spanish weaponry and the fact that they actively sought allies from among the native population. The thing that made the outcome a foregone conclusion, leaving the Aztec and their counterparts in the Americas without a chance, was the impact of disease upon the native population. Diseases to which the Precolumbian people had no natural immunity decimated the population. This demographic decline had several serious implications. Indigenous culture was subject to a series of policies, all of which had a weakening of the Prehispanic culture as an end result and an increasing acculturation into a new society with a new dominant language and customs.

Control over Land and Labor

In the century that followed the Spanish conquest, Indian land was subject to abandonment as plagues ravaged the local populations and their owners succumbed to illnesses. We know that procedures were in place to accommodate abandoned lands in Prehispanic times. Such lands were retained under the control of the local leaders, be they caciques or calpulli leaders (Gibson 1964: 282). Times were changing, however, and customs were not always followed. Aztec landholdings ended up in Spanish hands, either because they were sold, or because they were appropriated by the Spanish. As we shall see, however, one must be careful to paint a picture with broad brush strokes. A discussion of transactions involving land in eighteenth-century Cholula shows that lands remained in indigenous hands well after the fall of Tenochtitlan.

The Encomienda Policy

An institution that played an important role in the first half century of the colonial period was the *encomienda* policy. Derived from the Spanish verb, *encomendar,* or "entrust," the term *encomienda* referred to a situation in which native populations were entrusted to their Spanish overlords. The institution of an encomienda was one in which privileged Spanish colonists were entrusted with the care of native populations in their area. The *encomendero,* as the Spanish overlord was known, was responsible for the conversion to Christianity and ensuring the security of the indigenous population. In return, the Indians were responsible for paying tribute and providing labor.

The impact of this policy was considerable. It provided a tool for the Spanish to convert the Indians to Christianity. Although in theory the encomenderos were not supposed to enslave the Indians who lived on their land, in reality this happened all too often. Mistreatment also ensued: Indians were jailed, overtaxed, and sometimes killed (Gibson 1964: 78).

The institution of encomienda soon ran into trouble, but more from the Spanish Crown and not so much from organized Indian resistance. The original arrangement under which the encomiendas were set up stipulated that these territories and their attendant population were to be "entrusted" to the Conquistadors. As they took control, most of these encomenderos quickly saw their personal wealth increase dramatically. That caught the eye of an ever-weary Crown in Spain. Fearing that these new landowners would represent a challenge to the influence of the Spanish king, policies were instituted to emasculate any threat before it could threaten the Crown. For example, encomiendas were to stay in the hands of the original landowner/Conquistador. This was later extended to subsequent generations. Still, because of the limits imposed on who could inherit, the *encomiendas* eventually reverted to the Crown. As the encomiendas slowly were made to disappear, a new administration, closely monitored by the Spanish Crown and much more loyal to it, took over (Gibson 1964: 81). This new administration grew out of a system of government already in place during the days of encomienda. It was referred to as *corregimiento*.

The Institution of Corregimiento

The Spanish Crown was represented in Mexico and other parts of the Americas under its control by several layers of civil administrators. The principal representative of the king was the viceroy. Below him were people known as *oidores,* and below those were administrators called *corregidores*. This hierarchy was firmly in place in the late 1520s, less than a decade after the fall of Tenochtitlan. It served to disseminate all of the royal orders.

The corregidores are of interest to us here, if we want to follow how Spanish rule affected the indigenous population, because they were the ones who directly interacted with the Indians. These officials, who served the Crown and not themselves, were salaried administrators (Gibson 1964: 83); however, these salaries were drawn initially from the tributes generated within the administrative districts. The corregidores also received their food, fodder, fuel, and Indian service from the Indians (Gibson 1964: 83). Corregimiento survived much longer than encomienda; they were made obsolete only by new laws in 1786 (Gibson 1964: 84).

Corregimiento touched many aspects of the life of the indigenous population. The corregidores were instructed to ensure that people were converted to Christianity. Other specifications stated that tributes were exacted only in the amounts designated. It was forbidden to compel Indians to sell their produce at subnormal prices or to take goods from the Indians without compensation (Gibson 1964: 90–91).

Although a corregidor represented the level of local administration, direct contact between him and the Indians was limited. The native population may have seen their corregidor only a few times a year. Face-to-face interaction was done by Indian officials who worked for the corregidor (Gibson 1964: 91). The courts were the only venues where face-to-face contacts may have been more frequent.

Twentieth-century bas-relief carvings representing Spanish Conquistadors. (Alison Wright/ Corbis)

The Congregación Policy

As the Spanish were witness to this precipitous demographic decline, they were forced to find solutions that affected them as well: how to retain a labor force sufficiently large and manageable to attend to the tasks at hand. The Spanish found an answer in a policy that they instituted in the late sixteenth and early seventeenth centuries, a policy that they called *congregación*.

Congregación entailed the resettlement of scattered native populations into compact communities. This approach had antecedents in that similar efforts had already been undertaken in earlier periods; however, in those cases the rationale had been that such a policy would increase administrative efficiency as well as the ease of conversion of the people involved (Gibson 1964: 282). This time around, the congregación policy was aimed at reconstituting a labor force that would otherwise remain too scattered across the landscape and therefore difficult to control. Removing people from their ancestral lands has implications regarding landownership. Agricultural lands would be retained in the case of moving people over only short distances; in other cases, when people were moved over great distances, the law provided that new lands be assigned.

It is interesting in this case to observe how congregación rules reflected a great practicality. Because the goal of congregación was to create controllable workforces and to preserve the ability to produce food, this led, at times, to rulings against the Spanish landowners. In those cases where people were brought together in locations where available land was inadequate, land then had to be taken away from the Spanish and given to the Indian community that was brought in. Although the Spanish did receive compensation for their loss of property, it shows clearly that the combination of a workforce and the ability to produce sufficient amounts of food were of primary importance.

Once moved, people were forbidden to return to their old homes. Resistance to being moved did exist, but it ended up being local and directed against specific regulations. Aztecs complained that Spanish cattle would destroy their crops; they argued that the accommodations were better in their ancestral lands; they expressed fear that they would not be as well protected against intruders in the new locations. These objections were mostly ignored, although adjustments were occasionally made (Gibson 1964: 284).

The most important result of the policy of forceful removal of people was the mixing of settlers of mixed-ethnic origins in a new community. Different backgrounds, sometimes speaking different languages, meant that it became increasingly difficult to retain one's culture. In other words, whereas disease and warfare in the early stages had torn huge gashes into the proverbial fabric of society, later events, like congregación, continued to weaken the cultural bonds that had survived.

A CASE STUDY: The Transfer of Land
Ownership in Eighteenth-Century Cholula

During the sixteenth and seventeenth centuries property transactions occurred primarily between the indigenous population and the Spanish land owners. These exchanges had mostly come to an end by the second half of the eighteenth century because of political changes; however, properties continued to be exchanged between various categories of buyers and sellers. Whenever a transaction occurred, the sellers had to apply for a license from Spanish officials. When indigenous Cholulans wanted to sell property (land or the house on it), they were required to indicate why they wanted to sell, and on what they would spend their proceeds (von Deylen 2003: 129).

A tax had to be paid in cases of land sales. It is of interest that in case the seller was an indigenous person, there was no tax to be paid; all nonnative sellers had to pay an 8 percent tax (von Deylen 2003: 129). In case land was originally purchased from an indigenous person and then later sold again, the tax became applicable in the second case. This situation might seem odd in that it favored the indigenous party in the transaction. Lest we think that ideas of charity played a role, we should also know that the price that an indigenous seller could obtain depended heavily on the social status that he or she occupied as well as on the status of the party to whom they were selling. Here, the Spanish made up more than the difference.

In documents pertaining to late colonial property transactions in Cholula, it appears that the sales price of property varied widely depending on these factors. For example, if a nonaristocratic indigenous person sold property, the average price tended to be 25 pesos. On the other hand, when indigenous leaders sold land, about 100 pesos or more exchanged hands. In this case, it did not matter if these noblemen sold to other indigenous nobility or to Spanish buyers (von Deylen 2003: 130). The author of the study notes laconically "that clearly the indigenous nobility was not interested in reduced sales prices" (von Deylen 2003: 130).

The descendants of indigenous nobility were most active in these transactions. Documents from Cholula show how they bought up small landholdings from the macehuales, as well as larger tracts of land from both fellow nobility and the Spanish land owners. They also occasionally bought expensive houses (von Deylen 2003: 131). It is perhaps more surprising that within the group of macehuales almost 50 percent of the known cases involving the sale of land involved women owners. On the other hand, about 30 percent of the purchasers were women. The documents show that Indians continued to be property owners, and that they were sometimes in a position to acquire, rather than be forced to sell (von Deylen 2003: 143).

POLITICS

After the dust settled and the conflict with Spain had ended, Indian control over a central government was permanently lost. Even though the Spanish initially appointed descendants of the royal families that had once ruled the Triple Alliance, they eventually became absorbed into the lower levels of nobility in New Spain (Gibson 1964: 166). The Spanish very astutely realized that they were vastly outnumbered. Their solution was to retain the indigenous nobility in a position of power, but only at the level of townships and cities, rather than on any higher level.

Political power in Spanish towns resided with the municipal council. There were two principal offices, those of alcalde and regidor, within these councils (Gibson 1964: 167). This was the level of municipal governance that the Spanish allowed (perhaps because they were forced to) the Indians to continue to exert some political power (Gibson 1964: 167). Shortly after the conquest, when required to maintain control over their communities, the Aztecs put forth the existing tlahtoani as gobernador and continued to refer to him by his Nahuatl title (Gibson 1964: 167).

Within a few decades, however, by the middle of the sixteenth century, the Spanish instituted another position aimed at diluting native power even at this low level of community control. Elected or appointed non-tlahtoani gobernadores, or *gobernadoryotl,* were introduced, serving side by side with the tlatoani. Over time, power shifted from the indigenous nobility to these non-tlahtoani rulers (Gibson 1964: 168).

After their defeat, the inhabitants of Tenochtitlan saw a sequence of indigenous rulers for another 43 years. When Cuauhtemoc died in 1525, he was succeeded by Juan Velazquez Tlacotzin, who died soon thereafter as well. His successor, Andrés de Tapia Motelchichtzin, was of Aztec origin, but apparently not of high nobility. Sources refer to him as not being a nobleman, but only a noble warrior. One source even calls him a former slave (Gibson 1964: 168). He was succeeded by Pablo Xochiquentzin, an aristocrat, who served until his death in 1536. Descendants of the former ruling dynasty managed to get restored to a position of local tlahtoani by the late 1530s. The grandson of Axayacatl, Diego Huanitzin, became ruler around that time. He was the first to receive the title of tlahtoani of Tenochtitlan under Spanish rule. Tizoc's grandson, Diego Tehuetzqui, ruled from the late 1540s through the 1554. The last of the rulers who were lineal descendants of the Prehispanic ruling family was Luis de Santa Maria Cipac, a grandson of Ahuizotl. He became gobernador in 1563 and died in 1565. Over time, these rulers, whose powers were limited to local affairs, became acculturated into the dominant Spanish culture (Gibson 1964: 170).

The position of indigenous rulers in other communities was precarious. Although the precedent of elections for high-ranking officials was maintained by the Spanish, they also started heavily to influence the outcome of these events. We know of encomenderos who deposed or exiled native officials who were not cooperative enough in the eyes of the new rulers.

Traditions were maintained under Spanish rule. From the sixteenth through the eighteenth centuries newly elected Indian officials traveled to Mexico City to receive confirmation of their office from the viceroy. This echoes the travels undertaken by the various tlatoque to Tenochtitlan to receive confirmation from the Aztec emperors (Gibson 1964: 179).

THE INTRODUCTION OF CHRISTIANITY: IMPLEMENTATION AND IMPLICATION

Christianity was one of the pillars upon which the Spanish Crown based its justification for the conquest of the Americas. Conversion to Christianity was one of the main goals for such institutions as encomienda and corregimiento; however, we should not consider the Church as a monolithic bloc, faithfully serving the Crown in its pursuit of conversion. We should instead identify two powerful factions within the Church, each with its own agenda: the secular clergy and the regular Mendicant friars (Gibson 1964: 98).

Among the Mendicant friars, the Franciscans, Dominicans, and Augustinians were primarily interested in converting as many people as possible. They engaged in mass baptisms toward that end, which was an approach that came to an end with criticism of the superficial nature of such conversions.

The friars set out to eliminate non-Christian elements in society immediately. Temples were closed and destroyed, the Aztec priestly class was abolished, and human sacrifice was discontinued. Catholic churches were often built on top of the ruins of former Aztec temples. Processions and images of Catholic saints were introduced.

As Christianity was introduced, the native population continued to interpret elements as reflecting similar values or entities that they had known in Prehispanic days. For example, the community of saints was not perceived as an intermediary between God and man, but rather as a collection of deities. Native people were very interested in the crucifixion, especially in the aspects of sacrifice associated with it. God was not seen as exclusive and omnipotent. Heaven and hell took on properties of vaguely similar Prehispanic notions. Confession existed in Aztec times; however, the Aztec custom of going to confession only in times of crisis clashed with the Christian custom of going to confession at least once a year (Gibson 1964: 101).

Colonial-period Aztecs continued their Prehispanic religious practices well into the eighteenth century, and sometimes even later. For example, in 1803 one entire town in the Basin of Mexico was still worshipping idols in caves. Aside from such practices, special values were attached to springs and hills.

Over time, the impact of the Church, although important, got caught up in local politics. It suffered as a result. The Mendicant orders initially had courageously taken the side of the Indians against the abuses of the encomenderos; however, as the Church itself came to rely more and more on Indian payment of taxes and Indian labor, it eventually became more difficult to criticize the encomenderos for doing the same. This led to a waning in the influence of the Church. The conversion program suffered because of it. An approach by the Church that was sometimes heavy-handed was not exactly conducive to bringing in more converts either. The Church employed execution of those it deemed to be idolators. Lifetime imprisonment and torture were also favored (Gibson 1964: 117).

How effective was the Church in its efforts to convert people? The best answer lies in today's religious practices among indigenous people. We can all still witness ceremonies that harken back to Prehispanic days, clearly proving that the Church was not fully effective in its efforts.

The story of Mexico's first indigenous saint, Juan Diego, can shed more light on this topic. According to traditional Catholic sources, Juan Diego was born in 1474 with the name "Cuauhtlatoatzin" ("the talking eagle") in Cuautlitlán, which today is part of Mexico City, Mexico.

Father Peter of Ghent, one of the first Franciscan missionaries active in Mexico, baptized Juan Diego in 1524, when Juan was 50 years old. About 7 years later, on December 9, 1531, when Juan Diego was on his way to morning Mass, the Blessed Mother appeared to him on Tepeyac Hill, the outskirts of modern Mexico City. She asked him to go to the bishop and to request in her name that a shrine be built at Tepeyac, where she promised to pour out her

Juan Diego, an Aztec peasant to whom it is believed the Virgin of Guadalupe appeared on several occasions, was canonized by Pope John Paul II in July 2002. (Lynsey Addario/Corbis)

grace upon those who invoked her. The bishop, who did not believe Juan Diego, asked for a sign to prove that the apparition was true. On December 12, Juan Diego returned to Tepeyac. Here, he was told by the Blessed Mother to climb the hill and to pick the flowers that he would find in bloom. He obeyed, and although it was wintertime, he found roses flowering. He gathered the flowers and took them to Our Lady who carefully placed them in his mantle and told him to take them to the bishop as "proof." When he opened his mantle, the flowers fell on the ground and there remained impressed, in place of the flowers, an image of the Blessed Mother, the apparition at Tepeyac.

With the bishop's permission, Juan Diego lived the rest of his life as a hermit in a small hut near the chapel where the miraculous image was placed for veneration. Here, he cared for the church and the first pilgrims who came to pray to the Mother of Jesus.

Much deeper than the "exterior grace" of having been "chosen" as Our Lady's "messenger," Juan Diego received the grace of interior enlightenment. From that moment, he began a life dedicated to prayer and the practice of virtue and boundless love of God and neighbor. He died in 1548 and was buried in the first chapel dedicated to the Virgin of Guadalupe. He was beatified on May 6, 1990 by Pope John Paul II in the Basilica of *Santa Maria di*

Cipriano Gil, born in Mexico and now living in San Francisco, carries a statue of the Virgin of Guadalupe, the patron saint of Mexico. Every year as December 12 approaches, those who worship her march in processions and pilgrimages in her honor. (Lonny Shavelson/ZUMA/Corbis)

Guadalupe, Mexico City (http://www.vatican.va/news_services/liturgy/saints/ns_lit_doc_20020731_juan-diego_en.html).

A most telling detail is that at the canonization ceremony at the Basilica, the Pope held a Mass that borrowed from Aztec traditions, including a reading from the Bible in Nahuatl. The Pope urged the Catholic Church in Mexico to be respectful of indigenous traditions and to incorporate them into religious ceremony when appropriate (García Samper, Asunción et al. 2002).

One could argue that in this admonition the Pope indirectly acknowledged the strength with which the indigenous religious traditions have continued to survive, even until today. The figure of Juan Diego, Mexico's first saint and one of Latin America's few saints overall, is one that many anthropologists would see as an example of the syncretism that took place in the immediate aftermath of the Spanish conquest. This syncretism, or the mixing of elements from different religions, is also present in the construction of Spanish places of worship on top of the ruins of Precolumbian places of worship. Thus, when the population attended church in colonial times, there may have been the reminder in the back of their minds that they were performing ceremonies in a place where their ancestors performed their own before the Spanish arrived.

A Nahua Indian woman holds her daughter on her knee. (Danny Lehman/Corbis)

FUTURE DIRECTIONS

Archaeological Investigations of Rural Areas

The core of the Aztec realm, the Basin of Mexico, has traditionally been the main focus of research. Up until the last decade of the twentieth century, this has led to an almost-absurd situation. Tenochtitlan and its environs were hardly known archaeologically, given that most of the ruins were covered by one of the largest cities in the Western Hemisphere; however, because it was the seat of Aztec power, that is where people concentrated their research. On the other hand, archaeological information is more readily available in the surrounding Aztec provinces, yet interest in working in the hinterlands was minimal for a very long time. Work in these former Aztec provinces, however, is important for two main reasons: it allows us to fill in some of the blanks that exist in our knowledge of Aztec material culture, and it provides us with a counterpoint to what must be an exception to the rule in the Aztec world: the capital itself. In other words, research into life in the rural areas outside the capital will give us insights that pertain to much greater portions of the Aztec realm than information gathered in the capital itself (Smith 1994: 313).

Reassessment of Aztec Culture

As we come to understand Aztec culture better, we come to realize that this is not a culture dedicated only to cruelty and aggression. There are ample references in early colonial-period writings that the Nahuatl-speaking people worked collectively on farms, developed incredible crafts and art forms, were keenly interested in poetry, cared deeply for their children, loved telling stories, and were drawn to the excitement of the marketplace (Carrasco 2003: 135). A priest, who had spent 20 years with the Mexica, wrote "no people love their children as much as these people" (Carrasco 2003: 135).

There is no better insight than this with which to end this volume.

REFERENCES

Bandelier, Fanny R. 1932. *A History of Ancient Mexico by Fray Bernardino de Sahagún.* Translated by Fanny R. Bandelier from the Spanish version of Carlos Maria de Bustamante. Nashville: Fisk University Press.

Berrelleza, Román, and Juan Alberto. 1991. A Study of Skeletal Materials from Tlatelolco. In *Aztec Ceremonial Landscapes.* Edited by David Carrasco, pp. 9–10. Niwot: University of Colorado Press.

Read, Kay Almere, and Jason J. González. 2000. *Handbook of Mesoamerican Mythology.* (Handbooks of World Mythology). Santa Barbara: ABC-CLIO.

Sharer, Robert. 1994. *The Ancient Maya,* 5th ed. Stanford: Stanford University Press.

Smith, Michael. 1994. Economies and Polities in Aztec-Period Morelos. In *Economies and Polities in the Aztec Realm.* Edited by Mary G. Hodge and Michael E. Smith, pp.

313–348. (Studies on Culture and Society, volume 6) Albany: Institute for Mesoamerican Studies.

———. 1996. *The Aztecs (The Peoples of America)*. Oxford: Blackwell Publishers, Ltd.

von Deylen, Wiebke. 2003. *Ländliches Wirtshaftsleben in Spätkolonialen Mexiko. Eine Mikrohistorische Studie in Einem Multiethnishen Distrikt: Cholula 1750–1810*. Hamburg: Hamburg University Press.

Glossary

ACAMAPICHTLI: Name of first Aztec ruler (AD 1372–1391).

ACATLAYIACAPAN VEICALPULLI: Location in the Sacred Precinct in Tenochtitlan.

AHUAUHTLI: Green amaranth. Also refers to eggs of the axayacatl. Eaten by the Aztecs.

AHUIZOTL: River otter, also name of one of the Aztec rulers (AD 1486–1502).

ALCOHUA: Name of one of eight tribes leaving Aztlan.

ALTEPETL: City.

AMANTECA: Term to refer to feather workers.

AMATE: Aztec paper. Term derived from the Nahuatl word *amatl,* referring to a wild fig. Aztec papermakers would use the bark of various types of fig trees.

ATEMOTZLI: Month in the solar year calendar. It marked the end of the dry season.

ATEMPAN: Location in the Sacred Precinct in Tenochtitlan. Gathering place for children and lepers before their sacrifice.

ATLAHAUHCO: Monastery inside the Sacred Precinct in Tenochtitlan. Served as residence to priests.

ATLALLI: Land that is irrigated.

ATLATL: Spear thrower.

ATLAULICO: Temple in the Sacred Precinct of Tenochtitlan. Located near Coatlan temple.

ATLCAHUALO: Aztec month in the solar year calendar.

ATOCTLI: Fertile alluvial soil.

ATOLLI: Maize gruel.

AUIANIME: Female companions of unmarried Aztec soldiers.

AXAYACATL: Water bug; eaten by the Aztecs. Also name of Aztec ruler (AD 1468–1481).

AXOLOTL: Salamander. Eaten by the Aztecs.

AZTLAN: "Place of the herons," referred to as mythical homeland of the Aztecs.

CACAHUACUAUHUITL: General term for cacao tree.

CALMECAC: School attended by offspring of ruling class. Its students were prepared to become priests, warriors, and governors.

CALMIL: House-lot garden.

CALPANPILLI: Son of a tlahtoani and a concubine.

CALPIXQUE: Tax collectors.

CALPOLEHQUEH: Hightest rank among commoners, leaders of the calpulli.

CALPULLI: Ward, or neighborhood in a city. There were eighty such units or wards in Tenochtitlan. Often considered to have been made up by members of the same "clan." Also referring to a series of buildings located around the inside portion of the Sacred Precinct wall in Tenochtitlan. Visiting lords would do penance in these buildings.

CEMANAHUAC: Term used to refer to our physical world. The term translates as "that which is entirely surrounded by water." See also Teo-Atl.

CENTEOTL: Goddess of corn.

CENTZONTOTOCHTINITEUPAN: Temple in the Sacred Precinct of Tenochtitlan, dedicated to the gods of wine.

CHALCA: Name of one of eight tribes leaving Aztlan.

CHALCHIUHTLICUE: Name of female deity, a.k.a. "jade her skirt." Goddess of water.

CHAPULTEPEC: "Hill of the Grasshopper." Alleged to have been the first place in the Valley of Mexico where the Aztecs settled. An inhospitable place, according to descriptions.

CHAYOTLI: Chayote, a root consumed by the Aztecs.

CHICOMECATL: Name given to a building said to have been inside the Sacred Precinct in Tenochtitlan. Dedicated to the god Chicomecatl.

CHICOMOSTOC: "Place of seven caves." Alleged to have been visited by the Aztec on their migration from Aztlan to the Valley of Mexico.

CHICUNAUHAPAN: River that had to be crossed before entering Mictlan.

CHILILICO: Name given to a building said to have been inside the Sacred Precinct in Tenochtitlan.

CHIMALPOPOCA: Aztec ruler (AD 1415–1426).

CHINAMPAS: Floating gardens.

CIHUACOATL: Name referring to Snake Goddess, patron deity of the city of Colhuacan. The term also refers to the political position of a person standing-in during a period between two emperors.

CINTEUPAN: Temple in the Sacred Precinct of Tenochtitlan, dedicated to the goddess Chicomecoatl.

CITALCO: One of thirteen levels of heaven.

CITLALTÉPETL: Nahuatl term to refer to Mexico's tallest mountain, known to us as Pico de Orizaba.

CIVAPIPILTI: Name of a goddess.

COATEPANTLI: "Serpent wall," originally thought to have surrounded the Sacred Precinct in Tenochtitlan.

COATEPEC: "Snake Mountain," place where Huitzilopochtli was born. Term also applied to the pyramid supporting the temples of Tlaloc and Huitzilopochtli.

COATLAN: Temple in the Sacred Precinct of Tenochtitlan, located near a structure called Atlaulico.

COCOAAPAN: Pond located within the Sacred Precinct in Tenochtitlan. Bathing area for priests.

CODEX: Manuscript. Plural: codices.

COMALLI: Ceramic griddle, used to cook tortillas.

COYOLXAUHQUI: Goddess, sister of Huitzilopochtli.

CUAHCHICH: Elite warriors who usually fought in pairs.

CUAUHPIPILTIN: Commoners who have distinguished themselves on the battlefield.

CUAUHTEMOC: Aztec ruler (AD 1520–1525).

CUAUHTLALLI: Humus (i.e., soil enriched by decayed trees).

CUETLACHTLI: Term used to refer to a legendary monster.

CUEXPALCHICACPOL: "Youth with a baby's lock," title given to a warrior who had failed to take a prisoner after three battles.

CUICACALLI: "Houses of song," places where people would receive instructions in singing and poetry—especially pertaining to generating war poetry.

CUITLAHUAC: Aztec ruler (AD 1520).

CULHUACAN: City name, featured in the Aztec migration story.

EPCOATL: Name given to a temple said to have been inside the Sacred Precinct in Tenochtitlan.

ETZALCUALIZTLI: Month in the solar year calendar. Dedicated to Tlaloc and the tlatoques.

HILHUICATITLAN: Tall stone column located inside the Sacred Precinct at Tenochtitlan.

HUAUHTLI: "Green," as in vegetable manner. Traditionally interpreted as amaranth.

HUEHUETL: Upright wooden drum.

HUEHUETLATOANI: Title given to Aztec ruler. Meaning "old king," or "supreme king."

HUEHUETLATOLLI: Literally meaning "the Ancient Word," a form of verbal arts.

HUEI TECUILHUITL: Month in the solar year calendar. This month was dedicated to Xilonen.

HUEI TOZOZTLI: Month in the solar year calendar. Dedicated to Centeotl, goddess of corn.

HUEXOTZINCA: Name of one of eight tribes leaving Aztlan.

HUITLACOCHE: Fungus growing on corn.

HUITZIL: Name of a mythical priest said to have led the Aztecs out of Aztlan.

HUITZILIHUITL: Aztec ruler (AD 1391–1415).

HUITZILINQUATE: Temple in the Sacred Precinct of Tenochtitlan.

HUITZILOPOCHTLI: Aztec patron god. The Aztec migrated from Aztlan, led by priests who carried effigies of their patron god. Brother of Coyolxauhqui.

HUITZNAOACCALPULLI: Name given to a building said to have been inside the Sacred Precinct in Tenochtitlan.

HUITZNAOACTEUCALLI: Temple in the Sacred Precinct of Tenochtitlan.

HUITZTEPECALCO: Location in the Sacred Precinct of Tenochtitlan where the priests would dispose of the maguey spines after bloodletting rituals.

ICHCAHUIPILLI: Quilted cotton vest, used as protection by warriors.

ICPALLI: Low chairs without feet. Made out of wicker or wood and equipped with a back.

ILHUICATL HUITZLAN: One of thirteen levels of heaven.

ILHUICATL TONATIUH: One of thirteen levels of heaven.

IN CUICATL: "Bird songs" (i.e., verbal arts, such as singing or poetry).

IN XOCHITL: "Flower songs" (i.e., verbal arts, such as singing or poetry).

ITEPEIOC: Name given to a building said to have been inside the Sacred Precinct in Tenochtitlan.

ITZCOATL: Aztec ruler (AD 1426–1440).

IXIPTLA: Refers to the status taken on by sacrificial victims, as representatives of the god to whom they would be sacrificed.

IXTACIHUATL: Volcano on the southern edge of the Basin of Mexico.

IZCAHUITLI: Tiny aquatic worms. Eaten by the Aztecs.

IZCALLI: Month in the solar year calendar. It was dedicated to Xiuhtecutli, god of fire. This month was followed by the five Nemontemi days.

IZTACCINTEUTLITEUPAN: Temple in the Sacred Precinct of Tenochtitlan. Dedicated to the goddess Cinteotl.

MACEHUALTIN: Commoners, making up the bulk of the population. Required to work communal land, and to serve in the Aztec army.

MACUAHUITL: Wooden sword with a cutting edge made of obsidian blades.

MACUILEIPACTLI: Name given to a building said to have been inside the Sacred Precinct in Tenochtitlan.

MACUILMALINLITEUPAN: Temple in the Sacred Precinct of Tenochtitlan. It housed two statues.

MALINALCA: Name of one of eight tribes leaving Aztlan.

MALINALXOCHITL: Sister of Huitzilopochtli.

MALINTZIN: Name of a young woman, a.k.a. La Malinche, speaker of Nahuatl and Maya. Traveled with Cortés.

MATLATZINCA: Name of one of eight tribes leaving Aztlan.

MAYEQUEH: A category of commoners, laborers who were permanently employed on the lands of nobility.

MECATLAN: Name given to a building said to have been inside the Sacred Precinct in Tenochtitlan. Location where those who attended the statues of the gods learned how to play the horn.

MEXICA: Term to refer to Aztecs. See also Tenochca.

MEXICOCALMECAC: Name given to a temple said to have been inside the Sacred Precinct in Tenochtitlan. Dedicated to Tlaloc.

MICTECACIHUATL: God of death, one of two deities living in Mictlan. See also Mictlantecuhtli.

MICTLAN: One of three destinations for the soul of a deceased person. See also Tlalocan.

MICTLANTECUHTLI: God of death, one of two deities living in Mictlan. See also Mictecacihuatl.

MILPA: Field.

MIXCOATL: God of war, sacrifice, and hunting; a.k.a. "Cloud Serpent."

MIXCOPANTEZONPANTLI: Name given to a temple said to have been inside the Sacred Precinct in Tenochtitlan. Dedicated to the god Mixcoatl. Backdrop for severed heads displayed on stakes.

MIZCOATEUPAN: Name given to a building said to have been inside the Sacred Precinct in Tenochtitlan, dedicated to Mizcoatl.

MOCTECUHZUMA XOCOYOTZIN: Aztec ruler (AD 1502–1520).

MOCUICALLI: Name given to a temple said to have been inside the Sacred Precinct in Tenochtitlan. Location where foreign spies were executed.

NAHUALOZTOMECAH: Disguised merchants, acting as spies.

NAHUATILPIANI: "He who keeps the law," a law-abiding citizen.

NAHUATL: Language spoken by the ancient Aztecs.

NAPPATECUTLIYTEUPAN: Temple in the Sacred Precinct of Tenochtitlan.

NEMONTEMI: Five extra days added to complete the solar year calendar. These days followed the month Izcalli.

NETLALILOIA: Name given to a building said to have been inside the Sacred Precinct in Tenochtitlan. A space at the foot of this structure served as a repository of the flayed human victims.

NETOTILOIAN: Part of the Sacred Temple Precinct at Tenochtitlan.

NOTLATILOIAN: Location in the Sacred Precinct of Tenochtitlan, storage space for human skin.

OCHPANIZTLI: Month in the solar calendar. Dedicated to Toci, mother of the gods.

OCOTL: Torches made out of pine wood.

OCTLI: Alcoholic beverage made from the fermented sap of the agave plant.

OMACAMA: Statues housed in one of the temples inside the Sacred Precinct in Tenochtitlan.

OMECIHUATL: Two-Lady, name of a deity.

OMETECUHTLI: Two-Lord, name of a deity.

OMETEOTL: Supreme gods, creators, parents of gods.

OMETOCHTLI: Deity of fertility, a.k.a. "Two Rabbit."

OMEYOCAN: Most important levels in the Aztec concept of heaven; considered to represent the combination of the twelfth and thirteenth levels. This was a place of duality and the place where Ometeotl lived.

OZTOMECAH: Vanguard merchants.

PACHTONTLI: Month in the solar calendar, also known as Teotleco. It was dedicated to the arrival of all the gods.

PANQUETZALIZTLI: Month in the solar calendar. During this month, feasts took place to honor Huitzilopochtli, god of war.

PETATL: Mat, used to sleep on at night and as a seat during the day.

PETLACALLI: Wickerwork baskets.

PIPILTIN: Ruling class.

POCHTECA: Term used to refer to long-distance traders who also acted as spies. See Naualoztomeca.

POIAUHTLA: Name given to a temple said to have been inside the Sacred Precinct in Tenochtitlan. Served as backdrop for ceremonies during the Etzalqualiztli festival.

POPOCATEPETL: "Smoking mountain," a reference to a volcano on the southern edge of the Basin of Mexico.

POZTECPATLI: Fracture medicine.

QUACHTLI: Large-sized blanket.

QUAHUITL: Standard unit of linear measurement, approximately 2.5 m.

QUAUCALLI: Temple in the Sacred Precinct of Tenochtitlan. Served as a prison for statues of foreign gods.

QUAUCHXICALCO: Round temple in the Sacred Precinct of Tenochtitlan. It did not have a roof.

QUAUCHXICALCO THE SECOND: Copy of Quauchxicalco. Located in the Sacred Precinct at Tenochtitlan.

QUAUCHXICALCO THE THIRD: Copy of the preceding two structures. Formed backdrop for Tzompantli within the Sacred Precinct of Tenochtitlan.

QUAUHPILLI: "Eagle Lord," a title created during the reign of Emperor Moctecuhzuma Ilhuicamina I (AD 1440–1468). This title was bestowed upon commoners who had distinguished themselves in battle. The title was abolished under Moctecuhzuma Xocoyotzin (AD 1502–1520).

QUAXICALCO: Name given to a temple said to have been inside the Sacred Precinct in Tenochtitlan. The emperor would retire here and do penance in honor of the sun god.

QUECHOLLI: Month in the solar calendar. It was dedicated to Mixcoatl.

QUETZALCOATL: Name of a deity, a.k.a. "The Feathered Serpent"; also a title given to the two highest-ranking Aztec priests. They presided over the Tlaloc and Huitzilopochtli temples in the Sacred Precinct in Tenochtitlan.

TALUD-TABLERO: Architectural traits typical of Teotihuacan and Teotihuacan-inspired sites. Consists of a slope (talud) and a rectangular area with a raised border (tablero).

TEALTIANIMEH: Slave bathers.

TECCALCO: Name given to a temple said to have been inside the Sacred Precinct in Tenochtitlan. Place where captives were burned during the Teutleco festival.

TECCIZCALCO: Name given to a building said to have been inside the Sacred Precinct in Tenochtitlan.

TECHIELLI: Small temple in the Sacred Precinct in Tenochtitlan.

TECOANIMEH: Slave dealers.

TECPAN: Residence of a village leader. Derived from *teuctli*—see later—and "*pan*" indicating "place."

TECPILLI: Son of a teuctli, member of the ruling class.

TECUICATL: Food item consumed by the Aztecs, consisting of green algae (*Spirulina geitlerii*) collected from lakes and turned into loaves.

TECUILHUITONTLI: Month in the solar year calendar. Dedicated to Uixtocihuatl.

TECUXCALLI: Name given to a temple said to have been inside the Sacred Precinct in Tenochtitlan.

TELPOCHCALLI: School whose students were drawn from the ranks of commoners and lower-ranking nobility associated with the calpulli.

TEMALACATL: Round stone located in the Sacred Precinct at Tenochtitlan. Slaves were tied to it and forced to fight before being executed.

TEMEZCALLI: Bath or steam bath.

TENOCHCA: Term to refer to Aztecs. See also Mexica.

TENOCHTITLAN: Name of the Aztec capital, literally meaning "among the stone cactus fruit."

TEO-ATL: Body of water thought to surround the earth.

TEOOCTLI: Inebriating drink served to sacrificial victims.

TEOTIHUACAN: Name of a giant metropolis located in the northern portion of the Basin of Mexico. Predated the Aztecs.

TEOTL: Term referring to a deity or sacred power.

TEOTLECO: Month in the solar calendar, also known as Pachtontli. It was dedicated to the arrival of all the gods.

TEPANECA: Name of one of eight tribes leaving Aztlan.

TEPEILHUITL: Month in the solar calendar of the year, also referred to as Huei Pachtli. During this month, people honored hills, where the rain clouds were formed.

TEPONAXTLI: Two-toned wooden drum.

TEPOZTOPILLI: Thrusting spears.

TETEOINNAN: Patroness of curers, midwives; a.k.a. "Mother of Gods."

TETLANMA: Name given to a building said to have been inside the Sacred Precinct in Tenochtitlan.

TETLANMANCALMECAC: Monastery located inside the Sacred Precinct of Tenochtitlan. Dedicated to the goddess Chantico.

TETLEPANQUETZQUI: Category of sorcerer; "he who prepares fire for people."

TEUCCALLI: "Lord's house."

TEUCTLAHTOH: Category of tlahtoani, especially a tlahtoani subordinate to a higher-ranking tlahtoani.

TEUCTLI: Leader of a village; these people were in charge of a teuccalli, or Lord's House.

TEUNACAZTLI: *Cymbopetalum penduliflorum,* a spice added to chocolate.

TEUPAN: Temple in the Sacred Precinct of Tenochtitlan.

TEUTLACHCO: Ballcourt located inside the Sacred Precinct at Tenochtitlan.

TEUTLALPAN: Craggy land, a grove said to be within the Sacred Precinct of Tenochtitlan.

TEUTLECO: Name of a festival.

TEXCACALCO: Name given to a building said to have been inside the Sacred Precinct in Tenochtitlan.

TEXCATL: Round stone, used to sacrifice people on top of the pyramids.

TEYALUALOANIMEH: Spying merchants.

TEYOLIA: Aztec concept of soul.

TEZCAAPAN: One of two sacred springs inside the Ceremonial Precinct in Tenochtitlan. See also Tozpalatl.

TEZCACOACTLACOCHCALCO: Armory located in the Sacred Precinct in Tenochtitlan.

TEZCATALCHO: Ballcourt located inside the Sacred Precinct in Tenochtitlan.

TEZCATLIPOCA: Deity, known as "Smoking Mirror."

TEZONMOLCO: Name given to a building said to have been inside the Sacred Precinct in Tenochtitlan. Dedicated to Xiuhtecutli, god of fire.

TEZOQUITL: Firm, dark clayey soil.

TEZOZOMOC: King of the Tepanecs.

TIACHCAUH: Master of youths at the Telpochcalli.

TIAMICQUEH: Traders, dealers.

TIANQUIZPAN TLAYACAQUE: Officials in charge of maintaining order in the market square.

TIANQUIZTLI: Great market in the Aztec capital, Tenochtitlan. Also used to refer to the Pleiades constellation. Its movement through the sky was used as a marker in the celebration of the 52-year cycle.

TITITL: Month in the solar year calendar. It was dedicated to Tona.

TIZAAPAN: Inhospitable location where Aztecs settled during their migration.

TIZOC: Aztec ruler (AD 1481–1486).

TLACATECCATL: Term referring to either a generic term of high-ranking officer, or to one of two of the highest-ranking Aztec officers. See also Tlacochcalcatl.

TLACATECOLOTL: Sorcerer.

TLACHCALCO: Name given to a building said to have been inside the Sacred Precinct in Tenochtitlan. It housed a statue of the god Macuiltotec.

TLACOCHCALCO: Building in the Sacred Precinct of Tenochtitlan. Served as an armory.

TLATLACOHTIN: Slaves, representing the lowest social class.

TLACAXIPEHUALITZLI: "Feast of Flaying of Men," held during the second of the 18 months of the solar calendar. Accomplished warriors would receive honorific titles and elaborate garments.

TLACHTLI: Ball game.

TLACOCHCALCATL: Term referring to either a generic term of high-ranking officer, or to one of two of the highest-ranking Aztec officers. See also Tlacateccatl.

TLACOHCOHUALNAMACAQUEH: Peddlers.

TLACUILO: Trained scribe. The occupation of scribe was hereditary.

TLAHTOANI: Member of the ruling class, or pipiltin. Leader of a community, elected from among the nobility. This position was not hereditary. The term means "he who speaks."

TLAHTOHCAPILLI: Son of a tlahtoani, member of the ruling class.

TLAHUICA: Name of one of eight tribes leaving Aztlan.

TLAHUIZTLI: War suit, worn over body armor by elite warriors.

TLAHZOLLALLI: Sand enriched by decayed matter.

TLALAHUIAC: Land to which fertilizer is added.

TLALCOLHUALLI: Land that is bought or sold.

TLALCOZTLI: Fine, fertile yellow-reddish soil.

TLALHUITECTLI: Land that is worked down, or packed.

TLALMANTLI: Flatland (land that is neither hilly nor hollowed).

TLALOC: God of water.

TLALOCAN: One of three destinations to which a soul could go. Considered to be a warm and pleasant place, associated with the god Tlaloc. See also Mictlan.

TLALXICO: Temple in the Sacred Precinct of Tenochtitlan. Dedicated to the god of hell.

TLAMACAZQUI: Full priests. Term means "giver of things."

TLAMACAZTON: "Little priests," a term referring to first-year students of the priesthood, attending the calmecac school.

TLAMANALCO: Location at the foot of Iztacihuatl and Popocateptl; name of convent where de Sahagún lived and worked.

TLAMATINIME: "Knowers of things," wise men trained in verbal arts; teachers in the calmecac.

TLAMATZINCO: Temple in the Sacred Precinct of Tenochtitlan. Dedicated to the god Tlamatzincatl.

TLAMEMES: Professional carriers. They would carry goods to the market and tribute to Tenochtitlan.

TLANAMACANIMEH: Peddlers.

TLAQUETZALLI: Term meaning "precious thing."

TLATELOLCO: Settlement next to Tenochtitlan, and location of the largest market in the Aztec empire.

TLAXCALLI: Tortillas.

TLAXILACALLI: Concept referring to a rural territorial unit.

TLAXOCHIMACO/MICCAILHUILTONTLI: Month in the solar year calendar. Dedicated to Huitzilopochtli, god of war.

TLAYOLTEUHUIANI: "He who puts the deified heart into objects," a term used to refer to "artist."

TLAZOHPILLI: Son of a tlahtoani and a legitimate wife; member of the ruling class.

TLENAMACAC: "Fire priests." High-ranking priests, responsible for human sacrifice.

TLILALPAN: Pond in the Sacred Precinct of Tenochtitlan. Literally "black water."

TLILANCALMECAC: Name given to a temple said to have been inside the Sacred Precinct in Tenochtitlan. Served as an oratory.

TOCHINCO: Name given to a temple said to have been inside the Sacred Precinct in Tenochtitlan. Dedicated to Umetochtli, god of wine.

TOCI: Mother of the gods.

TOLTECA: Prime official artist.

TONALPOHUALLI: Sacred calendar, comprising 260 days.

TONATIUH: Sun god.

TOXCATL: Month in the solar year calendar. Dedicated to Tezcatlipoca.

TOXIUHMOLPILLIA: "Binding of the Years," a term used to refer to the New Fire ceremony.

TOZOZTONTLI: Month in the solar year calendar. Dedicated to Tlaloc.

TOZPALATL: One of two sacred springs inside the Ceremonial Precinct in Tenochtitlan. See also Tezcaapan.

TULA: Name of archaeological site in the northern portion of the Basin of Mexico. Succeeded Teotihuacan, preceded the Aztec culture.

TULNOAC: Temple in the Sacred Precinct of Tenochtitlan.

TZAPOTL: "Sweet," term used to refer to fruits that taste sweet.

TZOALLI: Amaranth dough.

TZOMPANTLI: Skull racks as seen inside the Sacred Precinct at Tenochtitlan. There were several locations with this name.

TZONMOLCOCALMECAC: Temple in the Sacred Precinct of Tenochtitlan. Here, priests would build and distribute the new fire.

UMACTL: Wooden statue inside the Quauchxicalo temple.

VEITZOMPANTLI: Skull rack placed in front of the temple of Huitzilopochtli, in the Sacred Precinct at Tenochtitlan.

XALATOCTLI: Sandy alluvial soil.

XALLALLI: Infertile sandy soil.

XIACATECUTLI: Temple in the Sacred Precinct of Tenochtitlan, dedicated to the god of merchants.

XIHUITL: Solar year calendar, comprising 365 days. Term also used to refer to turquoise, grass, or comet.

XILOCAN: Structure in the Sacred Precinct in Tenochtitlan.

XILONEN: Goddess of green corn.

XIPE TOTEC: Deity, taking care of agricultural fertility; also patron of the goldsmiths, a.k.a., "Our Lord with the Flayed Skins."

XIQUIPILLI: Army unit consisting of 8,000 men.

XIUHMOLPILLI: Calendrical cycle comprising 52 years.

XIUHTECUHTLI: Deity of fire and paternalism, a.k.a. "Turquoise Lord."

XIUHTILMAHTLI: Blue and white mantle worn by the emperor in peacetime.

XOCHIMILCA: Name of one of eight tribes leaving Aztlan.

XOCHIMILCO: Population center in the southern portion of the Basin of Mexico. Important food-producing center.

XOCHIPALCO: Lodging facility for visiting dignitaries, located in the Sacred Precinct at Tenochtitlan.

XOCHIPILLI: Deity of solar warmth, flowers, feasting, and pleasure, a.k.a. "Flower Prince."

XOCHIYAOYOTL: Flower war.

XOCOTL: "Sour," term used to refer to fruits that taste sour.

XOCOTL HUETZI: Month in the solar year calendar. Dedicated to the god of fire, Xiuhtecuhtli.

XOXOALLI: Inflammation of the feet and the ankles.

XUCHICALCO: Name given to a building said to have been inside the Sacred Precinct in Tenochtitlan.

YACATECUHTLI: God of commerce, patron of merchants, a.k.a. "Nose Lord."

YOLTEOTL: "God in his heart," a term used to refer to "artist."

YOPICO CALMECAC: Temple in the Sacred Precinct of Tenochtitlan.

YOPICO TZOMPANTLI: Skull rack located inside the Sacred Precinct of Tenochtitlan.

YOPIOCO: Temple in the Sacred Precinct of Tenochtitlan.

Chronology

Pre-1100 AD   Aztecs live in "Aztlan" homeland.

1100–1250 AD   Days of wandering.

1250 AD   Traditional arrival date of the Aztecs in the Basin of Mexico.

1325 AD   Traditional founding date for Tenochtitlan, the Aztec capital.

1372 AD   Acamapichtli becomes first Aztec ruler.

1391 AD   Huitzilihuitl succeeds Acamapichtli.

1415 AD   Chimalpopoca accedes to the throne. Tlatelolco becomes the most important Aztec market.

1426 AD   Civil war in the Tepanec kingdom.

1426 AD   Aztec ruler, Chimalpopoca, is murdered.

1426 AD   Chimalpopoca is succeeded by Itzcoatl.

1428 AD   Aztecs defeat Tepanec rebel factions.

1428 AD   Aztecs ally themselves with Texcoco and Tlacopan to form the Triple Alliance.

1428–1440 AD   Itzcoatl orders Aztec books destroyed.

1440 AD   Moctecuhzuma Ilhuicamina succeeds Itzcoatl.

1440–1450 AD   Moctecuhzuma Ilhuicamina consolidates Aztec territories.

1450–1458 AD   Construction of Templo Mayor is started.

1450–1454 AD   Drought hits Basin of Mexico. Social unrest ensues.

1462 AD(?)   Atototzli, Moctecuhzuma Ilhuicamina's daughter, may have succeeded him.

1468 AD   Axayacatl becomes ruler.

1468–1481 AD   Tenochtitlan annexes Tlatelolco.

1478 AD   (?)Tarascan armies beat back Aztec invasion.

1481 AD   Tizoc takes over from Axayacatl.

1486 AD   After suffering military defeats, Tizoc is removed from power.

1486 AD   Ahuizotl replaces Tizoc. The Aztecs take leadership of the Triple Alliance.

1518 AD   Moctecuhzuma II receives reports of foreigners arriving in the Gulf Coast region.

1519 AD   Cortés sets out from Cuba to the mainland.

1519 AD   Spanish arrive on Cozumel; proceed to Potonchan on the Gulf Coast.

1519 AD   Cortés and Malintzin meet in the Potonchan region.

1519 AD   The Spanish arrive in what is now the state of Veracruz. Emissaries of the Aztec ruler await them.

1519 AD   While in Veracruz, the Spanish form an alliance with the local Totonacs.

1519 AD   The Spanish move inland, accompanied by indigenous allies.

1519 AD   The Spanish arrive in Tenochtitlan. Cortés and Moctecuhzuma II meet for the first time.

1520 AD   Spanish troops land in Veracruz to apprehend Cortés.

1520 AD   Cortés leaves Tenochtitlan, and returns to Veracruz.

1520 AD   Hostilities erupt between Aztecs and Spanish troops left behind in Tenochtitlan, resulting in "La Noche Triste" and subsequent stalemate.

1520 AD   Cortés convinces the newly arrived troops to support him and returns to Tenochtitlan.

1520 AD   Moctecuhzuma II is taken hostage and his brother, Cuitlahuac, is chosen to replace him.

1520 AD   Moctecuhzuma II dies.

1520 AD   Savage street fighting in Tenochtitlan continues unabated. Cuitlahuac dies of smallpox.

1520 AD   Cuauhtemoc succeeds Cuitlahuac.

1521 AD   Fall of Tenochtitlan; Cuauhtemoc is captured.

1525 AD   Cortés orders the execution of Cuauhtemoc.

Sources for Further Study

Acosta Saignes, Miguel
1946 Migraciones de los Mexica. *Memorias de la Academia Mexicana de la Historia* 5 (2): 177–187. [The author addresses the issue of the origins of Aztec culture.]

Acuña, René, editor
1984–1987 *Relaciones Geográficas del Siglo XVI.* 9 vols. Universidad Nacional Autónoma de México, Mexico City. (Originally written 1578–1582) [These Relaciones contained answers to a questionnaire sent out in 1578 by the Spanish Crown. The information contained in these documents is very valuable in reconstructing Aztec culture.]

Alcina Franch, José
1992 *Códices Mexicanos.* Madrid. [The author presents an overview of Mexican manuscripts, an area in which he specialized.]

Alva Ixtlilxochitl, Fernando de
1975–1977 *Obras históricas.* 2 vols. Translated by Edmundo O'Gorman. Universidad Nacional Autónoma de México, Mexico City. (Originally written 1600–1640). [This publication makes available the works of an important early colonial writer, great-grandson of the king of Texcoco.]

Alvarado Tezozomoc, Fernando
1975 *Crónica Mexicáyotl.* Translated by Adrián León. (Originally written in 1609). Universidad Autónoma de México, Mexico City. [The author was of Aztec descent and worked as an interpreter during the early colonial period.]

Anales de Cuauhtitlan
1945 *Códice Chimalpopoca: Anales de Cuauhtitlan y leyenda de los soles.* Translated by Primo Feliciano Velázquez. Universidad Autónoma de México, Mexico, Instituto de Investigaciones Históricas, Mexico. [Modern edition of a colonial-period document.]

Anales de Cuauhtitlan
1975 In *Códice Chimalpopoca: Anales de Cuauhtitlan y leyenda de los soles.* Translated by Primo Feliciano Velázquez, pp. 3–68. Universidad Autónoma de México, Mexico. (Reprint of 1945 edition)

Anawalt, Patricia
1981 Custom and control: Aztec sumptuary laws. *Archaeology* 33(1): 33–43.

Anders, Ferdinand
1978 Der altamerikanische Federmosaikschild in Wien. *Archiv für Völkerkunde,* XXXII, pp. 67–88. Vienna. [The author discusses an Aztec shield decorated with feathers and alleged to have belonged to the Aztec emperor. It is currently in the collections of the Ethnographic Museum in Vienna.]

Anderson Arthur J. O., Frances F. Berdan, and James Lockhart
1976 *Beyond the Codices: The Nahua View of Colonial Mexico.* Berkeley: University of California Press. [Emphasis on the descendants of the Aztecs and their approach to history.]

Armillas, Pedro
1950 Teotihuacan, Tula y los Toltecas. *Runa* (3): 37–70. [Armillas argues in favor of identifying Teotihuacan as the site referred to as Tollan in Mesoamerican oral traditions.]

Armillas, Pedro
1951 Mesoamerican fortifications. *Antiquity* 25: 77–86. [The discovery of fortified sites in Mesoamerica gradually brought our perceptions about native cultures into perspective. They were not peace-loving cultures, but frequently engaged in warfare.]

Armillas, Pedro
1971 Gardens on swamps. *Science* 174: 653–661. [Discussion of the role played by the *chinampas* in supporting complex and extensive urban centers in the southern portion of the Basin of Mexico.]

Arnold, Philip
1999 *Eating Landscape. Aztec and European Occupation of Tlalocan.* Boulder: University Press of Colorado. [The Aztecs viewed the landscapes in which they lived as requiring constant nourishment, hence the title "eating landscape."]

Bandelier, Fanny R.
1932 *A History of Ancient Mexico by Fray Bernardino de Sahagún.* Translated by Fanny R. Bandelier from the Spanish version of Carlos Maria de Bustamante. Nashville: Fisk University Press. [English translation of one of the most important early Spanish chroniclers of Mexican history.]

Batres, Leopoldo
1902 *Archaeological Explorations in Escalerillas Street, City of Mexico, by Leopoldo Batres, General Inspector of Archaeological Monuments, Year 1900.* Mexico: J. Aguilar Vera and Co. [Batres, who is best known for his work on the Pyramid of the Sun in Teotihuacan, writes about the recovery of Teotihuacan materials in the Aztec capital Tenochtitlan.]

Bayard Morris, J.
1991 *Five Letters of Cortés to the Emperor.* (Reissue of 1969 edition). New York: W. W. Norton and Company. [While in the Americas, Cortés sent five letters to Emperor Charles V. They are reproduced in this volume.]

Berdan, Frances

1975   *Trade, Tribute, and Market in the Aztec Empire.* Unpublished Ph.D. dissertation. Department of Anthropology, University of Texas, Austin.

Berdan, Frances

1982   *The Aztecs of Central Mexico: An Imperial Society.* New York: Holt, Rinehart, and Winston.

Berdan, Frances

1994   Economic Alternatives under Imperial Rule. The Eastern Aztec Empire. In *Economies and Polities in the Aztec Realm.* Edited by Mary G. Hodge and Michael E. Smith, pp. 291–312. (Studies on Culture and Society, volume 6). Albany: Institute for Mesoamerican Studies. [Berdan reviews what happened when territories became incorporated into the Aztec empire. She focuses on the eastern Aztec empire.]

Berdan, Frances

1996   The Tributary Provinces. In *Aztec Imperial Strategies.* Edited by Frances F. Berdan, Richard E. Blanton, Elizabeth H. Boone, Mary G. Hodge, Michael E. Smith, and Emily Umberger, pp. 115–135. Washington, D.C.: Dumbarton Oaks. [Berdan discusses one of two categories of Aztec provinces, the other one being strategic provinces.]

Berdan, Frances

2000   Principles of Regional and Long-Distance Trade in the Aztec Empire. In *The Ancient Civilizations of Mesoamerica. A Reader.* Edited by Michael E. Smith and Marilyn A. Mason, pp. 191–203. Oxford: Blackwell Publishers. [Reprint of an earlier article on Aztec trade.]

Berdan, Frances

2002   Aztec Society: Economy, Tribute and Warfare. In *Aztecs.* Edited by Eduardo Matos Mactezuma and Felipe Solis Olguín, pp. 38–47. London: Royal Academy of Arts. [Contribution in catalogue from a world-class exhibit on the Aztec in London.]

Bernard, H. Russell and Salinas Pedraza, Jesús

1989   *Native Ethnograhpy: A Mexican Indian Decribes His Culture.* Newbury Park: Sage Publications.

Blanton, Richard E.

1996   The Basin of Mexico Market System and the Growth of Empire. In *Aztec Imperial Strategies.* Edited by Frances F. Berdan, Richard E. Blanton, Elizabeth H. Boone, Mary G. Hodge, Michael E. Smith, and Emily Umberger, pp. 47–84. Washington, D.C.: Dumbarton Oaks. [Blanton presents a model in which the markets in Central Mexico acted as an engine fueling political and economic growth in the Basin.]

Blanton, Richard E., and Mary G. Hodge

1996   Appendix 2. Data on Market Activities and Production Specializations in *Tlatoani* Centers in the Basin of Mexico and Areas North of the Basin (excluding Texcoco and Tenochtitlan-Tlatelolco). In *Aztec Imperial Strategies.* Edited by Frances F.

Berdan, Richard E. Blanton, Elizabeth Hill Boone, Mary G. Hodge, Michael E. Smith, and Emily Umberger, pp. 243–246. Washington, D.C.: Dumbarton Oaks Research Library and Collection. [Presentation of data culled from written documents, both colonial and modern.]

Boksenbaum, Martin, Paul Tolstoy, Garman Harbottle, J. Kimberlin, and Mary Neivens
1987   Obsidian Industries and Cultural Evolution in the Basin of Mexico before 500 B.C. *Journal of Field Archaeology* 14: 65–75.

Boone, Elizabeth Hill
1985   The Color of Mesoamerican Architecture and Sculpture. In *Painted Architecture and Polychrome Monumental Sculpture in Mesoamerica.* Edited by Elizabeth H. Boone, pp. 173–186. Washington, D.C.: Dumbarton Oaks. [This volume is the end result of a symposium held at Dumbarton Oaks in Washington, D.C. Among other things Dr. Boone discusses and evaluates the presence of Teotihuacan-style architecture in the context of the Aztec capital.]

Boone, Elizabeth Hill
1987   Templo Mayor research. In *The Aztec Templo Mayor.* Edited by Elizabeth H. Boone, pp. 5–69. Washington, D.C.: Dumbarton Oaks. [This volume resulted from a Dumbarton Oaks conference on the archaeological research carried out at the Templo Mayor in Mexico City.]

Boone, Elizabeth Hill
1992   Pictorial Codices of Ancient Mexico. In *The Ancient Americas. Art from Sacred Landscapes.* Edited by Richard F. Townsend, pp. 197–210. Chicago: The Art Institute of Chicago. [The author discusses a variety of manuscripts related to the history of Prehispanic Mexico.]

Boone, Elizabeth Hill
2000a   *Stories in Red and Black. Pictorial Histories of the Aztecs and the Mixtecs.* Austin: University of Texas Press. [Insightful analysis into how two Precolumbian cultures used the format of painted documents to relate their past and how they continued this tradition after the arrival of the Spanish. The author emphasizes how the pictorial format allows for the information to be understood across cultural and linguistic barriers.]

Boone, Elizabeth Hill
2000b   Venerable Place of Beginning. The Aztec Understanding of Teotihuacan. In *Mesoamerica's Classic Heritage. From Teotihuacan to the Aztecs.* Edited by Davíd Carrasco, Lindsay Jones, and Scott Sessions, pp. 371–395. Boulder: University of Colorado Press. [Boone discusses how the site of Teotihuacan was never a lost site, and how it continued to play an important role in the worldview of the Aztecs.]

Boserup, Esther
1973   *The Conditions of Agricultural Growth.* Chicago: Aldine. [Boserup evaluates how people adapt when confronted with growing populations and limited agricultural resources.]

Broda, Johanna

1970   El Tributo en Trajes Guerreros y la Estructura del Sistema Tributario Mexica. In *Economía Política e Ideología Prehispánico*. Edited by Pedro Carrasco and Johanna Broda, pp. 115–174. Mexico City: UNAM. [Overview of the Aztec tribute system and the role played by textiles within it.]

Brumfiel, Elizabeth M.

1980   Specialization, Market Exchange, and the Aztec State: A View from Huexotla. *Current Anthropology* 21: 459–478. [A contribution on craft specialization and market exchange by an author who focuses on social inequality.]

Brumfiel, Elizabeth

1983   Aztec State Making: Ecologys and the Origin of the State. *American Anthropologist* 85: 261–284. [On the role played by environment in the development of a complex society.]

Calnek, Edward

1976   The Internal Structure of Tenochtitlan. In *The Valley of Mexico*. Edited by Eric Wolf. Albuquerque: University of New Mexico Press.

Calnek, Edward

1978a   The Internal Structure of Cities in America: Pre-Columbian Cities; The Case of Tenochtitlan. In *Urbanization in the Americas from its Beginnings to the Present*. Edited by Schaedel, Richard, Jorge Hardoy, and Nora Scott Kinzer. The Hague: Mouton Publishers.

Calnek, Edward E.

1978a   The City–State in the Basin of Mexico: Late Prehispanic Period. In *Urbanization in the Americas from its Beginnings to the Present*. Edited by Richard Schaedel et al., pp. 463–470. The Hague: Mouton. [Presentation of what was known at the time on the origins and development of the Aztec state.]

Carrasco, Davíd

1999   *City of Sacrifice. The Aztec Empire and the Role of Violence in Civilization*. Boston: Beacon Press. [The author discusses Aztec history and the role that violence played in these developments.]

Carrasco, Davíd

2003   Toward the Splendid City: Knowing the Worlds of Moctezuma. In *Moctezuma's World. Visions of the Aztec World*. Revised Edition. Edited by Davíd Carrasco and Eduardo Matos Moctezuma, pp. 99–148. Boulder: University Press of Colorado. [The author pursues two controversies: Did the Aztec build real cities and what was the extent of human sacrifice and cannibalism?]

Carrasco, Pedro

1971   Social Organization of Ancient Mexico. In *Handbook of Middle American Indians*. Edited by Robert Wauchope. Vol. 10. Austin: University of Texas Press.

Carrasco, Pedro
1977   Los Señores de Xochimilco en 1548. *Tlalocan* 7: 229–265. [Discussion of the rulers of early colonial Xochimilco.]

Carrasco, Pedro
1984   Royal Marriages in Ancient Mexico. In *Explorations in Ethnohistory: Indians of Central Mexico in the Sixteenth Century.* Edited by Herbert R. Harvey and Hanns J. Prem, pp. 41-81. Albuquerque: University of New Mexico Press.

Carrasco, Pedro
1991   The Territorial Structure of the Aztec Empire. In *Land and Politics in the Valley of Mexico. A Two Thousand Year Perspective.* Edited by H. R. Harvey, pp. 93–112. Albuquerque: University of New Mexico Press. [Reviews and discusses the categories of territory within the empire and the types of tributary obligations and land tenure that prevailed.]

Caso, Alfonso
1959   La tenencia de la tierra entre los antiguos Mexicanos. *Memorias del Colegio Nacional* 4: 29–54. Mexico. [Caso defines land tenure among the Mexica.]

Charlton, Thomas H., David C. Grove, and Philip K. Hopke
1978   The Paredon, Mexico, Obsidian Source and Early Formative Exchange. *Science* 201: 807–809.

Chimalpahin, Domingo Francisco de San Antón Muñón
1965   *Relaciones originales de Chalco Amequemecan.* Translated by Sylvia Rendón. Mexico City: Fondo de Cultura Económica. (Originally written 1606–1631). [A modern publication of the study of the town of Chalco by Nahua historian Chimalpahin.]

Clendinnen, Inga
2000   *Aztecs. An Interpretation.* Cambridge: Cambridge University Press. (Reprint of 1991 edition)

Cline, Howard F.
1972   The Relaciones Geográficas of the Spanish Indies, 1577–1648. In *Handbook of Middle American Indians.* Edited by Robert Wauchope. Vol. 12, part one. *Guide to Ethnohistorical Sources*, pp. 183–247. Austin: University of Texas Press. [Discussion of a series of questionnaires sent by Madrid starting in 1578. The replies to these questions, to the extent that they have been preserved, present a unique window onto early colonial Mexico.]

Codex Borgia
1976   *Codex Borgia.* Edited by Karl Nowotny. Graz: Akademische Druck-U Verlagsanstalt. [Screenfold facsimile beautifully produced by the company in Austria.]

Codex Chimalpopoca
1975   *Códice Chimalpopoca: Anales de Cuauhtitlán Y Leyenda de los soles.* Translated and edited by P. F. Velázquez. Mexico: UNAM-IIH. [Publication of a colonial period document on the history of the Aztecs.]

Codex Mendoza

1992   *Codex Mendoza.* Edited by Frances F. Berdan and Patricia R. Anawalt. Berkeley: University of California Press. [This modern publication places this codex firmly within the reach of the interested lay public.]

Coe, Sophie

1994   *America's First Cuisines.* Austin: University of Texas Press. [Coe reviews the contributions made by the Americas to our cuisine.]

Coe, Sophie, and Michael D. Coe

1996   *The True History of Chocolate.* London: Thames and Hudson, Ltd. [This work is the logical result of Sophie Coe's work on *America's First Cuisines.* The historical context of chocolate consumption forms the main portion of this book.]

Conrad, Geoffrey W., and Arthur Demarest

1984   *Religion and Empire. The Dynamics of Aztec and Inca Expansion.* Cambridge: Cambridge University Press. [Both authors review the interaction between political organization and religion. They discuss such concepts as empire, hegemony, macrostate, and confederation.]

Cook, S. F., and W. Borah

1979   Indian Food Production and Consumption in Central Mexico before and after the Conquest (1500–1650). In *Essays in Population History: Mexico and California,* vol. 3, pp. 129–176. Los Angeles: University of California Press. [The authors argue that the Aztec diet before the arrival of the Spanish led to malnourishment and undernourishment. They suggest that the indigenous people had no choice but to resort to cannibalism.]

Cook, Sherburne, and L. B. Simpson

1948   *The Population of Central Mexico in the Sixteenth Century.* Ibero-Americana, no. 13. Berkeley and Los Angeles: University of California Press. [The authors provide a census of the population in Central Mexico in the years following the Spanish conquest. They used written documents to compute the numbers.]

Cortés, Hernando

1962   *Five Letters of Cortés to the Emperor.* Edited and translated by J. Bayard Morros. New York: Norton. (Originally written 1519–1526) [Modern edition of the correspondence between Cortés and Emperor Charles V.]

D'Olwer, Luis Nicolau, and Howard F. Cline

1973   Bernadino de Sahagún, 1499–1590. A. Sahagún and his works. In *Handbook of Middle American Indians.* Edited by Robert Wauchope. Vol. 13, part two. *Guide to Ethnohistorical Sources,* pp. 186–207. Austin: University of Texas Press. [The authors have put together an exhaustive historiography of one of the most important writers on Mexican history.]

Dalton, George

1971   *Economic Anthropology and Development: Essays on Tribal and Peasant Economies.* New York/London: Basic Books.

Darras, Véronique, and Fred W. Nelson

1987   Nota informative primeros resultados de la caraterización química por medio de los elementos traza de los yacimientos de obsidiana en la región de Zináparo-Purpero, Michoacán. *Trace* 12: 76–79. [Results of the compositional analysis of obsidian retrieved from sources in Michoacán.]

de Durand-Forest, Jacqueline

1996   Response from Jacqueline de Durand-Forest. *Nahua Newsletter*, November. [Part of an exchange among Aztec scholars on the topic of pochtecas.]

Díaz del Castillo, Bernal

1908–1916   *The True History of the Conquest of New Spain.* Translated by Alfred Percival Maudslay. Five vols. London: Hakluyt Society. [Older edition of the report on the conquest of the New World by one of the original participants and self-confessed eyewitness to the fall of Tenochtitlan.]

Díaz del Castillo, Bernal

1963   *The Conquest of New Spain.* Translated by J. M. Cohen. New York: Penguin. (Originally written 1560s). [Modern edition of the report on the conquest of the New World by one of the original participants and self-confessed eyewitness to the fall of Tenochtitlan.]

Diehl, Richard

1981   Tula. In *Archaeology.* Edited by Jeremy A. Sabloff, pp. 277-295. Handbook of Middle American Indians, Supplement, 1. Austin: University of Texas Press.

Durán, Diego

1967   *Historia de Las Indias de Nueva España.* 2 vols. Edited by Angel M. Garibay K. Mexico City: Porrúa. (Originally written between 1570 and 1581). [Modern edition of the contributions of a Dominican Friar whose observations are considered key to a better understanding of Aztec culture.]

Durán, Diego

1994   *The Aztecs: The History of the Indies of New Spain.* Translated by D. Heyden and F. Horcasitas, New York. (Written in 1581) [Modern edition of the contributions of a Dominican Friar whose observations are considered key to a better understanding of Aztec culture.]

Duverger, Christian

1993   *La Flor Letal. Economía del Sacrificio Azteca.* Mexico: Fondo de Cultura Económica. [Discussion of the role sacrifice played in Aztec society.]

Ekholm, Gordon F.

1946   Wheeled Toys in Mexico. *American Antiquity* 11(4). [On the presence of wheeled Toys and the complete lack of their application to transportation.]

Elam, J. Michael, Christopher Carr, Michael D. Glasscock, and Hector Neff

1992   Utrasonic Disaggregation and INAA of Textural Fractions of Tucson Basin and Ohio Valley Pottery. In *Chemical Characterization of Ceramic Pastes in Archaeology.*

Edited by Hector Neff, pp. 93–111. Madison: Prehistory Press. [Presentation of advanced compositional analysis of pottery.]

Elson, Christina M., and Michael E. Smith
2001 Archaeological Deposits from the Aztec New Fire Ceremony. *Ancient Mesoamerica* 12(2): 157–174. [The authors found tangible proof of the Aztec New Fire ceremony.]

Ericson, J. E., and J. Kimberlin
1977 Obsidian Sources, Chemical Characterization Hydration Rates in West Mexico. *Archaeometry* 19: 157–166.

Evans, Susan T.
1980 Spatial Analysis of Basin of Mexico Settlement Problems with the Use of the Central Place Model. *American Antiquity* 45: 866–875. [Attempts to apply theoretical models to the data observed in the field.]

Evans, Susan T.
1985 Cerro-Gordo Site; a Rural Settlement of the Aztec period in the Basin of Mexico. *Journal of Field Archaeology* 12(1):1-18.

Evans, Susan T.
1991 Architecture and Authority in an Aztec Village: Form and Function of the Tecpan. In *Land and Politics in the Valley of Mexico. A Two Thousand Year Perspective.* Edited by H. R. Harvey, pp. 63–92. Albuquerque: University of New Mexico Press. [Provides information on the dwellings in which rural elite lived. Provides a counterbalance to the data favoring the big cities.]

Evans, Susan T.
1992 The Productivity of Maguey Terrace Agriculture in Central Mexico during the Aztec Period. In *Gardens of Prehistory. The Archaeology of Settlement Agriculture in Greater Mesoamerica.* Edited by Thomas W. Killion, pp. 92–115. Tuscaloosa: University of Alabama Press. [Discusses one technique of agricultural production available to the Aztecs: terrace agriculture.]

Evans, Susan T.
1999 Aztec Palaces. In *Palaces of the Ancient New World.* Edited by Susan Toby Evans and Joanna Pillsbury. Washington, D.C.: Dumbarton Oaks. [Publication of a presentation given at a Dumbarton Oaks symposium.]

Evans, Susan Toby
2001 Tenochtitlán: Palaces. In *Archaeology of Ancient Mexico and Central America. An Encyclopedia.* Edited by Susan Toby Evans and David L. Webster, pp. 718–719. New York and London: Garland Publishing, Inc. [Updates our understanding on the layout of Aztec palaces.]

Ferriz, Horatio
1985 Canlona, a Prehispanic Obsidian-Mining Center in Eastern Mexico? *Journal of Field Archaeology* 12: 363-370.

Finer, Samuel E.

1975   State- and Nation-Building in Europe: The Role of the Military. In *The Formation of National States in Western Europe.* Edited by Charles Tilly. Princeton: Princeton University Press. [Discussion on political theory related to Europe.]

Fuentes, Patricia de

1963   *The Conquistadors: First-Person Accounts of the Conquest of Mexico.* London: Cassell. [A modern edition of eyewitness accounts penned by those who participated in the conquest.]

Gamio, Manuel

1917   Investigaciones Arqueológicas en Mexico, 1914–1915. *Annals of the XIX International Congress of Americanists.* Washington, D.C., pp. 125–133. [Gamio was very active in the Valley of Teotihuacan in the early portion of the twentieth century.]

Gamio, Manuel

1921   Vestigios del Templo Mayor de Tenochtitlan descubiertos recientemente. *Ethnos,* vol. I (8–12), November 1920–March 1921, pp. 205–207. [Gamio relates the discovery of remains of the Great Temple.]

Garcia Samper, Asuncion and Rossana Enrique

2002   *El Santo Juan Diego el Mensajero Indigena de la Virgen de Guadalupe.* Mexico: Centro de Estudios Mesoamericanos.

Gerhard, Peter

1970   A Method for Reconstructing Political Boundaries in Central Mexico. *Journal de la Société des Américanistes* n.s. 59, pp. 27–41.

Gibson, Charles

1964   *The Aztecs under Spanish Rule. A History of the Indians of the Valley of Mexico, 1519–1810.* Stanford: Stanford University Press. [Classic reference work. This study includes a detailed study of such topics as religion, encomienda and corregimiento, tribute, labor, production, and exchange during the colonial period. The meticulous endnotes and extremely detailed references make this a resource one keeps coming back to over and over.]

Gibson, Charles

1971   Structure of the Aztec Empire. In *Handbook of Middle American Indians.* Edited by Robert Wauchope. Vol. 10. Austin: University of Texas Press. [Outline of the political, economic, and religious organization in Prehispanic Aztec society.]

Glass, John B.

1975   "A Survey of Native Middle American Pictorial Manuscripts" and "A Census of Native Middle American Pictorial Manuscripts." In *Handbook of Middle American Indians.* 14. Edited by Robert Wauchope and Howard F. Cline, pp. 3–80, 81–225. Austin: University of Texas Press. [Meticulous and laboriously compiled overview of what we know about native pictorial manuscripts pertaining to Mesoamerica.]

Gorenstein, Shirley
   1966   The Differential Development of New World Empires. *Revista Mexicana de Estudios Antropologicos* XX: 41–67.

Gorenstein, Shirley
   1985   *Acambaro: Frontier Settlement on the Trascan-Aztec Border.* Vanderbilt University Publications in Anthropology, No. 32. Nashville: Vanderbilt University. [Discussion of the rare phenomenon of a fortified border in Mesoamerica: the region between Aztec and Tarascan territories.]

Gussinyer, Jordi
   1970   Un adoratorio azteca decorado con pinturas. *Boletin del INAH* 40: 30–35. [Contribution on the presence of Teotihuacan influences in the arts and architecture of the Aztecs.]

Gussinyer, Jordi
   1972   Rescate de un adoratorio azteca en México, D.F. *Boletin del INAH*, segunda época 2: 21–30. [Report on the emergency excavations in what used to be Tenochtitlan.]

Hare, Timothy S., and Michael E. Smith
   1996   A New Postclassic Chronology for Yautepec, Morelos, Mexico. *Ancient Mesoamerica* 7: 281–297. [The authors discuss the chronology of a provincial Aztec community.]

Harner, M.
   1977   The ecological basis for Aztec sacrifice. *American Ethnologist* 4: 117–135. [Harner argues that in Precolumbian times the Aztec diet was lacking in protein and that cannibalism was the only avenue available to compensate for this lack.]

Harris, M.
   1978   The Cannibal Kingdom. In *Cannibals and Kings,* pp. 147–166. New York: Random House. [The author favors the absolute necessity of cannibalism as an answer to a diet insufficient in protein among the Prehispanic Aztec.]

Harvey, Herbert R., and Barbara J. Williams
   1986   Decipherment and Some Implications of Aztec Numerical Glyphs. In *Native American Mathematics.* Edited by Michael P. Closs, pp. 237–259. Austin: University of Texas Press. [Contribution outlining the thinking behind the Aztec numerical system.]

Hassig, Ross
   1982   Precolumbian Markets in Precolumbian Mexico. *American Antiquity* 47: 46–51. [Discussion of the role played by markets and how they were organized.]

Hassig, Ross
   1988   *Aztec Warfare. Imperial Expansion and Political Control.* Norman: University of Oklahoma Press. [Hassig analyses in a very methodical way the ways in which Aztecs and their contemporaries engaged in warfare.]

Hassig, Ross

1993   *Trade, Tribute, and Transportation: The Sixteenth Century Political Economy of the Valley of Mexico.* Norman: University of Oklahoma Press. [Hassig discusses in detail the economic and political structure in the Valley of Mexico before and after the conquest.]

Hassig, Ross

2001   *Time, History and Belief in Aztec and Colonial Mexico.* Austin: University of Texas Press. [Hassig goes against established thinking favoring the use of cyclical time by Precolumbian people, including the Aztecs. Instead he argues that for the Aztecs, time was linear and predominantly used by the rulers to achieve their political ends.]

Healan, Dan M., Janet M. Kerley, and George J. Bey III

1983   Excavation and Preliminary Analysis of an Obsidian Workshop in Tula, Hidalgo, Mexico. *Journal of Field Archaeology* 10(2):127-145.

Hernández, Francisco

1945   *Antiguedades de la Nueva España.* Mexico City: Pedro Robredo. [Twentieth-century publication of a work compiled in the sixteenth century by the personal physician of Phillip II of Spain.]

Heyden, Doris

1987   Symbolism of Ceramics from the Templo Mayor. In *Aztec Templo Mayor.* Edited by Elizabeth H. Boone, pp. 109–130. Washington, DC.: Dumbarton Oaks.

Heyden, Doris

1987   *The Eagle, the Cactus, the Rock: The Roots of Mexico-Tenochtitlan's Foundation Myth and Symbol.* BAR International Series 484. BAR, Oxford. [Heyden focuses on the origins of Aztec society.]

Hicks, Frederic

1978   Los calpixque de Nezahualcoyotl. *Estudios de Cultura Náhuatl* 13: 129–152. [On the use of tax collectors by the king of Texcoco.]

Hicks, Frederic

1984   Rotational Labor and Urban Development in Prehispanic Tetzcoco. In *Explorations in Ethnohistory:* Indians of Central Mexico in the Sixteenth Century. Edited by Herbert R. Harvey and Janns J. Prem, pp. 147–174. Albuquerque: University of New Mexico Press.

Hicks, Frederic

1987   First Steps Toward a Market-Integrated Economy in Aztec Mexico. In *Early State Dynamics.* Edited by Henri J. M. Claessen and Pieter van de Velde, pp. 91–107. Leiden: E. J. Brill. [Reviews evidence to support the application of an economic model to the Aztecs.]

Hicks, Frederic
1991 Gift and Tribute: Relations of Dependency in Aztec Mexico. In *Early State Economics*. Edited by Henri J. M. Claessen and Pieter van de Velde, pp. 197–212. New Brunswick: Transactions Publishers. [Relates to the use of gift giving and tribute receiving in the development of political hierarchies.]

Hicks, Frederic
1994 Cloth in the Political Economy of the Aztec State. In *Economies and Polities in the Aztec Realm*. Edited by Mary G. Hodge and Michael E. Smith, pp. 89–111. (Studies on Culture and Society, volume 6). Albany: Institute for Mesoamerican Studies. [The Aztec economy was one based on barter. Textile played an important role in this context.]

Hirth, Kenneth G. and Angulo, Jorge
1981 Early State Expansion in Central Mexico; Teotihuacán in Morelos. *Journal of Field Archaeology* 8(2): 135-150.

Hodge, Mary G.
1994 Polities Composing the Aztec Empire's Core. In *Economies and Polities in the Aztec Realm*. Edited by Mary G. Hodge and Michael E. Smith, pp. 43–71. (Studies on Culture and Society, volume 6) Albany: Institute for Mesoamerican Studies.

Hodge, Mary
1996 Political Organization of the Central Provinces. In *Aztec Imperial Strategies*. Edited by Frances F. Berdan, Richard E. Blanton, Elizabeth H. Boone, Mary G. Hodge, Michael E. Smith, and Emily Umberger, pp. 17–45. Washington, D.C.: Dumbarton Oaks. [The late Dr. Hodge examines the relationships between communities, regional states, and the imperial capital. Her deliberate emphasis on the provinces is intended to counterbalance the overemphasis on Tenochtitlan.]

Hodge, Mary G.
1998 Archaeological Views of Aztec Culture. *Journal of Archaeological Research* 6: 197–238.

Humboldt, Alexander von
1810 *Vues des Cordillères et Monuments des Peuples de l'Amériques*. Paris: F. Schoell. [Reminiscences about a voyage to the New World, including Mexico, by one of the world's most famous explorers.]

Isaac, Barry
1983 Aztec Warfare: Goals and Battlefield Comportment. *Ethnology* XXII, 2: 121–131.

Jiménez Moreno, Wigberto
1974 La migracíon mexica. In *Atti del XL Congresso Internazionale degli Americanisti, Roma and Genova, 1972*. Vol. I, pp. 167–172. [The author discussed the migrations that took the Aztecs from Aztlan to Central Mexico.]

Kaufman, Terrence

1976   Mesoamerican Indian Languages. In *Encyclopedia Britannica, Macropedia*, vol. 11, pp. 956–963. New York: Encyclopedia Britannica. [Overview article by a leading linguist active in Mesoamerican studies.]

Kirchhoff, Paul

1954   Land Tenure in Ancient Mexico, a Preliminary Sketch. *Revista Mexicana de Estudios Antropológicos* 14: 351–361. [The author who coined the term *Mesoamerica* tries to define Aztec forms of land tenure.]

Kirchhoff, Paul

1958   La ruta de los Tolteca-Chichimeca entre Tula y Cholula. In *Miscellanea Paul Rivet: Octogenaria Dictata* I: 485–494. Mexico City: UNAM. [Kirchhoff reconstructs migration routes of the Aztec ancestors.]

Las Casas, Fray Bartolomé de

1958   *Apologética historia sumaria.* Biblioteca de Autores Españoles, vol. 105. Madrid: Ediciones Atlas. [Deals with the works of one of the most active protectors of native peoples.]

León-Portilla, Miguel

1990a   *Aztec Thought and Culture. A Study of the Ancient Nahuatl Mind.* (The Civilization of the American Indian Series) Translated by Jack Emory Davis. Norman: University of Oklahoma Press. (Paperback edition) [The author provides much-needed information on aspects of Aztec culture. His work counterbalances the prevailing view that Aztecs were a violent people, incapable of writing poetry, philosophy, or developing complex religious beliefs.]

León-Portilla, Miguel

1990b   *The Broken Spears: The Aztec Account of the Conquest of Mexico.* Boston: Beacon Press. [The author provides a historical overview of the Spanish conquest of the Aztec empire. As indicated in the title, he does so from the perspective of the vanquished.]

León-Portilla, Miguel

1992   Pasado de los Aztecas. In *Azteca. Mexica. Las Culturas del México Antiguo.* Edited by José Alcina Franch, Miguel León-Portilla, and Eduardo Matos Moctezuma, pp. 87–98. Madrid: Lunwerg Editores. [Essays on Aztec thought, science, commerce, and religion by one of Mexico's leading scholars.]

León-Portilla, Miguel

2002   Aztec Codices. Literature and Philosophy. In *Aztecs.* Edited by Eduardo Matos Moctezuma and Felipe Solis Olguín, pp. 64–71. London: Royal Academy of Arts. [Descriptive study of Aztec manuscripts in the catalogue of a world-class exhibit on the Aztec.]

Lopez, Ruth

2002   *Chocolate: The Nature of Indulgence Chocolate.* New York: Harry N. Abrams. [Exhibit catalogue. Relates origin of chocolate and the consumption of it by Aztec and Maya people.]

López-Austin, A.

1973   *Hombre-dios: Religíon y Política en el Mundo Nahuatl.* Mexico City: UNAM. [The author discusses the close connections that existed between religion and politics in the Aztec world.]

López Luján, Leonardo

1989   *La Recuperación Mexica del Pasado Teotihucano.* Mexico: INAH/GV editores/Asociación de Amigos del Templo Mayor. (Colección Divulgación). [Discussion of how the Aztecs looked with reverence to Teotihuacan as a place of importance in their history.]

López Luján, Leonardo

1999   Water and Fire: Archaeology in the Capital of the Mexica Empire. In *The Archaeology of Mesoamerica. Mexican and European Perspectives.* Edited by Warwick Bray and Linda Manzanilla, pp. 32–49. London: British Museum Press. [Reviews of contributions to Mexican archaeology by European scholars.]

López Luján, Leonardo

2001   Tenochtitlán: Ceremonial Center. In *Archaeology of Ancient Mexico and Central America. An Encyclopedia.* Edited by Susan Toby Evans and David L. Webster, pp. 712–717. New York and London: Garland Publishing, Inc. [Overview article in a recent publication offering a synopsis of the role ceremonies played in Tenochtitlan.]

López Luján, Leonardo

(In press)   *La Casa de las Aguilas: un Ejemplo de Arquitectura Sacra Mexica.* Instituto Nacional de Antropología e Historia, Mexico/Princeton University/Mexican Fine Arts Museum Center. [Details investigations carried out in a building inside the Sacred Precinct in Tenochtitlan.]

López Luján, Leonardo, Hector Neff, and Saburo Sugiyama

2000   The 9-Xi Vase. A Classic Thin Orange Vessel Found at Tenochtitlan. In *Mesoamerica's Classic Heritage. From Teotihuacan to the Aztecs.* Edited by Davíd Carrasco, Lindsay Jones, and Scott Sessions, pp. 219–249. Boulder: University of Colorado Press. [The authors review evidence of Aztec-period retrieval of Teotihuacan objects at the site of Teotihuacan. The Aztec would rebury these Teotihuacan items in Aztec structures in Tenochtitlan.]

Marcus, Joyce

1992   *Mesoamerican Writing Systems. Propaganda, Myth, and History in Four Ancient Civilizations.* Princeton: Princeton University Press. [Contribution by a preeminent epigrapher on the writing systems of the Aztec, Mixtec, Zapotec, and Maya cultures. The author argues that writing systems played an important role in the competition for prestige among rulers of these four cultures.]

Marcus, Joyce

2001 Breaking the Glass Ceiling: The Strategies of Royal Women in Ancient States. In *Gender in Pre-Hispanic America*. Edited by Cecilia F. Klein, pp. 305–340. Washington, D.C.: Dumbarton Oaks Research Library and Collection.

Matos Moctezuma, Eduardo

1964 El adoratorio decorado de las Calles de Argentina. *Anales del INAH* 17: 127–138. [The author reports on his discovery of an Aztec altar once used inside the Sacred Precinct of the Aztec capital.]

Matos Moctezuma, Eduardo

1979 Una máscara olmeca en el Templo Mayor de Tenochtitlan. *Anales de Antropología* XVI, pp. 11–19. [Relates the discovery of an Olmec mask from the Great Temple in Mexico City.]

Matos Moctezuma, Eduardo

1988 *The Great Temple of the Aztecs: Treasures of Tenochtitlan.* New York: Thames and Hudson. [Publication of the findings to date by the leading archaeologist working at the Great Temple in Mexico City.]

Matos Moctezuma, Eduardo

1990 Imperial Tenochtitlan. In *Mexico. Splendors of Thirty Centuries,* pp. 212–234. New York: The Metropolitan Museum of Art. [Matos Moctezuma discusses the history of the Aztec capital and the impression it made on the Spanish when they first saw it. This chapter in a museum catalogue also reviews and illustrates various outstanding examples of Aztec art.]

Matos Moctezuma, Eduardo

1992 Templo Mayor. Guide officiel. INAH-SALVAT, Mexico. [Government publication of the Templo Mayor aimed at visitors to the capital.]

Matos Moctezuma, Eduardo

1995 *Life and Death in the Templo Mayor.* Translated by Bernard R. Ortiz de Montellano and Thelma Ortiz de Montellano). Niwot: University Press of Colorado. [Findings of the archaeological investigations into the Templo Mayor.]

Matos Moctezuma, Eduardo

1999 *Excavaciones en la Catedral y el Sagrario Metropolitanos. Programma de Arqueología Urbana.* Mexico: Instituto Nacional de Arqueología e Historia. [The author details the recovery of archaeological information from what used to be the ceremonial center of the Aztec empire.]

Matos Moctezuma, Eduardo

2002 The Templo Mayor, the Great Temple of the Aztecs. In *Aztecs*. Edited by Eduardo Matos Moctezuma and Felipe Solis Olguín, pp. 48–55. London: Royal Academy of Arts. [Update on the research at the Templo Mayor by one of the main protagonists in this endeavor.]

Matos Moctezuma, Eduardo
2003   Aztec History and Cosmovision. In *Moctezuma's Mexico. Visions of the Aztec World*. Revised Edition. Edited by David Carrasco and Eduardo Matos Moctezuma, pp. 3–97. Boulder: University Press of Colorado. [Matos Moctezuma presents a synopsis of Aztec culture. Beautifully illustrated with photos of well-known objects and manuscripts.]

Matos Moctezuma, Eduardo, and Leonardo López Luján
1993   Teotihuacan and its Mexica Legacy. In *Teotihuacan: Art from the City of the Gods*. Edited by K. Berrin and E. Pasztory, pp. 156–165. New York: Thames and Hudson/The Fine Arts Museum of San Francisco. [The authors discuss the influence Teotihuacan had in Aztec architecture. They illustrate this point by referring to the construction of at least four Teotihuacan-style temples inside the sacred precinct in Tenochtitlan.]

Medina, Andrés, and Naomi Quezada
1975   *Panorama de las artesanías otomíes del Valle del Mezquital*. Mexico City: Universidad Nacional Autónoma de México, Instituto de Investigaciones Antropológicas. [Reviews artisanal production in the state of Hidalgo.]

Millón, René
1981   Teotihuacan: City, State, and Civilization. In *Archaeology*. Edited by Jeremy A. Sabloff, pp. 198-243. Handbook of Middle American Indians, Supplement, 1. Austin: University of Texas Press.

Minc, Leah, Mary Hodge, and James Blackman
1994   Stylistic and Spatial Variability in Early Aztec Ceramics. In *Economies and Polities in the Aztec Realm*. Edited by Mary G. Hodge and Michael E. Smith, pp. 133–173. (Studies on Culture and Society, volume 6) Albany: Institute for Mesoamerican Studies. [Early Aztec ceramic exchange centered on subregional markets associated with city–states.]

Molíns Fábregas, N.
1952–1953   El Códice Mendocino y la economía de Tenochtitlan. *Revista Mexicana de Estudios Antropológicos,* xiii, pp. 2–3, 315. [On the Codex Mendoza, one of the most important colonial documents on the Aztec tax requirements.]

Motolinia, Fray Torribio de Benavente o
1971   *Memoriales o Libro de las Cosas de la Nueva España y de los Naturales de Ella*. Mexico: Universidad Nacional Autónoma de México. [Relates the history of the conquest of Mexico by a colonial writer.]

Mundy, Barbara E.
1996   *Mapping of New Spain: Indigenous Cartography and the Maps of the Relaciones Geográficas*. Chicago: University of Chicago Press.

Neff, Hector, Ronald L. Bishop, and Edward V. Sayre
1988   A Simulation Approach to the Problem of Tempering in Composition Studies of Archaeological Ceramics. *Journal of Archaeological Science* 15: 159–172.

Neff, Hector, Ronald L. Bishop, and Edward V. Sayre

1989   More Observations on the Problem of Tempering in Compositional Studies of Archaeological Ceramics. *Journal of Archaeological Science* 16: 57–69.

Nelson, Fred W., K. Nielson, N. Mangelson, M. Hill, and Ray T. Matheny

1977. Preliminary Studies of Analysis of Obsidian Artifacts from Northern Campeche, Mexico. *American Antiquity* 42: 209–226.

Nichols, Deborah L.

1994   The Organization of Provincial Craft Production and the Aztec City–State of Otumba. In *Economies and Polities in the Aztec Realm*. Edited by Mary G. Hodge and Michael E. Smith, pp. 175–193. (Studies on Culture and Society, volume 6) Albany: Institute for Mesoamerican Studies. [Paper examines models of spatial organization of provincial craft production during the Late Postclassic period.]

Nicholson, Henry B.

1966   "The Problem of the Provenience of the Members of the 'Codex Borgia Group': A Summary." In *Suma Antropológica en Homenaje a Roberto J. Weitlaner*, pp. 145–158, Mexico City. [Nicholson contributes his insights into the origins of a group of manuscripts known as the Borgia group.]

Nicholson, H. B.

1971   Prehispanic Central Mexican Historiography. In *Investigaciones Contemporáneas de México: Memorias de la Tercera Reunión de Historiadores Mexicanos y Norteamericanos, Oaxtepec, Morelos, 4–7 de Noviembre de 1969*, pp. 38–81. Mexico City and Austin: Universidad Nacional Autónoma de México, El Colegio de México and University of Texas. [Nicholson compiles information on indigenous contributions to our understanding of Aztec history.]

Nicholson, Henry B.

1973a   Bernadino de Sahagún, 1499–1590. B. Sahagún's Primeros Memoriales, Tepepolco, 1559–1561. In *Handbook of Middle American Indians*. Edited by Robert Wauchope. Vol. 13, part two. *Guide to Ethnohistorical Sources*, pp. 207–218. Austin: University of Texas Press. [Nicholson reviews part of the lifework of Sahagún.]

Nicholson, Henry B.

1973b   Phoneticism in the Late Prehispanic Central Mexican Writing System. In *Mesoamerican Writing Systems*. Edited by Elizabeth P. Benson, pp. 1–46. Washington, D.C.: Dumbarton Oaks Research Library and Collections. [Nicholson attacks the issue of how better to understand the writing systems prevalent in Central Mexico.]

Nicholson, Henry, and Eloise Quiñones Keber

1991   Ballcourt Images in Central Mexican Native Tradition Pictorial Manuscripts. In *The Mesoamerican Ballgame*. Edited by Gerard van Bussel, Paul van Dongen, and Ted Leyenaar, pp. 119–133. Leiden: (Mededelingen van het Rijksmuseum voor Volkenkunde, No. 26). [Analysis of the ball game and ballcourts in the Aztec empire.]

Nowotny, Karl Anton

1960   *Mexicanische Kostarbeiten aus Kunstkammern der Renaissance im Museum für Völkerkunde Wien und in der Nationalbibliothek Wien.* Vienna: Museum für Völkerkunde. [This contribution highlights the Aztec treasures that made it to Europe during the early days of Spain's colonial adventure. Some of these objects include feather works.]

Offner, Jerome A.

1982   Aztec Legal Process: the Case of Texcoco. In *The Art and Iconography of Late Post-Classic Central Mexico.* Edited by Elizabeth Hill Boone, pp. 141-158. Washington, DC.: Dumbarton Oaks Research Library and Collections.

Offner, Jerome

1983   On the Inapplicability of "Oriental Despotism" and the "Asiatic Mode of Production" to the Aztecs of Texcoco. *American Antiquity* 46: 43–61.

Offner, Jerome

1983b   *Law and Politics in Aztec Texcoco.* Cambridge: Cambridge University Press. [One of the few extensive studies of the Aztec legal system. Concentrates on Texcoco because of superior source material.]

Olguín, Felipe Solís

2002   Art at the Time of the Aztecs. In *Aztecs.* Edited by Eduardo Matos Moctezuma and Felipe Solis Olguín, pp. 56–63. London: Royal Academy of Arts. [Descriptive study of Aztec art in the catalogue of a world-class exhibit on the Aztec].

Olmo Frese, Laura del

1999   *Análisis de la Ofrenda 98 del Templo Mayor de Tenochtitlan.* Mexico: INAH. (Colección Científica). [As research continues in the Templo Mayor area, archaeologists keep finding more evidence of Aztec ceremonial behavior. The author presents the analysis of one particular ceremonial offering.]

Ortiz de Montellano, Bernard R.

1990   *Aztec Medicine, Health, and Nutrition.* New Brunswick: Rutgers University Press. [The author reviews Aztec diet, the Aztec way of diagnosing and explaining illnesses, and how they attempted to cure them. De Montellano rejects the notion that Aztec cannibalism was practiced on a large scale to offset a perceived lack of protein in the diet.]

Otis Charlton, Cynthia

1994   Plebeians and Patricians. Contrasting Patterns of Production and Distribution in the Aztec Figurine and Lapidary Industries. In *Economies and Polities in the Aztec Realm.* Edited by Mary G. Hodge and Michael E. Smith, pp. 195–219. (Studies on Culture and Society, volume 6) Albany: Institute for Mesoamerican Studies. [Lapidary production played a role in showing visible wealth. Figurine production was geared toward household consumption rather than being a display of wealth.]

Parker, Geoffrey
1999   The Political World of Charles V. In *Charles V and his Time, 1500–1558.* Edited by Hugo Solis, pp. 113–225. Antwerpen: Mercatorfonds. [Parker gives us an insight into the political scene in Europe with which Emperor Charles V had to deal.]

Parsons, Jeffrey R.
1971   *Prehistoric Settlement Patterns in the Texcoco Region, Mexico.* Memoirs No. 3. Ann Arbor: Museum of Anthropology, University of Michigan. [Parsons undertook a key element of archaeological research: a settlement pattern study.]

Parsons, Jeffrey R.
1976   The Role of Chinampa Agriculture in the Food Supply of Aztec Tenochtitlan. In *Cultural Change and Continuity: Essays in Honor of James B. Griffin.* Edited by Charles E. Cleland, pp. 233–262. New York: Academic Press. [The Aztecs were capable of sustaining incredible population growth. One technique that allowed them to do so involved the use of raised fields, or *chinampas.*]

Parsons, Jeffrey R.
1980   Comment of Brumfiel, Specialization, Exchange, and the Aztec State. *Current Anthropology* 21: 471–472. [This is part of the format of *Current Anthropology:* authors are invited to a conversation with their critics.]

Parsons, Jeffrey R., Elizabeth M. Brumfiel, Mary H. Parsons, and David Wilson
1982   *Prehispanic Settlement Patterns in the Southern Valley of Mexico: The Chalco–Xochimilco Region.* Memoirs No. 14, Ann Arbor: Museum of Anthropology, University of Michigan.

Parsons, Jeffrey R., and Mary H. Parsons
1990   *Maguey Utilization in Highland Central Mexico.* Anthropological Papers, Ann Arbor: Museum of Anthropology, University of Michigan.

Pasztory, Esther
1998   *Aztec Art.* Norman: University of Oklahoma Press.

Payne, Stanley E., and Michael P. Closs
1986   A Survey of Aztec Numbers and Their Uses. In *Native American Mathematics.* Edited by Michael P. Closs, pp. 213–235. Austin: University of Texas Press. [One of a few studies dedicated to Aztec use of numbers.]

Plunket Nagoda, Patricia and Uruñuela, Gabriela
1994   Impact of the Xochiyaoyotl in Southwestern Puebla. *In Economies and Polities in the Aztec Realm.* Edited by M. Hodge and M. Smith, pp. 433-446. *Studies on Culture and Society, 6.* Albany: State University of New York at Albany, Institute for Mesoamerican Studies.

Pohl, John M. D., and Angus McBride
1991   *Aztec, Mixtec, and Zapotec Armies.* (Men-at-War Series). Oxford: Osprey Publishing.

Polgar, Steven

1975   Population, Evolution, and Theoretical Paradigms. In *Population, Ecology, and Social Evolution.* Edited by Steven Polgar, pp. 1–26. The Hague: Mouton.

Pollard, Helen Perlstein

1982   Ecological Variation and Economic Exchange in the Tarascan State. *American Ethnologist* 9: 250–268. [Deals with the arch enemies of the Aztec empire.]

Pospisil, Leopold

1971   *Anthropology of Law: A Comparative Theory.* New York: Harper and Row.

Prescott, W. H.

1843   *History of the Conquest of Mexico.* New York: Random House. [One of the earliest American publications introducing the world of the Aztecs to the general public.]

Price, T. Jeffrey, and Michael E. Smith

1992   Agricultural Terraces. In *Archaeological Research at Aztec-Period Rural Sites in Morelos, Mexico. Volume I: Excavations and Architecture.* Edited by Michael Smith, pp. 267–291. Monographs in Latin American Archaeology No. 4. Pittsburgh: University of Pittsburgh. [The authors address the use of agricultural terraces in the overall context of Aztec food production.]

Quiñones Keber, Eloise

1995   *Codex Telleriano–Remensis. Ritual, Divination, and History in a Pictorial Aztec Manuscript.* Austin: University of Texas Press. [This manuscript contains invaluable information about the Aztec calendar, mythology, rituals, history, and politics.]

Radin, Paul

1920   The Sources and Authenticity of the History of the Ancient Mexicans. *University of California Publications in American Archaeology and Ethnology* 17, no. 1: 1–150. [Radin discusses primary-source documents related to the history of Mexico. Included in his work is the so-called Historia de los Mexicanos por Sus Pinturas.]

Read, Kay Almere, and Jason J. González

2000   *Handbook of Mesoamerican Mythology.* (Handbooks of World Mythology). Santa Barbara: ABC-CLIO.

Rice, Prudence M.

1987   *Pottery Analysis: A Sourcebook.* Chicago: University of Chicago Press. [Still the Bible for those interested in pottery analysis.]

Robertson, Donald

1959   *Mexican Manuscript Painting of the Early Colonial Period: The Metropolitan Schools.* New Haven: Yale University Press. [Insightful and carefully researched work on early colonial painted manuscripts. The author was known to abstain from publishing until he was completely satisfied with his research.]

Román Berrelleza, and Juan Alberto
  1991 A Study of Skeletal Materials from Tlatelolco. In *Aztec Ceremonial Landscapes*. Edited by David Carrasco, pp. 9–10. Niwot: University of Colorado Press.

Rounds, J.
  1982 Dynastic Succession and the Centralization of Power in Tenochtitlan. In *The Inca and Aztec States 1400–1800*. Edited by George A. Collier, Renato I. Rosaldo, and John D. Wirth, pp. 63–89. New York: Academic Press. [Discusses the policy adopted by the Aztecs to guarantee a smooth succession from one emperor to the next. Includes a discussion on the position of *cihuacoatl,* or stand-in for the emperor, during the interregnum.]

Rupprich, H.
  1956 *Dürer: schriftlicher Nachlass.* Berlin: Deutscher Verein für Kunstwissenschaft. [The famous German artist left us with a description of objects from the New World That he saw at the court in Brussels. It is unknown what happened to these artifacts.]

Sahagún, Fray Bernadino de
  1959–1975 *Florentine Codex: General History of the Things of New Spain.* Translated and edited by C. E. Dibble and A.J.O. Anderson. Santa Fe: The School of American Research/University of New Mexico. [Monumental scholarly endeavor by Dibble and Anderson. Their translation makes one of the most important Spanish-language resources on Precolumbian cultures available to an English-speaking audience.]

Sanders, William T.
  1956 The Central Mexican Symbiotic Region. In *Prehistoric Settlement Patterns in the New World*. Edited by Gordon R. Willey, pp. 115–127. New York: Viking Fund Publications in Anthropology No. 23. Wenner-Gren Foundation for Anthropological Research. [On the ecology of Central Mexico.]

Sanders, William T., A. Kovar, T. Charlton, and R. A. Diehl
  1970 *The Natural Environment, Contemporary Occupation and Sixteenth Century Population of the Valley (Teotihuacan Valley Project Final Report).* University Park: Pennsylvania State University. [Sanders and his colleagues spent enormous amounts of energy studying the ecology and settlement patterns in the Valley of Teotihuacan, which is part of the Valley of Mexico.]

Sanders, William T., Jeffrey R. Parsons, and Robert S. Santley
  1979 *The Basin of Mexico: Ecological Processes in the Evolution of a Civilization.* New York: Academic Press. [Sanders and his colleagues undertook a massive regional survey of the Valley of Mexico, identifying a wide range of archaeological sites.]

Sanders, William T., and Robert S. Santley
  1983 A Tale of Three Cities: Energetics and Urbanization in Prehispanic Central Mexico. In *Prehistoric Settlement Patterns: Essays in Honor of Gordon R. Willey*. Edited by Evon Z. Vogt and Richard M. Leventhal, pp. 243–291. Albuquerque: University of New Mexico Press.

Sanders, William T., and David Webster

1988   The Mesoamerican Urban Tradition. *American Anthropologist* 90: 521–546.

Sandstrom, Alan R., and Paula E. Sandstrom

1986   *Traditional Papermaking and Paper Cult Figures of Mexico.* Norman: University of Oklahoma Press.

Santley, R. S., and E. K. Rose

1979   Diet, Nutrition and Population Dynamics in the Basin of Mexico. *World Archaeology* 1(2): 185–207. [The authors reject the notion that the Aztec resorted to cannibalism to offset an alleged lack of protein in their diet.]

Santley, Robert, Michael Berman, and Rani Alexander

1991   The Politicization of the Mesoamerican Ballgame and Its Implications for the Interpretation of the Distribution of Ballcourts in Central Mexico. In *The Mesoamerican Ballgame.* Edited by Vernon J. Scarborough and David Wilcox, pp. 3–24. Tucson: University of Arizona Press. [The authors discuss the nexus between ballgame and politics in Mesoamerica.]

Saville, Marshall H.

1920   The Goldsmith's Art in Ancient Mexico. Museum of the American Indian, New York: Heye Foundation, *Indian Notes and Monographs,* No. 7.

Séjourné, Laurette

1966   Arquitectura y pintura en Teotihuacan. Siglo XXI Mexico.

Seler, Eduard

1902–1923   *Gesammelte Abhandlungen zur Amerikanischen Sprach- und Altertumskunde.* 5 volumes. Berlin: Akademische Druck-U, Verlagsanstalt. (Reprinted Graz, Austria, 1960). [Mammoth undertaking by this respected German scholar. His notes and contributions, although more than a century old in some cases, are invaluable because of his insights and because he recorded monuments no longer in existence.]

Sharer, Robert J.

1994   *The Ancient Maya.* (5th ed.) Stanford: Stanford University Press. [Sharer updates Morley's standard reference for anyone interested in the ancient Maya. Given the pace of Maya archaeological research, this work deserves to be updated at least once every 10 years.]

Simons, Bente Bittmann, and Thelma D. Sullivan

1972   The Pochteca. *Atti del XL Congresso Internazionale degli Americanisti* 4: 203–212. [On the Aztec long-distance traders, the *pochteca.*]

Sisson, Edward

1983   Recent Work on the Codex Borgia Group. *Current Anthropology* 24: 653–656.

Smith, Michael E.

1984 The Aztlan Migrations of the Nahuatl Chronicles: Myth or History? *Ethnohistory* 31(3): 153–186. [Smith wades in on the controversies surrounding the Aztec migration story.]

Smith, Michael E., Patricia Aguirre, Cynthia Heath-Smith, Kathryn Hirst, Scott O'Mack, and Jeffrey Price

1989 Architectural Patterns at Three Aztec-Period Sites in Morelos, Mexico. *Journal of Field Archaeology* 16: 185–203.

Smith Michael

1992 *Archaeological Research at Aztec-Period Rural Sites in Morelos, Mexico. Volume 1. Excavations and Architecture.* Pittsburgh: University of Pittsburgh Monographs in Latin American Archaeology, no. 4. [This is a site report describing archaeological excavations directed by Michael Smith and Cynthia Heath-Smith at the Aztec rural sites of Cuexcomate and Capilco in the Mexican state of Morelos. These are the most completely excavated Aztec rural sites thus far. This fieldwork has generated important new insights into the nature of peasant households, social classes, trade, ritual, and agricultural practices in a provincial area of the Aztec empire.]

Smith, Michael E.

1993 Houses and the Settlement Hierarchy in Late Postclassic Morelos: A Comparison of Archaeology and Ehnohistory. In *Prehispanic Domestic Units in Western Mesoamerica: Studies of the House, Compound and Residence.* Edited by Robert S. Santley and Kenneth G. Hirth, pp. 191–206. Boca Raton: CRC Press. [Smith presents information recovered from his excavations into provincial Aztec centers in Morelos.]

Smith, Michael E., Cynthia Heath-Smith, Ronald Kohler, Joan Odess, Sharon Spanogle, and Timothy Sullivan

1994 The Size of the Aztec City of Yautepec: Urban Survey in Central Mexico. *Ancient Mesoamerica* 5: 1–11. [The authors provide data on the extent of a provincial Aztec community.]

Smith, Michael, and Cynthia Heath-Smith

1994 Rural Economy on Late Postclassic Morelos. An Archaeological Study. In *Economies and Polities in the Aztec Realm.* Edited by Mary G. Hodge and Michael E. Smith, pp. 349–376. (Studies on Culture and Society, volume 6) Albany: Institute for Mesoamerican Studies. [Presentation of information collected at excavations far away from the Aztec capital. The choice of a rural site rather than an urban one reflects the deep-rooted desire on the part of the two editors to counterbalance the multitude of Tenochtitlan-centered studies.]

Smith, Michael

1994 Economies and Polities in Aztec-Period Morelos. In *Economies and Polities in the Aztec Realm.* Edited by Mary G. Hodge and Michael E. Smith, pp. 313–348. (Studies on Culture and Society, volume 6) Albany: Institute for Mesoamerican Studies. [Focus on Smith's work in outlying areas of the Aztec empire.]

Smith, Michael, and Frances Berdan

1994   Province Descriptions. In *Aztec Imperial Strategies.* Edited by Frances Berdan, Richard Blanton, Elizabeth Hill Boone, Mary Hodge, Michael Smith, and Emily Umberger, pp. 265–349. Washington, D.C.: Dumbarton Oaks.

Smith. Michael E., and Mary G. Hodge

1994   An Introduction to Late Postclassic Economies and Polities. In *Economies and Polities in the Aztec Realm.* Edited by Mary G. Hodge and Michael E. Smith, pp. 1–42. (Studies on Culture and Society, volume 6) Albany: Institute for Mesoamerican Studies.

Smith, Michael E., and T. Jeffrey Price

1994   Aztec-Period Agricultural Terraces in Morelos, Mexico: Evidence for Household-Level Agricultural Intensification. *Journal of Field Archaeology* 21 (1994): 169–179.

Smith, Michael E.

1996   The Strategic Provinces. In *Aztec Imperial Strategies.* Edited by Frances F. Berdan, Richard E. Blanton, Elizabeth H. Boone, Mary G. Hodge, Michael E. Smith, and Emily Umberger, pp. 137–150. Washington, D.C.: Dumbarton Oaks. [This articles deals with one of two categories of provinces within the empire. The others were called tributary provinces.]

Smith, Michael E.

1997   Life in the Provinces of the Aztec Empire. *Scientific American,* September, pp. 76–83. [Smith answers the question: How did Aztec farmers live outside the Valley of Mexico?]

Smith, Michael E., and Cynthia Heath-Smith

2000   Rural Economy in Late Postclassic Morelos. An Archaeological Study. In *The Ancient Civilizations of Mesoamerica. A Reader.* Edited by Michael E. Smith and Marilyn A. Mason, pp. 217–235. Oxford: Blackwell Publishers.

Smith, Michael E.

2003a   A Quarter-Century of Aztec Studies. *Mexicon* XXV (1) (February): 4–10.

Smith, Michael E.

2003b   *Tlahuica Ceramics: The Aztec-Period Ceramics of Morelos, Mexico.* Albany: Institute of Mesoamerican Studies Monographs, vol. 13. [Because of lower population densities, Tlahuica sites have preserved much invaluable data on Aztec life and culture.]

Smith, Michael E.

2003c   *The Aztecs,* 2nd Ed. Malden: Blackwell Publishing.

Soustelle, Jacques

1962   *Daily Life of the Aztecs on the Eve of the Spanish Conquest.* Translated from the French by Patrick O'Brian. Stanford: Stanford University Press. [Eloquent and engaging presentation on Aztec daily life by the late Jacques Soustelle, one of the leading

French scholars on the Aztec. This translations allows English-speaking audiences to also get the feeling of "being there."]

Standley, Paul C.
1944 The American Fig Tree. In Von Hagen, *The Aztec and Maya Papermakers*, pp. 94–101. Mineola, New York: Dover Publications (1999 reprint). [Contribution on Prehispanic paper making.]

Stern, Theodore
1950 *Rubber-Ball Games of the Americas*. New York: J. J. Augustin

Stross, Fred H., Thomas R. Hester, Robert F. Heizer, and Robert N. Jack
1976 Chemical and Archaeological Studies of Mesoamerican and Californian Obsidians. In *Advances in Obsidian Glass Studies: Archaeological and Geochemical Perspectives*. Edited by R. E. Taylor, pp. 240–258. Park Ridge: Noyess Press.

Suárez de Peralta, Joan
1878 *Noticias Históricas de la Nueva España*. Edited by Justo Zaragoza. Madrid: Imprenta de Manuel G. Hernández. [Essays on the history of Mexico.]

Tezozomoc, Hernando Alvarado
1878 *Crónica Mexicana*. Bibliotéca Mexicana. Edited by J. M. Vigil, pp. 223–701. Mexico City. (Originally written in 1598) [History of the Spanish conquest as written by the descendant of Moctecuhzuma II.]

Thomas, Hugh
1995 *Conquest. Montezuma, Cortés, and the Fall of Old Mexico*. New York: Simon and Schuster.

Tilly, Charles
1975 Reflections on the History of European State-Making. In *The Formation of National States in Western Europe*. Edited by Charles Tilly. Princeton: Princeton University Press. [Volume on long-term aspects of European social and political history edited by one of the leading scholars in the field.]

Torquemada, Fray Juan de
1975 *Monarquía Indiana*. 3 vols. Mexico City: Editorial Porrúa. [Written by theologian and cardinal de Torquemada.]

Townsend, Richard F.
2000 *The Aztecs*. (Revised edition). London: Thames and Hudson.

Trigger, Bruce G.
1972 Determinants of Urban Growth in Preindustrial Societies. In *Man, Settlement, and Urbanism*. Edited by Peter J. Ucko, Ruth Tringham, and G. W. Dimbleby, pp. 575–599. Cambridge: Schenkman.

Trombold, Charles D., James F. Luhr, Toshiaki Hasenaka, and Michael D. Glasscock
1993   Chemical Characteristics of Obsidians from Archaeological Sites in Western Mexico and the Tequila Source Area: Implications for Regional and Pan-Regional Interaction within the Northern Mesoamerican Periphery. *Ancient Mesoamerica* 4: 255–270. [Chemical analysis of obsidian is what makes possible the reconstruction of trade in this commodity.]

Umberger, Emily
1987   Antiques, Revivals, and References to the Past in Aztec Art. *Res: Anthropology and Aesthetics* 13: 62–105. [Umberger's article reviews evidence of Teotihuacan objects retrieved from Aztec structures in Tenochtitlan, specifically the Templo Mayor area.]

Umberger, Emily
1996   Aztec Presence and Material Remains in the Outer Provinces. In *Aztec Imperial Strategies*. Edited by Frances F. Berdan, Richard E. Blanton, Elizabeth H. Boone, Mary G. Hodge, Michael E. Smith, and Emily Umberger, pp. 151–179. Washington, D.C.: Dumbarton Oaks. [An attempt to identify Aztec colonies in the outer provinces based on correlating written sources and material evidence. The correlation is not a good one.]

Vaillant, George
1941   *Aztecs of Mexico*. Doubleday, New York. [The author outlines his theory that the mythical site of Tollan should be identified as the site of Teotihuacan.]

Van Bussel, Gerard
2002   Catalogue. Object 299. In *Aztecs*. Edited by Eduardo Matos Moctezuma and Felipe Solis Olguín, p. 475. London: Royal Academy of Arts. [Description of a famous Aztec shield in the collections of the Museum für Völkerkunde in Vienna. The author is a curator at the Vienna museum.]

Van Zantwijk, R.
1985   *The Aztec Arrangement: The Social History of Pre-Spanish Mexico*. Norman: University of Oklahoma Press.

Vega Sosa, Constanza
1979   *El Recinto Sagrado de Mexico-Tenochtitlan. Excavaciones 1968–69 y 1975–76*. Mexico: Instituto de Antropología e Historia. [Overview of excavations carried out in the Sacred Precinct in Mexico City.]

Vollemaere, Antoon
1992   *De Mythe van Aztlan*. Mechelen: Quetzal Press. [The author retraces the Aztecs back to their homeland, Aztlan, which he believes was located in the Southwestern United States.]

von Hagen, Victor W.
1944   *The Aztec and Maya Papermakers*. New York: J. J. Augustin. (Dover Reprint, 1999)

Warren, J. Benedict

1973   An Introductory Survey of Secular Writings in the European Tradition on Colonial Middle America, 1503–1818. In *Handbook of Middle American Indians.* Edited by Robert Wauchope. Vol. 13. Part Two. *Guide to Ethnohistorical Sources,* pp. 42–137. Austin: University of Texas Press. [Compendium of three centuries worth of writings on Middle America.]

White, Benjamin

1973   Demand for Labor and Population Growth in Colonial Java. *Human Ecology* 1: 217–236. [Studies the relationship between demographic pressures and ecological context.]

White, Christine D., Michael W. Spence, Fred J. Longstaffe, Hilary Stuart-Williams, and Kimberley R. Law

2002   Geographic Identities of the Sacrificial Victims from the Feathered Serpent Pyramid, Teotihuacan: Implications for the Nature of State Power. *Latin American Antiquity* 13 (2): 217–236. [This study addresses the political and military structure of early Teotihuacan through the analysis of oxygen–isotope ratios in skeletal phosphate from forty-one victims of a sacrifice associated with the Feathered Serpent Pyramid.]

Williams, Barbara J.

1991   The Lands and Political Organization of a Rural Tlaxilacalli in Tepetlaoztoc, c. A.D. 1540. In *Land and Politics in the Valley of Mexico. A Two Thousand Year Perspective.* Edited by H. R. Harvey, pp. 187–208. Albuquerque: University of New Mexico Press. [Williams provides an analysis of the data from Tepetlaoztoc relating to the territorial and political organization of the community within one generation after the Spanish conquest.]

Williams, Barbara J.

1994   The Archaeological Signature of Local Level Polities in Tepetlaoztoc. In *Economies and Polities in the Aztec Realm.* Edited by Mary G. Hodge and Michael E. Smith, pp. 73–87. (Studies on Culture and Society, volume 6) Albany: Institute for Mesoamerican Studies. [Williams presents data on what lower-tier political entities look like in the material record.]

Wood, Michael

2000   *Conquistadors.* Berkeley: University of California Press. [Easy-to-read book on the Spanish side of the story by author and PBS filmmaker Michael Wood.]

Wyllie, Cherra

1994   *How to Make an Aztec Book: An Investigation Into the Manufacture of Central Mexican Codices.* Unpublished MA thesis, New Haven: Department of Anthropology, Yale University.

Index

Time periods are listed chronologically in the entry for Chronology.

About the Author

Dirk Van Tuerenhout is a native of Belgium. He studied archaeology and ancient history at the Catholic University of Leuven, in Belgium. He received a doctorate in Anthropology from Tulane University in New Orleans. His fieldwork and dissertation centered on the Precolumbian Maya. He has conducted excavations in Belize and Guatemala. He has taught at universities and colleges in New Orleans, Pennsylvania, and Houston. Currently he is the curator of anthropology at the Houston Museum of Natural Science. Among other things, he is responsible for the John P. McGovern Hall of the Americas dedicated to American Indian cultures from North, Central, and South America.